Hebrews

Biblical Interpretation Series

EDITORS
R. ALAN CULPEPPER
ELLEN VAN WOLDE

ASSISTANT EDITORS
DAVID E. ORTON
ROLF RENDTORFF

EDITORIAL ADVISORY BOARD
JANICE CAPEL ANDERSON
MIEKE BAL
PHYLLIS A. BIRD
ERHARD BLUM
WERNER H. KELBER
EKKEHARD STEGEMANN
VINCENT L. WIMBUSH
JEAN ZUMSTEIN

VOLUME 75

HEBREWS

Hebrews

Contemporary Methods–New Insights

EDITED BY

Gabriella Gelardini

Society of Biblical Literature
Atlanta

Copyright © 2005 by Koninklijke Brill NV, Leiden,
The Netherlands

This edition published under license from Koninklijke Brill NV,
Leiden, The Netherlands by the Society of Biblical Literature.

All rights reserved. No part of this work may be reproduced or transmitted in any form or by any means, electronic or mechanical, including photocopying and recording, or by any means of any information storage or retrieval system, except as may be expressly permitted by the 1976 Copyright Act or in writing from the Publisher. Requests for permission should be addressed in writing to the Rights and Permissions Department, Koninklijke Brill NV, Leiden, The Netherlands.

Authorization to photocopy items for internal or personal use is granted by Brill provided that the appropriate fees are paid directly to The Copyright Clearance Center, 222 Rosewood Drive, Suite 910, Danvers, MA 01923, USA. Fees are subject to change.

Library of Congress Cataloging-in-Publication Data

Hebrews : contemporary methods, new insights / edited by Gabriella Gelardini.
   p. cm. – (Biblical interpretation series ; v. 75)
   Originally published: Leiden ; Boston : Brill, 2005.
   Includes bibliographical references and index.
   ISBN 978-1-58983-386-9 (paper binding : alk. paper)
   1. Bible. N. T. Hebrews–Criticism, interpretation, etc. I. Gelardini, Gabriella.
BS2775.52.H42   2008
227'.8706–dc22   2008040686

CONTENTS

Foreword vii
   Harold W. Attridge

Introduction 1
   Gabriella Gelardini

PART ONE

CULTIC LANGUAGE, CONCEPTS,
AND PRACTICE IN HEBREWS

Does the Cultic Language in Hebrews Represent
Sacrificial Metaphors? Reflections on Some Basic
Problems 13
   Ekkehard W. Stegemann and Wolfgang Stegemann

Some Remarks on Hebrews from the Viewpoint of
Old Testament Exegesis 25
   Ina Willi-Plein

Characteristics of Sacrificial Metaphors in Hebrews 37
   Christian A. Eberhart

Covenant, Cult, and the Curse-of-Death: Διαθήκη in
Heb 9:15–22 65
   Scott W. Hahn

The Epistle to the Hebrews as a "Jesus-Midrash" 89
   Elke Tönges

Hebrews, an Ancient Synagogue Homily for *Tisha be-Av*:
Its Function, its Basis, its Theological Interpretation 107
   Gabriella Gelardini

PART TWO

SOCIOLOGY, ETHICS, AND RHETORIC IN HEBREWS

Portraying the Temple in Stone and Text: The Arch
  of Titus and the Epistle to the Hebrews 131
  Ellen Bradshaw Aitken

How to Entertain Angels: Ethics in the Epistle to
  the Hebrews 149
  Knut Backhaus

The Intersection of Alien Status and Cultic Discourse
  in the Epistle to the Hebrews 177
  Benjamin Dunning

Reflections of Rhetorical Terminology in Hebrews 199
  Hermut Löhr

PART THREE

TEXTUAL-HISTORICAL, COMPARATIVE, AND INTERTEXTUAL APPROACHES TO HEBREWS

Locating Hebrews within the Literary Landscape
  of Christian Origins 213
  Pamela M. Eisenbaum

Hebrews and the Heritage of Paul 239
  Dieter Georgi

Paul and Hebrews: A Comparison of Narrative Worlds 245
  James C. Miller

Constructions and Collusions: The Making and
  Unmaking of Identity in Qoheleth and Hebrews 265
  Jennifer L. Koosed and Robert P. Seesengood

Indices
  Index of Modern Authors 281
  Index of Ancient Sources 289

FOREWORD

Despite generations of learned commentators, the Epistle to the Hebrews remains an object of fascination for students of the origins of Christianity. Some of that fascination arises from the complexity of the work itself, with its elaborate, sustained, dare I say "metaphorical" treatment of the death of Christ, its rich but often subtle vocabulary, and its complex intertextual relations with the sacred scriptures of Israel and the literature of Second Temple Judaism. While the text is intricate, its contemporary readership has become more complex as well. Rhetorical and sociological analyses of early Christian texts and communities, building on traditional literary and historical criticism, have increased in complexity and sophistication. As interpreters generally have become sensitive to the political commitments of ancient texts and their postmodern readers, new questions and perspectives have emerged. At the same time, readers committed to a Christian stance in the contemporary world have turned with renewed enthusiasm to the movement's earliest voices. Scholarship on the New Testament thus continues to evolve, influenced by trends in the humanities generally and by efforts to find new ways to appropriate Scripture for contemporary religious life. It is no surprise then that scholarship on the Epistle to the Hebrews has also continued to develop.

When I set out to write a commentary on this most intriguing epistle some twenty years ago, the major issues had been stable for a generation or so. Most scholars had long since ceased to worry about Pauline authorship, but debates still raged about the dating of the epistle and its relations with other ancient sources, the Dead Sea Scrolls and Philo marking the ends of the usual spectrum, although "Gnostic" texts still appeared on the horizon of some scholarly analyses. Debate also continued about the character of the addressees. Were they Jews to be converted or saved from "relapsing" to Judaism? Or were they Gentiles whose faith needed to be strengthened in the face of persecution, or were they something in between? Questions redolent of the history of ideas still were prominent. What world of thought or imagination did it come from—Jewish apocalyptic, Greek philosophy, odd mythology? Some new analytical methods were just capturing the attention of exegetes. The groundbreaking work of Hans Dieter Betz on the rhetoric of Galatians suggested to other scholars that some sort of rhetorical analysis might be appropriate for Hebrews. Attempts to analyze the social situation of early Christian communities seemed a promising avenue.

The evolving world of scholarly discourse is well represented in these essays. Some are concerned with literary issues, such as the character and function of the text's figurative language (Eberhart, Stegemann and Stegemann) or its argumentative structures (Löhr). Seesengood and Koosed's essay explores the functions of the pointedly indeterminate author, comparing the similarly indeterminate "I" of Qoheleth. Intertextual issues loom large in the analyses by Hahn of the "covenant" language, by Tönges, in her exploration of the "midrashic" character of Hebrews, and by Gelardini, in her effort to relate Hebrews to a lectionary cycle. Attempts to understand the function of Hebrews now utilize various sociological and anthropological models. Willi-Plein invokes the categories of cultural anthropology in a new approach to the structure of Hebrews' play on sacrificial motifs. Aitken adopts a postcolonial perspective as she sets Hebrews in the context of Flavian Rome. Issues of "identity" formation in early Christianity and Judaism of the imperial period appear in several essays. Eisenbaum offers a general theoretical framework for this question. Backhaus uses the notion of a symbolic universe to describe what Hebrews does for its community. Dunning explores discourse about the "alien" as a way of unpacking Hebrews' rhetoric. While Pauline authorship is not an issue on the table, the affinities of the text with Pauline Christianity elicit new theological and literary analyses by Georgi and Miller, essays that contribute to the ongoing dialogue about the theological significance of Hebrews.

The conversation continues and will no doubt develop further as collaborative work on Hebrews proceeds in scholarly organizations such as the Society of Biblical Literature, whose Annual Meeting will soon host a new program unit on the text. One area that I hope will be further explored in that context is the history of reading Hebrews. There remain stories to be told about how the text functioned in the ongoing shaping of Christian doctrine and community identity. It is a delight to see a new cohort of young scholars ready to address the whole range of issues that this text presents.

Harold W. Attridge
New Haven, Conn., U.S.A.

INTRODUCTION

Habent sua fata libelli—the volume you are looking at is a unique one, and just as any other book holds its own history, this one does too.

It began on a gray winter day in 1999 during my stay at Harvard University as a visiting scholar, as Ellen B. Aitken and I cruised westwards on Interstate highway 90 heading toward Amherst, Massachusetts, the small town probably best known for one of its 19th-century residents, America's great if not greatest poet Emily Dickinson. Ellen and I were wondering why the renowned Society of Biblical Literature (SBL) had granted so little attention to the so-called Epistle to the Hebrews in its Annual Meeting, which had just taken place in Boston. Had it not been the merit of Hebrews scholarship of the last forty years to bring the *auctor ad Hebraeos* from the margin to the center of New Testament theology? Was this writer not currently considered the third great theologian of the New Testament, next to Paul and John? We agreed that something needed to be done. An apt occasion arose, but not immediately. It was Kristin De Troyer who suggested to me that I might put together a session on Hebrews for the International Meeting of the SBL in Rome in 2001. I didn't ponder long. Remembering the conversation with Ellen, I contacted her, and thanks to her help the SBL International Meeting had its first Hebrews Seminar. Another followed in Berlin (2002), then one in Cambridge (2003), and a further one in Groningen (2004). I became its official chair, and Ellen, Harold W. Attridge and Pamela M. Eisenbaum its unofficial steering committee. In these four years, twenty-four (!) papers on Hebrews were read. The idea to put forth a volume originated in Berlin. We are thrilled that starting in 2005, the SBL Annual Meeting will have its own Consultation on Hebrews too.

The present volume comprises a selection of twelve of the finest papers given in these sessions (2001: Aitken; 2002: Backhaus, Eisenbaum, Löhr; 2003: Dunning, Eberhart, Gelardini, Georgi, Miller, Stegemann and Stegemann, Tönges; 2004: Koosed and Seesengood) and two additional papers by scholars who intended to participate in the sessions but were prevented by other obligations ([2003]: Hahn,

Willi-Plein). The fourteen contributors form an intriguing international group of senior scholars alongside an aspiring group of younger scholars. Most of them either have written a monograph on Hebrews or are currently doing so.

Yet not only in terms of its authors does this volume offer exciting diversity. The complexity of Hebrews, which has often been described as a "riddle," has always invited the application of new methods. Hence, the reader of this volume might encounter a postmodern reading of Hebrews (Stegemann and Stegemann), an investigation of its textual history (Eisenbaum), or an approach to it via the sociology of knowledge (Backhaus) for the first time. Many new insights are offered here, such as the correlation of the political theology of Hebrews with that of Flavian Rome (Aitken), the interpretation of Hebrews based on the Palestinian Triennial Cycle (Gelardini) or the elaborate semantic-syntactical exegesis of διαθήκη (Hahn).

The fourteen essays are grouped into three parts. *Part One, "Cultic Language, Concepts, and Practice in Hebrews,"* considers cultic language and concepts (Stegemann and Stegemann, Willi-Plein, Eberhart), the importance of the covenant in Hebrews (Hahn, Gelardini), and Hebrews as a Midrash on Jesus (Tönges).

Ekkehard W. Stegemann and *Wolfgang Stegemann* bring a postmodern sensibility to Hebrews, by reflecting on what is done when sacrificial language is declared to be "metaphorical." The view inherent to this declaration is closely linked to a representation of history as a reproduction of an objective entity. Based on such an epistemological paradigm, one must conclude that since Hebrews' sacrificial language lacks any historical referent outside the text, it can only be metaphorical, and hence must be a theological interpretation of the *brutum factum historicum* of the crucifixion. But exactly this ontological presupposition in our "Western episteme" reveals its particular cultural and Eurocentric perspective. Historical facts are always interpretations by means of language and are influenced by the cultural and individual idiosyncrasies of the historian. In our—and by this is meant the Westerners'—understanding of reality, the perception of the death of Jesus on the cross as a so-called real historical event only allows for political, social, forensic, or psychological dimensions of its representation. Other forms of representing his death, such as in terms of an atoning sacrifice, appear in our spectrum of perceptions *a priori* as an additional, mythical and hence metaphorical *inter-*

pretation. The authors opt in conclusion to perceive the sacrificial language of Jesus' death not just as an *interpretation* of the crucifixion but also as a possible *representation*.

Ina Willi-Plein reads Hebrews' cultic concepts from a viewpoint of Old Testament exegesis and history of religion. Out of the set of ideas that seem to constitute the cultic system of the final stage of the Old Testament texts, she observes that Hebrews seems to prioritize the heavenly sanctuary within the Israelite framework of conceptions of cultic space, the office of the high priest, the cultic performance of the Day of Atonement, and the application of blood in the holy of holies. Since the service done by the high priest culminates in the ritual of the Day of Atonement, and since the author of Hebrews is doing theology by interpreting Scripture, Willi-Plein embarks on a close reading of Lev 16. From this perspective, she concludes that Christ's sin-offering in Hebrews should neither be viewed as a vicarious dying nor as an expiatory self-sacrifice. Rather, authorized by God, it is the Son's bringing of uncontaminated life (i.e., blood)—caused through innocent suffering—into the sanctuary in order to remove pollutions due to sin.

Christian A. Eberhart offers a *Wirkungsgeschichte* of sacrificial metaphors in the Hebrew Bible, the New Testament, and Hebrews. After providing a *Traditionsgeschichte* of the Judean sacrificial cult, Eberhart shows how the author of Hebrews builds on two types of traditional cult metaphors, one of *blood* and the other of *sacrifice*, which he ultimately connects: Christ's sacrifice implies his exaltation from earth to heaven where he now serves as the heavenly high priest; his blood guarantees the necessary cultic purification for those who approach the heavenly sanctuary.

Scott W. Hahn applies a semantic-syntactic and social-scientific method to Heb 9:15–22. In order to elucidate the meaning of "covenant" and overcome the long-standing interpretive *crux* of this passage, he suggests entering into Hebrews' own culture, which perceives liturgy and law as a unity. However, Heb 9:15–18 appears to be counter-evidence for this integration. In Heb 9:16–17, the author appears to use διαθήκη in a sense quite different from his customary usage, stepping outside Israelite-Jewish cultic categories in order to draw an analogy from Greco-Roman law, whose relevance is anything but clear. Hahn argues that the solution to the puzzle of Heb 9:16–17 is not to abandon the cultic-covenantal framework of the author's thought, with its close relationship between liturgy and law, but to enter into that framework more deeply. If it is understood that the context for these verses is the broken first (Sinaitic) covenant mentioned in Heb 9:15, one can see that the author is drawing out the *legal* implications of the *liturgical* ritual that established the first covenant.

Elke Tönges brings an intertextual and form-critical lens to Hebrews. By examining Hebrews' many quotations, their introductory formulas, and their interpretation, and moreover, the text's treatment of theological themes and heroes from the Septuagint, Tönges argues that the author and the audience are from a Jewish milieu. This also finds expression in the exegetical method of the author, who produces implicit and explicit midrash with his text. Therefore, she concludes, Hebrews with its *Sitz im Leben* in the ancient synagogue bears signs of structures known from the oldest homiletic midrashim. Unlike later midrashim with messianic content in the rabbinic corpus, Hebrews as a homiletic midrash in early form accredits messianic qualities exclusively to Christ. That is why Hebrews may be called a "Jesus-Midrash."

Gabriella Gelardini offers a form-critical, historical, and intertextual analysis of Hebrews. She starts by acknowledging that Hebrews is frequently categorized formally as an ancient synagogue homily with its consequent *Sitz im Leben* within the Sabbath gathering. By considering the liturgical conventions in ancient production and reception aesthetics of synagogue homilies, she makes clear that Hebrews must have functioned as the interpretation, teaching, and application of a first reading from the Torah (*sidrah*) and a second reading from the Prophets (*haphtarah*). Gelardini shows that the *sidrah* must stem from Exod 31:18–32:35 (breaking of the covenant) and the *haphtarah* from Jer 31:31–34 (covenant renewal). As is usual for homilies conforming to the *petichta* type, the *sidrah* in the introduction of the homily is not quoted but rather referred to in midrashic manner, except that it quotes—as it should—the last verse prior to (or first verse of) the *sidrah*, namely Exod 31:17b in Heb 4:4. As expected, the complementary *haphtarah* is quoted explicitly in the central part of the homily. The fact that these readings appear so central for the theme and structure of the homily, and moreover serve as its hermeneutical key, does justice to the obvious importance and extraordinary quantity of quotations from the LXX in Hebrews. The reconstructed two readings are part of the liturgical reading cycle, the Palestinian Triennial Cycle in early form, and both of them hint at the most important day of fast in Jewish tradition, *Tisha be-Av*. This suggestion is confirmed when the central quotations and the theological concepts in Hebrews are compared with extra-biblical text and information on *Tisha be-Av*.

Part Two, "*Sociology, Ethics, and Rhetoric in Hebrews*," considers socio-ethical matters in the first three contributions (Aitken, Backhaus, Dunning) and rhetoric in the fourth contribution (Löhr).

Ellen Bradshaw Aitken explores Hebrews in political and ideological terms. She sees the author of Hebrews as articulating resistance to the imperial rule, ideology, and propaganda expressed in the events and monuments surrounding the triumph of Vespasian and Titus, a triumph bestowed upon them by the Roman Senate for their victory in the First Jewish War and the destruction of Jerusalem in 70 CE. According to Aitken, the resistance is expressed by means of Christology, by depicting to whom the "real" triumph belongs and where the "real" temple is, and by promoting an ethic for the community that is consonant with the identity of the true triumphant ruler and that values solidarity with those who are perceived to be suffering under Flavian rule. The author's use of the theology of the Roman triumph is, moreover, an act of appropriating the religio-political strategies of the oppressor for the community's own ends; it is likely that he thus empowers those who are dispossessed.

Knut Backhaus investigates the ethical concepts of Hebrews by means of a sociology of knowledge. While there is widespread agreement on the moral purpose of Hebrews, there is also some embarrassment as to the particular form of such an ethos. If the main objection against the ethical program of Hebrews, namely, that it contains merely historical but no normative value, proves false, then the question of the relationship of the ethical exhortations and the general theology arises. Backhaus' elaborate examination of semantics and cultic and sociomorphic imagery in the paraenetical passages leads him to the following conclusion: The general theological conception of Hebrews legitimates the referential system that safeguards and determines both the perception of reality and the self-understanding of the community addressed. So the general theological conception as well as the particular ethical instructions serve the same purpose, i.e., the systematic and practical conceptualization of an interpretative sphere that protects the self-definition of the community from the cognitive majority and the pressure of cultural assimilation and enables the individual to internalize specifically Christian standards of practice. It is this cognitive, normative, and emotional orientation that is of ethical relevance, either directly in the biographical process of the second socialization or indirectly by means of habitualization and institutionalization.

Benjamin Dunning embarks upon a sociological reading of Hebrews by drawing from observations of religious groups—especially Mormons of 19th-century America. Mormons employed the rhetorical motif of outsiderhood as a self-designation in order to build and maintain social and religious identity. Dunning sees in Heb 11 and 13 textual traces of a similar dynamic. The rhetoric of alien identity found in these chapters performs a specific function with respect to identity formation for the communities that put it to work: it allows certain groups of early Christians to conceptualize and maintain their own distinctive insider status within the vast cultural field of socio-cultic identities in the Roman Empire, while at the same time leaving the issue of actual cultic practice in unresolved tension. This is done paradoxically by using a rhetoric of outsider status, rooted in a collective memory of Abraham and other great heroes of the faith.

Hermut Löhr pays attention to the rhetoric of Hebrews, investigating its semantics for rhetorical *termini technici*. The expressions that catch his eye are κεφάλαιον (Heb 8:1), ἀναγκαῖον (Heb 8:3), πρέπειν (Heb 2:10; 7:26), ἀδύνατον (Heb 6:4–8, 18; 10:4; 11:6), and Hebrews' self-designation λόγος τῆς παρακλήσεως (Heb 13:22). Even though these terms do not offer any direct or unambiguous evidence for the use of rhetorical handbooks by the author of Hebrews, it remains striking to Löhr that the author uses words and phrases whose rhetorical effect is to strengthen an argument by citing (pseudo-)logic or other necessity, possibility, or appropriateness. The expressions employed not only reveal the author as rhetorically skilled, especially in the sphere of argumentation, but point, moreover, to the field of deliberative rhetoric.

Part Three, "*Textual-Historical, Comparative, and Intertextual Approaches to Hebrews*," begins with a study of the textual history of Hebrews (Eisenbaum). The two essays that follow provide a comparison of Hebrews with Paul (Georgi, Miller), after which it is compared with Qoheleth on the question of authorship (Koosed and Seesengood).

Pamela M. Eisenbaum investigates the textual history of Hebrews in the framework of new proposals regarding Christian/Jewish origin and identity constructions. Her interest focuses specifically on the "afterlife" of Hebrews in the papyri rather than on the origin of the text, which allows her to contextualize the text within a literary landscape of early Christian texts. This investigation leads her to make fresh suggestions about the authorship along with the occasion, the date, and the addressees of Hebrews: Eisenbaum argues that the author or scribal editor deliberately concealed his identity as an implicit form of pseudonymity. Hebrews can be viewed as a quintessential example of a "theological essay," and thus its genre makes more sense within the context of the early second century. And finally, Hebrews is directed to an ideal audience imagined by the author, and its "supersessionism" is possibly a desperate attempt to construct anew a unique form of Judeo-Christian religiosity in which Rome is the common enemy of Jews and believers in Jesus.

Dieter Georgi examines the problem of succession, namely, of Paul's heritage in Hebrews, in a typological as well as a historical way. He starts out by reflecting on the *topos* of "school" in modern and ancient times, and deconstructs the common hermeneutical supposition that a school organized around a founder is something unitary. Georgi considers this step necessary in order to prevent misleading historical interpretations of the fact that Hebrews is placed at the end of the textual canon, an order that was only given in the third generation. With $\mathfrak{P}^{46}$, one of the oldest manuscripts, Hebrews was placed right after Romans, which offers a hermeneutical key: the author of Hebrews, an independent member of the "Pauline school," interprets Paul, in particular Romans, so that righteousness, justification, and Christology no longer function as points of polemics against or division from Jewish tradition, but rather provide a common basis. Thus, under the reign of Domitian and after the First Jewish War, the author of Hebrews understands "his" Paul as a new offer for synagogue and church in the Diaspora, not only for their survival but also for their flourishing in a world that seemed overcome by the powers of a demonized state.

In the stage of proof reading we were taken aback by the sudden death of Dieter Georgi on March 1, 2005. It is saddening that this greatly esteemed scholar was prevented from participating in the joy over the completion of this common book project. May his contribution in this volume—it was his last one—add to the high standing he had and still has in the field of New Testament studies.

James C. Miller compares the undisputed Pauline writings with Hebrews on the basis of the narrative worlds found in them. When speaking of narratives, he is asking about the stories found in these corpora that portray something of the "symbolic worlds" created by the authors. The questions that guide his inquiry are as follows: What events recounted in these writings form a meaningful sequence of events? What characters take part in these events and in what settings do they occur? Which of these stories constitute leading elements of a "narrative world" in these writings? In Miller's reconstruction of Hebrews' narrative world he sees the overarching narrative element as God's speaking and promises to the people of God throughout time. The four subplots are the story of the first and second covenant, the story of Jesus, the story of God's people in the past, and the story of God's people in the present. In Paul's texts the main narrative element seems to be God as the one sovereign creator. God's creation has been corrupted by the entrance of sin and death, but God, through Jesus Christ and the Spirit, is in the process of setting all of creation aright. Adam and Jesus stand as pivotal figures within this narrative. The three subplots are God's people, the story of Jesus, and the story of Paul himself. In comparing and contrasting the two authors, Miller focuses particularly on the priesthood, the story of Jesus and the two covenants.

Jennifer L. Koosed and *Robert P. Seesengood* apply a combination of newer approaches such as reader-response criticism, reception history, intertextuality and cultural criticism to the question of authorship for Qoheleth and for Hebrews. Koosed and Seesengood sketch the main historical stages of scholarship, showing how the various answers and constructions regarding authorship suited the interpreters' particular interests. Though both texts are anonymous, Qoheleth was long attributed to Solomon and Hebrews *inter alia* to Paul. This imputed authorship may have been what "saved" these texts. Nevertheless, it was philological analysis of both writings that eventually established the vast acceptance of the anonymity of these texts. Koosed and Seesengood conclude that this move in the modern/postmodern era may have served the needs of scholarship once again, since the erasure of the author and tradition guaranteed the erasure of authority.

Style and abbreviations in this volume conform to the guidelines given in Patrick H. Alexander et al., eds., *The SBL Handbook of Style: For Ancient Near Eastern, Biblical, and Early Christian Studies* (3d ed.; Peabody, Mass.: Hendrickson, 2003); abbreviations for works not listed in *The SBL Handbook of Style* follow Siegfried M. Schwertner,

Internationales Abkürzungsverzeichnis für Theologie und Grenzgebiete [IATG²]: Zeitschriften, Serien, Lexika, Quellenwerke mit bibliographischen Angaben (2d rev. and enl. ed.; Berlin: de Gruyter, 1992).

As editor I wish to express in conclusion my gratitude to several individuals who supported this project and helped to bring it to a successful end: First of all my thanks go to all authors in this volume, for their participation and cooperation in providing what was needed in due time, even when this required an extra effort in certain instances. I wish also to thank Prof. Dr. Ekkehard W. Stegemann (member of the Editorial Advisory Board of the Biblical Interpretation Series) for suggesting and recommending, and one of the editors of this series, R. Alan Culpepper, for accepting, the first proposal exclusively dedicated to Hebrews in their series. I wish to thank Patrick H. Alexander as well (Publishing Director, Brill Academic Publishers, Inc.) for his sensitive supervision of this project; throughout the entire process it was a delight working with him. I am especially grateful to the copy editor of this volume, Catherine Playoust (Harvard University). Her intelligent, professional, and very efficient work, paired with a meticulous concern for details, was indispensable and improved the quality of this volume greatly. And finally I acknowledge with gratitude the support of the Freiwillige Akademische Gesellschaft, Basel, whose financial contribution on behalf of this project was essential.

College, seminary, and doctoral students, but also younger and established scholars interested in Hebrews in general or in contemporary issues on Hebrews in particular, might enjoy the privilege of having relevant essays on Hebrews compiled in one single book. To my knowledge this is the first volume ever collecting essays on Hebrews from different authors. In this sense—as was stated in the opening—this volume is unique. May more follow in the future.

Gabriella Gelardini
Basel, Switzerland
January 2005

PART ONE

CULTIC LANGUAGE, CONCEPTS,
AND PRACTICE IN HEBREWS

DOES THE CULTIC LANGUAGE IN HEBREWS REPRESENT SACRIFICIAL METAPHORS? REFLECTIONS ON SOME BASIC PROBLEMS

Ekkehard W. Stegemann and Wolfgang Stegemann

> Metaphysics—the white mythology which reassembles and reflects the culture of the West: the white man takes his own mythology, Indo-European mythology, his own logos, that is, the mythos of his idiom, for the universal form of that he must still wish to call Reason.
> Jacques Derrida[1]

1. *Metaphors, History and Representation*

The letter to the Hebrews seems to be a good example of the interpretation of the death of Jesus in terms of sacrificial metaphors. We speak of "metaphorical language" if a certain point of reference outside a document's framework, in our case the crucifixion of Jesus, is spoken of in terms that stem from the semantic field of cultic sacrifices. The presupposition is that the historical referent here bears no features of a cultic sacrifice. Let us explain this argument briefly with regard to Hebrews.

It is not unknown to Hebrews that Jesus has been crucified (Heb 2:9; 6:6; 12:2). However, the document's mentioning of the crucifixion is rather marginal. Apart from a short notice about the loss of honor (Heb 12:2, ὑπέμεινεν σταυρὸν αἰσχύνης καταφρονήσας), which hints at a typical idea connected with the crucifixion, other circumstances of the death of Jesus do not play any significant role. In the center of the document's Christology the death of Christ is brought up in terms of (atoning) sacrifices for sins, particularly modeled after the atonement ritual at Yom Kippur (cf. Heb 9:11–14 which is contrasted with 9:7–10). Like the high priest who performs his atoning

---

[1] Jacques Derrida, "White Mythology," in *Margins of Philosophy* (Chicago: Chicago University Press, 1982), 213.

ritual at Yom Kippur by passing through a tabernacle, Christ has passed through the heavens (Heb 1:3; 4:14; 8:1) and is seated at the right hand of the throne of the Majesty. In the heavenly tabernacle he is now a minister (Heb 8:2). And just as every high priest is appointed to offer gifts and sacrifices, so is Christ, as the heavenly and true high priest (Heb 8:3). But unlike the earthly high priest, who enters the second tent with the blood of goats and calves, Christ steps into the greater and more perfect tabernacle with his own blood, once and for all, obtaining an eternal redemption (Heb 9:12).

The death of Jesus which happened in Jerusalem is only one side of the coin. The other side shows the cultic performance of the exalted Christ, who offered himself in the true and heavenly tent as a blameless victim to God. His atoning sacrifice will cleanse our conscience from "dead works" (Heb 9:14).

There is no doubt that in Hebrews the semantic field of cultic sacrifices vastly predominates over that of the execution of Jesus. In his commentary on Hebrews, Martin Karrer therefore states with good reason that in Hebrews the crucifixion recedes behind a theological interpretation of the death of Jesus ("Die Kreuzigung tritt hinter der theologischen Deutung zurück").[2] The differentiation he has in mind is a distinction between the death of Jesus due to a Roman capital punishment and its theological interpretation in terms of cultic language, mainly as an atoning sacrifice.

There is also no doubt that most New Testament scholars consider the cultic language to be *metaphorical*. To say even more, no other document of the New Testament seems to make a more comprehensive use of sacrificial metaphors with regard to the death of Jesus than Hebrews. And nowhere else does the use of metaphorical language seem to be as obvious as in this document.

Here it is not possible to discuss the different conceptions or theories of metaphorical language. What interests us for the moment can be best put in the following question: What are we doing by calling the cultic language used in Hebrews metaphorical language?

The answer to this question is closely linked to how we see the issue of historical representation, which is a certain topic within the larger picture of an essentially realistic epistemology. This type of

---

[2] Martin Karrer, *Der Brief an die Hebräer: Kapitel 1,1–5,10* (ÖTKNT 20/1; Gütersloh: Gütersloher Verlagshaus, 2002), 59.

epistemology regards (historical) representation to be a reproduction of an objective entity. In the German context of historical research we call this objective entity "historischer Referent," so the English equivalent may be "point of historical reference" or simply "historical referent." If the semantics of a text or a passage lacks any point of historical reference outside the text, then the language is taken as metaphorical. Transferring this idea to the sacrificial language of Hebrews, the logic is as follows: since the sacrificial language regarding the death of Jesus in Hebrews lacks any (historical) referent outside the text, there is no doubt that the document makes use of the cultic language in a metaphorical way. On the contrary, the crucifixion of Jesus in Jerusalem, which is taken as the historical referent outside the relevant passages in Hebrews, neither shows any feature of the performance of a cultic sacrifice nor regards Jesus as a substitute for an animal victim. Consequently, we draw the conclusion that the sacrificial language of the textual passages in question is metaphorical, and we take it as a means toward a theological understanding of the death of Christ.

And to say even more—the sacrificial language of Hebrews looks like a very lucid example of a metaphorical interpretation of the death of Jesus, since in this biblical document the offering of Christ as the victim of the sacrificial ritual seems to take place in a *heavenly sanctuary*. Therefore, due to our epistemological paradigm, the sacrifice of Christ can *a priori* be ruled out as a potential historical referent, since from the perspective of our worldview heaven is no place for historical events. But exactly this ontological presupposition of our scientific paradigm is instructive, because it reveals its particular cultural perspective. Let us explain this argument a little bit further.

1.1. *Occidental Rationalism*

Twenty years ago, Martin Hengel published a small book on early Christian historiography which contains some principles concerning the historical-critical method. One of them seems to be really postmodern, if it is permissible to use this label with reference to a text of Martin Hengel.

Hengel's target here is Ernst Troeltsch's assertion concerning the "almighty" principle of analogy as a key to the critical procedure of historiography. Troeltsch postulates a kind of sameness of all reality which is transparent and available to all human beings regardless of their culture or historical epoch. In the context of historiography this means that everything in history is in principle of the same kind.

We don't hesitate to underline Hengel's response to this claim, when he writes:[3]

> Damit wird die ... gegenwärtige Wirklichkeitserfahrung zum entscheidenden Kriterium dafür gemacht, was in der Vergangenheit geschehen sein kann und was nicht.
>
> With that [premise] the present experience of reality gains the rank of a definitive criterion for what may have happened in the past and what may have not.

What is more, it is not only the aspect of time, the dominance of the present time, that is at stake here. Hengel's argument has to be broadened. The system of measurement for the experience of reality comes from a particular culture and its worldview, which guides our decisions about what is false and what is true. Specifically, it comes from the European or Western culture, which invented the "Western episteme" (Michel Foucault). Or, to mention some other labels, because nowadays we have a lot of labels for this particular epistemology, we can call this culture-bound epistemological paradigm "Eurocentrism" and "logocentrism," like Derrida, who puts both labels together in his *Of Grammatology*. He also coined the phrase "white mythology," which in many aspects seems to point to the same features of the epistemology of the West for which Jürgen Habermas coined the phrase "occidental rationalism." Whichever label is used, behind it lies a shared insight about the loss of the absoluteness and universal validity of the Western epistemological paradigm, which started its dominance with the Enlightenment. Robert Young puts it well in his inspiring book, *White Mythologies: Writing History and the West*, which considers the "self-consciousness about a culture's own historical relativity" as a characteristic feature of Postmodernism. He writes:[4]

> Postmodernism itself could be said to mark ... the sense of the loss of European history and culture as History and Culture, the loss of their unquestioned place at the centre of the world. We could say that if, according to Foucault, the centrality of "Man" dissolved at the end of

---

[3] Martin Hengel, *Zur urchristlichen Geschichtsschreibung* (2d ed.; Stuttgart: Calwer, 1984), 107.

[4] Robert Young, *White Mythologies: Writing History and the West* (London: Routledge, 1990; 2d ed. 2004), 20.

the eighteenth century as the "Classical Order" gave way to "History," today at the end of the twentieth century, as "History" gives way to the "Postmodern," we are witnessing the dissolution of "the West."

1.2. *The Epistemological Paradigm of the West Distinguishes Between the* brutum factum historicum *and its Interpretation*

The underlying historical paradigm deserves another critical observation. Recall Martin Karrer's statement quoted above, in which he makes a distinction between the crucifixion of Jesus as a historical event and its additional theological interpretation in terms of sacrifices. And perhaps so do we all. So it's not our intention to blame Martin Karrer for a supposedly problematic distinction but to make us all a little bit more aware of an epistemological premise we all take for granted.

First of all: This type of scientific paradigm assumes that we are generally able to distinguish between a historical event and its later interpretation. In other words, this strategy of argumentation presupposes the existence of something like a *brutum factum* from which we can discern its subsequent interpretation. In our case, the *brutum factum* is the death of Jesus due to his crucifixion by Roman soldiers. The interpretation is the understanding of this death as an atoning sacrifice. And because the historical referent lacks any feature of a real cultic sacrificial ritual, the interpretation must be a theological and metaphorical one. But is there really any such thing as a pure historical fact, a *brutum factum historicum*, a kind of historical thing-in-itself, without interpretation and influences of the cultural and individual idiosyncrasies of the historian?

Secondly: This type of scientific paradigm does not take into consideration that the so-called *brutum factum* cannot be perceived without the use of language and therefore within the setting or patterns of a certain culture. It is our suspicion that there is no such thing as a *brutum factum historicum*, because two elements are always required for the process of historical research: the historical data; and the historian, whose perception of the data as well as his interpretation is inevitably culture-bound. In our—and by this is meant here the Westerners'—understanding of reality, the perception of the death of Jesus on the cross as a so-called real historical event only allows for political, social, forensic, or psychological dimensions of its representation. Other forms of representing his death, such as in terms of an atoning sacrifice, appear in our spectrum of perceptions *a priori* as an additional and metaphorical *interpretation*, or, to reactivate a former notion, as *mythical*.

So we conclude: The decision between a metaphorical and a non-metaphorical interpretation of the death of Jesus depends on our assessment of the historical referent to which a textual passage is related. Therefore it depends on the respective model of reality that, as far as our model is concerned, we take as universally valid. We easily admit that the metaphorical use of sacrificial language is very helpful and deepens our interpretation of the crucifixion—but just as *interpretation* of the crucifixion, not its *representation*. On the contrary, the discourses of the social and legal aspects of the crucifixion of Jesus in Jerusalem are in our view not interpretations of the historical events but their representation.

Our question was: What are we doing by calling the cultic language in Hebrews metaphorical? As a quite global answer we would say: we are *demythologizing* the relevant texts by reading them as metaphors, which means we are reducing them to the "rationalistic" standards of our culture. On the other side, how does our reading change if we take the cultic discourse in Hebrews as non-metaphorical? What follows from this for the main subjects of this discourse? The next section will give some answers to these questions.

2. *Some Basic Ideas in Hebrews*

2.1. *The Way from Earth to Heaven's Sanctuary Through the Self-Sacrifice of Christ*

Our thesis is that the cultic language of Hebrews is not metaphorical and does not substitute for a real meaning of the death of Christ but speaks of Christ as the real high priest and of his death as a real sacrifice. Hebrews thus distinguishes between two cults, the earthly cult (that means the cult in Jerusalem) and the heavenly one. And by making comparisons between them, the author of Hebrews underlines at the same time what is incomparable. The intention is to emphasize that through the self-sacrifice of the high priest Jesus Christ, the heavenly cult is surpassing the earthly cult, which is only "a shadowy copy"[5] of it. This means there is a surpassing role for

---

[5] Harold W. Attridge, *Hebrews: A Commentary on the Epistle to the Hebrews* (Hermeneia; Philadelphia: Fortress, 1989), 216.

Christ as the eternal high priest in heaven, a surpassing sacrifice (i.e., the death of Christ the sinless high priest as self-sacrifice), a surpassing sacrificial act ("once and for all"), a surpassing sacrificial effect (perfect and lasting atonement of sins), and a surpassing place for the cult (earth and heaven or, better, from earth to heaven). The concept of comparing the two cults includes not only underlining the contrasts between them as qualitative differences, but also the earthly cult's role as prefigurement and at the same time shadow; it is ὑπόδειγμα and σκιά (Heb 8:5), a "shadowy copy," and ἀντίτυπα τῶν ἀληθινῶν (Heb 9:24), a "copy of what is real or true."[6]

Attridge rightly hinted at the Platonic language or motif here. This "Platonizing"[7] concept seems to have an analogy in the basic (soteriological) concept of Hebrews. The Platonic and especially the Philonic[8] version of the ascent or rise of the soul from the sensible to the ideal world, however, does not occur as such. Rather Hebrews' concept is that Christ as the heavenly Son of God arrived in the world (Heb 10:5) and returned to heaven by offering his body (Heb 10:10) on earth. This death is the true and unique sacrifice once and for all, the true and unique effective or perfect atonement of sins, and, most importantly for our thesis, the removal of the separation between earth and heaven. By re-entering the heavenly sanctuary after and through his death, Christ became the forerunner (Heb 6:20), the πρόδρομος, of all who as believers have been and will be perfectly atoned for by his self-sacrifice. Thus, Christ has "inaugurated" the way and the believers have the παρρησία, the confidence, in this access to the heavenly sanctuary (Heb 10:19–22). The death of Christ on earth has removed the demarcation between heaven and earth. The earth is now open to heaven, or the way on earth is now paved for those sanctified by his blood as a living way to heaven. However, only Christ himself has taken this way already and has arrived in the heavenly sanctuary to worship as high priest at the presence of God; thus he has found for himself, or arrived at, eternal redemption (Heb 9:12). He has already overcome or made his way through the veil that separates the heavenly sanctuary from earth (the commentary "that is his flesh" in Heb 10:19–20 may well

---

[6] Translations follow Attridge, *Hebrews*, 216, 260, 263.
[7] Attridge, *Hebrews*, 263. Cf. Erich Grässer, *An die Hebräer* (3 vols.; EKKNT 17; Zürich: Benziger and Neukirchen-Vluyn: Neukirchener, 1990–1997), 2:190–193.
[8] See Philo, *Opif.* 71.

hint at his death, so that either the flesh is the veil that has been overcome by Christ through his death and has to be overcome by the believers by their death or at the moment of the second appearance of Christ, or "the flesh" is an abbreviation for the sacrificial death as such). But the way for the believers to heaven "has not yet been manifested" (Heb 9:8, see below) as long as the creation, the world, exists. Since the second tabernacle on earth, the *sanctissimum*, is a shadowy copy and prefiguration of the heavenly sanctuary, heaven itself is the sanctuary. But there is just one single room there (Heb 9:8), with the throne of God and no courts. The earth is, so to speak, the court, separated from the heavenly sanctuary by a veil ("the flesh"?), through which Christ has already gone his way to heaven. On the earth, but outside the gate, stands the altar, the θυσιαστήριον (Heb 13:10–12). So the believers do not have here a *polis* which remains, but are seeking for the future one in heaven (Heb 13:14). The believers' way to heaven on earth is inaugurated through Christ, but now they have to bear his reproach outside (Heb 13:13) and lead their life as already sanctified inhabitants of heaven. And since there is no sacrifice on earth any more for them (and perhaps in Jerusalem, too, literally, for the temple has been already abolished?), their way of life, their conduct, and their belief are like a sacrifice. Only here does the author metaphorically apply the cultic language (Heb 13:15–16), as for example Paul does in his letters.

2.2. *The Perfect and Lasting Atonement Includes the Cleansing of the Conscience*

Connected with this basic cultic idea of the way from earth to heaven is the idea of the two covenants. The superior ministry of Christ makes him the mediator of the greater or better covenant (Heb 8:6), announced in Jer 31. The key verses of this chapter, namely Jer 31:33–34 (as indicated by their repetition in Heb 10:16–17), refer to the concept of perfection and perpetuity of sanctification, which presupposes the total removal of sins, the περιελεῖν (Heb 10:11) or ἀφαιρεῖν (Heb 10:4), including the cleansing of the conscience/consciousness of sins (Heb 10:2). In the old covenant there was neither a perfect nor a lasting atonement. The sins were not taken away since the blood of animals was not able to do it (Heb 10:4). And the fact that there was no cessation of offering indicates the lack of cleansing of the conscience, so that Yom Kippur is, rather, a yearly remembrance of sins (Heb 10:3). The new covenant, however, includes the internalizing of the laws and the notion that God will not remember their sins and iniquities any longer. What has the cleansing or perfection of conscience, συνείδησις, in common with these essentials of the new covenant? First of all, as Attridge rightly says: "The reference to remembrance of sins under the old covenant contrasts with the promise that they will be forgotten under the new,"[9] or, more precisely, that they will not be remembered (Heb 8:12; 10:17). Remembrance of sins by God obviously has an anthropological aspect, namely a "bad conscience" (Heb 10:22). Conversely, a "good conscience" (Heb 13:18), that is, a conscience cleansed from a bad conscience, has a theological aspect: God does not remember the sins, since they are perfectly removed. As Philo says in *Det.* 146, the message of God is sent into the heart and mirrored in the conscience. And secondly, the internalizing of the laws, their being written on the hearts and minds, transposes the laws into the most internal and conscious part of the human being: heart and mind, which build the conscience. There is no external education necessary any longer, no external threat of punishment nor promise of reward or praise. So the first covenant's offerings are unable κατὰ συνείδησιν τελειῶσαι τὸν λατρεύοντα (Heb 9:9), that is, they are not able "to perfect in conscience the person who ministers."[10] In other words, in respect of or with regard to his conscience (κατὰ συνείδησιν) they do not lead to perfection, for the "bad conscience" remains as an indication of the non-remission of sins. Inside the person or as God's internal message to him he is aware or conscious of the inability of the offerings in regard to the perfect or total atonement or cleansing. The sins are not taken away and God is remembering them. Thus the conscience of sins (Heb 10:2) is just the inward equivalent of the external practice of sacrificial repetition.

3. *Two Exegetical Details (Heb 9)*

Hebrews 9:1–10 alludes to the yearly Yom Kippur and its inability to take away sins. In connection with the rite wherein the high priest enters the second tabernacle only once a year, Heb 9:8–10 comments:

---

[9] Attridge, *Hebrews*, 272.
[10] Attridge, *Hebrews*, 230.

"The Holy Spirit signifies that the way into the sanctuary has not yet been revealed while the first tabernacle maintains its standing, which is a symbol for the present time, according to which gifts and sacrifices are offered which are unable to perfect in conscience the person who ministers, (being) only fleshly ordinances, about foods and drinks and various ablutions imposed until a time of correction."[11] What does "while the first tabernacle maintains its standing" mean? First of all, we agree that this verse should not be related to the destruction of the temple. But if the second tabernacle symbolizes the heavenly sanctuary and the high priest's entrance into it once a year symbolizes Christ's entering once and for all into the heavenly sanctuary, which is part of "the greater and more perfect tabernacle, which is not manufactured, that is, not of this creation" (Heb 9:11–12),[12] then we suggest that the "*stasis* of the first tabernacle" means the existence of "this creation." The perfect passive πεφανερῶσθαι of the verb φανερόω in Heb 9:8 therefore could be translated by "has not yet been revealed," in the sense of "has not yet appeared, has not yet been manifested publicly" (as Christ has already appeared or has been manifested for the abolition of sin; cf. πεφανέρωται in Heb 9:26). The access of the way is opened by Christ's sacrifice and he has already arrived in the sanctuary of the "greater tabernacle," but as long as the created world exists this access has not been manifested to the believers. This will take place when Christ "will a second time appear, apart from sin [that is, without atonement, since his death at the first appearance is atonement once and for all] (and) for salvation, to those who await him" (Heb 9:28).[13] Christ himself will take them on the way to heaven which he has opened for them by his death, that is, by the removing of sins and by sanctifying them. So even if the "first tabernacle maintains (still) its *stasis*," the "time of correction" (Heb 9:10) already has come with the first appearance of Christ. The "fleshly ordinances" concerning foods and so on have been abrogated and the written laws have been substituted, corrected by the new covenant written on the hearts and minds of the believers.

Hebrews often contrasts the perpetuity and perfection of Christ's self-sacrifice to the sacrificial activity of the first covenant (cf. Heb

---

[11] Attridge, *Hebrews*, 230–231.
[12] Attridge, *Hebrews*, 244.
[13] Attridge, *Hebrews*, 260.

10:1, εἰς τὸ διηνεκὲς οὐδέποτε δύναται τοὺς προσερχομένους τελειῶσαι; Heb 10:14, μιᾷ γὰρ προσφορᾷ τετελείωκεν εἰς τὸ διηνεκὲς τοὺς ἁγιαζομένους). Astounding, however, is the future tense καθαριεῖ in Heb 9:14: he will cleanse the conscience from dead works, so that we might serve the living God. Of course it is possible to translate the future tense with a present tense.[14] The logic presupposed by this interpretation is as follows: if the blood of animals sanctifies (in the past and now), how much more can and should and will (from the point of view of the effect of the animals' blood) and does (at present) the blood of Christ sanctify. But the indicative of the future tense could be an expression of the "pure future" of an activity, either of a lasting activity (I shall continue to do something) or of an event which will take place at some point in the future (e.g., our body shall undergo a transfiguration once in the future, but this has not yet taken place). If we apply these meanings to Heb 9:14, it is clear that the first one makes better sense, since the removing of sins has taken place. But is the cleansing of the conscience already perfect? In Heb 9:14 it says not the conscience of "sins" (as in Heb 10:2), but the cleansing of the conscience of "dead works." Maybe the author reckons with the possibility of remains, of relics of sins of the past in the conscience, which accompany their life until the end of time. Maybe the author reckons with a long life repenting, a μετανοίας ἀπὸ νεκρῶν ἔργων (Heb 6:1), initiated by the starting of belief in Christ and not ceasing before the end of creation.

Prof. Dr. theol. Ekkehard W. Stegemann
Ordinarius für Neues Testament
Universität Basel, Theologische Fakultät
Nadelberg 10, CH-4051 Basel, Switzerland
ekkehard-w.stegemann@unibas.ch

Prof. Dr. theol. Wolfgang Stegemann
Lehrstuhl für Neues Testament
Augustana-Hochschule
Waldstrasse 11, D-91564 Neuendettelsau, Germany
wolfgang.stegemann@augustana.de

---

[14] As is done by Attridge, *Hebrews*, 244.

SOME REMARKS ON HEBREWS FROM THE VIEWPOINT OF OLD TESTAMENT EXEGESIS

Ina Willi-Plein

1

The Epistle to the Hebrews presupposes the cultic concept of the OT *Endgestalt* and its interpretation by written and oral tradition.[1] Concepts of cultic space, ritual performance, priestly service, and the function of sacrifice were developed throughout the history of OT Israel from the very beginning of Israelite settlement and still after the end of the Second Temple period. Before assuming that the Epistle is speaking "metaphorically," one should know the "basic" idea(s) of the cultic system precisely, but there are still many questions left for discussion by OT scholars. Among others, at least the following main problems should be mentioned:

(1) The semantic diversity and complex history of what we use to subsume under the title of OT "sacrifice";[2]

---

[1] The following observations will not include the problem of the old/new covenant (Heb 8:13). For this, and above all for the assumption that the Epistle to the Hebrews has to be interpreted as a text for Jewish (which need not mean non-Christian) addressees, cf. Frank Crüsemann, "Der neue Bund im Neuen Testament: Erwägungen zum Verständnis des Christusbundes in der Abendmahlstradition und im Hebräerbrief," in *Mincha: Festgabe für Rolf Rendtorff zum 75. Geburtstag* (ed. Erhard Blum; Neukirchen-Vluyn: Neukirchener, 2000). On p. 53, Crüsemann makes reference to Erich Grässer (*An die Hebräer* [3 vols.; EKKNT 17; Zürich: Benziger Verlag and Neukirchen-Vluyn: Neukirchener, 1990–1997], 1:41), who remarks that nothing is against the "Gleichursprünglichkeit von Brief und Überschrift."

[2] Cf. the considerations in Ina Willi-Plein, *Opfer und Kult im alttestamentlichen Israel: Textbefragungen und Zwischenergebnisse* (SBS 153; Stuttgart: Katholisches Bibelwerk, 1993), 25–28, with the enumeration of three possible answers to the question of what sacrifice (*Opfer*) "is": a gift; a meal prepared by humans for God or in his presence (cf. Alfred Marx, *Les offrandes végétales dans l'Ancien Testament: Du tribut d'hommage au repas eschatologique* [VTSup 57; Leiden: Brill, 1994]); or a performance of world reality as it is or should be. The problem results from the fact that in Hebrew a general term for the various kinds of what we would call sacrifice does not exist. The only general term in Hebrew for sacrificial performances seems to be *qorban* קרבן (also in the NT: Matt 27:6; Mark 7:11), "coming near," which implies a concept of space with the throne in its center. Friedhelm Hartenstein calls this "Symbolik des

(2) Israelite mental conceptions of cultic space (holy places, buildings, correspondence of earth and heaven, etc.),[3] in both horizontal and vertical dimensions;

(3) The "mental iconography"[4] of divine presence in the cult, or the problem of human access to the royal palace (throne/abode) of God. What does it mean in this context that God is in heaven, and we are on earth, but also, that divine Presence (שכינה)[5] is located in his "dwelling place" (משכן) in the sanctuary (with its two focal points of the altar of burnt offering and the inner room of the holy of holies) while his throne is in heaven? This leads immediately to the next point.

(4) The role and function of human participants in cultic performances (priests, temple staff, individual making an offering, community). If priests are seen as servants organized in some kind of functional hierarchy with the high priest at the top, and if the latter may be seen on the mental background of palatial service, then the priests' function is a double one: service before the heavenly King, and communication between "outside" and "inside" or—which is not the same—between human and divine. From

---

'Zentrums'": Friedhelm Hartenstein, *Die Unzugänglichkeit Gottes im Heiligtum: Jesaja 6 und der Wohnort JHWHs in der Jerusalemer Kulttradition* (WMANT 75; Neukirchen-Vluyn: Neukirchener, 1997), 22–23. Christian Eberhart (*Studien zur Bedeutung der Opfer im Alten Testament: Die Signifikanz von Blut- und Verbrennungsriten im kultischen Rahmen* [WMANT 94; Neukirchen-Vluyn: Neukirchener, 2002]) presumes a general (semantic) meaning of all sacrificial lexemes as "gift." However, Rainer Kessler questions with good reason "ob man wirklich gut daran tut, mit Christian *Eberhart* 'Die Bedeutung *der* Opfer im Alten Testament' ergründen zu wollen": Rainer Kessler, "Die Theologie der Gabe bei Maleachi," in *Das Manna fällt auch heute noch: Beiträge zur Geschichte und Theologie des Alten, Ersten Testaments: Festschrift für Erich Zenger* (ed. Frank-Lothar Hossfeld et al.; HBS 44; Freiburg i. Br.: Herder, 2004), 404–405.

[3] Cf. several publications of Friedhelm Hartenstein, e.g., besides idem, *Unzugänglichkeit*, esp. 22 (and passim) and 44 (and passim), also idem, "'Der im Himmel thront, lacht' (Ps 2,4)," in *Gottessohn und Menschensohn: Exegetische Studien zu zwei Paradigmen biblischer Intertextualität* (ed. Dieter Sänger; BThSt 67; Neukirchen-Vluyn: Neukirchener, 2004), esp. 169–170.

[4] For this term, which was introduced to OT discussion by Tryggve N. D. Mettinger, *No Graven Image? Israelite Aniconism in Its Ancient Near Eastern Context* (ConBOT 42; Stockholm: Almqvist & Wiksell, 1995), esp. 20 (with n. 25), see Friedhelm Hartenstein, *Das "Angesicht JHWHs:" Studien zu seinem höfischen und kultischen Bedeutungshintergrund in den Psalmen und in Exodus 32–34* (Habil. theol., Marburg, 2000; FAT; Tübingen: Mohr Siebeck, forthcoming), 7 (with n. 35).

[5] See Bernd Janowski, "'Ich will in eurer Mitte wohnen.' Struktur und Genese der exilischen Schekina-Theologie," in idem, *Gottes Gegenwart in Israel* (Beiträge zur Theologie des Alten Testaments 1; Neukirchen-Vluyn: Neukirchener, 1993), 119–147.

the human point of view, the priests are mediators who bring the community's need to God; but with regard to their service in the presence of God, they are paying homage to the almighty King.

(5) What, then, is the supposed (main) purpose and the special need of cult, sacrifice, and ritual? Or, with regard to Hebrews (or to the final shape of the OT and to early Judaism), what is the major aim: to overcome sin or to worship?

Out of the set of ideas that seem to constitute the cultic system of the final stage of OT texts, Hebrews seems to prioritize the heavenly sanctuary, the office of the high priest, the cultic performance of the Day of Atonement,[6] and the application of blood in the holy of holies. Why precisely these elements seemed to be fitting as basic elements for the new (christological) system presented in Hebrews has to be discussed by NT scholars. Nevertheless, from the point of view of OT exegesis, we may offer some background information and ask some questions.

2

What strikes an exegete of the OT at first glance is the extraordinary importance of Psalm interpretation for the theological argument of Hebrews, together with its persistent use of the rhetorical device of comparative amplification (*a minori ad maius*).

---

[6] For OT study on כפר and the Day of Atonement, cf. fundamentally Bernd Janowski, *Sühne als Heilsgeschehen: Traditions- und religionsgeschichtliche Studien zur Sühnetheologie der Priesterschrift* (2d rev. and enl. ed.; WMANT 55; Neukirchen-Vluyn: Neukirchener, 2000); Jacob Milgrom, *Leviticus 1–16: A New Translation with Introduction and Commentary* (AB 3; New York: Doubleday, 1991), esp. 1009–1084; and the recent study of Rolf Rendtorff, "Erwägungen zu *kipper* in Leviticus 16," in *Manna*, 499–510. About the scapegoat: Bernd Janowski and Gernot Wilhelm, "Der Bock, der die Sünden hinausträgt. Zur Religionsgeschichte des Azazel-Ritus Lev 16,10.21f.," in *Religionsgeschichtliche Beziehungen zwischen Kleinasien, Nordsyrien und dem Alten Testament: Internationales Symposion Hamburg 17.–20. März 1990* (ed. Bernd Janowski, Klaus Koch and Gernot Wilhelm; OBO 129; Göttingen: Vandenhoeck & Ruprecht, 1993), 109–169; Bernd Janowski, "Azazel und der Sündenbock: Zur Religionsgeschichte von Leviticus 16,10.21f. (I 1993. II 1990)," in idem, *Gottes Gegenwart*, 285–302; and most recently, Dominic Rudman, "A Note on the Azazel-goat Ritual," *ZAW* 116 (2004): 396–401. Janowski ("Azazel und der Sündenbock") concludes that the term לעזאזל after a rather complicated linguistic and semantic development meant "for the elimination of (a?) god's anger."

(1) During pre-Sinaitic times the status of the angels is surpassed by that of the Son (Heb 1, referring to Pss 2:7; 97:7; 14:4 LXX; 45:7 LXX, etc.). In Heb 2:6–8, this is deduced from, or demonstrated by, an exegesis of Ps 8.
(2) During the period that was initiated by the revelation on Mount Sinai, Moses' authority as a legislator is surpassed by the Son's legal authority (Num 12:7 LXX). In Heb 3 and 4:1–3, this is deduced from, or demonstrated by, the interpretation of Ps 95.
(3) After this series of comparative amplifications, the central theme of the epistle is how communication takes place between Israel and God in the period after Sinai and before the eschatological fulfillment. It is performed in the cult that was established on Mount Sinai and is executed by the priests in the tabernacle and the temple. So the core of priestly service seems to be the ritual of atonement by which the communication disrupted by human sin can be restored so that divine forgiveness may be granted.

Hebrews shares the mental conception of cult that characterizes OT texts—at least those of exilic and post-exilic origin (especially Malachi)—namely, the concept of an audience before the great King's throne, during which one has the opportunity to make a request and to find favor. In this context, homage and gift[7] are of great importance.

If the temple or the tabernacle is seen as a palace of the King to whose throne the requests of his human subjects are brought, then an introduction needs to be performed by palatial guides, that is, by appointed priests and especially the high priest. Priesthood (ἱερωσύνη) for the earthly sanctuary was entrusted to the tribe of Levi, although in Gen 14 King Melchizedek is in transparent disguise presented as a pre-Sinaitic priest of Jerusalem whose priesthood was approved by Abraham's tithe.

In this connection the vertical concept of space, with its correspondence between earthly and heavenly sanctuary, assumes great importance. Since Jerusalem is the place where God will put his name, the place of his residence (משכן) where his Presence (שכינה) is experienced, it is the very place of transition (imagined in a verti-

---

[7] However, we would not agree with Eberhart (*Bedeutung der Opfer*, passim) that *every* sacrifice is a gift.

cal axis)[8] and access to God's throne in heaven—the true aim of every cult.

The connection between earthly and heavenly sanctuary is not metaphorical, but may rather be described as "real presence." By amplification of reality the throne in heaven corresponds to the throne of the Cherubim with the *kapporet* as a propitiatory (ἱλαστήριον). That is why the minister (λειτουργός) in heaven corresponds to and at the same time surpasses the earthly high priest: Levitical priesthood is surpassed by Christ's priesthood.

Again, this can only be deduced from, or demonstrated by, the interpretation of a Psalm, in this case Ps 90:4. The decisive argument is the reference to the pre-Sinaitic priest Melchizedek as a priest without genealogy: exactly because Melchizedek was no Levite, it is the christological reference to the non-Levite Christ that proves the latter to be the heavenly high priest (Heb 8:3). For the Psalm addresses him as a high priest, although he is descended from the tribe of Judah and therefore cannot be a high priest on earth.

But is there really gradual increase (in the sense of a climax) in the series of amplifying arguments? Is it more important that Christ surpasses Aaron or the high priest than that he surpasses Moses, while at the same time one can realize "that Aaron's authority is confined to the sanctuary and even there, ... he is still subject to the higher authority of Moses"?[9] Of course not. It is Aaron's ministry in the sanctuary that is surpassed by Christ's. Since the service done by the high priest culminates in the ritual of the Day of Atonement, we have to examine that ritual; since the author of Hebrews is doing theology by interpreting Scripture, the main task will be to read the central text of Lev 16, which is the only biblical text dealing with the Day of Atonement.

---

[8] Cf. the idea of the vertical cosmic axis in Babylon and also in Israel, as demonstrated by Friedhelm Hartenstein, *Unzugänglichkeit*, esp. 56, 111 (and passim); and idem, "Wolkendunkel und Himmelsfeste: Zur Genese und Kosmologie des himmlischen Heiligtums JHWHs," in *Das biblische Weltbild und seine altorientalischen Kontexte* (ed. Bernd Janowski and Beate Ego; 2d ed.; FAT 32; Tübingen: Mohr Siebeck, 2004), esp. 145–148.

[9] Milgrom, *Leviticus 1–16*, 57.

3

In the last two or three decades, much exegetical investigation has been done on this subject,[10] and especially on two main questions:

(1) What is "atonement" (כפר *Pi'el*) and what relation does it have to "sin," "sin-offering" (חטאת), and "sacrifice" in general?
(2) What is the precise task of the scapegoat and the etymological and semantic meaning of *Azazel*?

To begin with the latter, Janowski's[11] considerations on *Azazel* seem after all to come nearest to a probable explanation, and at the same time they seem to prove the "foreign" (Anatolian) origin of the ritual. It is the youngest element[12] of the rather young ritual of the youngest OT holiday. Perhaps it is a finishing touch, inspired by contact with post-Hittite ritual specialists (who made a deep impression on many members of Ancient Near Eastern societies). The ritual of the day could work without the scapegoat, and so it is not disconcerting that Hebrews does not mention it.

As we have seen above, the main task of a high priest is to maintain communication with God. This is the case on Yom Kippur, too. The main point is Aaron's or the high priest's entering the holy of holies and thus getting access to the throne, "for in the cloud I will be seen above the kapporet" (Lev 16:2).[13] This is why Aaron has to "put the incense on the fire before the Lord so that the cloud from the incense covers the kapporet...lest he die" (Lev 16:13).[14]

---

[10] See the bibliography noted above on כפר, the Day of Atonement, and the scapegoat. With regard to the festival calendar, etc., see also Corinna Körting, *Der Schall des Schofar: Israels Feste im Herbst* (BZAW 285; Berlin: de Gruyter, 1999).

[11] Janowski, "Azazel und der Sündenbock."

[12] By this remark I partially revoke my own view given in Willi-Plein, *Opfer und Kult*, 104–107.

[13] Cf. Milgrom's discussion of the cloud (*Leviticus 1–16*, 1024), and for the problem of "seeing" God: Friedhelm Hartenstein, "Die unvergleichliche 'Gestalt' JHWHs: Israels Geschichte mit den Bildern im Licht von Deuteronomium 4,1–40," in *Die Sichtbarkeit des Unsichtbaren: Zur Korrelation von Text und Bild im Wirkungskreis der Bibel: Tübinger Symposion* (ed. Bernd Janowski and Nino M. Zchomelidse; Arbeiten zur Geschichte und Wirkung der Bibel 3; Stuttgart: Deutsche Bibelgesellschaft, 2004), esp. 50 (with n. 6). The problem has also been discussed in Hartenstein, "'Angesicht JHWHs.'"

[14] The translation here and in the following is taken or at least adapted from Milgrom's in *Leviticus 1–16*.

The *kapporet* is the point of intersection of heaven and earth in the sanctuary.[15]

Aaron has to change his clothes before beginning the ritual of the day. Several explanations for the use of the special linen garments, which are called "sacral vestments" (Lev 16:32), have been given in tradition;[16] the most plausible one is "that the angels were dressed in linen, see Ezek 9:2–3, 11; 10:2; Dan 10:6; cf. Mal 2:7"[17]—it is not improbable that Malachi may be dated to the same period as the composition of Lev 16.

When entering the *adyton*, Aaron thus enters the place of access to heaven; therefore he has to wear the same garments as the servants in heaven. After the central ceremony of atonement, when returning to the "ordinary" service of the sanctuary by sacrificing the burnt offerings for himself and for the people (Lev 16:24), which are "effecting atonement for himself and for the people," he has to change his clothes again. This shows that atonement is also part of everyday-service, which now (from Lev 16:23 onwards)[18] can start again. The two assistants who had to take away the ceremonial detritus (the scapegoat and the carcasses of the sin-offerings of priests and people) may—after ceremonial purification—"reenter the camp" (Lev 16:28).

The passage Lev 16:29–31 then impresses the date and character of the day, and Lev 16:32 makes sure that the genealogical succession will be followed. Leviticus 16:33–34 gives a short summary: the objects[19] for making atonement are the sanctuary (in the sense of the holy of holies?), the tent of meeting, and the altar of burnt offering; the persons concerned (those who benefit from the act of atonement) are the priests and "all the people of the congregation."

All this shows clearly that the purpose of the special ritual of the day is the "repair" of communication with God that has been endangered by contamination of the sacred place and persons. The contamination is removed by the special sin-offerings of the special ceremony in which Aaron acts as a heavenly servant in the inner room of God's house. To be able to do so, he has to bring the

---

[15] Willi-Plein, *Opfer und Kult*, esp. 108.
[16] We will not discuss here their historical (Egyptian?) origin.
[17] Milgrom, *Leviticus 1–16*, 1016.
[18] Or perhaps after the general conclusion in Lev 16:20.
[19] Cf. Rendtorff's important observations in "Erwägungen zu *kipper*" on the use of the different prepositions.

blood of the sin-offering for himself and after that also the blood of the sin-offering for the people into the *adyton* and to apply it to the *kapporet*. He can only do so because the *kapporet* is covered by the cloud of incense. The general clause Lev 16:16 clearly pronounces the purpose of all this: "He shall כפר what is holy of the pollutions of the sons of Israel and of their transgressions regarding all their sins."

What distinguishes the ceremony from other sin-offerings is not the means but the purpose: to repair "the tent of meeting that abides (or: of him who abides?) with them in the midst of their pollution." So כפר *Piʿel* seems to designate an action of repair or purgation.[20] It is complemented by the scapegoat ceremony with the general confession of "all the iniquities and transgressions of the Israelites, regarding all their sins" (Lev 16:21): the scapegoat is used as a transportation vehicle[21] to remove all "detritus" to the desert, the area of chaos, away from the camp where the tent of meeting grants communication with God. As for the scapegoat itself, it is the remnant of the election of one goat out of two for the sin-offering of the people.[22] "The purpose of the lots is clearly to leave the selection of the animals[23] to the Lord."[24]

Aaron enters the *adyton* by (means of) a bull as a sin-offering and a ram for a burnt offering (Lev 16:3). The addressees of the text know what a sin-offering is: it may be performed on various occasions, and it is always a ceremony showing, or rather performing[25]

---

[20] Here I follow Milgrom rather than Janowski, although the ceremony may still be summarized as "Sühne als Heilsgeschehen." Heb 9:11–14, too, speaks of purgation!

[21] Willi-Plein, *Opfer und Kult*, 106 (so the scapegoat is used for an elimination ritual).

[22] The casting of lots is here (and often) a technique of binary choice: "for the Lord" versus "not for the Lord." The meaning of "Azazel" does not matter for the context, but certainly it is not the name of a demon.

[23] We would prefer the singular: "the animal."

[24] Cf. Milgrom, *Leviticus 1–16*, 1020.

[25] I should like to insist on my interpretation of sin-offering חטאת as a performance, but contrary to Eberhart's objection (*Bedeutung der Opfer*, 259), I am not of the opinion that "die חטאת werde zum Träger bzw. 'Symbol' für Unreinheit oder Sünde und Tod." The misinterpretation of my ideas results from the double meaning of חטאת—on the one hand, as the result of a disruptive action against life (sin, חטא), and on the other hand, as a ritual that enacts (and thus overcomes) that chaotic danger. The latter might perhaps be seen as a "symbol," but in both cases חטאת is and functions as a verbal noun belonging to the factitive-resultative *Piʿel* of the verb חטא. This implies a critical reconsideration of the so-called *Piʿel privativum*; cf. Willi-Plein, *Opfer und Kult*, 98 n. 8: The *privativum* results from the construction with (directional) מן.

and thus eliminating, "sin" or fault. This is done by application of blood, which means application of (non-guilty) life (Lev 17:11).[26]

For this purpose an animal has to be slaughtered, but only in order to gain the (innocent) blood which is innocent life, belonging to God. So a sin-offering is no act of violence, no expiatory killing, and probably even no gift to God,[27] for life has always belonged to God. Rather, it is a presentation of life, an act which was authorized, according to the priestly writer (P), by God himself to remove the bad pollutions of sin.

But the presence of the tent of meeting and the holy of holies is more than that: it is the point of meeting of heaven and earth, the point of direct ascent[28] to God's throne. How can that be done without offending his majesty by so many pollutions and thus interrupting the way to come before the throne and to receive acceptance and grace? The ritual of Yom Kippur solves the problem by giving the high priest full access at least once a year, for the moment of total acceptance. The minister in heaven, however, always has access to the throne and thus can always intercede on behalf of the people. This is perpetual priesthood according to the order of Melchizedek.

So from the point of view of OT exegesis we would conclude: Christ has entered the heavenly sanctuary not by slaughtering, not even by sacrificing himself, but by bringing uncontaminated life into the sanctuary—his own life after his own innocent suffering. If any metaphor is present in this context in Hebrews, it is at Heb 9:11–14, where Christ's priestly purgation is said to have been done by his blood—which, after all, is a metaphor for his life. He "gave" his life for the benefit of others (ὑπέρ)[29] and thus entered the heavenly

---

[26] "The blood *is* the life": On the function of *Beth essentiae* in nominal clauses of identification, cf. Ernst Jenni, *Die hebräischen Präpositionen* (3 vols.; Stuttgart: Kohlhammer, 1992–2000), 1:84–85.

[27] Eberhart (*Bedeutung der Opfer*, 273) stresses that "kultische Reinigung [ist] nur möglich durch das, was vom heiligen Gott selbst kommt," and interprets blood application as a ritual of purgation. From this he establishes (p. 287, with reference to Lev 6:17–21) the holiness of animal blood (we would prefer to speak of the holiness of life). Between all this and the assessment of sin-offering (or its blood) as a gift there seems to be tension. God as the owner of life has conceded ("given") the blood "upon the altar to make an atonement" (Lev 17:11); so at best one could say that life/the blood is given back to its owner.

[28] We cannot discuss here its relation to the altar of "ascending" burnt offering (עולה).

[29] On ὑπέρ following the verbal expression for vicarious suffering or death, cf. Cilliers Breytenbach, "Gnädigstimmen und opferkultische Sühne im Urchristentum

sanctuary to do his priestly service forever: it is "making propitious" for the benefit of humanity. This is done once and for all, ἐφάπαξ, and even this statement may be part of the exegesis of the OT (LXX) text—taking up and interpreting[30] ἅπαξ τοῦ ἐνιαυτοῦ of Lev 16:34 LXX: τοῦ ἐνιαυτοῦ as referring to the high priest, ἅπαξ to Christ.

The sanctuary on earth is a "shadow" (σκιά, Heb 8:5) of that in heaven;[31] however, the sanctuary in heaven is no "metaphor," but a mental reality. Neither is it even a cult sublimation. The sublimation of cult—probably in times of great distance from or even non-existence of the temple—can be found in Hebrews, too, in the parenetical final parts of the epistle (Heb 13), when θυσία αἰνέσεως is mentioned (Heb 13:15) and the inventory of cult is metaphorized.[32]

But there is no metaphorization in the central conclusion of Heb 10:19–21: Christ is the high priest "over" God's house, and by his mediatory service he enables those who are ready to accept purgation and grace to "come forward" (Heb 10:22) and follow his leadership in faith (Heb 12:1–3).

Reading the Epistle to the Hebrews with its topic of Christ as the heavenly high priest against the background of the final shape of the OT,[33] the literal understanding of which the author obviously took

---

und seiner Umwelt," in *Opfer: Theologische und kulturelle Kontexte* (ed. Bernd Janowski and Michael Welker; stw 1454; Frankfurt a. M.: Suhrkamp, 2000), esp. 238–239.

[30] Such interpretation is according to the 11th rule of the 32 *Middot* of Eliezer (Günter Stemberger, *Einleitung in Talmud und Midrasch* [8th ed.; Munich: C. H. Beck, 1992], 35–36), which—like "Parallelen in den hellenistischen Normen von *synthesis* und *diairesis*" (p. 36)—allows the structuring and subdivision of clauses to be changed if reasons for a better interpretation can be given in this manner. This can be assumed for the LXX text of Lev 16:34, if τοῦ ἐνιαυτοῦ was understandable as a genitive of time, meaning "every year" (in this sense Xenophon, *Vect.* 4.23: LSJ, 568). ἅπαξ would then mean "(no more than) once," the subdivision of the clause could be understood to occur after ἅπαξ rather than before it, and the whole passage ἐξιλάσκεσθαι περὶ τῶν υἱῶν Ισραηλ ἀπὸ πασῶν τῶν ἁμαρτιῶν αὐτῶν {·} ἅπαξ <·> τοῦ ἐνιαυτοῦ ποιηθήσεται could be translated, "to effect purgation on behalf of the Israelites for all their sins one time; every year shall it be done." In this structure ἅπαξ could be specified as "once and for all," ἐφάπαξ.

[31] This idea may have a larger Hellenistic context, but it should also be seen against a possible background of the positive semantic connotations of "shadow" in biblical Hebrew.

[32] It can be no more than an assumption that great distance from or non-existence of the temple is what lies at the root of cult sublimation, "metaphorization," and the idea of the Holy Spirit as the "spirit of holiness" for a community without a sanctuary in their center.

[33] In this context we need not make any difference between the Hebrew and the Greek text.

for granted, does not lead to the conclusion that Christ's "blood" is meant to be (or equated with) an expiatory sacrifice.[34] From the point of view of OT exegesis, not only the relation between vicarious dying and sacrifice[35] but also the symbolic significance of blood in biblical texts deserve to be reconsidered.[36]

Prof. Dr. theol. Ina Willi-Plein
Professorin für Altes Testament und spätisraelitische Religionsgeschichte
Universität Hamburg.
Fachbereich 01: Evangelische Theologie, Institut für Altes Testament
Sedanstrasse 19, D-20146 Hamburg, Germany
ina.willi-plein@theologie.uni-hamburg.de

---

[34] Even less is there any connection (as is sometimes considered in the literature) with the ritual of Passover. Passover is no sacrifice at all, cf. Willi-Plein, *Opfer und Kult*, esp. 111 and 125.

[35] Cf. Bernd Janowski, "'Hingabe' oder 'Opfer'? Zur gegenwärtigen Kontroverse um die Deutung des Todes Jesu," in *Mincha*, 93–119.

[36] Just after finishing the main text of this article I had the opportunity to read the manuscript of a very informative article by Friedhelm Hartenstein, "Zur symbolischen Bedeutung des Blutes im Alten Testament," in *Deutungen des Todes Jesu* (ed. Jörg Frey and Jens Schröter; WUNT; Tübingen: Mohr Siebeck, forthcoming). I was pleased to find in it some ideas parallel to mine.

CHARACTERISTICS OF SACRIFICIAL METAPHORS IN HEBREWS*

Christian A. Eberhart

The Epistle to the Hebrews is the only writing of the New Testament extensively employing sacrificial images and metaphors. Most of these images belong to the well-developed interpretive concept of the sacrifice of Jesus. However, the precise meaning and implications of this concept change throughout the writing. Two passages from the Epistle to the Hebrews illustrate this change, and lead us right into the center of the problem:[1]

ὃς ἐν ταῖς ἡμέραις τῆς σαρκὸς αὐτοῦ δεήσεις τε καὶ ἱκετηρίας πρὸς τὸν δυνάμενον σῴζειν αὐτὸν ἐκ θανάτου μετὰ κραυγῆς ἰσχυρᾶς καὶ δακρύων προσενέγκας καὶ εἰσακουσθεὶς ἀπὸ τῆς εὐλαβείας

In the days of his flesh, he [Christ] *offered/sacrificed* prayers and supplications, with loud cries and tears, to the one who was able to save him from death, and he was heard for his godly fear. (Heb 5:7)

οὕτως καὶ ὁ Χριστὸς ἅπαξ προσενεχθεὶς εἰς τὸ πολλῶν ἀνενεγκεῖν ἁμαρτίας ἐκ δευτέρου χωρὶς ἁμαρτίας ὀφθήσεται τοῖς αὐτὸν ἀπεκδεχομένοις εἰς σωτηρίαν.

So Christ, *having been offered/sacrificed* once to take away the sins of many, will appear a second time, not to deal with sin, but to save those who are awaiting him. (Heb 9:28)

These passages are two examples of how the author of Hebrews[2] appropriates the concept of the sacrifice of Jesus. Both examples refer

---

* In honor of Robert Jewett, on the occasion of his 70th birthday.

[1] All biblical passages are accompanied by my own translations. Cult references and metaphors in the translations are italicized.

[2] Hebrews does not mention the name of its author. This person seems to have been known to the community of the addressees (cf. Heb 13:18–19), but the "limits of historical knowledge preclude positive identification of the writer" (William L. Lane, *Hebrews 1–8* [WBC 47A; Dallas: Word Books, 1991], xlix). In the church of antiquity and in current scholarship, proposals for Hebrews' authorship include Paul, Barnabas, Luke, Clement of Rome, Apollos, Silas (Silvanus), Philip, Priscilla and Aquila, Jude, Aristion, and Epaphras. See Lane, *Hebrews 1–8*, xlix–li; Werner G. Kümmel, *Einleitung in das Neue Testament* (21st ed.; Heidelberg: Quelle und Meyer,

to the passion of Jesus, and both employ sacrificial metaphors using the cultic term προσφέρω.³ Yet despite these common features, the two passages refer to different contents. According to Heb 5:7, it is Jesus who sacrifices *something*—in this case, "prayers and supplications" to God. According to Heb 9:28, however, *Jesus himself* is sacrificed. So in the first passage the sacrifice is an act of human religious behavior, while later it is a person, implying particularly the death of this human being. Investigating the characteristics of sacrificial metaphors in Hebrews, therefore, depends on the meaning of sacrifice itself: What is a sacrifice, and which ritual element constitutes its climax? The answer to this question necessitates a study of the Israelite or Judean sacrificial cult as a necessary precondition for understanding sacrificial metaphors in the NT—it will, thus, be a study in *Traditionsgeschichte*. The comprehensiveness of this study is naturally limited by the scope of this essay. I will, however, try to outline some basic features of the sacrificial cult as it appears in the HB/OT, some of which need to be emphasized against the general opinion of current scholarly interpretation.⁴ Furthermore, I will study how sacrifices are used as metaphors both in the HB/OT and in the NT. Conveying concepts such as "offering" and "acceptability," these metaphors comply with the nature of sacrifices in the HB/OT. The author of Hebrews appropriates this tradition, but gradually reframes the contents of sacrificial metaphors by referring them explicitly to the death of Jesus. Thus, the sacrifice of Jesus has two effects: it becomes the initial step of his exaltation and office as the heavenly high priest; and it purifies human beings so that they may approach the heavenly sanctuary.

1983), 345–347; Robert Jewett, *Letter to Pilgrims: A Commentary on the Epistle to the Hebrews* (New York: Pilgrim, 1981), 10; Craig R. Koester, *Hebrews: A New Translation with Introduction and Commentary* (AB 36; New York: Doubleday, 2001), 42–46.

³ The Septuagint frequently uses προσφέρω in cultic contexts. The verb is also common in Hebrews (cf. Konrad Weiss, "φέρω," *TWNT* 9:67–70; Harold W. Attridge, *The Epistle to the Hebrews: A Commentary on the Epistle to the Hebrews* [Hermeneia; Philadelphia: Fortress, 1989], 143).

⁴ For a more comprehensive investigation see Christian A. Eberhart, *Studien zur Bedeutung der Opfer im Alten Testament: Die Signifikanz von Blut- und Verbrennungsriten im kultischen Rahmen* (WMANT 94; Neukirchen-Vluyn: Neukirchener, 2002).

1. Reflections on the Judean Sacrificial Cult

1.1. Scholarly Interpretations: The Meaning of Ritual Blood Application

The cultic texts of the HB/OT contain no articulation of how a sacrifice "works." Even in the book of Leviticus, the regulations given for the five types of sacrifice (burnt offering, cereal offering, communion sacrifice, sin offering, and guilt offering) in Lev 1–7 are primarily concerned with the correct performance of ritual steps, but omit any explicit statement on how a sacrifice "functions." This might be due to the fact that sacrifices were part of everyday life and did not need any explicit definition. This common knowledge remained unmentioned in the priestly texts to which Leviticus belongs, and has thus been lost for the modern reader because in today's religious practice actual sacrifices are no longer offered.

It seems like this lack of a clear definition is reflected in academic scholarship, because there are almost as many theories on sacrifice as there are scholars studying the subject matter.[5] A closer look, however, reveals that today, despite these different theories, most scholars agree with the idea that the killing of an animal or a living being is the basis of the sacrificial ritual. This killing happens in favor of a human individual or group, thus making a sacrifice a vicarious process. For example, according to René Girard and Walter Burkert, the sacrificial animal serves as a substitute for the human being.[6] And according to Hartmut Gese, atonement accomplished

---

[5] For a summary of the most prominent theories on sacrifice see Josef Drexler, *Die Illusion des Opfers: Ein wissenschaftlicher Überblick über die wichtigsten Opfertheorien ausgehend vom deleuzianischen Polyperspektivismusmodell* (Münchener Ethnologische Abhandlungen 12; Munich: Anacon, 1993), 1–2; Peter Gerlitz, "Opfer I. Religionsgeschichte," *TRE* 25:253–254.

[6] Girard claims that sacrifices are a way of controlling violence and conflicts found at the heart of human society by offering a space where these destructive powers can be exercised in the act of killing. Therefore a sacrifice may be interpreted as a legalized form of collective murder directed at sustaining the human society. See René Girard, *La violence et le sacré* (Paris: Grasset, 1972); idem, *Ausstossung und Verfolgung: Eine historische Theorie des Sündenbocks* (Frankfurt: Fischer, 1992), 48–69. Burkert holds that the experience of hunting has a positive and conciliatory effect on society in that it provides food and requires a special organization of the human community. A sacrifice, then, is the ritualized repetition of the climax of a hunt because it allows people to re-experience the killing of an animal. As with Girard's approach, killing is understood as the precondition for human society to persist. See Walter Burkert, *Homo Necans: Interpretationen altgriechischer Opferriten und Mythen* (RVV 32; Berlin: de Gruyter, 1972), 6–9; idem, *Greek Religion* (trans. John Raffan; Cambridge: Harvard University Press, 1985), 55–59. For a more thorough presentation and critique of Girard's and Burkert's theories, see Eberhart, *Studien*, 196–199, 203–221.

through sacrificial blood rites became the center of the Judean cult.[7] However, this scholarly consensus has been challenged by Jacob Milgrom. He insists that in the case of the sin offering, the חַטָּאת, the sacrificial blood effects the ritual cleansing of the sanctuary, which is subject to defilement itself.[8] According to this interpretation, sacrifices cannot be understood as vicarious processes, and animal slaughter appears no longer as the climax of the sacrificial ritual.

Milgrom's theory is corroborated by a number of further biblical passages. For instance, the *"torah* of the sin offering," the תּוֹרַת הַחַטָּאת (Lev 6:17–23 MT [ET 6:24–30]), deals with the consequences of the understanding that not only the blood but also the meat of the sin offering are most holy. Whatever coincidentally touches this meat or blood needs to be treated in a special fashion because it has attained sanctity: כֹּל אֲשֶׁר־יִגַּע בִּבְשָׂרָהּ יִקְדָּשׁ וַאֲשֶׁר יִזֶּה מִדָּמָהּ עַל־הַבֶּגֶד אֲשֶׁר יִזֶּה עָלֶיהָ תְּכַבֵּס בְּמָקוֹם קָדֹשׁ: וּכְלִי־חֶרֶשׂ אֲשֶׁר תְּבֻשַּׁל־בּוֹ יִשָּׁבֵר וְאִם־בִּכְלִי נְחֹשֶׁת בֻּשָּׁלָה וּמֹרַק וְשֻׁטַּף בַּמָּיִם (Lev 6:20–21). This transfer of sanctity must also depend upon conscious physical contact while the central blood application[9] rites are carried out during a sin offering ritual.

Another passage dealing with the special quality of sacrificial blood is Lev 17:11:

כִּי נֶפֶשׁ הַבָּשָׂר בַּדָּם הִוא וַאֲנִי נְתַתִּיו לָכֶם עַל־הַמִּזְבֵּחַ לְכַפֵּר עַל־נַפְשֹׁתֵיכֶם כִּי־הַדָּם הוּא בַּנֶּפֶשׁ יְכַפֵּר:

> For the life of the flesh[10] is in the blood, and I have given it to you to make atonement for yourselves on the altar, because the blood makes atonement through the life.

---

[7] Gese's understanding of atonement is based on the assumption that the human identity that has been defiled by sin is transferred to the sacrificial animal. When slaughtered, the animal vicariously suffers the death which the human being deserves. A second aspect of atonement is the rite of applying the sacrificial blood in the sanctuary where God resides. Because this blood still "contains" the human identity, the blood rite is a way of establishing contact between the earthly and the divine sphere (cf. Hartmut Gese, "Die Sühne," in *Zur biblischen Theologie: Alttestamentliche Vorträge* [2d ed.; Tübingen: Mohr Siebeck, 1983], 95–99).

[8] According to Milgrom, the blood of the חַטָּאת functions as "the purging element, the ritual detergent" at the ritual of the Day of Atonement, the יוֹם הַכִּפֻּרִים (Jacob Milgrom, *Leviticus 1–16: A New Translation with Introduction and Commentary* [AB 3; New York: Doubleday, 1991], 254).

[9] Here and in the following, the term "application" or "to apply" in the context of blood rites comprises both the "smearing" (נתן) and the "sprinkling" (נזה Hiphil) of sacrificial blood. Either way, this blood is brought into physical contact with something or somebody.

[10] In translations of Lev 17:11, the Hebrew word בָּשָׂר is often rendered as "creature" (NIV, *Traduction Oecumenique de la Bible*: "créature") or "body" ("Leib," cf. *Die*

This statement as well as its reiteration in Lev 17:14 gives an alternative rationale for the holiness of animal blood. Here, it is the fact that blood contains life which accounts for its special quality. This life belongs to God and must, therefore, not be consumed in the process of eating meat. Instead, it has been given for atonement on the altar, which means it can cleanse the altar (as well as the rest of the sanctuary) from defilement through human sins and impurities.[11]

These rationales for the special quality of blood are helpful to understand some aspects of the covenant at Mount Sinai (Exod 24:1–11) or of the ordination ceremony of Aaron and his sons (Exod 29 and Lev 8). During the covenant at Mount Sinai, an altar is built (Exod 24:4), and burnt offerings and communion sacrifices are offered (Exod 24:5). Moses collects the sacrificial blood in basins and, after having read the words of "the book of the covenant" (סֵפֶר הַבְּרִית) to the people (Exod 24:7), dashes half of it onto the people. In analogy to "the book of the covenant," Moses calls this blood "the blood of the covenant" (Exod 24:8, דַּם־הַבְּרִית). The story reaches its climax when Moses and Israel's representatives climb on Mount Sinai. There they not only see Israel's God (Exod 24:10a, וַיִּרְאוּ אֵת אֱלֹהֵי יִשְׂרָאֵל)[12] but even have a celebration including eating and drinking (Exod 24:11b).[13] For human beings, however, the direct encounter with the holy God usually has fatal consequences (cf. Gen 32:31 MT [ET 32:30]; Exod 19:21–24; 33:20). This is why the narrative of the covenant at Mount Sinai explicitly mentions: "But God did not raise his hand against the leaders of the Israelites" (Exod 24:11a, וְאֶל־אֲצִילֵי בְּנֵי יִשְׂרָאֵל לֹא שָׁלַח יָדוֹ). The fact that Moses and Israel's representatives

---

Bibel nach der Übersetzung Martin Luthers [1984]). While בָּשָׂר can certainly have these meanings, it may be pointed out that the context of Lev 17:11 deals with the prohibition of consuming blood in the process of eating meat. In Lev 17:11, therefore, the proper rendering of בָּשָׂר is "flesh."

[11] This particular consequence of human sins and impurities is often neglected. However, the HB/OT consistently states that God's sanctuary and holy name may be subject to defilement (Lev 15:31b; 16:16b; 20:3; Num 19:13, 20). Cf. Jacob Milgrom, "Atonement in the OT," *IDBSup* 79.

[12] In Exod 24:10 (and 24:11), the Septuagint weakens the offensiveness of the statement that the Israelites see God: καὶ εἶδον τὸν τόπον, οὗ εἱστήκει ἐκεῖ ὁ θεὸς τοῦ Ἰσραηλ ("and they saw the location where Israel's God stood").

[13] The remark in Exod 24:11 about eating and drinking might be surprising. The joyous celebration is, however, included in one of the two types of sacrifice which have been offered, the communion sacrifice (Exod 24:5). Its ritual includes the consumption of the sacrificial meat (cf. Lev 7:11–27).

survive implies that they themselves are in a holy state.[14] This is due to the previous covenant, consisting both of Israel's agreement to follow the words of "the book of the covenant," and of the rite with "the blood of the covenant."

In Exod 29 and Lev 8, the accounts of the ordination ceremony of Aaron and his sons feature analogous structures. After the main altar has been consecrated by means of the holy anointing oil and sacrificial blood (Exod 29:36–37; Lev 8:11), Aaron and his sons wash and dress in special priestly vestments (Exod 29:5–6; Lev 8:7–9, 13). Then their consecration is carried out in a threefold fashion: first by pouring the holy anointing oil on Aaron's head (Exod 29:7, 29; Lev 8:12); second by smearing sacrificial blood on the ears, thumbs, and toes of Aaron and his sons (Exod 29:20; Lev 8:23–24); and third by a particular sprinkling rite:

וַיִּקַּח מֹשֶׁה מִשֶּׁמֶן הַמִּשְׁחָה וּמִן־הַדָּם אֲשֶׁר עַל־הַמִּזְבֵּחַ וַיַּז עַל־אַהֲרֹן עַל־בְּגָדָיו וְעַל־בָּנָיו וְעַל־בִּגְדֵי בָנָיו אִתּוֹ

> Then Moses took some of the anointing oil and some of the blood that was on the altar. And he sprinkled [them] on Aaron and his vestments, and also on his sons and their vestments. (Lev 8:30; cf. Exod 29:21)

This curious combination of anointing oil and sacrificial blood corroborates the interpretation suggested above, that blood application rites actually effect purification. Not only the sacrificial blood but also the anointing oil is holy. This holiness is due respectively to the unique ingredients of the anointing oil (cf. Exod 30:22–33) and to the special quality of blood as a symbol of life. It is transferred to human beings as well as their vestments upon physical contact during application rites. Therefore, upon completion of this ceremony, Aaron and his sons are "holy" (Exod 29:1, 44; Lev 8:30, קדשׁ Pi‛el) and can serve as priests in the presence of God.

The stories of the covenant on Mount Sinai and the priests' ordination share similar objectives and ritual procedures. In either case, human beings face the danger of approaching the holy God. The preparation for this encounter comprises ritual consecration: the blood of sacrifices is applied to human beings so that Israel becomes God's

---

[14] Cf. Ernest W. Nicholson ("The Covenant Ritual in Exodus XXIV 3–8," *VT* 32 [1982]: 83): "the making of the covenant here was also a matter of Israel becoming Yahweh's holy people."

holy people and ordinary people become priests. Now Moses and Israel's representatives as well as the priests are prepared for the presence of the holy God and survive.

1.2. *Some Considerations of Cultic Terminology*

However, do terminological considerations warrant our interpretive tendency not to over-emphasize the importance of sacrificial slaughter? It has been pointed out that a basic term for sacrifice in the HB/OT is זבח, which means "to slaughter." And derived from this root, the Hebrew term for "altar," מִזְבֵּחַ, is nothing but the "place of slaughter."[15] Furthermore, the Greek equivalent of the noun זֶבַח, "sacrifice," is θυσία, which once again can refer to slaughter. Therefore basic considerations of Hebrew and Greek terminology seem to suggest that, in fact, the crucial action in a sacrifice is the killing of an animal.

However, the meaning of these central cultic terms needs to be revised, and indeed broadened. According to Jan Bergman, זבח is a comprehensive term encompassing not only animal slaughter, but the whole ritual process of the זֶבַח including the sharing of the meat and the burning of certain portions on the altar.[16] A מִזְבֵּחַ, then, is the place where the sacrifice comprising all of these ritual steps is carried out. It is important to notice that only such a broader meaning helps one to understand the ritual procedure practiced during the time of the post-exilic temple. This procedure is reflected in the sacrificial regulations of Lev 1–7, according to which animal slaughter is never to be carried out on the central altar, but somewhere in the forecourt or on the side of the altar (Lev 1:11; Ezek 40:39–41), which are areas of lesser sanctity.[17] At the post-exilic temple, therefore, the central altar is no longer the place of killing. It is actually the "altar of burnt offering," the מִזְבַּח הָעֹלָה, which indicates that the burning of the sacrificial material is the main ritual element to be carried out there.

A similar correction is necessary regarding the meaning of the Greek equivalent of זבח, namely the verb θύω. This word can refer

---

[15] Cf. Gary A. Anderson, "Sacrifice and Sacrificial Offerings, Old Testament," *ABD* 5:873.
[16] Jan Bergman, Helmer Ringgren, and Bernhard Lang, "זָבַח," *ThWAT* 2:513.
[17] Cf. Milgrom, *Leviticus 1–16*, 164.

to profane slaughter, but it has a broader meaning as well. A more appropriate rendering of θύω would be "to sacrifice," and according to Johannes Behm, θύω has the original meaning of "to smoke."[18] A broader meaning of the noun θυσία is attested in the Septuagint, where this term also appears as the translation of "cereal offering," מִנְחָה (see, e.g., Lev 2). Consisting of vegetable materials, this type of sacrifice naturally comprises no slaughter; rather, the only ritual step to be carried out at the sanctuary is the burning rite on the central altar.

So both the Hebrew term זֶבַח and the Greek term θυσία need to be understood in a broader sense. Another general Hebrew term for sacrifices, קָרְבָּן, literally means "what is brought near" and will be translated as "offering," just like its Greek rendering προσφορά. Once more, neither the Hebrew nor the Greek term stresses or alludes to animal slaughter. Instead, both express the inherent dynamics of a sacrificial ritual which, throughout its performance, "moves" toward the most holy altar, thus "approaching" God who resides in the sanctuary. Therefore a first conclusion of this survey of the sacrificial cult in the HB/OT is that the slaughter of animals is rather insignificant.

1.3. *Animal Slaughter and Burning Rite in the Context of Sacrificial Rituals*

Further observations will support this particular conclusion. For example, in the story of the "competition" between Elijah and the prophets of Baal in 1 Kgs 18:21–40, the crucial task is the preparation of burnt offerings. This text is a narrative, which implies that it will focus on certain features deemed important for the general plot while omitting less important information. In this story, the rough outline of the process of preparing a burnt offering is given no less than three times (1 Kgs 18:23, 26, 33). In these passages several actions of the ritual are mentioned: the selection of the sacrificial animal; the cutting up of the animal's body (1 Kgs 18:23, 33); the "preparation" of the animal (1 Kgs 18:26); putting the wood in order on the sacrificial altar (1 Kgs 18:33); and placing the pieces of the animal on the altar (1 Kgs 18:23, 33). Finally, the fire falling down from heaven (1 Kgs 18:38) also belongs to the sacrificial ritual. There is, however, no explicit mention of animal slaughter. The fact that

---

[18] Johannes Behm, "θύω," *ThWAT* 3:180–181.

the slaughter has happened is, of course, implied in further ritual actions like the cutting up of the animal's body. But the slaughter as such is clearly not the emphasis of the sacrifices, and therefore remains unmentioned.[19]

Finally, it may be pointed out that scholars arguing for the importance of animal slaughter for sacrificial rituals tend to neglect one type of sacrifice consisting not of animals, but of wheat, oil, and frankincense. This is the "cereal offering," the מִנְחָה, which has already been mentioned above (see 1.2). Even though the ritual of this type of sacrifice does not feature slaughter it is still considered a full "offering," קָרְבָּן (cf. Lev 2:1 [bis], 4, 7, 12; 7:38), like all other types of sacrifice.[20] Most interestingly, the law on the sin offering, the חַטָּאת, in Lev 4:1–5:13, stipulates that in case of neediness, a grain offering can be substituted for the customary animal offering (Lev 5:11–13). This substitute grain offering remains a fully valid sin offering, and as such an "offering," קָרְבָּן, for God. Therefore the cereal offering may be considered a serious challenge to traditional sacrificial theories as developed by Girard, Burkert, and Gese, because it demonstrates that a sacrifice can function without killing, and hence without a victim. This, of course, leads us now to the question of which ritual element may be considered the climax of the cereal offering.

The answer to this question lies in a brief reflection on the ritual of the cereal offering. Leviticus 2 distinguishes various kinds of cereal offerings, depending on how its basic materials of wheat, oil, and frankincense are prepared. At the sanctuary, however, each kind of cereal offering is handed over to the priest, who then takes a handful

---

[19] The narrative of Abraham's sacrifice (Gen 22:1–14) seems to contradict this conclusion because of its particular emphasis on Isaac's imminent death. It can, however, be shown that this narrative cannot be understood as a paradigm for sacrifices in general (cf. Christian A. Eberhart, "Die Prüfung Abrahams—oder: Wo aber ist das Opfer im Neuen Testament? Exegese von 1. Mose 22 aus christlicher Sicht," in *Wo aber ist das Opferlamm? Opfer und Opferkritik in den drei abrahamitischen Religionen* (ed. Ulrich Dehn; EZW-Texte 168; Berlin: Evangelische Zentralstelle für Weltanschauungsfragen, 2003), 32–33.

[20] Even though the cereal offering is one of the five types of sacrifices listed in the sacrificial laws in Lev 1–7, modern scholarship has in fact tended to deny this, thus questioning the status of this sacrifice. Gary A. Anderson, for instance, in writing his very comprehensive article on HB/OT sacrifice and sacrificial offerings, which generally offers a careful analysis of biblical data, nonetheless distinguishes *four* types of sacrifice while omitting the cereal offering ("Sacrifice and Sacrificial Offerings: Old Testament," 5:877–881).

of it in order to burn it on the main altar: וְהֵבִיאָהּ אֶל־בְּנֵי אַהֲרֹן הַכֹּהֲנִים וְקָמַץ מִשָּׁם מְלֹא קֻמְצוֹ מִסָּלְתָּהּ וּמִשַּׁמְנָהּ עַל כָּל־לְבֹנָתָהּ וְהִקְטִיר הַכֹּהֵן אֶת־אַזְכָּרָתָהּ הַמִּזְבֵּחָה אִשֵּׁה רֵיחַ נִיחֹחַ לַיהוָה (Lev 2:2; cf. 2:9, 16). The rest of the cereal offering is for the priest (Lev 2:3). This means that, at the sanctuary, the only ritual element with cultic significance is the burning rite on the altar. At the same time, the burning rite is the only ritual element common to *all* five types of sacrifice.[21] These observations are important enough to suggest that, rather than animal slaughter, it is the burning of at least some of the sacrificial material on the main and most holy altar which is the central ritual element of sacrifices. In the priestly texts, the verb קטר *Hiphil* usually describes this action.[22] Furthermore, two interpretive terms denote the implications of what happens during the burning rite: the technical terms אִשֶּׁה ("fire offering") and רֵיחַ נִיחֹחַ ("pleasing odor"). The first of these describes the fact that the fire on the altar transforms a material offering given by a human individual or community. The second technical term, רֵיחַ נִיחֹחַ, refers to the process of sacrificial smoke ascending to heaven. It conveys the idea that God smells the odor of the sacrifice and thus receives it.

This interpretation of sacrifices in the HB/OT is corroborated by a number of further passages. Starting with the cereal offering, the addition of frankincense to the wheat and oil probably serves the sole purpose of rendering the burning as the crucial element of the ritual more impressive (Lev 2:1, 16). The burnt offerings in 1 Kgs 18:21–40 have already been addressed above. Here the lack of any explicit mention of animal slaughter corresponds to the emphasis on the "fire of the Lord" (1 Kgs 18:38, אֵשׁ־יְהוָה) falling down from

---

[21] In the context of the five types of sacrifice, the burning rite occurs, among others, at the following passages:
Lev 1:9, 13, 17; 8:21:   Burnt offering (עֹלָה);
Lev 2:2, 9, 11, 16:   Cereal offering (מִנְחָה);
Lev 3:5, 11, 16:   Communion sacrifice (זֶבַח שְׁלָמִים);
Lev 4:10, 19, 26, 31, 35; 16:25: Sin offering (חַטָּאת);
Lev 7:5:   Guilt offering (אָשָׁם).

[22] The verb קטר *Hiphil* must be distinguished from שׂרף. Both refer to the burning of materials, and both can occur in cultic texts on sacrifice. However, שׂרף is used to describe the burning of sacrificial remains without any cultic significance (e.g., Lev 4:12, 21). On the contrary, the verb קטר *Hiphil* always describes the burning rite on the main altar. This burning rite occurs as part of the sacrifice and has a specific cultic significance.

heaven and consuming the sacrificial animals on which previously even water had been poured. The God who answers with fire determines the competition between Elijah and the prophets of Baal, and is thus identified as the real God: וְהָיָה הָאֱלֹהִים אֲשֶׁר־יַעֲנֶה בָאֵשׁ הוּא הָאֱלֹהִים (1 Kgs 18:24b). A further well-known example of God responding to a burnt offering occurs at the end of the flood, when Noah and his family leave the ark. The first thing Noah does is to offer a sacrifice, and God smells its odor and decides not to harm humankind again: וַיָּרַח יְהוָה אֶת־רֵיחַ הַנִּיחֹחַ וַיֹּאמֶר יְהוָה אֶל־לִבּוֹ לֹא־אֹסִף לְקַלֵּל עוֹד אֶת־הָאֲדָמָה בַּעֲבוּר הָאָדָם (Gen 8:21a). Another type of sacrifice is the communion sacrifice, the זֶבַח שְׁלָמִים. The largest part of its sacrificial meat is for the person offering it, who will usually consume it at a celebration. However, more than half of the sacrificial law in Lev 3 is dedicated to the precise description of the burning rite, and which pieces of the sacrificial animal are to be burnt.[23] Finally, there is no doubt that the characteristic and most prominent feature of the sin offering is the central blood rite (Lev 4:5–7, 16–18, 25, 30, 34). However, the formula about atonement and forgiveness (Lev 4:20b, 26b, 31b, 35b) always occurs right after the description of the burning on the altar (Lev 4:19–20a, 26a, 31a, 35a), thus demonstrating the importance of this ritual element also for the sin offering. In his study on the history of the sacrifice in Ancient Israel, Rolf Rendtorff holds that the incorporation of this burning rite into the ritual of the sin offering is the reason why this ritual has become a sacrifice.[24]

Observations like these suggest that the burning rite is the ritual element to be considered in any attempt to understand how sacrifices in the HB/OT "function." The burning rite thus marks the final step and, in the case of burnt offering and cereal offering, also the climax of the sacrificial ritual, which is essentially a dynamic movement through sacred space toward the center of holiness, thus an "approach" (root קרב) to God. Transformed by the fire of the altar, the material offering given by a human individual or community is "transported" to heaven in the ascending smoke. It is, therefore, the

---

[23] For a detailed study on the communion sacrifice throughout different periods of Israelite history see Christian A. Eberhart, "Beobachtungen zum Verbrennungsritus bei Schlachtopfer und Gemeinschafts-Schlachtopfer," *Bib* 83 (2002): 88–96.
[24] Rolf Rendtorff, *Studien zur Geschichte des Opfers im Alten Israel* (WMANT 24; Neukirchen-Vluyn: Neukirchener, 1967), 234. See also idem, *Leviticus 1,1–10,20* (BKAT 3/1; Neukirchen-Vluyn: Neukirchener, 2004), 171.

burning rite which determines the quality of a cultic ritual as "offering for God," קָרְבָּן לַיהוָה.[25]

1.4. *The Metaphorization of Sacrificial Language in the Hebrew Bible/Old Testament*

In Israelite and Judean history, sacrificial rituals formed the center of the daily temple worship in Jerusalem. Sacrifices could not be offered anywhere else because the cult was centralized, and thus limited to, the sanctuary in Jerusalem (cf. Deut 12:1–28). However, the concept of sacrifice was not confined to this space. By means of metaphorization it transcended the walls of this sanctuary and was implemented into the general religious language. In this process, ritual elements of the sacrificial cult as well as its qualities and attributes came to be applied to different theological concepts in order to find new dimensions of expression. Such metaphors already appear in the HB/OT, for example in Ps 51:19 MT (ET Ps 51:17):

זִבְחֵי אֱלֹהִים רוּחַ נִשְׁבָּרָה לֵב־נִשְׁבָּר וְנִדְכֶּה אֱלֹהִים לֹא תִבְזֶה

> The *sacrifices of God* are a broken spirit; O God, you will not despise a broken and contrite heart.

In this passage, the "sacrifices of God" are not those of the regular cult, which requires very specific materials for every type of sacrifice. Instead, a particular spiritual condition of the worshiper, namely, the precondition for righteous behavior, appears as the equivalent of such sacrifices. The common aspect of the material sacrifices and this particular spiritual condition is their acceptability to God.

Another passage featuring sacrificial metaphors is Sir 35:1–3. Displaying his familiarity with the actual temple cult,[26] Sirach even refers to specific types of sacrifice, namely προσφορά (offering), (θυσία) σωτηρίου (communion sacrifice), σεμίδαλις (cereal offering), and (θυσία) αἰνέσεως (thank offering), as well as to ἐξιλασμός (atonement), and allocates all of these to individual acts of righteous religious practice. Furthermore, the continuation in Sir 35:5 LXX (ET 35:8) is highly instructive, as it explicitly describes how the acceptance of these various sacrifices is thought to "function":

---

[25] For a more thorough presentation of the importance and meaning of the burning rite see Eberhart, *Studien*, 183–184; 361–381.

[26] Cf. John J. Collins, *Jewish Wisdom in the Hellenistic Age* (OTL; Louisville: Westminster John Knox, 1997), 90.

προσφορὰ δικαίου λιπαίνει θυσιαστήριον, καὶ ἡ εὐωδία αὐτῆς ἔναντι ὑψίστου.

The *offering of the righteous* enriches the altar, and its *pleasing odor is before the Most High*.

With its particular stress on the aspect that God smells the pleasing odor, the רֵיחַ נִיחוֹחַ, this cultic metaphor confirms the above interpretation of sacrifices with emphasis on the burning rite (see 1.3). In addition, the recurrent insistence of these metaphors on religious practice or human actions being acceptable to God allows the conclusion that the actual sacrifice of the temple worship is essentially an "offering for God" (קָרְבָּן לַיהוָה) which itself is supposed to be acceptable to God.[27]

In this process of metaphorization, the central idea of cultic concepts is picked up and situated in a different context, namely that of ethical lifestyle and religious practice. This means, however, that sacrificial metaphors generally witness to the interpretation of sacrifices by the contemporary Judean community. As such, they do not give a "definition" of how sacrifices "function," but convey the essence of sacrifices more explicitly than do the cultic texts of the HB/OT. Therefore sacrificial metaphors contain important information for modern scholars who attempt to understand actual sacrificial rituals. By referring to the burning rite and choosing the aspect of acceptability, the metaphors in Ps 51:19 and Sir 35:1–5 support the interpretation of sacrificial rituals proposed above (see 1.3).

Summary of section 1: The previous study of basic features of the sacrificial cult in the HB/OT has shown that, contrary to traditional scholarly theories, animal slaughter is not the climax of sacrificial rituals. Following the approach of Jacob Milgrom, we may assume that the different blood application rites have instead the function of cleansing either the sanctuary or human beings. However, the burning rite on the main altar is part of *all* five types of sacrifice, even of the cereal offering, which is carried out with vegetable material. The altar fire transforms the sacrificial material and transports

---

[27] It is worth noting that for Sirach, the ethical demands of the law are not more important than sacrifices. He clearly states: "Do not appear before the Lord empty-handed, because all of this [that you offer] is in fulfillment of the law" (Sir 35:4 [ET 35:6–7]). Cf. Theophil Middendorp, *Die Stellung Jesu Ben Siras zwischen Judentum und Hellenismus* (Leiden: Brill, 1973), 84–85.

it to God. In numerous biblical passages, the burning rite appears as the climax of the sacrificial ritual. Therefore it may be considered the key to the interpretation of sacrificial rituals, determining the quality of all types of sacrifice as "offering for God." This understanding is corroborated by sacrificial metaphors as they witness to the contemporary Judean community's interpretation of sacrifices.

2. *Sacrificial Metaphors in the New Testament*

When the early Christian community used sacrificial metaphors, it chose as its point of reference the temple cult of Jerusalem, which was still being celebrated until 70 CE. However, Early Christianity did not create these metaphors, but picked up a tradition which had been developed for many centuries and to which the HB/OT bears witness. Therefore a question of particular interest will be whether the NT writings feature any substantial changes to this tradition. Our study of selected NT sacrificial metaphors starts by considering references to the "blood (of Jesus)," followed by an investigation of the metaphor of "sacrifice." In a final step, cult metaphors in Hebrews will be studied. This approach will allow us to assess special developments featured in Hebrews.

2.1. *The New Testament Metaphor of "Blood"*

In NT sacrificial metaphors, all basic elements of the Judean cult have been appropriated. 1 John 1:7, for instance, alludes to blood application rites:

> ἐὰν δὲ ἐν τῷ φωτὶ περιπατῶμεν ὡς αὐτός ἐστιν ἐν τῷ φωτί, κοινωνίαν ἔχομεν μετ' ἀλλήλων καὶ τὸ αἷμα Ἰησοῦ τοῦ υἱοῦ αὐτοῦ καθαρίζει ἡμᾶς ἀπὸ πάσης ἁμαρτίας.
>
> But if we walk in the light, as he [God] is in the light, we have fellowship with one another, and the *blood of Jesus* his Son *cleanses us from all sin.*

This passage is part of a fundamental statement about the nature of God and about ethical aspects of Christian behavior: because "God is light" and not darkness (1 John 1:5), Christians are supposed to refrain from sinful actions and adopt a righteous lifestyle. While the contrasting categories of light and darkness "belong to the universal language of religious symbolism,"²⁸ the cultic image of the cleansing power of blood refers more specifically to a Judean background. However, both the universal and the cultic motif convey the concepts of cleanness, righteousness, and holiness. The example for all of these is God's holiness. Human sin, which appears as the general human condition (1 John 1:10), is removed through the blood of Jesus.

Another sacrificial metaphor is found in Rev 7:14:

> καὶ εἶπέν μοι· οὗτοί εἰσιν οἱ ἐρχόμενοι ἐκ τῆς θλίψεως τῆς μεγάλης καὶ ἔπλυναν τὰς στολὰς αὐτῶν καὶ ἐλεύκαναν αὐτὰς ἐν τῷ αἵματι τοῦ ἀρνίου.
>
> And he [the elder] said to me: These are they who have come out of the great tribulation. They have *washed their robes and made them white in the blood of the Lamb.*

This passage belongs to an eschatological vision of God's heavenly throne surrounded by a multitude of people from all cultures and countries of the world (Rev 7:9). All of these people have "come out of the great tribulation." First mentioned in Dan 12:1 as "a time of distress" (עֵת צָרָה), the theme of God's people suffering from persecution became a classic feature of apocalyptic texts (cf. Mark 13:7–23; *Did.* 16:4–5). It is usually coupled with the idea that the ones who persist will eventually be saved. Here, this salvation is illustrated with the cultic image of robes washed and made white in the blood of the Lamb. Such white robes are worn by martyrs (cf. Rev 3:5; 6:11). The idea that robes are purified through blood is, of course, paradoxical. In the HB/OT, however, it is part of the consecration of priests, as we have seen above (Exod 29:20–21; Lev 8:23–24, 30; see 1.1). There, even the robes of the priests are explicitly said to be consecrated through the application of sacrificial blood. A similar image occurs, for example, in Jacob's last address to his sons: Judah's garments are washed in wine and the "blood" of grapes (Gen 49:11). In Rev 7:14, therefore, the white color of the robes cannot be understood literally. Instead, it is a symbolic reference to purity and holiness.²⁹ This holiness is the result of the martyrs' faithfulness and persistence. Furthermore, just as Israel needs

---

²⁸ John R. W. Stott, *The Epistles of John: An Introduction and Commentary* (TNTC; Leicester: Inter-Varsity Press; Grand Rapids: Eerdmans, 1964), 70.

²⁹ Cf. Pierre Prigent, *L'Apocalypse de Saint Jean* (2d ed.; CNT 14; Geneva: Éditions Labor et Fides, 1988), 126.

purification in order to approach God on Mount Sinai (Exod 24; see 1.1), and as priests need consecration during their ordination process (Exod 29/Lev 8), holiness is a necessary prerequisite for the martyrs to approach the throne of the holy God where they are to serve continuously:

> διὰ τοῦτό εἰσιν ἐνώπιον τοῦ θρόνου τοῦ θεοῦ καὶ λατρεύουσιν αὐτῷ ἡμέρας καὶ νυκτὸς ἐν τῷ ναῷ αὐτοῦ
>
> For this reason they are before the throne of God, and serve[30] him day and night in his temple. (Rev 7:15)[31]

In these passages, the means of consecration is the "blood of Jesus" (1 John 1:7) and the "blood of the Lamb" (Rev 7:14). Both expressions refer to the crucifixion of Jesus and illustrate how human sinfulness is removed. However, it should be pointed out that the "mode" of this salvation is purification analogous to cultic blood rites. It is a subtle but important difference that, in this metaphor, the death of Jesus as such does not remove sin, just as animal slaughter as such is not the event which consecrates human beings in the HB/OT.[32] Instead, the death of Jesus is the precondition for the availability of his blood, hence for salvation.

2.2. *The New Testament Metaphor of "Sacrifice"*

Other metaphors in the NT appropriate different aspects of the HB/OT sacrificial cult. In opening the paraenetic section of his letter to the Romans, Paul writes:

---

[30] The Greek term λατρεύω refers to cultic service (cf. Acts 7:7, 42; Heb 8:6; 9:9, 14).

[31] David E. Aune suggests that the washing of the robes is "part of the ritual purification required after the shedding of blood" (*Revelation 6–16* [WBC 52B; Nashville: Thomas Nelson, 1998], 474). Such an explanation, however, neglects the danger involved in encountering God, cf. Gen 32:31; Exod 19:21–24; 33:20.

[32] In his comments on 1 John 1:7, Stephen S. Smalley claims that the "blood" of Jesus "must be interpreted above all against the specific background of the cultic observances on the Day of Atonement (Lev 16; but cf. also the Passover story and ritual, Exod 12)" (*1, 2, 3 John* [WBC 51; Waco: Word Books, 1984], 25). In these biblical passages, however, sacrificial blood is never applied to human beings, but to the lintel and the two doorposts of the houses of the Israelites (Exod 12:13, 23), and to the tent of meeting as well as the altar of burnt offering (Lev 16:14–16, 18; see also v. 20a). Therefore a much closer analogy is found in Exod 24:1–11 and Exod 29/Lev 8. Smalley also explains with reference to Lev 17:11 that "as a means of atonement..., the 'blood' of a victim was thus its life yielded up in death" (*1, 2, 3 John*, 24). But this traditional understanding of sacrifices (see above) does not account for the fact that 1 John 1:7 mentions a process of cleansing from sins.

Παρακαλῶ οὖν ὑμᾶς, ἀδελφοί, διὰ τῶν οἰκτιρμῶν τοῦ θεοῦ παραστῆσαι τὰ σώματα ὑμῶν θυσίαν ζῶσαν ἁγίαν εὐάρεστον τῷ θεῷ, τὴν λογικὴν λατρείαν ὑμῶν·

Therefore, I urge you, brothers, by God's mercy, to *present*[33] your bodies as a *living sacrifice, holy and acceptable to God*, which is your spiritual service. (Rom 12:1)

In this metaphor, the addressees are expected to present *themselves* as a sacrifice. Paul uses general traditional attributes of the sacrificial cult such as "holy" and "acceptable" (see 1.1, 4) to describe its special quality. The content of this service is determined in the following verses and consists of "renewing your minds" (Rom 2:2) and detailed exhortation on a righteous lifestyle—therefore the sacrifice is "living." To claim that "ζῶσαν is probably chosen to contrast the thought of a sacrifice which consists in the quality of daily living . . . with a sacrifice which consists in killing an animal"[34] is hardly adequate. This explanation fails to explain what the metaphorical value of the term θυσία might be for the context of Romans if animal slaughter as its supposedly central ritual element would be turned into the contrary. In the HB/OT, however, ritual killing is rather insignificant for the meaning of sacrifices, as has been shown above (1.1). It is also important to recapitulate that the Greek term θυσία does not necessarily refer to animal slaughter, but has a broader meaning comprising specifically the burning rite. It can, therefore, be the translation of מִנְחָה, "cereal offering," which is essentially given to the officiating priest who then burns a portion of it. Considering how the sacrificial metaphor is employed in Rom 12:1, it is clear that the nature of a sacrifice is understood as an "offering," the climax of which is to "present" oneself to God.

Another passage from a Pauline writing is instructive because of its similar usage of sacrificial metaphors. In Phil 4:18, Paul writes:

ἀπέχω δὲ πάντα καὶ περισσεύω· πεπλήρωμαι δεξάμενος παρὰ Ἐπαφροδίτου τὰ παρ' ὑμῶν, ὀσμὴν εὐωδίας, θυσίαν δεκτήν, εὐάρεστον τῷ θεῷ.

---

[33] The Greek verb παριστάνω refers to sacrificial service; cf. Heinrich Schlier, *Der Römerbrief* (HTKNT 6; Freiburg: Herder, 1977), 355.

[34] James D. G. Dunn, *Romans 9–16* (WBC 38B; Dallas: Word Books, 1988), 710. In a similar fashion, Joseph A. Fitzmyer comments that Paul "implicitly compares Christians with animals slaughtered in Jewish or pagan cults, but he corrects the comparison by adding 'living' and the following phrase. It is not a cult that offers dead animals to God" (*Romans: A New Translation with Introduction and Commentary* [AB 33; New York: Doubleday, 1993], 640).

I have received everything and more; I have abundantly, having received from Epaphroditus the things you sent, *a pleasing odor, an acceptable sacrifice, pleasant to God.*

In his expression of gratitude, Paul first uses business terminology when, in fact, drawing up a receipt for having received the gifts (maybe bread or beverages, etc.).[35] Then he turns to a different figurative background and employs sacrificial terminology, calling these gifts a "sacrifice," θυσία. Once again, it is clear that these metaphors do not convey the notion of slaughter. Just as in the Judean cult a sacrifice may be considered an "offering for God," so here objects of everyday life can be labeled in the same fashion, provided they please the addressee. This central nature of sacrifices is explicitly linked to the ritual element through which the offering as such becomes manifest, namely, the burning rite. The Greek term ὀσμὴ εὐωδίας ("pleasing odor"), a translation of the Hebrew interpretive term רֵיחַ נִיחֹחַ, obviously points to this ritual element.

Before turning to sacrificial metaphors in the Epistle to the Hebrews, one more NT passage shall be studied:

> Γίνεσθε οὖν μιμηταὶ τοῦ θεοῦ ὡς τέκνα ἀγαπητὰ καὶ περιπατεῖτε ἐν ἀγάπῃ, καθὼς καὶ ὁ Χριστὸς ἠγάπησεν ἡμᾶς καὶ παρέδωκεν ἑαυτὸν ὑπὲρ ἡμῶν προσφορὰν καὶ θυσίαν τῷ θεῷ εἰς ὀσμὴν εὐωδίας.
>
> Therefore be imitators of God, as beloved children. And walk in love, just as Christ loved us, too, and gave himself for us as an *offering and sacrifice to God, as a pleasing odor.* (Eph 5:1–2)

This passage features a number of elements familiar from previous cultic metaphors. First of all, the motif of sacrifice is again employed in a paraenetic context (Eph 4:25–6:9). As in 1 John 1:7, the example of proper conduct is God (Eph 5:1), even though Christ also appears as role model (Eph 5:2). This statement is, furthermore, dominated by three occurrences of the word "love," and the further context again contains the dualism of light and darkness (Eph 5:8–9).

The terminology of the sacrificial metaphor is similar to that of Phil 4:18 (see above). The traditional exegesis, however, interprets the metaphor in Eph 5:2 as a reference to the death of Jesus.[36] Yet

---

[35] Cf. Adolf Deissmann, *Light from the Ancient East: The New Testament Illustrated by Recently Discovered Texts of the Graeco-Roman World* (trans. Lionel R. M. Strachan; 2d ed.; London: Hodder and Stoughton, 1911), 111–112, 335.

[36] Cf. Markus Barth, *Ephesians: Translation and Commentary on Chapters 4–6* (AB 34A;

how this death could serve as an example for the detailed paraenetic instructions remains rather unclear. With regard to the previous investigation of both the sacrificial cult in the HB/OT and the NT sacrificial metaphors, it may instead be proposed that in Eph 5:2, the words "offering and sacrifice for God" do not refer to the moment of the death of Jesus. The sacrifice of Jesus is rather a reference to his whole life, which serves as an example of Christian love. The words Jesus spoke and the actions he performed, but also the fact that as part of this life he willingly suffered death on the cross, serve as the true example of love because they are an expression of a righteous and divine life. The verse demonstrates that the life of Jesus also has salvific value; hence NT soteriological concepts do include incarnational aspects.

2.3. *Cult Metaphors in Hebrews*

Despite the limited scope of this study, I hope to have established a background detailed enough to finally show the development and characteristics of sacrificial metaphors in the Epistle to the Hebrews. Let us start with the first sacrificial metaphor in this text, which occurs in Heb 5:7:

> ὃς ἐν ταῖς ἡμέραις τῆς σαρκὸς αὐτοῦ δεήσεις τε καὶ ἱκετηρίας πρὸς τὸν δυνάμενον σῴζειν αὐτὸν ἐκ θανάτου μετὰ κραυγῆς ἰσχυρᾶς καὶ δακρύων προσενέγκας καὶ εἰσακουσθεὶς ἀπὸ τῆς εὐλαβείας
>
> In the days of his flesh, he [Christ] *offered/sacrificed* prayers and supplications, with loud cries and tears, to the one who was able to save him from death, and he was heard for his godly fear.

In this opening statement of a lengthy clause on Christ's solidarity with human beings, his sacrifice clearly does not refer to his death. Instead, it corresponds to sacrificial metaphors found elsewhere in biblical literature (see 2.1). In keeping with the image of pious prayer known from Judean traditions (cf. Pss 22; 116:8; 3 Macc 1:16),[37]

Garden City, N. Y.: Doubleday, 1974), 558: "The author [of Eph] designates Jesus Christ's death as an atoning sacrifice offered by the pouring out of blood." See also Wolfgang Stegemann, "Der Tod Jesu als Opfer: Anthropologische Aspekte seiner Deutung im Neuen Testament," in *Abschied von der Schuld? Zur Anthropologie und Theologie von Schuldbekenntnis, Opfer und Versöhnung* (ed. Richard Riess; Stuttgart: Kohlhammer, 1996), 125: "So wird zum Beispiel Eph 5,2 Jesu Tod explizit mit Opferterminologie ausgesagt."

[37] See also Attridge, *Hebrews*, 150–151.

Christ's emotional appeal to God is vividly described here by employing the cultic term προσφέρω. Christ offers δεήσεις τε καὶ ἰκετηρίας, which implies that he turns to God. This phrase also implies what is then explicitly mentioned: God hears his prayer.[38]

The text of Heb 5:7 does not say precisely what Christ prays for. Yet the author of Hebrews "heightens the agony motif by alluding to loud cries and tears, which are not reported elsewhere in the gospel tradition.... [I]t is at least clear that total involvement in mortality is communicated."[39] In addition, the observation that God is called "the one who was able to save him [Christ] from death," a customary circumlocution (cf. 1 Sam 2:6; Hos 13:14), certainly alludes to the content of Christ's prayer.[40] It does not matter if this is understood as an allusion to the struggle in Gethsemane, or as referring to general mortality as a feature of human existence already implied in the first words in Heb 5:7, "in the days of his flesh." Either way, in a subtle fashion Hebrews associates sacrificial terminology with the death of Christ.

The next sacrificial metaphor with reference to Jesus is found in Heb 7:27:

> ὃς οὐκ ἔχει καθ' ἡμέραν ἀνάγκην, ὥσπερ οἱ ἀρχιερεῖς, πρότερον ὑπὲρ τῶν ἰδίων ἁμαρτιῶν θυσίας ἀναφέρειν ἔπειτα τῶν τοῦ λαοῦ· τοῦτο γὰρ ἐποίησεν ἐφάπαξ ἑαυτὸν ἀνενέγκας.
>
> He [Christ] has no need, like the high priests, to offer sacrifices daily, first for his own sins and then for those of the people. He did this once for all when he *offered himself*.

Hebrews 7 explores the image of Christ as the holy and blameless high priest. As such, he appears in opposition to the human high priest, who is still defiled by sin and will always be so. While the human high priest therefore needs to offer (ἀναφέρω) many sacrifices *for* himself, Christ has offered *himself* once. This new quality of Christ's sacrifice is the crucial difference between Heb 7:27 and 5:7, since in 5:7 the sacrifice consisting of prayers and supplications is not a self-sacrifice, and might have occurred repeatedly. Thus in Heb 7,

---

[38] It is beyond the scope of this study to determine how Christ's prayer was "heard" by God. Multiple ways of understanding this passage are presented in James Swetnam, "The Crux at Hebrews 5:7–8," *Bib* 81 (2000): 347–361.

[39] Jewett, *Letter*, 88.

[40] Cf. Koester, *Hebrews*, 289.

the author of Hebrews finally adapts sacrificial metaphors to fit his/her overall christological program set out in Heb 2:14 that salvation is accomplished through Christ's death. It should be emphasized, however, that the adaptation of the sacrificial metaphor changes the content it usually conveys. While in passages like Rom 12:1, Phil 4:18, Eph 5:2, and Heb 5:7 the metaphorical terminology refers to aspects of acceptability, holiness, and offering (see above), Heb 7:27 introduces with the self-sacrifice both a reference to and a focus on the crucifixion. In the discussions within this article so far, this has only occurred in cultic metaphors mentioning the "blood (of Jesus)" (cf. 1 John 1:7; Rev 7:14).

One question remains unanswered for the moment: How exactly is this salvation through self-sacrifice accomplished? It will be answered in Heb 9, where the sacrificial concept is fully developed. In Heb 9:1–10, the imagery of the Day of Atonement, the יוֹם הַכִּפֻּרִים, is introduced.[41] This means that Hebrews, in fact, adopts Judean traditions of atonement through blood application, which have been outlined above (1.1), in order to merge them with the concept of "Christ's sacrifice." Thus the author of Hebrews states:

> οὐδὲ δι' αἵματος τράγων καὶ μόσχων διὰ δὲ τοῦ ἰδίου αἵματος εἰσῆλθεν ἐφάπαξ εἰς τὰ ἅγια αἰωνίαν λύτρωσιν εὑράμενος.
>
> He [Christ] *entered into the sanctuary* once for all, not with the *blood of goats and calves*, but with *his own blood* to obtain an eternal redemption. (Heb 9:12)

So here, in fact, Christ's blood substitutes for the blood of sacrificial animals. Due to his superior quality, however, the effect of this new blood application lasts forever. The mode of this redemption corresponds, once again, to Judean atonement traditions: "how much more will the *blood of Christ*, who through the eternal Spirit *offered himself unblemished to God* (ἑαυτὸν προσήνεγκεν ἄμωμον τῷ θεῷ), *purify* (καθαριεῖ) our consciences from acts that lead to death, so that we may serve the living God" (Heb 9:14). This ritual cleansing through blood application rites is characteristic of the Day of Atonement,

---

[41] Hebrews refers to the regulations of the Day of Atonement in Lev 16 when mentioning the "tent" (cf. Heb 9:2, 3, 6). "Significantly, the author makes no mention of the second Temple—which had its critics—but declares that Christ's sanctuary is greater than even the Mosaic Tabernacle, the memory of which was widely revered" (Koester, *Hebrews*, 413).

and will be referred to again in Heb 9:21–22.[42] As was shown above in the outline of blood rites in the HB/OT, the covenant ceremony at Mount Sinai (Exod 24:1–11) also features blood application rites which consecrate the Israelites (1.1). In Heb 9:19–20 the author of Hebrews, probably seeking to ground his/her christological concept in the Judean traditions as firmly as possible, also describes this application rite and, in addition, draws in the ceremony of the red heifer (Num 19:1–11). Redemption according to Hebrews, therefore, is a mixture of metaphors derived from the traditional sacrificial cult, expanded by the idea that the human conscience is purified.

At this point, the question of the purpose of Christ's death needs to be posed. So far in the christological development found in Hebrews, Christ's blood purifies and thus eliminates human sin. As has been pointed out already, it is strictly speaking not Christ's *death* which effects this purification.[43] The Greek term αἷμα can, of course, be a synonym for "death," or more precisely for "murder."[44] In cultic texts of the HB/OT, however, this is not the case, because αἷμα always refers to the actual blood of sacrificial animals. It has been demonstrated that a sacrifice can be offered without a victim (Lev 2; 5:11–13; see 1.3). At the covenant of Mount Sinai (Exod 24:1–11), at the ordination of Aaron and his sons (Exod 29; Lev 8), and at the ceremony of the Day of Atonement (Lev 16), sacrificial blood purifies upon physical contact, which means when it is actually applied to people or the sanctuary and its sacred objects. But this purification would not happen if the animal of, e.g., a sin offering were to be slaughtered without the subsequent blood application rite being carried out. Animal slaughter is a preparatory element in the sacrificial ritual, and certainly a necessary prerequisite for purifying blood rites. The moment of slaughter as such, however, has no particular significance. Thus, cultic metaphors like those in 1 John 1:7, Rev 7:14,

---

[42] Heb 9:21–22a explicitly mentions: καὶ τὴν σκηνὴν δὲ καὶ πάντα τὰ σκεύη τῆς λειτουργίας τῷ αἵματι ὁμοίως ἐρράντισεν. καὶ σχεδὸν ἐν αἵματι πάντα καθαρίζεται κατὰ τὸν νόμον ("And in the same way he sprinkled with the blood both the tent and all the vessels used for the service. Indeed, under the law almost everything is purified with blood"). Two aspects are of interest in this passage: The effect of blood application is purification, and the sanctuary as well as all of its vessels—and not only human beings—can be the objects of this purification. Heb 9:21–22 therefore shows that the interpretation of blood application rites suggested above was still accepted during the time of Early Christianity.

[43] Cf. Attridge, *Hebrews*, 251–252; Koester, *Hebrews*, 414.

[44] Cf. Johannes Behm, "αἷμα," *TWNT* 1:172–173; Eberhart, *Studien*, 224–226.

and Heb 9 mention the purifying effect of (the application of) Christ's blood. Without Christ's death this particular purification would be impossible. In sacrificial images, therefore, Christ's death is not the actual salvific event but the precondition for the availability of his blood.

The author of Hebrews provides indirect proof of this subtle distinction. His/her general christological program that salvation is accomplished through Christ's death (Heb 2:14) is stated again in Heb 9:15: θανάτου γενομένου εἰς ἀπολύτρωσιν τῶν ἐπὶ τῇ πρώτῃ διαθήκῃ παραβάσεων ("a death has occurred that redeems them from the transgressions under the first covenant"). But in order to prove this statement, the author of Hebrews needs to change the imagery that has been so thoroughly developed throughout the entire chapter. Hence s/he leaves cultic metaphors and chooses a secular legal background when arguing that succession takes effect upon the death of the testator:

> Ὅπου γὰρ διαθήκη, θάνατον ἀνάγκη φέρεσθαι τοῦ διαθεμένου· διαθήκη γὰρ ἐπὶ νεκροῖς βεβαία, ἐπεὶ μήποτε ἰσχύει ὅτε ζῇ ὁ διαθέμενος.

> In the case of a will, it is necessary to prove the death of the testator, because a will is in force only when somebody has died; it never takes effect while the testator is alive. (Heb 9:16–17)

This legal metaphor provides a sufficient background to argue that somebody's death has a positive effect. Based solely on cultic metaphors, this argument would have been impossible.

The focus of the whole argumentation in Heb 9 has been that Christ's sacrifice offered once for all is better than the repeated sacrifices offered in the Levitical cult. It may be pointed out that throughout this argumentation, the general validity of the cult has remained unquestioned. The soteriological concept of Christ's sacrifice and the purification it effects are developed in analogy to the Levitical sacrifice, which means that the latter is taken for granted so that the validity of the earlier can be derived from it:

> εἰ γὰρ τὸ αἷμα τράγων καὶ ταύρων καὶ σποδὸς δαμάλεως ῥαντίζουσα τοὺς κεκοινωμένους ἁγιάζει πρὸς τὴν τῆς σαρκὸς καθαρότητα, πόσῳ μᾶλλον τὸ αἷμα τοῦ Χριστοῦ, ὃς διὰ πνεύματος αἰωνίου ἑαυτὸν προσήνεγκεν ἄμωμον τῷ θεῷ, καθαριεῖ τὴν συνείδησιν ἡμῶν ἀπὸ νεκρῶν ἔργων εἰς τὸ λατρεύειν θεῷ ζῶντι.

> For if the sprinkling of the blood of goats and bulls and of the ashes of a heifer sanctifies those who have been defiled so that their flesh is

> purified, how much more will the blood of Christ, who through the eternal Spirit offered himself unblemished to God, purify our consciences from acts that lead to death, so that we may serve the living God. (Heb 9:13–14)

Based on this argumentation, Hebrews gradually introduces the claim that the heavenly cult with all of its features is "better" (κρείττων) than the Levitical one: Jesus has obtained a better ministry than the earthly priest (Heb 8:6) and is the mediator of a better covenant (Heb 7:22; 8:6); the tent of the sanctuary that is not made by hand is "greater and more perfect" than the earthly one (Heb 9:11); and the law (ὁ νόμος) is but a "shadow" of the "good things to come" (Heb 10:1). Further claims are that Christ's blood purifies better (Heb 9:14) and that the heavenly things need better sacrifices (Heb 9:23).

But the author of Hebrews aims for more. While thus far s/he has declared the superiority of the heavenly cult over the earthly one, s/he now sets out to fundamentally question the validity of the latter: ἀδύνατον γὰρ αἷμα ταύρων καὶ τράγων ἀφαιρεῖν ἁμαρτίας (Heb 10:4, "because it is impossible for blood of bulls and goats to take away sins"; see also Heb 10:11). This statement prepares the exclusive claim that only Christ's sacrifice is valid. Two observations shall, however, be made about this statement. First, Hebrews is interested in forgiveness of sins that is continuously effective and "makes complete" (Heb 10:1, τελειόω). Yet such a dimension of the elimination of sins is never intended in the sacrificial cult of the HB/OT. There the reality that human beings will always commit sins and become impure, and that they will be in need of forgiveness and purification at all times, forms the basis of the temple cult with its repetitive (in fact, daily) service. Hebrews' interpretation that this repetitiveness is a sign of inefficiency is, therefore, the result of the specific interest in continuous forgiveness. Second, the total denial of the validity of the Judean sacrificial cult in Heb 10:4 is inconsistent with Hebrews' own argument in Heb 9:13. There the effectiveness of this cult is the foundation of the metaphor of Christ's sacrifice.

The author of Hebrews now makes use of a homiletic midrash in order to develop the sacrificial metaphor further. S/he refers in Heb 10:5–7 to Ps 39:7–9 LXX, according to which God desires not sacrifices but the execution of the divine will (τοῦ ποιῆσαι ὁ θεὸς τὸ θέλημά σου). In the subsequent comment, the author of Hebrews understands this as proof for the abolition of Levitical sacrifices. They will be replaced by "the second" (τὸ δεύτερον), which refers to Christ's sacrifice (Heb 10:9). The author of Hebrews continues:

ἐν ᾧ θελήματι ἡγιασμένοι ἐσμὲν διὰ τῆς προσφορᾶς τοῦ σώματος Ἰησοῦ Χριστοῦ ἐφάπαξ.

By that will, we have been sanctified through the sacrifice of the body of Jesus Christ once for all. (Heb 10:10)

The metaphor of the sacrifice of Christ's body, motivated by a Septuagint variant,[45] has caused some scholarly discussion regarding its meaning. It has been observed that the terminology stands close to that in Rom 12:1.[46] In this passage the appeal "to present your bodies as a living sacrifice" refers to a righteous lifestyle (see 2.2). In fact, also in Heb 10:7 the phrase τοῦ ποιῆσαι ὁ θεὸς τὸ θέλημά σου ("to do your will, O God") can be understood in this sense, which would correspond to the reference to Christ's incarnation, ἰδοὺ ἥκω ("see, I have come").[47] With these features, the entire passage Heb 10:5–10 seems to return to the contents of traditional sacrificial metaphors which—with the image of Christ who "sacrificed prayers and supplications" (Heb 5:7)—have formed a point of departure in Hebrews. But considering how the metaphor of Christ's sacrifice has been developed throughout Hebrews, and given the ἐφάπαξ ("once for all") in Heb 10:10, it may be assumed that in Heb 10:5 the Septuagint variant featuring "body" has been chosen consciously. Its openness allows incorporating the new features of Hebrews' Christology which stresses suffering, and links the concept of Christ's sacrifice to his death.[48] The ambiguous notion of the "sacrifice of the body of Jesus Christ" (Heb 10:10), therefore, combines "an internal dimension of obedience and an external dimension in the offering of his

---

[45] Ps 40:7b MT (ET Ps 40:6b) reads אָזְנַיִם כָּרִיתָ לִּי ("ears you dug for me"). However, the best Septuagint manuscripts read σῶμα. For a discussion of the variants see Koester, *Hebrews*, 432–433.

[46] Cf. Jewett, *Letter*, 164; Klaus Berger, *Theologiegeschichte des Urchristentums: Theologie des Neuen Testaments* (2d ed.; Tübingen: A. Francke, 1995), 399, 459.

[47] Cf. William L. Lane, *Hebrews 9–13* (WBC 47B; Dallas: Word Books, 1991), 262.

[48] Attridge (*Hebrews*, 274) points out that "Hebrews exploits this contrast of sacrifice and willing obedience, yet the interpretive translation in the LXX of "body" for "ears" also serves the purpose of the argument. For Christ's conformity to the divine will is clearly an act that involves his body."

body through crucifixion."[49] As such, this statement forms a climax of the development of Hebrews' composite sacrificial metaphors.

The effect of Christ's sacrifice for the community is explained in Heb 10:19, 22:

> Ἔχοντες οὖν, ἀδελφοί, παρρησίαν εἰς τὴν εἴσοδον τῶν ἁγίων ἐν τῷ αἵματι Ἰησοῦ, ... προσερχώμεθα μετὰ ἀληθινῆς καρδίας ἐν πληροφορίᾳ πίστεως ῥεραντισμένοι τὰς καρδίας ἀπὸ συνειδήσεως πονηρᾶς καὶ λελουσμένοι τὸ σῶμα ὕδατι καθαρῷ·

> Therefore, brothers, since we have confidence to enter the sanctuary through the blood of Jesus, ... let us approach with a true heart in full assurance of faith, with our hearts sprinkled from an evil conscience and our bodies washed with pure water. (Heb 10:19, 22)

In this passage, the author of Hebrews picks up a theme that may be regarded as the purpose of the entire cult concept: approaching God. In Heb 4:16 as well as in Heb 10:22, the addresses are urged to "approach" (προσέρχομαι) the sanctuary and encounter the holy God who resides there.[50] This theme thus frames the whole section of cultic imagery in Heb 5–10. The "approach" is possible "through the blood of Jesus" (Heb 4:19), which is understood as purification from sin (cf. Heb 4:22). As has been shown earlier (see 1.1), in Judean cult traditions such purification is the only way of encountering the holy God. Christ's sacrifice grants this purity and therefore guarantees eternal access to God for humans. It has, however, yet another effect. At the heart of the Day of Atonement imagery in Heb 9:12, Christ's blood—which may only here be understood as synonymous with "death"—is also the means of access for Christ himself into the sanctuary (διὰ δὲ τοῦ ἰδίου αἵματος εἰσῆλθεν ἐφάπαξ εἰς τὰ ἅγια αἰωνίαν λύτρωσιν εὑράμενος). Through his death, Christ left the earth in order to serve as high priest in the heavenly sanctuary.

Throughout his/her writing, the author of Hebrews creates a new, composite Christology by combining elements of traditional cult metaphors. Evidence that this is a conscious, innovative process may be found at the end of the writing. There the metaphor of Christ's sacrifice that happens once for all time occurs in juxtaposition to

---

[49] Koester, *Hebrews*, 439, with reference to, among others, Harold W. Attridge, "The Uses of Antithesis in Hebrews 8–10," *HTR* 79 (1986): 9.

[50] Cf. Wilhelm Thüsing, "'Lasst uns hinzutreten...' (Heb 10,22): Zur Frage nach dem Sinn der Kulttheologie im Hebräerbrief," *BZ* 9 (1965): 1–17.

the continuous sacrifices of the Christian community consisting of praise and a righteous lifestyle:

Διὸ καὶ Ἰησοῦς, ἵνα ἁγιάσῃ διὰ τοῦ ἰδίου αἵματος τὸν λαόν, ἔξω τῆς πύλης ἔπαθεν.

Therefore Jesus also suffered outside the gate in order to *sanctify the people by means of his own blood.* (Heb 13:12)

Δι᾽ αὐτοῦ [οὖν] ἀναφέρωμεν θυσίαν αἰνέσεως διὰ παντὸς τῷ θεῷ, τοῦτ᾽ ἔστιν καρπὸν χειλέων ὁμολογούντων τῷ ὀνόματι αὐτοῦ. τῆς δὲ εὐποιΐας καὶ κοινωνίας μὴ ἐπιλανθάνεσθε· τοιαύταις γὰρ θυσίαις εὐαρεστεῖται ὁ θεός.

Through him then let us continually *offer to God a sacrifice of praise,* that is, the fruit of lips confessing his name. Do not neglect acts of kindness and fellowship, for such *sacrifices are pleasing to God.* (Heb 13:15–16)

Summary of section 2: The early Christian community continued a tradition of cult metaphors found already in the HB/OT. In the process of appropriation the contents of these metaphors generally remained without change. Thus the metaphor of the *blood (of Jesus),* which refers to the crucifixion, conveys the idea that Christians are purified and consecrated by means of this blood as a necessary prerequisite of approaching the holy God. In this image the death of Jesus appears as the precondition for the availability of his blood, hence for salvation. In NT writings with the exception of Hebrews, the metaphor of *sacrifice* conveys notions such as "offering" and "acceptability." It is particularly a reference to the burning rite of the Judean sacrificial cult. In the NT it is applied to both goods (Phil 4:18) and human beings, implying that the surrender of life is not at the center of this image. In christological contexts (Eph 5:2), therefore, the *sacrifice of Jesus* cannot be understood as an exclusive reference to the crucifixion. Instead it points to Christ's whole life as an example of Christian love.

The Epistle to the Hebrews builds on these two types of traditional cult metaphors, but ultimately connects them. While initially stating that *Christ sacrifices prayers* (Heb 5:7), Hebrews gradually develops the contents of this metaphor. It is combined with the imagery of the Day of Atonement, which is governed by blood application rites that effect purification (Heb 9). As a result, the ambiguous metaphor of the *sacrifice of the body of Jesus Christ offered once for all* (Heb 10:10) evolves to include a reference to the crucifixion. Hebrews thus establishes a new, composite christological image. Its effect is twofold: it implies Christ's transition from earth to heaven where he now serves as the heavenly high priest, and it communicates the cultic purification that Christians obtain in order to approach the heavenly sanctuary.[51]

Dr. theol. Christian Eberhart
Associate Professor of New Testament
Lutheran Theological Seminary Saskatoon
114 Seminary Crescent, Saskatoon, Saskatchewan S7N 0X3, Canada
c.eberhart@usask.ca

---

[51] I am grateful to Harold W. Attridge who, through his insightful and constructive comments on my presentation during the 2003 International SBL Conference in Cambridge, UK, has helped me to develop and refine my arguments.

COVENANT, CULT, AND THE CURSE-OF-DEATH:
Διαθήκη IN HEB 9:15–22

Scott W. Hahn

1. *Covenant and Cult in Hebrews*

The Book of Hebrews has typically been regarded as anomalous in biblical studies for a variety of reasons, one of which is its unusual emphasis on the concept of "covenant" (διαθήκη), which is treated differently and much more extensively in Hebrews than in any other New Testament book. Just over half of the occurrences of the word διαθήκη in the New Testament (17 of 33) are in Hebrews alone. Moreover, Hebrews is unique in the emphasis it places on "covenant" as a *cultic* and *liturgical* institution.

A new phase in modern studies of the biblical concept of "covenant" (בְּרִית MT, διαθήκη LXX) began in the middle of the last century with George E. Mendenhall's work comparing the form of Hittite vassal treaties to the Sinai covenant of Exodus.[1] Scholars since Mendenhall have either challenged or defended his arguments for the antiquity of the covenant concept in Israelite religion, but have generally stayed within the framework Mendenhall established for the discussion, viewing "covenant" as a legal institution and using the extant treaties between ancient Near Eastern states as the primary texts for comparison and engagement with the biblical materials.[2] Thus, covenants

---

[1] George E. Mendenhall, *Law and Covenant in Israel and the Ancient Near East* (Pittsburgh: The Biblical Colloquium, 1955).

[2] Notice how often "law" or "treaty" occurs in the titles of the following important studies on biblical covenants: Herbert B. Huffmon, "The Covenant Lawsuit," *JBL* 78 (1959): 285–295; Dennis J. McCarthy, *Treaty and Covenant* (AnBib 21; Rome: Pontifical Biblical Institute, 1963 [2d ed., 1978]); Meredith G. Kline, *Treaty of the Great King: The Covenant Structure of Deuteronomy: Studies and Commentary* (Grand Rapids: Eerdmans, 1963); Rintje Frankena, "The Vassal Treaties of Esarhaddon and the Dating of Deuteronomy," *OTS* 14 (1965): 140–154; Hayim Tadmor, "Treaty and Oath in the Ancient Near East: A Historian's Approach," in *Humanizing America's Iconic Book* (ed. Gene M. Tucker and Douglas A. Knight; Chico: Scholars Press, 1982), 125–152; George E. Mendenhall, "The Suzerainty Treaty Structure: Thirty Years Later," in *Religion and Law* (Winona Lake: Eisenbrauns, 1990), 85–100.

in biblical scholarship have generally been considered under the aspect of "law."

Scholarship has tended, however, to neglect the fact that even these ancient Near Eastern treaty-covenants had a pronounced cultic-liturgical dimension.³ The covenants were often concluded by lengthy invocations of nearly the entire Near Eastern pantheon, calling upon the gods to witness elaborate sacred oaths confirmed by ritual sacrifices and to enforce those oaths with blessings for faithfulness and curses for transgression.⁴ Thus, the establishment of covenants consisted essentially of a liturgy: ritual words and actions performed in the presence of Divinity. The liturgical dimension of covenant-making appears quite clearly in the OT, where the covenant is established through cultic ritual (e.g., Exod 24:4–11) and liturgical functionaries or "celebrants" (i.e., priests and Levites) mediate the covenant blessings and curses on behalf of God (Num 6:22–27; Deut 27:14–26).

Reflecting on the OT traditions of "covenant," the author of Hebrews, while not forgetting the legal dimension, places the *liturgical* (or cultic) in the foreground. This is most obvious in chs. 8–9 of Hebrews,⁵ in which the author contrasts two covenant orders: the old (Heb 8:3–9:10) and the new (Heb 9:11–28). Both covenant orders have a cultus which includes a high priest (Heb 8:1, 3; 9:7, 11, 25, ἀρχιερεύς) or "celebrant" (Heb 8:2, 6, λειτουργός) who performs ministry (Heb 8:5; 9:1, 6, λατρεία) in a tent-sanctuary (Heb 8:2, 5; 9:2–3, 6, 8, 11, 21, σκηνή), entering into a Holy Place (Heb 8:2; 9:2–3, 12, 24, ἅγια) to offer (Heb 8:3; 9:7, 14, 28, προσφέρω) the blood (Heb 9:7, 12, 14, 18–23, 25, αἷμα) of sacrifices (Heb 8:3–4, 9:9, 23, 26, θυσίαι) which effects purification (Heb 9:13, ἁγιάζω; Heb 9:14, 22–23, καθαρίζω) and redemption (Heb 9:12, 15, λύτρωσις) of worshippers (Heb 8:10, 9:7, 19, λαός; Heb 9:9, 14, λατρεύοντες) who

---

³ An exception is the essay by John M. Lundquist, "Temple, Covenant, and Law in the Ancient Near East and in the Hebrew Bible," in *Israel's Apostasy and Restoration: Essays in Honor of Roland K. Harrison* (ed. Gileadi Avraham; Grand Rapids: Baker, 1988), 293–305.

⁴ Cf. *ANET* 200–201; 205–206; 532–535, 538–541.

⁵ On the cultic background of Heb 9, see James Swetnam, "A Suggested Interpretation of Hebrews 9,15–18," *CBQ* 27 (1965): 375; Johannes Behm, "διαθήκη," *TDNT* 2:131–132; Ceslas Spicq, *L'Épître aux Hébreux* (2 vols.; Paris: Gabalda, 1952), 2:246–247; Albert Vanhoye, *Old Testament Priests and the New Priest According to the New Testament* (trans. J. B. Orchard; Studies in Scripture; Petersham, Mass.: St. Bede's, 1986), 176–177.

have transgressed cultic law (Heb 8:4; 9:19, νόμος).[6] The mediation of both covenants is primarily cultic, the sacred realm of liturgy.

The legal nature of the covenant is not absent, however. The two aspects of the covenant, legal and liturgical, are inextricably bound in a reciprocal relationship. On the one hand, cultic acts (i.e., sacrificial rites) establish the covenant (Heb 9:18–21, 23), and also renew it (Heb 9:7; 10:3). On the other hand, the covenantal law provides the legal framework for the cult, determining the suitable persons, materials, acts, and occasions for worship (Heb 7:11–28; 9:1–5). Thus, the liturgy mediates the covenant, while covenant law regulates the liturgy.

The legal and liturgical aspects of the covenant are united in Christ himself, who is simultaneously king (the highest legal authority) and high priest (the highest liturgical celebrant). This dual role of Christ as priest and king, running as a theme throughout the book, is announced already in Heb 1:3, where Christ "sits down at the right hand of the Majesty in heaven" (i.e., a royal act) after having "provided purification for sins" (a priestly function). It is brought to its quintessential expression by the use of Melchizedek—both "King of Salem" and "Priest of God Most High" (Heb 7:1)—as a principal type of Christ.

Hebrews' vision of a cultic covenant, with close integration of law and liturgy, is difficult for modern scholarship to appreciate. Western modernity, as heir to the Enlightenment concept of "separation of church and state," has tended to privatize liturgy and secularize law, resulting in an irreconcilable divorce between the two. On the occasions when liturgy does appear in the public square, it is generally either dismissed as superstition or critiqued (reductionistically) as ritualized politics. In any case, Hebrews confronts us with a radically different vision: law and liturgy as distinguishable but inseparable aspects of a single covenant relationship between God and his people.

It is my thesis in this study that, in order to understand the Book of Hebrews, we must be prepared to enter into its own cultural

---

[6] Cf. William L. Lane, *Hebrews 9–13* (WBC 47b; Dallas: Word, 1991), 235: "The manner in which the argument is set forth presupposes the cultic orientation of 9:1–10 and its leading motif, that access to God is possible only through the medium of blood (9:7). The basis for the exposition in 9:11–28 is not primarily theological. It is the religious conviction that blood is the medium of purgation from defilement.... The essence of the two covenants is found in their cultic aspects; the total argument is developed in terms of cultus.... The interpreter must remain open to the internal logic of the argument from the cultus."

worldview, with its unity of liturgy and law; and that doing so will elucidate a long-standing interpretive *crux*: the meaning of διαθήκη in Heb 9:15–18.

The methodology that I employ is in some ways classical textual exegesis, that is, examining the grammar and syntax of the text in the light of its historical and religious context. But since I emphasize the legal and liturgical aspects of the covenant in their integration, a more deliberate application of the social-scientific approach is appropriate. This methodology is associated with the scholars Bruce J. Malina, John J. Pilch, Richard Rohrbaugh, and others.[7] David A. deSilva has applied social-scientific methods specifically to the interpretation of Hebrews.[8]

Regrettably, most of the social-scientific study of the New Testament in the past decades has focused on the Greco-Roman world, not the significance of the unique cultural institutions of First and Second Temple *Israel* (or Judea) herself—the covenant, cult, priesthood, temple, etc.—and how these institutions shaped the cultural worldview of the New Testament authors. John Dunnill's monograph *Covenant and Sacrifice in the Letter to the Hebrews* represents a breakthrough in this regard.[9] Dunnill not only applies social-scientific methods to the analysis of the distinctly Israelite-Jewish values and cultural institutions characterizing the Book of Hebrews, but also incorporates methodological insights from the religious anthropology of Mary Douglas and Victor Turner.[10] In what follows, I will build on Dunnill's

---

[7] Bruce J. Malina, *The New Testament World: Insights from Cultural Anthropology* (3d ed.; Louisville, Ky.: Westminster/John Knox, 2001); idem, *Christian Origins and Cultural Anthropology: Practical Models for Biblical Interpretation* (Atlanta: John Knox, 1986); idem, *Windows on the World of Jesus: Time Travel to Ancient Judea* (Louisville, Ky.: Westminster/John Knox, 1993); John J. Pilch, *Introducing the Cultural Context of the New Testament* (New York: Paulist, 1991); John J. Pilch and Bruce J. Malina, *Handbook of Biblical Social Values* (Peabody, Mass.: Hendrickson, 1998); Richard Rohrbaugh, ed., *The Social Sciences and New Testament Interpretation* (Peabody, Mass.: Hendrickson, 1996); David G. Horrell, *Social-Scientific Approaches to New Testament Interpretation* (Edinburgh: T&T Clark, 1999); Philip F. Esler, ed., *Modelling Early Christianity: Social-Scientific Study of the New Testament in its Context* (London: Routledge, 1995).

[8] David A. deSilva, *Despising Shame: Honor Discourse and Community Maintenance in the Epistle to the Hebrews* (SBLDS 152; Atlanta: Scholars Press, 1995); idem, *Perseverance in Gratitude: A Socio-Rhetorical Commentary on the Epistle "To the Hebrews"* (Grand Rapids: Eerdmans, 2000).

[9] John Dunnill, *Covenant and Sacrifice in the Letter to the Hebrews* (SNTSMS 75; Cambridge: Cambridge University Press, 1992).

[10] Mary L. Douglas, *Natural Symbols: Explorations in Cosmology* (2d ed.; New York: Routledge, 1996); idem, *Purity and Danger: An Analysis of Concepts of Pollution and Taboo*

work while attempting to unravel the difficulties presented by Heb 9:15–18.

2. *Hebrews 9:15–18: A* Crux Interpretum

Hebrews' concept of covenant, with liturgy and law intertwined, may actually be at work in the one passage of Hebrews where the author seems to dispense with his usual cultic categories for understanding covenant. Ironically, the problematic passage occurs in the middle of Heb 9, the chapter with the densest concentration of cultic language and imagery in the book. In Heb 9:16–17, according to most commentators, the author abandons his Israelite, cultic understanding of διαθήκη, "covenant,"[11] and appeals to the Greco-Roman, secular definition of διαθήκη as "last will or testament."[12] In the usual translations, the author seems, in the course of Heb 9:15–18, to slip between the two quite distinct meanings in a facile manner:

> For this reason he is the mediator of a new covenant (διαθήκη), so that those who are called may receive the promised eternal inheritance, because a death has occurred that redeems them from the transgressions under the first covenant (διαθήκη). For where a will (διαθήκη) is involved, the death of the one who made it must be established. For a will (διαθήκη) takes effect only at death, since it is not in force as long as the one who made it is alive. Hence not even the first covenant (διαθήκη) was inaugurated without blood. (Heb 9:15–18 NRSV)

As can be seen, the NRSV follows the majority of commentators and translators by taking διαθήκη in the sense of "will" or "testament" in Heb 9:16–17, even though the word clearly has the meaning "covenant" in vv. 15 and 18, and indeed in every other occurrence in Hebrews.[13] Nonetheless, it is not difficult to see why this approach

---

(New York: Routledge, 1966); Victor W. Turner, *The Ritual Process: Structure and Anti-Structure* (Ithaca, N.Y.: Cornell University Press, 1966).

[11] On the use of διαθήκη with the meaning "covenant" in most Jewish Hellenistic literature, see Behm, *TDNT* 2:126–129.

[12] For διαθήκη in secular Greek, see Johannes Behm and Gottfried Quell, *TDNT* 2:106–134, esp. 124–126.

[13] Cf. NEB, JB, TEV, NIV, NAB (only the NASB translates "covenant" in vv. 16–17). Commentators endorsing "testament" in vv. 16–17 include: Gerhardus Vos, *The Teaching of the Epistle to the Hebrews* (Grand Rapids: Eerdmans, 1956), 27–48; George W. Buchanan, *To the Hebrews* (AB 36; Garden City: Doubleday, 1972), 151; Thomas G. Long, *Hebrews* (IBC; Louisville: John Knox, 1997), 99; Harold W. Attridge, *Hebrews* (Hermeneia; Philadelphia: Fortress, 1989), 253–256; Paul Ellingworth,

enjoys majority support.[14] In Heb 9:15, the context seems to demand the sense of "covenant," since only a covenant has a mediator (μεσίτης) and reference is made to the first διαθήκη, which the author clearly regards as a covenant. However, in Heb 9:16, the requirement for the "death of the one who made it" would seem to suggest the translation "will" or "testament," since covenants did not require the death of their makers. Likewise, in Heb 9:17, the statement that a διαθήκη takes effect only at death and is not in force while the maker is alive seems to apply only to a testament. However, in Heb 9:18, the topic returns again to "the first διαθήκη," that is, the Sinai event, which can scarcely be anything but a covenant.

Nevertheless, while the alteration between the meanings "testament" and "covenant" seems required semantically, the resulting argument is not logically satisfying. A "testament" simply is not a "covenant," and it is hard to see how the analogy between the two has any validity. In a "testament," one party dies and leaves an inheritance for another. In a "covenant," a relationship is established between two living parties, often through a mediator. Testaments do not require mediators, and covenants do not require the death of one of the parties. Moreover, it is hard to understand either the "new" or the "old" covenants—as portrayed in Hebrews—as a "testament." If the old covenant is understood as a "testament," God would be the "testator"; yet it is absurd to think of God dying and leaving an inheritance to Israel. In the new covenant, Christ indeed dies, but he is a mediator (Heb 9:15; 12:24), not a "testator." Moreover, he does not die in order to *leave* an inheritance to the Church, but rather to *enter* the inheritance himself (Heb 1:3–4; 2:9; 9:11–12; 10:12–13), which he then shares with his "brothers" (Heb 2:10–3:6).

Clearly, then, the mode of the inheritance of salvation in Hebrews is based on a Jewish covenantal and not a Greco-Roman testamentary model.[15] Therefore, it is hard to see how the analogy the

---

Commentary on Hebrews (NIGTC; Grand Rapids: Eerdmans, 1993), 462–463; Victor C. Pfitzner, *Hebrews* (ANTC; Nashville: Abingdon, 1997), 131; Craig R. Koester, *Hebrews* (AB 36; New York: Doubleday, 2001), 418, 424–426.

[14] See Swetnam, "Suggested Interpretation," 374–375, for a succinct summary of the case.

[15] Cf. Dunnill, *Covenant and Sacrifice*, 46–47: "Though Hebrews exhibits Alexandrian [i.e. Hellenistic] terminology... in every case the substance of the thought is Jewish... The Hellenistic element overlays a mind thinking in the categories of the Old Testament cultus." Although it came to be used in later periods, the institution of the testament is not native to Israelite-Jewish culture, which traditionally practiced *intestate* (non-testamentary) succession, in which the first-born son enjoyed a privi-

author draws in Heb 9:15–18 has any cogency. The awkwardness of the argument has led a few commentators to propose taking διαθήκη as "covenant" in Heb 9:16–17 (see below), but most retain the sense "testament" while expressing their discomfort:

> Among the many references to covenants, new and old, the word-play on διαθήκη which compares them to a secular will seems strangely banal, and the argument that Jesus' death was necessary because "where there is a will the death of the testator must be established" (9:16) is simply irrelevant to the theology of the new covenant.[16]

Basically the idea of testament fits into the passage very clumsily.[17]

> [The author] jumps from the religious to the current legal sense of διαθήκη ... involving himself in contradictions which show that there is no real parallel.[18]

Is it really the case that the author of Hebrews, usually so theologically and rhetorically brilliant, has committed here a logical and theological *faux pas*, a minor blunder tearing the otherwise seamless coherence of his homiletical masterpiece?[19] I am inclined to think

---

leged share. The first-born had no privileged status in Greco-Roman succession (see Larry R. Helyer, "The *Prōtotokos* Title in Hebrews," *Studia Biblica et Theologica* 6 [1976]: 17). The fact that the author of Hebrews thinks in terms of Israelite-Jewish inheritance custom can be seen in the strategic use of the concept πρωτότοκος (first-born) in Heb 1:6 and 12:23.

[16] Dunnill, *Covenant and Sacrifice*, 250–251.
[17] George D. Kilpatrick, "Διαθήκη in Hebrews," *ZNW* 68 (1977): 263.
[18] Behm, *TDNT* 2:131. Many other advocates of διαθήκη-as-testament also feel the tension caused by the abrupt switch in meaning, e.g., F. F. Bruce, *The Epistle to the Hebrews* (rev. ed.; NICNT; Grand Rapids: Eerdmans, 1990), 461; Pfitzner, *Hebrews*, 131; Ellingworth, *Hebrews*, 462; Swetnam, "Suggested Interpretation," 373. Currently it seems popular to defuse this tension somewhat by describing the author as engaged in "playful" rhetorical argument which—while not logically valid—would amuse the audience or readership with its clever word-play (Attridge, *Hebrews*, 253–254; similarly Long, *Hebrews*, 98–99). Unfortunately, in order to be rhetorically effective an argument must at least appear to be valid. A blatantly false example cited as proof, or a syllogism whose errors are apparent to all, tends to discredit the speaker and his argument. It is doubtful whether the argument of Heb 9:16–17 would have had even apparent validity under a testamentary interpretation.
[19] On the coherence and brilliance of Hebrews' thought and expression, see Attridge, *Hebrews*, 1: "[Hebrews is] the most elegant and sophisticated ... text of first-century Christianity.... Its argumentation is subtle; its language refined; its imagery rich and evocative ... a masterpiece of early Christian rhetorical homiletics"; Albert Vanhoye, *The Structure and Message of the Epistle to the Hebrews* (Subsidia Biblica 12; Rome: Pontifical Biblical Institute, 1989), 32–33: "Pause for a moment to admire the literary perfection of [this] priestly sermon.... One sees how the author is concerned about writing well ... [his] talent is seen especially in the harmony of his composition"; Dunnill, *Covenant and Sacrifice*, 8: "[The interpreter must] capitalize on the strong impression of the *unity* of its imaginative world which any

not. In what follows, I will propose that if διαθήκη is understood as "covenant" in Heb 9:16–17, there is a way of interpreting the passage which confirms the coherence of thought of the author, who seems to be explicating the *legal implications* of the *liturgical act* which established the first covenant.

First, I will point out certain frequently-overlooked difficulties with the usual interpretation of διαθήκη as "testament" in Heb 9:16–17; second, critique some previous attempts to understand διαθήκη as "covenant" in these verses; and finally, outline an original interpretive proposal which, I believe, has greater explanatory power than others offered to date.

2.1. *Difficulties with Διαθήκη as "Testament"*

The troubles with διαθήκη as "testament" in Heb 9:15–18 go deeper than the mere fact that the word so translated renders the argument of the passage obscure if not simply fallacious. John J. Hughes has pointed out these difficulties at length elsewhere.[20] I will summarize some of Hughes' observations here, focusing on the lexical, grammatical and legal problems with rendering διαθήκη as "testament" in these verses.

2.1.1. *Lexical Issues*

Outside of Heb 9:16–17 the author of Hebrews uses διαθήκη only in its Septuagintal sense of "covenant" (בְּרִית).[21] Moreover, the term διαθήκη (and the concept of "covenant") occurs more often and receives greater attention and emphasis in Hebrews than in any other New Testament book.[22] Most of the occurrences of the word (15 of 17) occur in the extended discussion of Christ-as-high-priest from

---

reading of Hebrews communicates.... It is generally agreed that Hebrews exhibits a marked theological *coherence*"; and Brooke F. Westcott, *The Epistle to the Hebrews: The Greek Text with Notes and Essays* (2d ed., 1892; repr., Grand Rapids: Eerdmans, 1980), xlvi–xlvii: "The style is... characteristic of a practised scholar. It would be difficult to find anywhere passages more exact and pregnant in expression.... The writing shows everywhere the traces of effort and care.... Each element, which seems at first sight to offer itself spontaneously, will be found to have been carefully adjusted to its place, and to offer in subtle details results of deep thought." Cf. also Swetnam, "Suggested Interpretation," 375.

[20] John J. Hughes, "Hebrews IX 15ff. and Galatians III 15ff.: A Study in Covenant Practice and Procedure," *NovT* 21 (1976–77): 27–96.

[21] Cf. Behm, *TDNT* 2:132; Lane, *Hebrews*, 230.

[22] Cf. Vos, *Hebrews*, 27.

Heb 7–10, with seven occurrences in Heb 9 alone. Since the word is central to the author's thought, and in every instance outside Heb 9:16–17 has the meaning "covenant," Hughes remarks: "As a matter of a priori concern one should at least be exceedingly cautious in attributing a meaning to διαθήκη in [Heb] 9:15–22 that is so foreign to the author's use of the word elsewhere."[23]

2.1.2. *Grammatical Issues*

Several scholars have noted grammatical irregularities in the use of φέρεσθαι (Heb 9:16b) and ἐπὶ νεκροῖς (Heb 9:17a).[24] If Heb 9:16b had testamentary practice in view, one would expect ὅπου γὰρ διαθήκη, διαθέμενον ἀνάγκη ἀποθανεῖν, "where there is a testament, it is necessary for the testator *to die*" (italics added). The circumlocution θάνατον ἀνάγκη φέρεσθαι τοῦ διαθεμένου seems unnecessary. The NRSV translates, "the death of the one who made it must *be established*" (italics added), but similar usage in the rest of the New Testament or the LXX cannot be found. Φέρω frequently occurs in legal contexts (biblical and non-biblical) but in the sense of "bring a report, claim, or charge," not a *death*. The expression should be φέρεσθαι ἀνάγκη τὸν λόγον τοῦ θανάτου, "it is necessary for the report of the death to be brought."[25]

Another grammatical strain occurs at Heb 9:17a, διαθήκη γὰρ ἐπὶ νεκροῖς βεβαία, which the NRSV renders, "a will takes effect only at death." A literal translation, however, would read "for a διαθήκη is confirmed *upon dead [bodies]*." Ἐπὶ νεκροῖς cannot be taken as "at death" (ἐπὶ νεκρῷ or ἐπὶ νεκρώσει), although this is the sense demanded by a testamentary interpretation of διαθήκη.[26] The use of the plural (νεκροῖς, "dead [bodies]") is particularly awkward if indeed the author was intending to speak of the death of the testator.[27]

Both of these grammatical irregularities become intelligible when διαθήκη is taken as "covenant" in the manner I will outline below.

---

[23] Hughes, "Hebrews IX 15ff.," 32–33.

[24] Cf. Kilpatrick, "Διαθήκη," 265; Westcott, *Hebrews*, 301.

[25] Lexicographers treat it as a special case of φέρω, being unable to produce any analogous citations. Cf. LSJ 1923a (def. A.IV.4, "announce"), BAGD 855b (def. 4.a.b, "establish"), L&N 667b–668a (§70.5, "show"). Note Ellingworth's honesty: "Exact parallels to this statement have not been found" (*Hebrews*, 464); and Attridge's polite understatement: "The sense of φέρεσθαι is somewhat uncertain" (*Hebrews*, 256).

[26] Lane, *Hebrews*, 232; George Milligan, *The Theology of the Epistle to the Hebrews* (Edinburgh: T&T Clark, 1899), 169.

[27] Attridge admits, "The phrase referring to the testator's death, 'for the dead' (ἐπὶ νεκροῖς), is somewhat odd" (*Hebrews*, 256). Likewise, Swetnam recognizes the oddity and offers a singular explanation for it ("Suggested Interpretation," 378).

2.1.3. Legal Issues

Hughes demonstrates that the characteristics of a διαθήκη in Heb 9:16–17 do not, in fact, correspond to those of secular Hellenistic or Roman διαθῆκαι. For example, the ratification or validation (βεβαίωσις) of wills in Hellenistic, Egyptian, and Roman law was not "over the dead [bodies]" (Heb 9:17, ἐπὶ νεκροῖς):

> It is simply untrue and completely lacking in classical and papyrological support to maintain that, given the legal technical terms (βέβαιος, ἰσχύω, and perhaps ἐγκαινίζω) and their consistent meanings, a will or testament was only legally valid when the testator died... It is impossible, not just unlikely, that [Heb 9:16–17] refer to any known form of Hellenistic (or indeed any other) legal practice.[28]

A Hellenistic will was legally valid (βέβαιος) not when the testator died, but when it was written down, witnessed, and deposited with a notary.[29] Moreover, the inheritance was not always subsequent to the death of the testator, as Heb 9:17 would imply. Distribution of the estate while the testator(s) was still living (*inter vivos*) was widespread in the Hellenistic world.[30] Only a few instances of *donatio inter vivos* known to the readers of Hebrews would have subverted the emphatic statement of Heb 9:17b (ἐπεὶ μήποτε ἰσχύει ὅτε ζῇ ὁ διαθέμενος)[31] and destroyed its rhetorical effectiveness.[32]

---

[28] Hughes, "Hebrews IX 15ff.," 61.

[29] Hughes, "Hebrews IX 15ff.," 60.

[30] Hughes, "Hebrews IX 15ff.," 62, citing Hans J. Wolff, "Hellenistic Private Law," in *The Jewish People in the First Century: Historical Geography, Political History, Social, Cultural and Religious Life and Institutions* (2 vols.; ed. Shemuel Safrai and Manahem Stern; CRINT, sec. 1; Assen: Van Gorcum, 1974), 1:534–560, here 543; and Rafal Taubenschlag, *The Law of Greco-Roman Egypt in Light of the Papyri 322 BC–640 AD* (2d ed.; Warsaw: Panstwowe Wydawnictwo Naukowe, 1955), 207–208.

[31] On μήποτε as a strong negative, see Ellingworth, *Hebrews*, 464. The sense would not be "wills do not usually have force while the testator lives," but "they *certainly* do not," or perhaps "they *never* do" (cf. NIV, ASV).

[32] Subsequent responses to Hughes' demonstration ("Hebrews IX 15ff.," published 1979) of the lack of correspondence between Heb 9:16–17 and Greco-Roman testamentary law have been surprisingly weak. Curiously, Attridge, publishing almost thirteen years after Hughes' seventy-page *NovT* article, makes no reference to Hughes or his arguments (Cf. Attridge, *Hebrews*, 255–256 n. 25, 419). Ellingworth, while aware of Hughes, does not rebut him, although his comment "ἀνάγκη is here used [in v. 16] not strictly of a legal requirement" (*Hebrews*, 464) seems a concession to Hughes' evidence that testaments were validated by a notary and not by death. Likewise, Koester, who feels Hughes' arguments more strongly, has to nuance and mitigate the sense of Heb 9:17 to accommodate Hughes' point that the language is not legally accurate (*Hebrews*, 418, 425). Koester also cites a papyrus death-notice as proof of his assertion that "legally people had to present evidence that the testator had died for a will to take effect" (*Hebrews*, 418, 425), but the papyrus cited does not actually mention a will or inheritance as being at issue in the notice of death.

2.2. Previous Proposals for Διαθήκη as "Covenant" in Heb 9:16–17

The various difficulties with reading διαθήκη as "testament" noted above have led several scholars to maintain the author's usual meaning "covenant" for διαθήκη in Heb 9:16–17.[33] These scholars have, in my opinion, moved the discussion in the proper direction by seeking to explain Heb 9:16–17 in terms of the cultic rituals involved in biblical and ancient Near Eastern covenant-making. In these rites, the covenant-maker (ὁ διαθέμενος) swore a self-maledictory oath (i.e., a curse), which was then ritually enacted by the death of animals representing the covenant-maker.[34] The bloody sacrifice of the animal(s) symbolized the fate of the covenant-maker should he prove false to his covenantal obligations.[35] The meaning of Heb 9:16–17 may be paraphrased as follows: Where there is a covenant, it is necessary that the death of the covenant-maker be represented (by animal sacrifices); for a covenant is confirmed over dead bodies (sacrificial animals), since it is never valid while the covenant-maker is still ritually "alive."

2.2.1. The Covenantal Background of Heb 9:16–17

As background for the covenantal interpretation of Heb 9:16–17, it may be useful to cite some relevant examples to demonstrate the following: (1) biblical and ancient Near Eastern covenant-making entailed the swearing of an oath, (2) this oath was a conditional self-malediction, i.e., a curse, (3) the content of the curse usually consisted of the covenant-maker's death, and (4) the curse-of-death was often pre-enacted through sacrificial rituals.

(1) Covenant-Making and Oath-Swearing. The swearing of an oath was closely associated with the making of a covenant. In fact, the two terms, oath (אָלָה) and covenant (בְּרִית), are sometimes used interchangeably, e.g., in Ezek 17:13–19:

---

[33] E.g., Westcott, *Hebrews*, 298–302; Milligan, *Hebrews*, 166–170; John Brown, *An Exposition of the Epistle of the Apostle Paul to the Hebrews* (ed. D. Smith; New York: R. Carter, 1862; repr. Edinburgh: The Banner of Truth Trust, 1972), 407–419; Hughes, "Hebrews IX 15ff.," 27–96; Lane, *Hebrews*, 226–252; Darrell J. Pursiful, *The Cultic Motif in the Spirituality of the Book of Hebrews* (Lewiston, N.Y.: Edwin Mellen, 1993), 77–79.

[34] E.g., Westcott, *Hebrews*, 301; Hughes, "Hebrews IX 15ff.," 40–42; Lane, *Hebrews*, 241–243.

[35] Hughes, "Hebrews IX 15ff.," 41; Lane, *Hebrews*, 242.

And he took one of the seed royal and made a *covenant* (בְּרִית) with him, putting him under *oath* (אָלָה). (The chief men of the land he had taken away, that the kingdom might be humble and not lift itself up, and that by keeping his *covenant* it might stand.) But he rebelled against him by sending ambassadors to Egypt, that they might give him horses and a large army. Will he succeed? Can a man escape who does such things? Can he break the *covenant* and yet escape? As I live, says the Lord GOD, surely in the place where the king dwells who made him king, whose *oath* he despised, and whose *covenant* with him he broke, in Babylon he shall die. . . . Because he despised the *oath* and broke the *covenant*, because he gave his hand and yet did all these things, he shall not escape. Therefore thus says the Lord GOD: As I live, surely my *oath* which he despised, and my *covenant* which he broke, I will requite upon his head. (italics added, RSV)

In light of Ezek 17:13–19 and similar texts, the close inter-relationship between "covenant" and "oath" is a commonplace among scholars who work with ancient Near Eastern covenant materials:[36]

> It is now recognized that the *sine qua non* of "covenant" in its normal sense appears to be its ratifying oath, whether this was verbal or symbolic (a so-called "oath sign").[37]

> [B]*erith* as a commitment has to be confirmed by an oath: Gen. 21:22ff.; 26:26ff.; Deut. 29:9ff. (10ff.); Josh. 9:15–20; 2 K. 11:4; Ezk. 16:8; 17:13ff.[38]

(2) Covenant Oath as Conditional Self-Malediction. The oath by which a covenant was ratified was a conditional self-malediction (self-curse), an invocation of the divinity to inflict judgment upon the oath-swearer should he fail to fulfill the sworn stipulations of the covenant.

---

[36] See Gordon P. Hugenberger, *Marriage as a Covenant: A Study of Biblical Law & Ethics Governing Marriage, Developed from the Perspective of Malachi* (VTSup 52; Leiden: Brill, 1994), 183–184. Curse (אָלָה) and covenant (בְּרִית) appear in semantic proximity in the following texts: Hos 10:4; Deut 29:11, 13 MT (ET 29:12, 14); Ezek 16 as shown above; and Gen 26:28. In Gen 24:1–67, אָלָה and שְׁבֻעָה are used interchangeably; and elsewhere (Deut 4:31; 7:12; 8:18; 31:20; Josh 9:15; 2 Kgs 11:4; Ezek 16:8; Ps 89:3) it is apparent that נִשְׁבַּע שְׁבֻעָה and כָּרַת בְּרִית are functionally equivalent. For a Phoenician example of the relationship between curse and covenant, see Ziony Zevit, "A Phoenician Inscription and Biblical Covenant Theology," *IEJ* 27 (1977): 110–118.

[37] Hugenberger, *Marriage as Covenant*, 4; citing James Barr, "Some Semantic Notes on the Covenant," in *Beiträge zur Alttestamentlichen Theologie: Festschrift für Walther Zimmerli zum 70. Geburtstag* (ed. Herbert Donner, Robert Hanhart, and Rudolf Smend; Göttingen: Vandenhoeck & Ruprecht, 1977), 23–28.

[38] Moshe Weinfeld, "בְּרִית *bᵉrîth*," *TDOT* 2:256. See also Hugenberger, *Marriage as Covenant*, 182–184.

A fourteenth-century BCE Hittite covenant expressed this principle as follows: "May the oaths sworn in the presence of these gods break you like reeds, you ... together with your country. May they exterminate from the earth your name and your seed."³⁹ Likewise, in Ezek 17:13–19, it is evident from the divine threats to enforce the oath that the making of the covenant involved a conditional curse-of-death (e.g., Ezek 17:16, 19). The word "curse," in fact, came to be functionally equivalent to "covenant" and "oath." Hugenberger remarks, "The fact that אָלָה (originally meaning "curse," cf. Gen 24:41; Deut 29:19 MT [ET 29:20]; 30:7; Isa 24:6; Jer 23:10; Pss 10:7; 59:13) is used [to mean "covenant"] serves to emphasize the hypothetical self-curse which underlies biblical oaths—that is, if the oath should be broken, a curse will come into effect."⁴⁰

(3) Death as the Content of the Curse. That the curse for covenant violation was typically death can be seen quite clearly in the passage from Ezekiel cited above (17:16), in the covenant curses of Lev 26 and Deut 28,⁴¹ and in other biblical passages which explicitly mention the violation of the covenant being sanctioned by death⁴² or mortal punishment.⁴³ Likewise, among extant ancient Near Eastern covenant documents, death by excruciating or humiliating means, accompanied by various other calamities, is frequently the content of the oath-curse.⁴⁴ At Qumran it is a commonplace that "the sword avenges the covenant"⁴⁵ resulting in death.⁴⁶ Dunnill's observation is apposite:

---

³⁹ *ANET* 206b.

⁴⁰ Hugenberger, *Marriage as Covenant*, 194. Sometimes the curse is only implicit. See Hugenberger, *Marriage as Covenant*, 200–201. Some biblical examples are 1 Sam 3:17; 14:44; 20:13; 25:22; 2 Sam 3:9; 3:35; 19:14 MT; 1 Kgs 2:23; 2 Kgs 6:31; Ruth 1:17; Jer 42:5, in all of which the content of the curse is left unexpressed, but may be presumed to be death.

⁴¹ Cf. Lev 26:14–39, esp. v. 30, but also vv. 16, 22, 25, 38; Deut 28:15–68, esp. vv. 20, 22, 24, 26, 48, 51, 61.

⁴² Deut 4:23, 26; 17:2–7; Josh 7:11, 15; 23:16; Jer 22:8–12 (both death and death-in-exile); Jer 34:18–21; Hos 8:11.

⁴³ E.g., to be "devoured" (Deut 31:16); "consumed" and "burned" (Isa 33:8–12; Jer 11:10, 16); "destroyed' (Hos 7:13 [cf. 6:7]).

⁴⁴ Cf. *ANET* 179–180, 201, 205, 532, 534, 538–541. Note, too, that while not all the curses are death *per se*, usually they are means of death: plague, famine, siege, military defeat, etc.

⁴⁵ See CD I, 3; I, 17–18; III, 10–11; 4Q266 2 I, 21; 4Q269 2 I, 6; 4Q390 1 I, 6. The reference to the "sword" is probably inspired by Lev 26:25.

⁴⁶ See CD XV, 4–5; 1Q22 1 I, 10.

> In both Greek and Hebrew [oaths] often take the form of a *conditional self-curse*, the swearer invoking upon his or her own head penalties to follow any breach of the undertaking.... Even where the context is non-legal and the vagueness of the penalty shows the formula on the way to becoming a figure of speech, in every case the invocation of death is the guarantee of sincerity, placing the whole person behind the promise made.⁴⁷

(4) The Curse of Death Ritually Enacted. Several ancient Near Eastern documents record the symbolic enactment of the curse-of-death during the covenant-making ritual. One of the most celebrated examples is the eighth-century treaty of Ashurnirari V and Mati'ilu, the King of Arpad, which includes the following enacted curse-ritual or *Drohritus*:

> This spring lamb has been brought from its fold ... to sanction the treaty between Ashurnirari and Mati'ilu. If Mati'ilu sins against (this) treaty made under oath by the gods, then, just as this spring lamb ... will not return to its fold, alas, Mati'ilu ... [will be ousted] from his country, will not return to his country, and not behold his country again. This head is not the head of a lamb, it is the head of Mati'ilu.... If Mati'ilu sins against this treaty, so may, just as the head of this spring lamb is torn off ... the head of Mati'ilu be torn off.⁴⁸

Hugenberger draws the following conclusion:

> In light of this and many similar examples [e.g., *ANET* 539f.], it is possible ... that the prominence of such cutting oath-signs in the ratification ceremony for covenants gave rise to the widespread terminology of "cutting" [כָּרַת] a covenant as well as "cutting" a curse.⁴⁹

The Bible records similar curse-rituals. Abraham's bisection of animals in the covenant of Gen 15 represented a self-curse of death for the covenant-maker—in this case, God himself. The significance

---

⁴⁷ Dunnill, *Covenant and Sacrifice*, 249. Cf. O. Palmer Robertson: "The death of the covenant-maker appears in two distinct stages. First it appears in the form of a symbolic representation of the curse, anticipating possible covenantal violations. Later the party who violates the covenant actually experiences death as a consequence of his earlier commitment" (*The Christ of the Covenants* [Grand Rapids: Baker, 1980], 11–12).

⁴⁸ *ANET* 532b.

⁴⁹ Hugenberger, *Marriage as Covenant*, 195; Quell, *TDNT* 2:108. In light of the evidence Hugenberger and others have adduced, Koester's statement that "there is little evidence that sacrifices represented the death of the one making the covenant" is puzzling (*Hebrews*, 418).

of the *Drohritus* is elucidated by Jer 34:18–20,[50] where the Lord addresses the leaders of Jerusalem and Judah, who had made a solemn covenant to release their slaves during the siege of Jerusalem but promptly reneged on their commitment when the siege was lifted:

> I will make the men who violated My covenant, who did not fulfill the terms of the covenant which they made before Me, [like] the calf which they cut in two so as to pass between the halves: The officers of Judah and Jerusalem, the officials, the priests, and all the people of the land who passed between the halves of the calf shall be handed over to their enemies, to those who seek to kill them. Their carcasses shall become food for the birds of the sky and the beasts of the earth. (NJPS)

Significantly, each of the biblical covenants that concern the author of Hebrews involves a *Drohritus* symbolizing the curse-of-death. The covenant (or covenants) with Abraham (Heb 6:13–18; 11:17–19) is confirmed by the bisection of animals (Gen 15:9–10), the rite of circumcision (Gen 17:10–14, 23–27), and the "sacrifice" of Isaac (Gen 22:13; Heb 6:14; 11:17–19).[51] The Sinai covenant is solemnized by the sprinkling of the people with the blood of the animal sacrifices after their solemn promise to obey the covenant stipulations (Exod 24:3–8), conveying the concept, "As was done to the animals, so may it be done to us if we fail to keep the covenant."

2.2.2. *The Exegesis of Heb 9:16–17 with Διαθήκη as "Covenant"*
The advocates of διαθήκη-as-covenant propose this biblical and ancient Near Eastern background of covenant-by-self-maledictory-oath as the context for Heb 9:16–17. In Heb 9:16, according to this view,

---

[50] The scholarly support for viewing Gen 15 as a self-maledictory ritual enactment in light of Jer 34 is strong, although some dispute it. See Quell, *TDNT* 2:116; Hugenberger, *Marriage as Covenant*, 195 n. 109.

[51] On the possibility that the covenant-making ceremonies in Gen 15 and 17 are not parallel accounts of the same event but intentionally different covenants, see T. Desmond Alexander, "A Literary Analysis of the Abraham Narrative in Genesis" (Ph.D. diss.; The Queen's University of Belfast, 1982), 49, 160–182. Heb 6:13–18 and 11:17–19 focus on the formulation of the Abrahamic covenant-oath found in Gen 22:15–18. On the self-maledictory symbolism of circumcision, see Meredith G. Kline, *By Oath Consigned: A Reinterpretation of the Covenant Signs of Baptism and Circumcision* (Grand Rapids: Eerdmans, 1968), 39–49, 86–89, esp. 43; Hugenberger, *Marriage as Covenant*, 196; and Dunnill, *Covenant and Sacrifice*, 177 n. 72. On the interrelationship of the three Abrahamic covenant-making rituals, see Dunnill, *Covenant and Sacrifice*, 177.

φέρεσθαι should be translated "bring into the picture" or "introduce."[52] The "death" (θάνατος) that must be "brought into the picture" (φέρεσθαι) is the death of the covenant-maker (ὁ διαθέμενος), symbolically represented by the sacrificial animals. Thus, Heb 9:16 (ὅπου γὰρ διαθήκη, θάνατον ἀνάγκη φέρεσθαι τοῦ διαθεμένου) should be translated, "For where there is a covenant, it is necessary to introduce the [symbolic] death of the covenant-maker." The following statement of Heb 9:17, "for a covenant is ratified over dead [bodies]," is a fairly accurate description of biblical and ancient Near Eastern covenant-making practice. Hebrews 9:17b, "since it [a covenant] is never in force while the covenant maker lives," makes sense if ὅτε ζῇ ὁ διαθέμενος ("while the covenant-maker lives") is understood symbolically, i.e., to mean "while the covenant-maker is still ritually alive, not yet having undergone the death represented by the sacrificial animals."

Hebrews 9:18–22, which speaks of the sprinkling of blood at the establishment of the first covenant at Sinai, follows naturally from Heb 9:16–17 (ὅθεν, "hence"). Hebrews 9:16–17 states that a covenant requires the ritual death of the covenant-maker; Heb 9:18–22 points out that in fact the first covenant was established in this way, with the blood of the representative animals being sprinkled over the people and all the implements of the covenant cult.

2.2.3. *Difficulties in the Case for Διαθήκη as Covenant*

In many respects the case for διαθήκη-as-covenant in Heb 9:16–17, as it has been argued to date, is appealing. It retains continuity with the author's Jewish, cultic understanding of the nature of "covenant," and produces a logically sound reading of Heb 9:15–18. However, there are at least two serious objections to the view as outlined above.

First, covenants were not always ratified by the ritual slaughter of animals. William Lane goes so far as to say, "The formulation [Heb 9:17, ἐπεὶ μήποτε ἰσχύει ὅτε ζῇ ὁ διαθέμενος] accurately reflects the legal situation that a covenant is *never* secured until the ratifier has bound himself to his oath by means of a representative death" (italics added).[53] While it is true that many covenants were solemnized in this way, one cannot assert that a "representative death" was *always*

---

[52] Hughes cites 2 Pet 2:11, John 18:29, and *1 Clem.* 55:1 as examples of similar usage ("Hebrews IX 15ff.," 42–43). See BAGD 855b (def. 4.a.β).
[53] Lane, *Hebrews*, 243.

necessary.⁵⁴ There was no monolithic form for covenant-making in the Bible or the ancient Near East. Moreover, it was the oath rather than the sacrifices that sufficed to establish a covenant, as Hugenberger and others have demonstrated.⁵⁵

Second, it does not seem plausible that the two phrases θάνατον ἀνάγκη φέρεσθαι τοῦ διαθεμένου, "it is necessary for the death of the covenant-maker to be borne," and ὅτε ζῇ ὁ διαθέμενος, "while the covenant-maker is alive," are intended in a figurative sense. The author *does* appear to be speaking of the actual death of the covenant-maker.⁵⁶

These two objections suggest that, although the reading of διαθήκη as "covenant" may be an improvement over the alternative "testament," a better case must be made for it.

2.3. *A New Proposal: The Broken Covenant and the Curse-of-Death*

An interpretation of Heb 9:16–17 that renders the text intelligible and coheres with the theological system expressed in the rest of the epistle is possible, if one recognizes that the particular covenant occupying the author's thought in Heb 9:15–22 is the first or Sinai covenant, seen as a *broken* covenant. It is not covenants in general, but the broken Sinai covenant that forms the context within which Heb 9:16–17 should be understood. In what follows I will offer my exegesis of Heb 9:16–17 phrase by phrase.

2.3.1. Ὅπου γὰρ διαθήκη *(Heb 9:16a)*

Hebrews 9:16–17 is a parenthetical explanation of the genitive absolute construction in Heb 9:15, θανάτου γενομένου εἰς ἀπολύτρωσιν τῶν ἐπὶ τῇ πρώτῃ διαθήκῃ παραβάσεων, "a death having occurred for the remission of transgressions *under the first covenant*" (italics added). The purpose of Heb 9:16–17 is to explain *why a death was necessary*, given the predicament of the broken first covenant.

---

⁵⁴ Brown, *Hebrews*, 415: "Far less have we evidence that the death of the sacrificial victim was necessary to the validity of every arrangement to which the word rendered 'covenant' may be applied"; Attridge, *Hebrews*, 254: "There are covenants recorded in scripture where no inaugural sacrifice is mentioned."

⁵⁵ Hugenberger, *Marriage as Covenant*, 196–197, and Weinfeld, *TDOT* 2:256 and scripture references cited therein.

⁵⁶ Robert P. Gordon, *Hebrews* (Sheffield: Sheffield Academic Press, 2000), 103–104: "V. 16b refers unmistakably to the death of the ratifier of the will/covenant as being essential for its implementation.... Interpreting this as the symbolic death of the ratifier... requires a lot of reading between the lines in v. 16b and even more so in v. 17"; cf. also Vos, *Hebrews*, 39.

In Heb 9:16, when the author says "For where there is a covenant," the reader must also incorporate from Heb 9:15 the concept παραβάσεων γενομένων, "transgressions having taken place." In other circumstances—for example, if there were no covenant in place, or if a different kind of relationship were in place (e.g., a trade contract)—transgressions would not result in death, or would simply not be of concern. However, the author of Hebrews emphasizes, ὅπου γὰρ διαθήκη, θάνατον ἀνάγκη φέρεσθαι τοῦ διαθεμένου, "*where there is a covenant*, it is necessary for the death of the covenant-maker to be endured [when transgressions have taken place]." The fact that a covenant is in force renders the situation of transgression deadly. The author's point becomes clearer when ὅπου is taken causally, i.e., not as "where" but as "whereas" or "since."[57] Verse 16 could be rendered, "*Since* there is a covenant, it is necessary for the death of the covenant-maker to be borne." Under different circumstances, the fact that there had been transgressions (παραβάσεις) may have been inconsequential or given rise to some lesser punishment, but "since there is a covenant"—particularly one that has been ratified by a bloody *Drohritus* (Heb 9:18-22), i.e., which entails a curse-of-death for violations—"the death of the covenant-maker must be borne."

2.3.2. θάνατον ἀνάγκη φέρεσθαι τοῦ διαθεμένου *(Heb 9:16b)*

A broken covenant of this kind demands the curse-of-death. The biblical and extra-biblical examples of death as the sanction for covenant-breaking (see above) support the author's assertion. Some commentators have voiced the opinion that "covenants or contracts, of whatever sort, simply do not require the death of one of the parties,"[58] but in the understanding of the author of Hebrews, covenants of this sort (ratified by sacrifice) certainly *do* require the death of one of the parties when broken.

An explanation of the circumlocution θάνατον ἀνάγκη φέρεσθαι τοῦ διαθεμένου is in order. Φέρω should be taken in its common meaning "to bear, to endure,"[59] rather than the otherwise-unattested

---

[57] Cf. BAGD 576a (def. 2b); L&N 782a (§89.35); LSJ 1242a (def. II.2). Ὅπου is clearly causal in 1 Cor 3:3, 4 Macc 14:11, 14, 19; possibly also in 4 Macc 2:14 and 6:34. Ὅπου occurs in Heb 6:20; 9:16 and 10:18. In both Heb 9:16 and 10:18 the causal meaning ("whereas, since") seems to provide a better reading than the usual rendering.

[58] Attridge, *Hebrews*, 256.

[59] BAGD 855a (def. 1c); L&N 807a (§90.64); LSJ 1923a (def. A.III). In Heb

meanings most modern versions and lexicons provided here for the phrase θάνατον φέρεσθαι.⁶⁰ The phrase διαθέμενον ἀνάγκη ἀποθανεῖν, "it is necessary for the covenant-maker to die," would be more succinct, but the difference in emphasis between "the covenant-maker must die" and "the death of the covenant-maker must be borne" is significant, if subtle. In the first formulation, the subject of the verbal idea is the *covenant-maker*, in the second, it is the *death*. The second formulation does not actually specify who must die, only that the covenant-maker's death must be endured. The author leaves open the possibility that the death of the covenant-maker might be borne by a designated representative, e.g., the high-priest Jesus. He only stresses that, because of transgression (Heb 9:15), *someone* must bear the curse-of-death, without specifying whom. In the view of the author, ultimately Christ endures the curse-of-death on behalf of the *actual* covenant-makers, i.e., those under the first covenant (Heb 9:15).

The concept of someone "bearing" (φέρω) the death of the covenant-maker in Heb 9:16, like the "bearing (ἀναφέρω) the sins of many" in Heb 9:28, may be shaped by the use of φέρω in Isa 53 LXX, where (ἀνα)φέρω is consistently used in the sense "bear something for another."⁶¹ Hebrews 9:28 (τὸ πολλῶν ἀνενεγκεῖν ἁμαρτίας) is a clear reference to Isa 53:12 LXX (καὶ αὐτὸς ἁμαρτίας πολλῶν ἀνήνεγκεν), which suffices to show that Isa 53 is in the mind of the author in Heb 9. Thus, it may well be that the use of φέρω in the sense of "bear on another's behalf" in Isa 53:3–4 elucidates the use of φέρω in Heb 9:16.

2.3.3. διαθήκη γὰρ ἐπὶ νεκροῖς βεβαία *(Heb 9:17a)*

The sense of Heb 9:17a ("a [broken] covenant is confirmed upon dead [bodies]") is that, after a covenant has been broken (the situation under the first covenant), the only means of enforcing the covenant is to actualize the covenant curses, which ultimately result in the death of the covenant-maker-turned-covenant-breaker.⁶²

---

[13]:13 φέρω is used in this sense (τὸν ὀνειδισμὸν αὐτοῦ φέροντες). Cf. also Heb 12:20 (οὐκ ἔφερον γὰρ τὸ διαστελλόμενον); Isa 53:4 LXX (οὗτος τὰς ἁμαρτίας ἡμῶν φέρει); Jer 51:22 LXX; Ezek 34:29; 36:6 LXX.
[60] See discussion above, esp. n. 25.
[61] Cf. Isa 53:3, 4, 11, 12.
[62] Cf. Lev 26:14–39, esp. v. 30, but also vv. 16, 22, 25, 38; Deut 28:15–68, esp. vv. 20, 22, 24, 26, 48, 51, 61. As was noted above for the ancient Near Eastern oath-curses, although not all the curses of Lev 26 and Deut 28 are *immediate* death,

The use of the plural ἐπὶ νεκροῖς, "dead bodies"—problematic under the testamentary reading—is not unexpected under the reading proposed here. The situation the author envisions is the first covenant, made by the people. Ὁ διαθέμενος and ἐπὶ νεκροῖς refer to the people of Israel in the collective singular and the plural form respectively. The grammatically-singular "people" (cf. Heb 9:19, λαός) is the "covenant-maker" (ὁ διαθέμενος) at Sinai, yet "dead bodies" (νεκροί, cf. Deut 28:26 LXX) would result if the curse-of-death was actualized upon them.

2.3.4. *ἐπεὶ μήποτε ἰσχύει ὅτε ζῇ ὁ διαθέμενος (Heb 9:17b)*
The bold statement of Heb 9:17b, "since it certainly is not in force while the covenant-maker lives,"[63] expresses the following principle: for the covenant-maker(s) to remain alive after violating the covenant indicates that the covenant has no binding force (μήποτε ἰσχύει). It is useful to recall the rhetorical question of Ezek 17:15: "But he rebelled against him... Will he succeed? Can a man escape who does such things? Can he break the covenant and yet escape?" (RSV). For the author of Hebrews, as well as for Ezekiel, the answer is an emphatic "No!" (cf. Heb 12:25!). The survival of the covenant-maker after the violation of his sworn commitment demonstrates the impotence of the covenant and the powerlessness of the oath-curse. A covenant is not *in force* if it is not *enforced*.

2.3.5. *ὅθεν οὐδὲ ἡ πρώτη χωρὶς αἵματος ἐγκεκαίνισται (Heb 9:18)*
Hebrews 9:18-22 explicitly concerns the first Sinaitic covenant, strengthening the case that this broken covenant is the assumed context of Heb 9:16-17. The sense of Heb 9:18, ὅθεν οὐδὲ ἡ πρώτη χωρὶς αἵματος ἐγκεκαίνισται, may be "Hence, neither was the first covenant inaugurated without blood," the emphasis being on the fact that, at its very inauguration, the first covenant liturgically pre-enacted the death of the covenant-maker should the covenant be transgressed.[64] Thus, the reader should not doubt that the Sinaitic covenant was one that entailed the curse-of-death. The flow of thought from Heb 9:16-17 to 9:18-22 could be paraphrased as follows: "A broken

---

virtually all the curses are *means* of death: plague, disease, enemy attack, wild animals, siege, famine, etc.
[63] For μήποτε as a strong negative ("certainly not") see Ellingworth, *Hebrews*, 464.
[64] Cf. Vanhoye, *New Priest*, 203.

covenant requires the death of the covenant-maker (Heb 9:16–17); hence, the first covenant liturgically portrayed the death of the covenant-maker by bloody sacrifice (Heb 9:18–21). Nearly everything about the first covenant was covered in blood, representing the necessity of death for the forgiveness of transgressions of the covenant (Heb 9:22, cf. 9:15)."

3. Conclusion and an Avenue for Further Study

At the beginning of this essay, we discussed the close integration of the legal and liturgical aspects of the covenant in the thought-world of Hebrews. However, Heb 9:15–18 appeared to be counter-evidence for this integration. In Heb 9:16–17, the author appears to use διαθήκη in a sense quite different from his customary usage, stepping outside Israelite-Jewish cultic categories in order to draw an analogy from Greco-Roman law, whose relevance is anything but clear.

I have argued that the solution to the puzzle of Heb 9:16–17 is not to abandon the cultic-covenantal framework of the author's thought, with its close relationship between liturgy and law, but to enter into that framework more deeply. If it is understood that the context for the statements of Heb 9:16–17 is the broken first covenant mentioned in Heb 9:15, one can see that the author is drawing out the *legal* implications of the *liturgical* ritual (i.e., bloody sacrifices) that established the first covenant: a broken covenant demands the death of the covenant-maker (Heb 9:16), and it is not being enforced while the offending covenant-maker lives (Heb 9:17).

Therefore, Heb 9:16–17 does not involve an abrupt, unmarked switch in context (from Jewish to Greco-Roman), nor does the author argue for a strained analogy between a "covenant" and a "testament." Verses 16–17 simply restate a theological principle summarized in the verse they seek to explicate (Heb 9:15): the first covenant entailed the curse-of-death for those who broke it (Heb 2:2; 10:28), which Christ takes upon himself as Israel's corporate representative (Heb 2:9, 14; 9:28), thus freeing those under the first covenant from the curse-of-death (Heb 2:15; 10:14) and providing for them a new and better covenant (Heb 9:28; 10:15–17; 12:22–24).

If I have been correct in my exegesis of Heb 9:16–17, then the statement of v. 17b certainly opens up an avenue for further study: ἐπεὶ μήποτε ἰσχύει ὅτε ζῇ ὁ διαθέμενος, "since [the covenant] is certainly not in force while the covenant-maker lives." According to my paradigm, the author is speaking about the broken Sinaitic covenant: having been broken (at the golden calf apostasy), it is not in force (or being enforced) until the covenant curse (i.e., death) is actualized upon the covenant-maker (Israel). The covenant-curse of death is only finally visited upon Israel when Christ dies as their representative (Heb 9:15). But this implies that, in the author's view, there is a extended hiatus in Israel's history between the violation of the first covenant (Exod 32:1–14) and the death of Christ, during which the first covenant was, in a sense, not "strong" or "in force" (μήποτε ἰσχύει), held in abeyance, its curses not being actualized. It is as if, after the golden calf, a verdict is reached, the sentence handed down, but the execution suspended indefinitely. What justified this suspension?

The answer is to be found in the narrative of Exod 32. After the covenant has been broken God threatens to enforce it: "Now let me alone, so that my wrath may burn hot against them and I may consume them; and of you I will make a great nation" (Exod 32:10 NRSV). But Moses pleads with God to relent, based on the divine oath to the Patriarchs: "Remember Abraham, Isaac, and Israel, your servants, how you swore to them by your own self" (Exod 32:13 NRSV). Moses is referring to God's oath at the Aqedah (Gen 22:15–18), the only record of God swearing by himself to the Patriarchs. On Mt. Moriah, after the near-sacrifice of Isaac, God spoke to Abraham:

> By Myself I swear, the LORD declares: Because you have done this and have not withheld your son, your favored one, I will bestow My blessing upon you and make your descendants as numerous as the stars of heaven and the sands on the seashore; and your descendants shall seize the gates of their foes. All the nations of the earth shall bless themselves by your descendants, because you have obeyed My command. (Gen 22:16–18 NJPS)

In Exod 32:13, Moses appeals to this oath, making the following argument to God: "You cannot annihilate Israel for violating their covenant-oath, for if you do, you would violate your own self-sworn oath to bless and multiply Abraham's descendants." In other words, the covenant *curses* of Sinai could not be enforced upon the people of Israel because of God's prior oath to Abraham to *bless* his descendants (i.e., Israel).

The Levitical priesthood, according to the narrative of the Pentateuch, is established in response to the golden calf apostasy (Exod

32:29). The author of Hebrews notes that "on the basis of [the Levitical priesthood] the law was given to the people" (Heb 7:11). This would refer to the fact that the bulk of the sacrificial system (Lev 1–7, 16), as well as the Deuteronomic Code, was given to Israel subsequent to the golden calf episode and the elevation of the Levites. The author of Hebrews may have held the view that this Levitical cultic system was "weak and useless" (Heb 7:18) because it was only a symbolic or pedagogical apparatus designed to remind Israel of her covenant violations (Heb 10:3) until one could come who was capable of bearing the curse-of-death of the (broken) covenant on behalf of the whole nation (Heb 2:9; 9:15), thus enabling God to enforce the first covenant without undermining his self-sworn oath to bless the "seed of Abraham" (Gen 22:15–18; Heb 6:13–20).

The author of Hebrews places considerable weight on divine oaths in general,[65] and devotes particular attention to this divine oath at the Aqedah (Gen 22:15–18) in Heb 6:13–20. He mentions the Aqedah again in Heb 11:17–19. Dunnill remarks:

> The story of the "Binding of Isaac" [is] a theme which has vastly greater significance, not only for this chapter but for the theology of the letter as a whole, than its rather brief appearance (11:17f.) would suggest. [It is of] fundamental importance for the letter's Christology... it acts as the organizing centre of Hebrews 11 and as a "foundation sacrifice" for the faith-covenant established through Jesus.[66]

In Jewish tradition, the Aqedah took place on the Day of Atonement, and the rituals of Day of Atonement were interpreted as a yearly anamnesis of Isaac's "sacrifice."[67] Thus, the author's theology of the Day of Atonement, articulated throughout Heb 9:1–28, may have an integral relation to the significance he sees in the Aqedah and the divine oath given there (Heb 6:13–20; 11:17–19).

In sum, it may be that the author of Hebrews regards the divine oath to Abraham at the Aqedah as a foundational act for Israel, which is renewed in Christ. The divine oath of the Aqedah is an expression of God's providential mercy, inasmuch as it prevents the

---

[65] Dunnill, *Covenant and Sacrifice*, 249: "Oaths and the finality they confer are deeply important in Hebrews, especially the unique status and revolutionary consequences of divine oaths." The author discusses the divine oath of Num 14:20–23 (through Ps 95:7–11) in Heb 3:7–4:11 and that of Ps 110:4 in Heb 7:20–22.
[66] Dunnill, *Covenant and Sacrifice*, 173.
[67] See Dunnill, *Covenant and Sacrifice*, 174–175.

full enforcement of the curses of the first covenant (Exod 32:13–14) until the coming of the Christ, who can bear the curse-of-death on behalf of all (Heb 2:9; 9:15) and restore for Israel the Abrahamic blessing (Heb 6:13–20; Gen 22:15–18). Christ's death is simultaneously the legal execution of the curses of the old covenant and the liturgical ritual of sacrifice which establishes the new. Hebrews' theology on this point would be strikingly similar to Paul's in Gal 3:6–25, which is unsurprising given the numerous connections between Galatians and Hebrews already noted by other scholars.[68] In any event, the complex of issues surrounding the divine oath at the Aqedah, the "weakness" of the Sinaitic covenant rituals, and the author's bold statement in Heb 9:17b certainly merits further study.

Scott W. Hahn, Ph.D.
Professor of Scripture and Theology
Franciscan University of Steubenville
808 Belleview Boulevard, Steubenville, Ohio 43952, U.S.A.
shahn@franciscan.edu

---

[68] E.g., Ben Witherington III, "The Influence of Galatians on Hebrews," *NTS* 37 (1991): 146–152.

THE EPISTLE TO THE HEBREWS AS A "JESUS-MIDRASH"

Elke Tönges

1. *Introduction*

My interest in the Epistle[1] to the Hebrews concerns the way in which it cites and transforms verses, stories, characters, and themes from the Hebrew Bible. The author does not just adopt these Jewish traditions, but forms them into an immense intertextual network. By writing in an elaborated Greek, he or she presents Jewish traditions from his/her own particular viewpoint. The text never refers to non-Jewish traditions, nor does it cite Greek or Roman literature. Rather, the author concentrates his/her literary composition on the words of God that she/he finds in Greek translation in the Scriptures of Israel. Therefore the Epistle to the Hebrews has mainly a Jewish background.

I want to examine the special kind of Jewish background that might be possible for our text. First I will consider—in the section on methodology—whether Hebrews contains any midrashic elements and whether it might be considered as a Jewish midrash. Therefore I will analyze how it uses quotations from the Hebrew Bible and their introductory formulas. The next step will be to examine the content of Hebrews and its theological impact. How does the text refer to figures from Israel's history? Finally I will return to the question of whether we may speak of the overall text of Hebrews as a midrash and will offer a hypothesis for a possible original *Sitz im Leben*.

---

[1] I will refer to our text as an "epistle," although by using this term I do not intend to describe its literary form. Translations of Hebrews and other biblical texts in this article are my own.

2. Methodological Approach

2.1. *The Epistle to the Hebrews—a "Jesus-Midrash"?*

If we want to call the Epistle to the Hebrews a "Jesus-Midrash," we have to define the *genre* midrash in a broad sense. The word *midrash* is used in rabbinic and New Testament exegesis in different ways. It may describe a literary genre, certain books, or a model for contemporary biblical-literary analysis.[2] A definition of what is meant when we talk about midrash is therefore in order: (1) the contents of a text, (2) its form, (3) a method, (4) or all of these. Moshe D. Herr emphasized in 1971 that "Midrash is the designation of a particular *rabbinic literature* constituting an anthology and compilation of homilies."[3] Arnold Goldberg worked on a descriptive terminology of the "form" midrash. Yet his definition from 1985, whereby a lemma means a dictum provided that a certain hermeneutical operation is performed,[4] seems too narrow.

Most of the books which are described as Midrashim were written from the second century CE on. However, early forms of midrashim were already known in the centuries before Christ. Goldberg comments that in early Judaism the periphrastic exegesis of the Torah was more important than in our transmitted Midrashim. The oldest Midrash books are the so-called "tannaitic" or "exegetic" Midrashim (*Mek. R. Yish., Sipra, Sipre Num., Sipre Deut.*). These were written from the third century on, but include much older material.

In terms of the methods employed, the author of the Epistle to the Hebrews is thoroughly Jewish. He or she uses exegetical terminology, rules of interpretation, and expository patterns (like the midrash) that are found elsewhere in Judaism. But the *christological* interpretation of the biblical writings makes a unique contribution.

As an interpretive activity the midrashic procedure is mostly oriented to Scripture, adapting it to the present for the purpose of instructing or edifying the reader or hearer. The literary expression can be described in two different ways. With the use of midrash in

---

[2] Cf. Lieve Teugels, "Midrash in the Bible or Midrash on the Bible? Critical Remarks about the Uncritical Use of a Term," in *Bibel und Midrasch: Zur Bedeutung der rabbinischen Exegese für die Bibelwissenschaft* (ed. Gerhard Bodendorfer and Matthias Millard; FAT 22; Tübingen: Mohr Siebeck, 1998), 44.

[3] Moshe D. Herr, "Midrash," *EncJud* 11:1507.

[4] Arnold Goldberg, "Form-Analysis of Midrashic Literature as a Method of Description," *JJS* 36 (1985): 159–174, esp. 162.

Ben Sira and Qumran, the term "midrash" is now employed more broadly to designate "interpretive rendering of the biblical text" (= implicit midrash) and various kinds of "text and exposition" patterns (= explicit midrash). Implicit midrash first appears as a process of rewriting.[5]

Some examples of passages in Hebrews that have been identified as midrash are:

(1) Heb 1–4: "Schriftgnosis mit paränetischem Midrasch"[6]
(2) Heb 1:1–14[7]
(3) Heb 1:1–2:18[8]
(4) Heb 2:5–8: "Ps 8:4–6 . . . followed by a midrashic commentary"[9]
(5) Heb 3:1–6: "exegetic midrash"[10]
(6) Heb 3:7–4:13: "selbständiger Midrasch über Ps 95"[11]
(7) Heb 3:12–4:11: "Psalm 95:7–11 together with a midrashic application of the passage to the situation of the readers"[12]
(8) Heb 3:16–19: "Methode des rabbinischen Midrasch"[13]
(9) Heb 5:1–7:28[14]

---

[5] E. Earle Ellis, *The Old Testament in Early Christianity: Canon and Interpretation in the Light of Modern Research* (WUNT 54; Tübingen: Mohr, 1991), 92; cf. 2 Chr 13:22; 24:27.

[6] Hans Windisch, *Der Hebräerbrief* (2d ed.; HNT 14; Tübingen: Mohr Siebeck), 1931), 8.

[7] See E. Earle Ellis, *Prophecy and Hermeneutic in Early Christianity: New Testament Essays* (WUNT 18; Tübingen: Mohr, 1978), 221–226.

[8] Ellis (*The Old Testament in Early Christianity*, 96 n. 69) suggests that Heb 1:1–2:18 is "perhaps" an instance of explicit midrash appearing as a "special pattern."

[9] Donald A. Hagner, *Hebrews* (NIBC 14; Peabody, Mass.: Hendrickson, 1998), 14.

[10] Otto Michel calls Heb 3:3–6a an "exegetic Midrash," which is influenced by the parallel text of Moses in Heb 3:2c (Otto Michel, *Der Brief an die Hebräer* [6th ed.; KEK 13; Göttingen: Vandenhoeck & Ruprecht, 1966], 92); cf. Scott Layton, "Christ over his House (Hebrews 3,6)," *NTS* 37 (1991): 473: "Heb 3,1–6 is a complex midrash on several texts."

[11] Peter S. Wick, "The Midrash on Deuteronomy 12:9–11 in Hebrews 3:7–4:13: A Key to the Overall Theological Concept of Hebrews" (paper presented at the international meeting of the SBL, Groningen, Netherlands, 26 July 2004). Cf. Otto Michel: "selbständiger Midrasch über Ps 95" (Michel, *Brief an die Hebräer*, 7). Martin Dibelius, "Der himmlische Kult nach dem Hebräerbrief," *TBl* 21 (1942): 7: "Midrasch über Ps 95." Windisch (*Hebräerbrief*, 30): "längere midraschartige Betrachtung über Ps 94,7–11."

[12] Hagner, *Hebrews*, 14.

[13] Friedrich Schröger, *Der Verfasser des Hebräerbriefes als Schriftausleger* (BU 4; Regensburg: Pustet, 1968), 113.

[14] Theme and initial texts (Heb 5:1–6; Ps 2:7; 110:4) + Exposition (Heb 5:7–10; [+ Inserted exhortation (Heb 5:11–6:12)] + Supplementary text (Heb 6:13–14; Gen 22:16–17) + Exposition (Heb 6:15–20) + Supplementary text (Heb 7:1–2; Gen

(10) Heb 7: "Midrasch über Ps 109,4 und Gen 14,17–20"[15]
(11) Heb 9: "midrash-like presentation of material drawn from the Pentateuch, but with no explicit quotation"[16]
(12) Heb 10: "quotation of Ps 40:6–8 with a brief midrashic commentary"[17]
(13) Heb 10:5–39: "proem Midrash"[18]
(14) Heb 10:1–18: "selbständige[r] Midrasch über die Einzigartigkeit des Opfers Christi"[19]
(15) Heb 11:8–19: "Abraham Midrash"[20]
(16) Heb 12: "midrashic treatment of OT material"[21]
(17) Heb 12:5–6: "Midrasch Haggadah"[22]

The above mentioned passages are *explicit midrashim*. They appear as clusters of texts and commentaries on a particular theme. Similar patterns may be found in Qumran (e.g. 4Q174) or in the texts of the first-century Jewish writer Philo of Alexandria.[23] The New Testament exegetical patterns display a number of differences from those of the rabbis. As I shall show later for the introductory formulas, this may represent an earlier stage of development of the art and genre as well as a divergent theological orientation. For example, the midrashim underlying Heb 5–7 are distinctive because of their christological dimension; they apply Ps 110:4 (109:4 LXX) to Jesus.

Perhaps Hebrews cites not just the traditions, themes, and persons of the people of Israel to illustrate Jesus' role and mission to the world, but also employs a traditional Jewish handling and creative writing of the well-known texts. Therefore, we might examine next the use of the quotations and introductory formulas in the next step.

14:17–20) + Exposition (Heb 7:3–27) + Concluding allusion to the initial text (Heb 7:28); cf. Ellis, *Prophecy and Hermeneutic*, 157 and Ellis, *The Old Testament in Early Christianity*, 99 n. 81.

[15] Windisch, *Hebräerbrief*, 59.
[16] Hagner, *Hebrews*, 14.
[17] Ibid.
[18] Ellis, *The Old Testament in Early Christianity*, 98, 107.
[19] Michel, *Brief an die Hebräer*, 184.
[20] Luis F. Mercado, "The Language of Sojourning in the Abraham Midrash in Hebrews 11:8–19: Its Old Testament Basis, Exegetical Traditions and Function in the Epistle to the Hebrews" (Th.D. diss., Harvard University, 1966), 2.
[21] Hagner, *Hebrews*, 14.
[22] Schröger, *Verfasser*, 189.
[23] Ellis, *The Old Testament in Early Christianity*, 96 n. 71: "E.g. Philo, *De Sacrif. Abel.* 76–87: Lev 2:14 + Commentary with verbal links and supplementary texts + Concluding allusion to the opening text + Final texts (Exod 6:7; Lev 26:12)."

2.2. Quotations

Some scholars claim to have found midrash texts elsewhere in the New Testament: 1 Cor 10:1–22 and the so-called "formula quotations" in Matthew's Gospel.[24] These formula quotations have the same formal structure as rabbinic midrashim defined by Goldberg.[25] How are the quotations used in Hebrews?

The Epistle to the Hebrews is structured around forty-four direct quotations referring to a total of fifty-three different texts from what would come to be called the Hebrew Bible. There are more than eighty further allusions to other texts of the Jewish canon.

Almost all quotations are taken from the Septuagint. However, it must be noted that the collection of Septuagint texts had not been completed by the end of the first century and that the author may only have had certain parts of the Septuagint available. Judging from the scriptural quotations, these texts would have included the Torah, the Psalms, and Jeremiah.

We know that in the case of the Epistle to the Hebrews, comparing Hellenistic or Jewish influence does not help to reveal the meaning of Hebrews in the first century. There are many texts which demonstrate a combined Hellenistic-Jewish influence, such as the writings of Philo of Alexandria, who wrote in Greek but used midrashic techniques. We also know that there were many Greek synagogues at the time of the composition of the Epistle to the Hebrews. Therefore Hebrews can quote the Hebrew Bible in Greek translation and still be a "Jewish" book, because the common language of the first century CE was Greek.

Hypothesis 1: From the choice and origin of its quotations, it can be seen that the Epistle to the Hebrews originated at the boundary between Hebrew-Jewish and Hellenistic-Jewish milieu.

To support the hypothesis, we might notice the following six points:

(1) We have already seen that the *auctor ad Hebraeos* had access to a number of different parts of the Septuagint. If we use the Jewish division of the Hebrew Scriptures into Torah, Prophets, and Writings

---

[24] Cf. Matt 1:23; 2:6, 15, 18, 23; 4:15–16; 8:17; 12:18–21; 13:35; 21:5 and 27:9–10.

[25] Arnold Goldberg, "Midrashsatz: Vorschläge für die descriptive Terminologie der Formanalyse rabbinischer Texte," *FJB* 17 (1989): 45–56.

(*Ketubim*), we see that twenty-two of the direct quotations in Hebrews are from the book of Psalms; some Psalms (95, 110 [94, 109 LXX]) are even mentioned twice, and a few are alluded to even more often. This is a common rabbinic method: the rabbis like to quote the text under discussion, as is done in Heb 3:7–4:11 and Heb 7.

(2) Next most frequent are quotations from the Torah, especially Genesis and Deuteronomy. The question is whether we already are finding signs in Hebrews of the three-part division of the Hebrew Bible. The author does not bother to discuss the development of the canon or to give us any hints in the text. The New Testament phrases "Law (of Moses) and Prophets"[26] or "Torah of Moses, Prophets, Psalms"[27] are not mentioned in Hebrews.

It should, however, be noted, that the Greek word νόμος appears only in Heb 7–10, which deals with cultic patterns. Here the argumentation about Jesus as high priest is interpreted in terms of the Melchizedek-Abraham tradition and cultic descriptions of the role and function of the priests. Therefore, νόμος describes the Levitical part of the law. However, the underlying meaning of νόμος here—and always—is the "Torah of Moses" which reveals the will of God (Heb 10:28; cf. 9:19).

(3) Most Jewish texts seek to place themselves in the long tradition of the prophets of Israel. Hebrews does this too. In the exordium, the author introduces the prophets as revealing God's message in an earlier time (Heb 1:1): "Having spoken of old in many forms and various ways to the fathers through the prophets." Texts from the prophetic books, such as Jer 31, are not just widely quoted but express the essence of the theological impact of the letter. Two quotations from 1 and 2 Samuel are eminently important. One cites God's promise in Nathan's prophecy (2 Sam 7:14 in Heb 1:5) and the other includes God's assurance that the faithful priest will receive from God an everlasting house (1 Sam 2:35 in Heb 2:17; 3:2, 6).

(4) Except for the book of Psalms, there are not many quotations from the Writings (*Ketubim*) in the Epistle to the Hebrews. Indeed, it seems that Hebrews does not even know the Greek word γραφή, using instead λόγος ζῶν (Heb 4:12).

---

[26] Cf. Luke 16:16 // Matt 11:13; Luke 16:29, 31; 24:27; Matt 5:17; 7:12; John 1:45; Acts 13:15; 24:14; 28:23; Rom 3:21.
[27] Cf. Luke 24:44.

An indication of the clear and consistent *christological* interpretation of texts from the Hebrew Bible is given in Heb 10:7. Here Christ speaks in the words of Ps 40:8 (39:8 LXX): "in the scroll of the book, it is written about me" (ἐν κεφαλίδι βιβλίου γέγραπται περὶ ἐμοῦ).

(5) We should further recognize that Hebrews is full of composite quotations which often append to one text a compilation from another (cf. Heb 10:37–38: Isa 26:20 and Hab 2:3–4). This practice appears frequently in other Jewish literature, and such study and interpretation of Scripture was an established practice in first-century Judaism.

We have to assume that biblical quotations that deviate from the text of the Septuagint were generally intentional alterations rather than unintentional lapses. The Epistle to the Hebrews uses this technique freely to show and draw out its textual impact. Therefore, Hebrews has a number of *textual alterations*, such as Heb 10:6, "in burnt offerings and sin offerings you did not have pleasure." The first words about the offerings, from Ps 40:7 (39:7 LXX), create verbal links within the larger exposition of Scripture, i.e., a pattern of *explicit midrash* (cf. Heb 10:38; Rom 10:12–13, 16, 18). However, there does remain the possibility that the author is using a different version of the Septuagint from the one known to us, rather than making a deliberate alteration. For instance, this question remains open for the use of "body" in Heb 10:5 rather than "ears" as in the Psalm verse being quoted here (Ps 40:7 [39:7 LXX]).

(6) Besides the quotations of Scripture from what would come to be called the Hebrew Bible, Hebrews includes allusions to the additional books in the Septuagint, specifically to the later Wisdom tradition (Heb 1:3: Wis 7:25–26; 11:25) and to the books of Maccabees (Heb 11:25: 2 Macc 6–7 and 4 Macc 15:2, 8).

We may conclude that the use of scriptural quotations in the Epistle to the Hebrews is consistent with the development of the Jewish canon as witnessed in the writings of Greek-speaking authors of the first century (cf. Josephus, *C. Ap.* 1.38–46). Hebrews therefore seems to be part of the Jewish discussion: it respects Jewish boundaries and thus enables the community it addresses to develop their ideas and understanding of the world and of God's plan in the context of and in discussion with Jewish positions and traditions.

Let me complete this point with Arnold Goldberg's well-known insight that rabbinic literature—and, I would add, the Epistle to the Hebrews—is "a literature of tradition, but also a literature of quotation."

2.3. *Introductory Formulas*

The Epistle to the Hebrews not only quotes texts from the Hebrew Bible, but also uses introductory formulas to introduce these quotations. These *formulae quaestionis* are important when we ask how Hebrews transforms the biblical texts and how it uses them to show that Jesus is the redeemer of the world. The formulas show that the Epistle to the Hebrews may be placed on the boundary between Hebrew-Jewish and Hellenistic-Jewish milieu.

The well-known phrase, "it was written" (γέγραπται), is used only once, in a quotation from Ps 40:8 (39:8 LXX) in Heb 10:7. In its place, phrases containing verbs like λέγειν or φανεῖν ("speak, say") or in some texts μαρτυρεῖν ("witness, bear testimony") are used (Heb 2:6; 7:17). This reflects the fact that Greek is richer in verbs of saying than is Hebrew. With these verbs a certain shift from a written text to oral speech is made. The quotations in the Epistle to the Hebrews are no longer written, but are becoming the spoken authoritative word.

Bruce Metzger has compared the use of introductory formulas in the Mishnah and in the New Testament. He suggests that when these formulas differ, they are two different *genres* rather than being two differing *interpretations of history*. He points out that the New Testament and the Mishnah each contain a number of examples where the subject of the verb of saying in the formula may be either the Scriptures or God: "Indeed, so habitual was the identification of the divine Author with the word of Scripture that occasionally personality is attributed to the passages itself."[28] In fact, "the author of Hebrews cites the words of Scripture as the words of God even where the OT does not so characterize them, and where the words are in the third person about God."[29]

The author of Hebrews even characterizes two quotations as words of Christ: Heb 2:12–13 and 10:5–7. These are not the words of the earthly Jesus of Nazareth, but rather words of Christ, who expresses

---

[28] Bruce M. Metzger, "The Formulas Introducing Quotations of Scripture in the NT and the Mishnah," *JBL* 70 (1951): 306.
[29] Ibid. Cf. Heb 1:6, 7, 8; 4:4, 7; 7:21; 10:30b.

his incarnation and his relation to God and his brothers and sisters in the words of Scripture (Ps 22:23 [21:23 LXX], etc.).

Another text shows the use of the Holy Spirit in an introductory formula which expresses the authority of the quotation. In 2 Sam 23:2, God's spirit speaks through David's words. It is possible that this text is the origin of the formula, "as the Holy Spirit says" (cf. Heb 3:7, quoting Ps 95 [94 LXX]). The Psalms are full of references to being God's word, and so fit easily with the intention of Hebrews that the Psalms should be heard as divine speech.

Various subjects are used to transmit the quotations: God, the Son, the Holy Spirit, Moses (Heb 9:20; 12:21), "someone" (Heb 2:6) and, at the end of the epistle, "we" (Heb 13:6).[30]

This change of authorities in introductory formulas is in its use similar to rabbinic literature. Texts that are quoted as God's word are cited in the rabbinic literature as words of an authoritative rabbi.

In addition, it is noteworthy that Hebrews is the only book in the New Testament to contain examples of the indefinite type of formula where the subject is "someone" and/or the source of the citation is left unspecified (Heb 2:6, "someone [τις] bore testimony to this somewhere [πού], saying"; Heb 4:4, "for he has spoken somewhere [πού]"; Heb 5:6, "since he [God] says elsewhere [ἐν ἑτέρῳ]"). This indefinite formula appears also in the Mishnah and the writings of Philo.[31] Hebrews uses these unspecific references to the Hebrew Bible to emphasize that the biblical text is not human writing, but the word of God (see Heb 5:12, λόγια τοῦ θεοῦ).

Hypothesis 2: Hebrews' view of the continuing activity of God in the historical event comprising the life, death, and resurrection of Jesus of Nazareth, as fulfilling or even surpassing divine revelation as recorded in the Hebrew Bible, is reflected even in the choice of

---

[30] A precise list of the quotations, noting their differences from the Septuagint text known to us, may be found in Michael Theobald, "Vom Text zum 'lebendigen Wort' (Hebr 4,12): Beobachtungen zur Schrifthermeneutik des Hebräerbriefs," in *Jesus Christus als die Mitte der Schrift: Studien zur Hermeneutik des Evangeliums* (ed. Christof Landmesser et al.; BZNW 86; Berlin: de Gruyter, 1997), 754.

[31] Philo, *Ebr.* 61, *Deus* 74; cf. William Leonard, *The Authorship of the Epistle to the Hebrews* (London: Vatican Polyglot, 1939), 275, 283; Herbert E. Ryle, *Philo and Holy Scripture* (London: Macmillan, 1895), xiv; Joseph A. Fitzmyer, "The Use of Explicit Old Testament Quotations in Qumran Literature and in the New Testament," *NTS* 7 (1960–61): 299–305.

formulas introducing quotations of Scripture in the Epistle to the Hebrews.

2.4. *Use of Interpretation Patterns*

Friedrich Schröger recognized different rhetorical styles. In his earlier work, *Der Verfasser des Hebräerbriefes als Schriftausleger*,[32] he distinguishes between typological elements, methods of scriptural interpretation, and rabbinic or Qumranic Midrashim. However, we cannot entirely accept these distinctions, since it is not possible to distinguish between exegetical methods like the seven middot (exegetical rules) of Hillel,[33] which are quite often used in rabbinic texts and which also have many parallels in Hellenistic rhetorical language and in rabbinic Midrashim, and interpretative methods of midrash itself.

Typology is not a method but what we might call a "spiritual" approach. Like the haggadah of the rabbis, it brings the text into the present by appropriating the prophetic and representational character of Old Testament characters, events and institutions.[34]

Some scholars have shown how *typological elements* are used in the Epistle to the Hebrews and have characterized them as "Hellenistic" or "Philonic" traditions. But E. Earle Ellis remarks that "in the New Testament typology appears, broadly speaking, as *creation typology* and *covenant typology*... In the covenant typology various persons, events and institutions of Old Testament Israel are viewed as prophetic prefigurements of New Testament realities."[35] This is the case in the Epistle to the Hebrews, where the covenant typology is found in chs. 8–10. There it expresses the "new covenant," which will be found in the house of Israel and Judah. Hebrews 8:8–12 quotes the whole text of Jer 31:31–34, focusing on just three topics: the new covenant, the end of sacrifices and the writing of Torah/law in the hearts and minds of the people. The heart plays an important role for Hebrews,

---

[32] Schröger, *Verfasser*.

[33] Cf. Günter Stemberger, *Einleitung in Talmud und Midrasch* (8th ed.; Munich: Beck, 1992), 25–40.

[34] Cf. Karl-Heinrich Ostmeyer, "Typos—weder Urbild noch Abbild," in *Bildersprache verstehen: Zur Hermeneutik der Metapher und anderer bildlicher Sprachformen* (ed. Ruben Zimmermann; Texte und Studien zu Handlung, Sprache und Lebenswelt 38; Munich: Fink, 2000), 218, 223; Leonhard Goppelt, *Typos: The Typological Interpretation of the Old Testament in the New* (trans. Donald H. Madvig; Grand Rapids: Eerdmans, 1982), 30–31, 152, 198, 201–202.

[35] Ellis, *The Old Testament in Early Christianity*, 166.

for it is the place where someone decides whether he or she is willing to follow the law (see Heb 3:8, 12). This stands in relation to the central question of the audience for which Hebrews was written: whether to return to the Jewish faith or to continue to believe in Jesus as the Messiah. In the central chapters Heb 8–10, Jesus is shown as realizing the new covenant and as resuming the prophecy of Jeremiah.[36] The author of Hebrews cites the prophetic text referring to a "new covenant" to show Jesus' superiority (Heb 8:6, "better covenant") compared to the covenant given at Mount Sinai and not to the covenant of Jeremiah. In Heb 10:15–17, Jer 31:33 is quoted as the word of the Holy Spirit. This is intended to direct the words of the text directly at the readers and listeners of the epistle, who understand themselves to be living at the end of time (Heb 1:2). This method of interpretation is comparable with the Pesher-Midrashim in Qumran.[37]

Besides the passages quoted directly from the Hebrew Bible, Hebrews includes a large number of allusions to certain stories or expressions, such as "consuming fire" (Heb 12:29, πῦρ καταναλίσκον; cf. Deut 4:24); or "pursue peace with everyone" (Heb 12:14, Εἰρήνην διώκετε; cf. Ps 34:15 [33:15 LXX]),[38] etc.

Summary: We have seen that the Epistle to the Hebrews is full of explicit quotations and implicit allusions to Scripture. Is it possible to assume that the "epistle" to the Hebrews as a whole is transmitted also in a familiar Jewish form? And what would that mean for our interpretation of the text?

3. *Theological Content*

3.1. *Introduction*

That the text "to the Hebrews" is a *Jewish* text can be seen not only from the kind and genre of quotations, but also from the theological

---

[36] Cf. Konrad Taut, *Anleitung zum Schriftverständnis? Die heiligen Schriften nach dem Hebräerbrief* (THEOS 20; Hamburg: Dr. Kovac (private), 1998), 89.

[37] For the genre Pesher-Midrashim and midrash eschatology in Pesharim, see Timothy H. Lim, *Pesharim* (Companion to the Qumran Scrolls 3; London: Sheffield Academic Press, 2002), 48–53.

[38] The injunction "pursue peace" is a common motif of Old Testament and later Jewish paraenesis. See Ps 34:15; *T. Sim.* 5:2; *m. 'Abot* 1:12; Matt 5:9; 1 Pet 3:11, which cites Ps 34:15. Harold W. Attridge, *The Epistle to the Hebrews* (Hermeneia; Philadelphia: Fortress, 1989), 367 with n. 10.

transformation and intention of the text. Hebrews explains Jesus' role and function for a group of people who are familiar with the stories and figures of the Hebrew Bible. The original readers are referred to as "Hebrews" or "Jews." Hebrews thus shows us an intra-Jewish discussion between Jews who refer to their "common" Judaism (*religio licita*) and others who believe that Jesus is the Messiah of Israel. When we read the text of Hebrews it is as though we were listening to one side of a telephone conversation. We must see whether the theological interpretations may fit the hypothesis that Hebrews is a *Jewish* text.

3.2. *The Eschatological Dimension in Hebrews*

Since in Hebrews the *eschatological perspective* is the underlying motive, it is important to examine and compare it with Jewish texts. The *auctor ad Hebraeos* characterizes herself/himself and the addressees as living in the last days, as described in the exordium of Heb 1:2: "at the end of these days."[39] This conviction is common for authors of New Testament texts and Jewish apocalyptic texts.[40] In Hebrews, history is divided into two ages: this age and the age to come (Heb 6:5, μέλλοντος αἰῶνος). The message has to be seen in connection with Ps 95 (94 LXX), quoted in Heb 3–4, which pronounces the nearness of the *eschaton*:[41] "Today, if you hear his voice, do not harden your heart as in rebellion."[42]

It should be noted that, like Hebrews, the Book of Revelation represents a comprehensive adaptation of the images and motifs of the Hebrew Bible, using midrashic techniques to verbalize the eschatological vision of the seer.

3.3. *Figures from the History of Israel*

The Epistle to the Hebrews mentions more than twenty important characters from the history of the people of Israel. In Heb 11, the

---

[39] For text-critical remarks see Attridge, *Hebrews*, 35.
[40] Cf. Peter von der Osten-Sacken, *Die Apokalyptik in ihrem Verhältnis zu Prophetie und Weisheit* (TEH 157; Munich: Kaiser, 1969), 39–43.
[41] According to Herbert Braun, *An die Hebräer* (HNT 14; Tübingen: Mohr, 1984), 95, and against Erich Grässer, *An die Hebräer* (3 vols.; EKKNT 17; Zürich: Benziger and Neukirchen-Vluyn: Neukirchener, 1990–1997), 1:187 n. 21.
[42] For the use and messianic-eschatological interpretation of Ps 95, see Str-B 1:164–165.

encomium of faith, fifteen biblical figures are cited, including Abel, Enoch, Noah, Jephthah, Samuel, and the prophets, and God's response to their faith and good deeds is described.

For the author of the Epistle to the Hebrews, it was enough just to mention the names and a few aspects of the biblical figures. When they heard the names of these biblical heroes, his/her readers and listeners were able to relate these references to the familiar biblical stories. By using this method, the author was able to reframe characters and biblical stories: stories from the Hebrew Bible became part of the history of Jesus and emphasized the superiority of Jesus Christ.

Further research is needed to assess the significance of the author's choice of biblical figures. Following Heinrich Zimmermann and William Loader, it might also be interesting to consider how the role of the high priest is transformed.[43] We can note, however, that a number of figures of great importance for the constitution of the people of Israel are frequently mentioned in our text.

Let me focus here on Abraham and Moses, who appear in several texts illustrating Jesus' superiority and his heavenly connection to God.

The image of Abraham as Father of the People of Israel is used at the beginning of our text to point out that Jesus had come to the children of Abraham (Heb 2:16). God's promise that Abraham would be made into a great people is even quoted in Heb 6:14: "Surely, I will bestow blessings on you and will multiply you" (Gen 22:17).

The children and grandchildren of Abraham, Isaac, and Jacob are mentioned three times in Heb 11. These texts seem to lay a strong accent on the family relationship of the forefathers of Israel.

The second figure widely used in Hebrews is Moses. The New Testament cites Moses and his deeds more than eighty times. Moses appears in different roles—as the mediator of the Torah, or as a prophet. Generally in the New Testament, as in Hebrews in particular, his role and function as mediator between God and the people

---

[43] The portrait of Christ as a high priest is singular in the New Testament. It derives from traditions that are based on a complex Jewish heritage. Cf. Heinrich Zimmermann, *Die Hohepriester-Christologie des Hebräerbriefes* (Paderborn: Ferdinand Schöningh, 1964), passim; William Loader, *Sohn und Hoherpriester: Eine traditionsgeschichtliche Untersuchung zur Christologie des Hebräerbriefes* (WMANT 53; Neukirchen-Vluyn: Neukirchener, 1981), passim; Windisch, *Hebräerbrief*, 12–14; Michel, *Brief an die Hebräer*, 165–169; Oscar Cullmann, *Die Christologie des Neuen Testaments* (Tübingen: Mohr, 1957), 83–110, etc.

of Israel is compared to Jesus' function and mission.[44] Hebrews characterizes Moses as the leading figure for the desert generation, authorized by God (Heb 3:1–6),[45] who is, like Jesus, a loyal, faithful and reliable mediator of God. Further on, the Epistle to the Hebrews mentions Moses as the transmitter of the Torah (Heb 9:19; 10:28). But it also criticises his "covenant" as antiquated and unworthy (Heb 8–10). Such criticism of the quality of the prophecy of Moses is well known in Midrash texts. For instance, his knowledge of God's thoughts and plans is far inferior to that of Balaam:

> *And there arose no prophet in Israel like Moses* (Deut 34:10). In Israel no prophet arose; but amongst the nations of the world there was one. Who is this? Balaam, the son of Beor. But there is a difference between the prophecy of Moses and the prophecy of Balaam. Moses did not know who was speaking to him, but Balaam knew who was speaking, for it is said: *'the oracle of one who hears the words of God'* (Num 24:16). Moses did not know when God would speak to him, until God spoke, but Balaam knew when he was speaking to him. (*Sipre Deut.* 357 to Deut 34:10 [my translation])

The only historical figures mentioned in Hebrews who do not belong to the people of Israel are Timothy and the brothers and sisters in Italy, who appear at the end of the epistle in the (probably spurious)[46] final greeting (Heb 13:23–24).

4. *May we Even Speak of the Overall Text of Hebrews as a "Jesus-Midrash"?*

As we have seen, the Epistle to the Hebrews demonstrates many similarities with other Jewish interpretations of Scripture. The author's methods and his/her ways of handling Scripture and interpreting it in a messianic and eschatological way show that the text is a part of the Jewish tradition.

---

[44] See Hubert Frankemölle, "Mose in Deutungen des Neuen Testaments," *KuI* 9 (1994): 72–84.

[45] Cf. the interpretation of Heb 3:1–6 in Elke Tönges, "Der Brief an die Hebräerinnen und Hebräer—Eine antijudaistische Schrift?" in *Christlich von Gott reden im Angesicht Israels: Symposion zum 60. Geburtstag von Klaus Wengst* (ed. Katharina von Bremen and Elke Tönges; Iserlohn: Institut für Kirche und Gesellschaft der Evangelischen Kirche von Westfalen, 2003), 85–91.

[46] See the discussion in Wolfgang Kraus, "Neuere Ansätze in der Exegese des Hebräerbriefes," *VF* 48 (2003): 67–68.

The use of Septuagint texts is also relevant: Hebrews alters certain biblical texts and presents them in a different (usually christological) way.[47]

But how do we deal with the *Jewish* text, published in the explicit *Christian* canon, the New Testament? The difference between rabbinic Midrashim and New Testament midrash is this: "While rabbinic midrash seeks to discover some hidden element within the Old Testament texts itself, the New Testament midrash with its eschatological orientation applies the text theologically to some aspect of Jesus' life and ministry. While for the rabbis the text is primary, the New Testament writers give primacy to Jesus and to the surrounding messianic events, or tradition of events, and only then use Old Testament texts to explain or illuminate them."[48]

Hagner presumes that Hebrews is "a carefully argued exposition, employing midrashic treatment of Scripture, repeatedly punctuated by exhortatory passages,"[49] whereas George W. Buchanan even goes so far to describe Hebrews as "a homiletic midrash based on Ps 110."[50] In my opinion, the central idea of Buchanan that Hebrews is Jewish exegesis in the form of a midrash cannot be denied, but relating it to Ps 110 (109 LXX) as *the* biblical basis for the midrash is exaggerated. Let us search for the *Sitz im Leben* of the midrash exegesis.

There is a possible *Sitz im Leben* of the familiar tannaitic Midrashim: during worship in the Hellenistic synagogue. Goldberg assumes in his form-critical analysis of periphrastic Midrash-sentences that it is possible that periphrastic biblical exegesis played a more central role in early Judaism than is apparent from our Midrash texts. He and Günter Stemberger also suppose that this biblical exegesis took place in the context of the service in the synagogue.[51] There is, however, a slight problem with this hypothesis: there are almost no texts to

---

[47] See Martin Karrer, "Der Weltkreis und Christus der Hohepriester. Blicke auf die Schriftrezeption des Hebräerbriefs," in *Frühjudentum und Neues Testament im Horizont Biblischer Theologie* (ed. Wolfgang Kraus and Karl-Wilhelm Niebuhr; WUNT 162; Tübingen: Mohr Siebeck, 2003), 151–179.

[48] Ellis, *The Old Testament in Early Christianity*, 94.

[49] Donald A. Hagner, *Encountering the Book of Hebrews: An Exposition* (EBS; Grand Rapids: Baker Academic, 2002), 29.

[50] George W. Buchanan, *To the Hebrews. Translation, Comment and Conclusions* (AB 36; Garden City, N.Y.: Doubleday, 1972), XIX.

[51] Arnold Goldberg, "Paraphrasierende Midrashsätze," *FJB* 18 (1990): 22; Stemberger, *Einleitung in Talmud und Midrasch*, 234, 238, 241–242.

support it. Goldberg ended his last lecture with the following task for his pupils: "The assumption of an early literary form with its *Sitz im Leben* within the synagogue sermon or homily should be examined further."[52]

There is another question which must be discussed in this context: the classification of the so-called Epistle to the Hebrews as a sermon or homily. Hebrews is full of parenetic phrases. The later Midrash form referred to as *homily* has the specific structure *yelammedenu—petichta—semikhah—inyan—chatima*, as does also a synagogue homily. Indeed, as we shall discuss in a moment, the one may be the same as the other. At the least, such a homily must consist of a *petichta* and *chatima*. The *petichta* opens the sermon and serves as a *prooemium*. It consists of a verse of the Hebrew Bible, apparently unrelated to the theme of the homily, and the interpretation of both this verse and the rabbinic commentary on it, finally connecting to the homily's theme. The *chatima* ends the homily, offering comfort and reassurance or an eschatological kerygma.

It is possible that the form of the Epistle to the Hebrews is that of an early homily or homiletic midrash.[53] While it does not conform precisely to the homiletic structure outlined above, it possibly reveals a version of the form that may have been developed in the context of an early first-century Hellenistic synagogue service. As such, the Epistle may have been an early homily or homiletic midrash that was written for "Hebrews" who believed in the messianic role and function of Jesus and sought to describe them in cultic, biblical terms. We do have a sort of *prooemium*, the interpretative key of our epistle, at Heb 1:1–5 (or Heb 1:1–13). If the closing verses of Hebrews, 13:20–25, are seen as a later addition, then it is possible to distinguish a possible *chatima* in Heb 13:18–19: "Pray for us; for we are persuaded that we have a good conscience since we desire to behave honorably in all things. I especially entreat you to do this so that I may be restored to you sooner."

In adding the closing verses of Hebrews as it has come down to us, an anonymous editor characterized its contents as λόγος τῆς

---

[52] Goldberg, "Paraphrasierende Midrashsätze," 22 (my translation).
[53] Cf. Windisch (*Hebräerbrief*, 124), who thinks the form of Hebrews is most likely that of the synagogal homily; Hartwig Thyen, *Der Stil der jüdisch-hellenistischen Homilie* (FRLANT 65; Göttingen: Vandenhoeck & Ruprecht, 1955), 17–18.

παρακλήσεως (Heb 13:22, "message of exhortation").[54] Hans-Friedrich Weiss has shown that this phrase is a *terminus technicus* for the reading of the sermon or homily that follows the reading of "Torah and Prophets."[55] It was used in the Hellenistic synagogues in connection with the exegesis of Scripture, with the intent that the faith of the congregation should be strengthened and related to their own situation through the exegesis of Scripture in a midrashic form. In particular, the doctrinal presuppositions of the congregation interact with the interpretation of texts from Scripture both in content and in structure.

It is clear that Heb 13:22–25 is full of problems. This passage was written by someone who wanted to use Hebrews as a true Epistle—i.e., as a written text. It therefore marks the transition from an oral to a written tradition. This is similar to what happened with the rabbinic literature at the end of the second century. It is only in Heb 13:22 that we find the signal that Hebrews may be a spoken text—a homily—which presents a logos-theology. Perhaps the editor already encountered Hebrews as a homily and assumed at the end of the text that it is must be a λόγος τῆς παρακλήσεως.

Dr. theol. Elke Tönges
Wissenschaftliche Assistentin am Lehrstuhl
für Neues Testament und Judentumskunde
Ruhr-Universität Bochum
Evangelisch-Theologische Fakultät, GA 8/145
Universitätsstrasse 150, D-44780 Bochum, Germany
elke.toenges@ruhr-uni-bochum.de

---

[54] Cf. Attridge, *Hebrews*, 404; cf. Acts 13:22–25.
[55] Cf. Hans-Friedrich Weiss, *Der Brief an die Hebräer* (KEK 13; Göttingen: Vandenhoeck & Ruprecht, 1991), 40.

HEBREWS, AN ANCIENT SYNAGOGUE HOMILY FOR *TISHA BE-AV*: ITS FUNCTION, ITS BASIS, ITS THEOLOGICAL INTERPRETATION

Gabriella Gelardini

Introduction

The thesis of this article is that the book of Hebrews is an ancient synagogue homily. This form-critical claim is not new in Hebrews scholarship, but the original approach here is that known aspects of production and reception aesthetics regarding ancient synagogue homilies are applied to Hebrews. It is firstly asked whether there is textual evidence of the synagogue as its *Sitz im Leben* (1.1 and 2.1). Secondly, the function of the ancient synagogue homily is considered, namely, that it ought to interpret a reading from the Torah and a complementary reading from the Prophets (1.2 and 2.2). Thirdly, the readings from the Torah (1.4 and 2.4) and the Prophets are reconstructed (1.5 and 2.3), and their central and structuring role in the text is shown. Fourthly, the basis of Hebrews in the liturgical reading cycle—in this case the Palestinian Triennial Cycle—and the place of the two readings it contains along with its theological interpretation are analyzed (1.3 and 2.5). And lastly, form-critical aspects are brought into consideration (1.6). The conclusions presented here constitute a distillation of what I have examined in my dissertation, "'Verhärtet eure Herzen nicht': Der Hebräer, eine Synagogenhomilie zu *Tischa be-Aw*" (Diss. theol., University of Basel, 2004).

1. *The Ancient Synagogue Homily in its Liturgical Context*

1.1. *The* Sitz im Leben *of the Ancient Synagogue Homily: The Sabbath Gathering*

All important literary sources for early Jewish practice, such as the New Testament,[1] Josephus,[2] Philo,[3] rabbinic texts,[4] as well as epigraphic evidence as found in the Theodotus Inscription,[5] presuppose a regular, liturgical, and non-sacrificial Sabbath gathering within the ancient synagogue. According to Lee I. Levine, this gathering was fashioned along the lines of the covenant-renewal ceremony as portrayed in Neh 8:1–8.[6] In Jewish tradition this passage is therefore perceived as one of the earliest postexilic literary sources to give a precise account of the various elements of such liturgical gatherings. From the proto-Sabbath gathering in Nehemiah, the reading and interpreting (teaching) of the holy Scriptures developed into the most important part of the Sabbath gathering of New Testament times.

1.2. *The Function of the Ancient Synagogue Homily: The Teaching of the Sacred Texts*

Nehemiah 8:8 states:[7] "So they *read* from the book, from the law of God [= Torah], with *interpretation* [= homily]. They gave the *sense* [= translation], so that the people understood the reading" (italics and comments added). Traditionally,[8] "giving the sense" was associated with the translation; as a rule, this meant a translation from Hebrew into Aramaic, with the Targumim as its literary remnants. "Interpretation," on the other hand, was perceived as the explanation or teaching of the read portion, hence, the homily—or, in Hebrew, the *derasha*. For this argument it is important to keep in mind that the homily had the function of explaining, teaching, and applying

---

[1] See Luke 4:16; Acts 13:14, 42, 44; 17:2; 18:4.
[2] E.g., Josephus, *C. Ap.* 2.175.
[3] E.g., Philo, *Somn.* 2.127.
[4] E.g., *t. Sukkah* 4:6.
[5] E.g., Kenneth C. Hanson, "The Theodotus Inscription," n.p. [cited 7 November 2004]. Online: http://www.kchanson.com/ANCDOCS/greek/theodotus.html.
[6] Lee I. Levine, *The Ancient Synagogue: The First Thousand Years* (New Haven: Yale University Press, 2000), 501.
[7] Biblical citations follow the NRSV.
[8] Levine, *The Ancient Synagogue*, 501.

the lection. By the first century this three-step procedure of reading, translating, and interpreting in the context of a weekly ceremony had become an universal Jewish practice. Levine states: "It was a unique liturgical feature in the ancient world; no such form of worship was known in paganism."[9]

1.3. *The Basis of the Ancient Synagogue Homily: The Palestinian Triennial Cycle*

It was said that the reading from the Torah was the basis of the synagogue homily. We do know that not only a passage from the Torah but another scriptural passage gave basis to the synagogue homily; the additional one usually was taken from the Prophets. That there were two reading portions prior to the delivery of the sermon is evidenced not least in several New Testament passages, such as Acts 13:14–41. It is assumed that the readings from the Torah were established earlier; the entire Torah was divided into portions and strictly read in *lectio continua*. The readings from the Prophets, on the other hand, were established later; these readings had to complement the readings from the Torah, and hence were never read *in toto* nor in *lectio continua*.[10]

---

[9] Levine, *The Ancient Synagogue*, 139; Charles Perrot, "The Reading of the Bible in the Ancient Synagogue," in *Mikra: Text, Translation, Reading and Interpretation of the Hebrew Bible in Ancient Judaism and Early Christianity* (ed. Martin J. Mulder and Harry Sysling; vol. 1 of *The Literature of the Jewish People in the Period of the Second Temple and the Talmud*; CRINT sec. 2; Assen: Van Gorcum, 1988), 137; See Matt 4:23; 9:35; 13:54; Mark 1:21–22, 39; 6:2; Luke 4:15, 31–32, 44; 6:6; 13:10; John 6:59; 18:20; Acts 9:20; 13:14–16; 19:8; Josephus, *A. J.* 16.43.

[10] Ben Zion Wacholder, Prolegomenon to *The Palestinian Triennial Cycle: Genesis and Exodus with a Hebrew Section containing Manuscript Material of Midrashim to these Books* (vol. 1 of *The Bible as Read and Preached in the Old Synagogue: A Study in the Cycles of the Readings from Torah and Prophets, as well as from Psalms and in the Structure of Midrashic Homilies*, by Jacob Mann; LBS; New York: Ktav, 1971; repr. of 1940 edition with new Prolegomenon), XV: Wachholder believes that the reading from the Prophets was introduced during the Second Temple period: "But we have to dispose first of a medieval legend that ascribed the origin of the custom of reciting several verses from the Prophets, called *haphtarah*, to the fourth decade of the second century BCE. When Antiochus IV, it is said, prohibited the reading of the Torah, the edict was evaded by a recitation of a Prophetic portion; and this substitute survived the persecution. There is nothing in our sources to substantiate the legend, except to say that the *haphtarah* originated in the days of the Second Temple." Levine (*The Ancient Synagogue*, 143) also sees the beginnings of the reading from the Prophets in Hasmonean times (cf. Prologue to Sirach; 2 Macc 2:13; 15:9): "The Hasmonean era—with its many upheavals and dramatic political, military, social, and religious developments—gave rise to messianic expectations and hopes of renewed grandeur in certain circles;

The reading pairs were organized in lectionary cycles; we know of the existence of two such cycles, the Palestinian Triennial Cycle (PTC) and the Babylonian Annual Cycle (BAC). As the name implies, the PTC provided a reading through the Torah in three years (or three and an half), and it was in use in ancient Palestine and in Palestinian Jewish colonies in the Diaspora; for instance, it had been adapted by the ancient Roman Jewish community.[11] The BAC provided a reading through the Torah in one year and was in use in the Diaspora; the BAC prevailed over the PTC and is nowadays used by most Jewish communities around the world.[12] Both their origins and their complex histories of development remain nebulous. The first explicit literary mentioning of two reading cycles is given in the Babylonian Talmud, which dates from Byzantine times. There, in *Meg.* 29b, the PTC is compared to the Babylonian one; the text reads: "In the west [= ancient Palestine], where the Torah is concluded in three years" (comment added). The wording and context of this imply, Levine argues, that the two reading cycles had by then long been established, and that both were integral parts of standard synagogue praxis.[13]

Nonetheless, the PTC seems to be the older lectionary cycle, since the oldest rabbinic corpora (haggadah, halakah, homiletic Midrashim, Targumim, and Piyyutim) are mostly based on the PTC. Despite poor evidence, Levine along with others is convinced that the readings from the Torah within the PTC were established no later than the third century BCE and the readings from the Prophets no later than the first century CE,[14] and that the PTC was followed prior to

---

apocalyptic speculation emerged, and eschatological groups such as the Dead Sea sect combed the Prophets for contemporary allusions. The use of the prophetic corpus—or variations of it, as the apocalyptic mode appears to be—seems to have flourished at the time, and it may well have been this climate that gave rise to such institutionalized recitations."

[11] See the brochure of the "Museo Ebraico di Roma," Lungotevere Cenci, 000186 Rome, Italy.
[12] Louis Jacobs, "Reading of Torah: History," *EncJud* 15:1247.
[13] Levine, *The Ancient Synagogue*, 140–141.
[14] Levine, *The Ancient Synagogue*, 138–139; Wacholder, "Prolegomenon," XII, XIV–XV: According to Deut 31:9–13, Moses decrees the public reading of the laws right after having them written down. The reading ought to take place every seven years during Sukkoth. That is perhaps why Josephus, Philo, the New Testament, and the Talmud ascribe the weekly study of the Scriptures to Moses. It then remains unclear whether Ezra (cf. Neh 8:14–15) picked up an existing custom or whether he was the one who introduced the public reading of certain passages during the feasts (fifth century BCE).

the Second Temple's destruction, as the oldest synagogue homilies seem to imply.[15] It is important at this point to keep in mind that if an ancient synagogue homily—as, for instance, the book of Hebrews—was based on a lectionary cycle, most likely it was based on the PTC, or maybe on an early form of it. But it remains to be mentioned that although there were local variants as to the readings, one must take into account the valuable advice of Charles Perrot, who states: "The readings of the [P]TC are a little like the ancient Jewish prayers: freedom of formulation must be joined by the recurrence of motifs already established by custom. Synagogues were not at the mercy of their own fantasies."[16]

1.4. *The Torah Reading, the* Sidrah

The Torah portion within the PTC was named *sidrah* (pl. *sedarim*). As mentioned above, the Torah was to be read in portions, no less than three verses at a time, and in *lectio continua*. According to the Mishnah, the earliest literary source giving an account of reading rules, the Torah reading had to continue on each Sabbath exactly where it had ended the week before, until the *entire* Torah was read through (*m. Meg.* 3:4; cf. also *t. Meg.* 3(4):10 and *b. Meg.* 24a).[17]

One can imagine that traditions to demarcate the *sedarim* evolved over time, depending on local liturgical traditions and theological preferences. It is important to remember that in the absence of a numerical system of reference, passages often were delimited by content and by narrative logic, and the introductory words gave a passage its name. This practice is already found in the oldest rabbinic corpus, the Mishnah (e.g., *m. Meg.* 4:5–6). The traditions of demarcation left their traces in MSS as early as the first century BCE, as Josef M. Oesch showed in his investigation of MSS from the Judean Desert; as part of the Oral Torah, the divisions in the text were to be handed down faithfully in scrolls manufactured for liturgical use. Two of the most important terms indicating a demarcation in Hebrew texts, *petucha* (opening) and *setuma* (closing), were already introduced

---

[15] Levine, *The Ancient Synagogue*, 135.
[16] Perrot, "Reading of the Bible," in *Mikra* (ed. Mulder and Sysling), 1:139.
[17] According to *m. Meg.* 3:10, the following passages were allowed to be read but not translated in public: Gen 35:22; 38; Exod 32:22–24; Num 6:24–27; 2 Sam 11:2–27; 13.

in the Mishnah as *termini technici*.[18] The PTC is known to have divided the Torah into 154, 161, 167, and 175 *sedarim*;[19] the BAC instead up to this day divides it into 54 *parashot*.[20]

The earliest reading rules in the Mishnah contain the introduction of special readings for upcoming feast and fast days (*m. Meg.* 4:5–6, cf. also *b. Meg.* 31b). It is assumed that these resemble a custom that had only become necessary after the destruction of the Second Temple and the forced cessation of its sacrifices. This might be indicated by the fact that the two readings during feast and fast days usually were accompanied by an additional Torah reading, the so-called *maftir*, named after the additional sacrifices at Temple times. It is important to keep in mind that the synagogue homily of New Testament times most likely did not yet know these special feast and fast readings; hence, if a feast or fast did come up, the regular Sabbath reading before or after would be theologically and narratively linked to the upcoming feast or fast, by means of the homily.

1.5. *The Reading from the Prophets, the* Haphtarah

The reading from the Prophets had to follow the Torah reading; the Hebrew term consequently became *haphtarah* (pl. *haphtaroth*), meaning the "conclusion" of the liturgical reading. The earliest and most important source to attest that the Torah reading was followed by a short reading from the Prophets is Acts 13:15 (cf. also Luke 4:17–20).

It was stated in 1.3 above that Levine believes the prophetic readings in the PTC were fixed by the first century CE. To him, Luke 4:17 is proof of this fact; the verse reads: "[A]nd the scroll of the prophet Isaiah was given to him [Jesus]. He unrolled the scroll and

---

[18] Perrot, "Reading of the Bible," in *Mikra* (ed. Mulder and Sysling), 1:156; Josef M. Oesch, *Petucha und Setuma: Untersuchungen zu einer überlieferten Gliederung im hebräischen Text des Alten Testaments* (OBO 27; Fribourg: Paulusdruckerei, 1979), 362–363.

[19] Perrot, "Reading of the Bible," in *Mikra* (ed. Mulder and Sysling), 1:140: scribes would often place the number of *sedarim* either in the margin or at the end of the scroll. Editorial Staff, "Triennial Cycle," *EncJud* 15:1386: 154 represent the minimum, 161 the maximum of possible Sabbaths in a year. 167 *sedarim* were in use by the Yemenites. The difference in number is caused by the fact that a feast or fast day could fall on a Sabbath. In this case, the regular reading was interrupted and substituted with a special reading of the day. The cyclic reading was picked up again on the consecutive Sabbath. To divide the Torah into 175 *sedarim* represented a custom in which the Torah was read in three and a half years, hence concluded twice in seven years.

[20] The alternative term *parashah* (pl. *parashoth*) derives from Nehemiah and means literally "read in portions" (cf. Neh 8:8: מְפֹרָשׁ).

found the place where it was written."[21] Yet whether the expression "found the place [εὗρεν τὸν τόπον]" indeed means that the *haphtaroth* were fixed and this is why Jesus "found" his reading is disputed by others.[22]

Once again, in the Mishnah (and Babylonian Talmud) we find the earliest rules regarding the *haphtaroth*; the most important factor was that the *haphtarah* had to follow the *sidrah* because it was supposed to complement it and had to be "similar" in content (*b. Meg.* 29b). Due to this different function, the *haphtaroth* were never intended to be read *in toto* nor in *lectio continua*; as a matter of fact, even within the same Sabbath gathering one was allowed to skip parts and jump between different prophetic books (*m. Meg.* 3:4; *b. Meg.* 24a). Its length originally had to be in the range of three to five verses (*m. Meg.* 3:4; *t. Meg.* 3:18; cf. also Luke 4:18–19 with a length of two verses). In *m. Meg.* 3:10 and *t. Meg.* 3:1–9 we are given lists of passages that were not only forbidden to be translated but even to be read in public.[23] Within the PTC, 50% of the *haphtaroth* were from the book of Isaiah, especially from chapters 40–66, and only 1.8% from the book of Jeremiah.[24]

1.6. *Form-Critical Aspects of the Ancient Synagogue Homily*

The most important sources for form-critical aspects of ancient synagogue homilies may be found in the oldest homiletic Midrashim. Even though they display a later state of textual development than the relevant New Testament texts, they do remain relevant in offering important form-critical clues for Hebrews, because they seem to use and recompose older material.[25]

Form criticism of rabbinic homiletic material has identified two types of homilies: the *petichta* (or *proem*) and the *yelammedenu*. The less frequent type, the *yelammedenu*, was a more spontaneous homily, which was inspired by questions posed from the audience to the preacher regarding the readings of the day. The more frequent type,[26] the

---

[21] Levine, *The Ancient Synagogue*, 142.
[22] E.g., Wacholder, "Prolegomenon," XX; Levine, *The Ancient Synagogue*, 142 n. 95.
[23] Especially Ezra 1 and 16 were forbidden.
[24] Wacholder, "Prolegomenon," XXXII.
[25] Joseph Heinemann, "Preaching: Homilies in the Midrashim," *EncJud* 13:997.
[26] Avigdor Shinan, "Sermons, Targums and the Reading from Scriptures in the Ancient Synagogue," in *The Synagogue in Late Antiquity* (ed. Lee I. Levine; Philadelphia: American Schools of Oriental Research, 1987), 98: So far 2,000 *petichtot* have been

petichta, usually required a careful literary composition. Both homily types could emphasize either the Torah reading, with a more exhortative connotation, or the reading from the Prophets, with a more comforting connotation (cf. e.g., Luke 4:21–27; Acts 13:16–41).[27]

Since in this investigation what is of interest is the more common, fully-composed homily (with a more exhortative connotation), it is important to understand the production-aesthetical requirements of *petichtot*. This homily usually consisted of three parts: the introduction (some times named *petichta* as well); the main part; and quite often a messianic and paraenetic ending (named *chatima*).[28] Whereas the structure of *petichta* and *chatima* are fairly well researched, the middle part is not. Recall that in the synagogue gathering the homily was delivered after the reading and the translation. Because the Torah had just been read, the introduction of the homily was *not* to quote the *sidrah* explicitly except for its initial verse; yet, the preacher (in Hebrew, the *darshan*) had to refer to it in midrashic manner. He would do so by quoting similar passages or passages associated with the *sidrah* of the day, and he would especially use passages from the book of Psalms. By taking associative leaps he had to end the introduction of his homily with the explicit quotation of the starting verse of the *sidrah*.[29] The more comforting middle part in this type of homily then had to contain an explicit and literal quotation of the *haphtarah*. The final part would end in exhortative and comforting applications of the scripture for the audience's situation. Such an aesthetics of production was required owing to the intended reception aesthetics suitable for oral societies. The preacher had the challenging task of entertaining his audience, from scholars to illiterate children.[30] The better he managed to commence at a remote point

---

found in midrashic literature. Since most of them end with the opening verse of the Torah reading, it is assumed that they were originally composed for use in the synagogue.

[27] Christoph Dohmen and Günter Stemberger, *Hermeneutik der Jüdischen Bibel und des Alten Testaments* (KStTh 1,2; Stuttgart: Kohlhammer, 1996), 108.

[28] Dohmen and Stemberger, *Hermeneutik*, 108–109; Günter Stemberger, *Einleitung in Talmud und Midrasch* (rev. 8th ed.; München: C. H. Beck, 1992), 241–244; Perrot, "Reading of the Bible," in *Mikra* (ed. Mulder and Sysling), 1:158.

[29] Ismar Elbogen, *Der jüdische Gottesdienst in seiner geschichtlichen Entwicklung* (Hildesheim: Georg Olms, 1995; 2d repr. of the 3d rev. ed., 1931), 196; Stemberger, *Einleitung*, 241–242.

[30] Avigdor Shinan, "Synagogues in the Land of Israel: The Literature of the Ancient Synagogue and Synagogue Archaeology," in *Sacred Realm: The Emergence of the Synagogue in the Ancient World* (ed. Steven Fine; Oxford: Oxford University Press, 1996), 140.

and move associatively towards the initial verse of the *sidrah*, the more the audience thought him a skilled and humorous rhetor.[31] A good example of this technique within an introduction may be found in *Gen. Rab.* 55:2–3 to Gen 22:1.[32]

2. *Hebrews, an Ancient Synagogue Homily for* Tisha be-Av

2.1. *The* Sitz im Leben *of Hebrews: The Sabbath Gathering*

Does the book of Hebrews hint at a context within the synagogue? I believe it does, because of at least seven observations. The interpretation of the sacred texts in the context of the Sabbath gathering must be perceived as (basically adult) education. For ancient

---

[31] Heinemann, "Preaching," 13:995: "The rabbis contrasted the synagogues and the houses of study and their sermons with the attractions of the circus and of the theater of the Roman-Hellenistic world. Remarkably enough, they succeeded in making the bulk of the people prefer the former: 'They that sit in the gate talk of me' (Ps 69:13) was given two different interpretations: '... those are the gentiles who sit in their theaters and circuses ... scoffing me ...; and ... those are Israel who sit in the synagogues and houses of study ... reading dirges and lamentations and *Ekhah*' (*Lam. Rab.*, Proem 17). However, the well-to-do would, at times, stay away from such 'vulgar' gatherings (*b. Git.* 38b). The audience expressed their approval and enjoyment; at times, they reacted with laughter, or, when the preacher did not succeed in arousing them, with indifference. The preachers would adapt their interpretations and examples to the level of the audience; and when addressing simple people they would not refrain from using very telling, even ribald, phrases or illustrations (*Lev. Rab.* 18,1 ...). The popularity of the aggadic sermon emerges clearly from the following statement: 'In times of old when the *perutah* [a small coin] was easy to come by, a man would desire to hear words of Mishnah and of Talmud; but now when the *perutah* is no longer easily found, and moreover we are suffering from the kingdom [i.e., Roman rule], a man desires to hear words of Scripture and words of *aggadah*' (*Pesiq. Rab Kah.* 101b)."

[32] "'The Lord tests the righteous ... (Ps 11:5).' Rabbi Jonathan said: This potter does not examine defective vessels, because he cannot give them a single blow without breaking them. What does he examine? Sound vessels, even if he hits them a few times for he will not break them. Thus, the holy One, blessed be He, does not test the wicked but the righteous.

Rabbi Jose son of R. Hanina said: This flax worker, when he knows that his flax is of good quality, the more he beats it the more it improves and the more it glistens. When it is of poor quality, he cannot give it one knock without it splitting. Thus, the Holy One, blessed be He, does not test the wicked but the righteous, for it is said: 'The Lord tests the righteous ... (Ps 11:5).'

Rabbi Lazar said: Regarding a householder who possesses two cows, one strong and the other feeble, upon which does he put the yoke? Upon the strong one. Thus, the Holy One, blessed be He, tests the righteous, for it is said: 'The Lord tests the righteous ... (Ps 11:5).'

Another interpretation: 'The Lord tests the righteous.' This is Abraham: 'And God tested Abraham (= Torah opening verse: Gen 22:1).'"

societies, with its embedded religions, education had a sacred/religious connotation to it. Learning and doing the law was portrayed as the highest ideal of a pious son (and daughter) of Israel. Hebrews' formal self-definition as word of exhortation, as τοῦ λόγου τῆς παρακλήσεως (Heb 13:22), belongs in the context of the synagogue and ought to help the audience to stay within or come back into the covenantal relationship with God; the only other use of λόγος παρακλήσεως in the New Testament is to be found in Acts 13:15 and refers explicitly to a synagogue homily following the two readings. The homily was delivered by teachers and leaders; the titles διδάσκαλος (Heb 5:12) and ἡγεμών (in participial form, Heb 13:7, 17, 24) are not only found in Hebrews but are also evidenced in epigraphic sources related to ancient synagogues.[33] Incidentally, as we learn from Heb 13:23, our author and teacher is one who travels, which might identify him as an itinerant preacher. Other didactical references may be found in Heb 5:11–6:2; 12:5–11. The teaching material was of course taken from the sacred texts. It is then not surprising that Hebrews is one of the books in the New Testament with the most quotations and explanations from the Hebrew Bible.

The implied listeners are addressed as ἐκκλησία in Heb 2:12 (cf. also Heb 12:23). They are also exhorted not to leave the communal gathering, the ἐπισυναγωγή, in Heb 10:25. When they are invited to "approach the throne" in Heb 4:16 and informed that they "have come to Mount Zion, to the city of the living God, the heavenly Jerusalem" in Heb 12:22, I believe reference is being made to places in an implicit sacred geography of the synagogue; "throne" and "heavenly Jerusalem" are highly cultic references, which only seem to make sense within a "cultic" building such as the Diaspora synagogue.[34] Finally, the deeds of charity (Heb 6:10; 13:3, 16) and hospitality (Heb 13:2) also belong in the context of ancient synagogues.

2.2. *The Function of Hebrews: The Teaching of the Sacred Texts*

It was stated in 1.2 that synagogue homilies functioned as teaching (interpretation, application) of a pair of readings through a teacher

---

[33] Carsten Claussen, *Versammlung, Gemeinde, Synagoge: Das hellenistisch-jüdische Umfeld der frühchristlichen Gemeinden* (StUNT 27; Göttingen: Vandenhoeck & Ruprecht, 2002), 285.

[34] For a more detailed treatment of this subject matter, see Gabriella Gelardini,

addressing a synagogue community. It seems as though Hebrews fits this description, since the author appears concerned to draw a certain teaching to the addressees' attention. He does so by referring to earlier delivered teachings, for instance in Heb 2:1 (τοῖς ἀκουσθεῖσιν), Heb 2:3 (λαλεῖσθαι), Heb 5:12 (διδάσκειν ὑμᾶς[35] ... τῶν λογίων τοῦ θεοῦ), and Heb 13:7 (ἐλάλησαν ὑμῖν τὸν λόγον τοῦ θεοῦ). Moreover, the author refers to the Hebrew Bible as authority; since he has the Greek translation as his basis, the Apocrypha must be regarded as an integral part of his "canon." He refers to Scripture by using λόγος (Heb 2:2), νόμος (Heb 7:5, 12, 19, 28 [twice]; 8:4; 9:19, 22; 10:1, 8, 28), νενομοθέτηται (Heb 7:11), ἐντολή (Heb 7:5, 16, 18; 9:19), δικαίωμα (Heb 9:1, 10), προφῆται (Heb 1:1), διαθήκη (Heb 8:9 [twice]; 9:4 [twice], 15, 20; 10:29), and κεφαλίδι βιβλίου (Heb 10:7). The seemingly countless explicit and implicit quotations and references to the LXX are introduced by the author with lexemes such as: εἶπον (Heb 3:10; 4:3, 4; 10:30; 13:5), φησιν (Heb 8:5), λαλέω (Heb 1:1, 2; 4:8), and λέγω (Heb 1:6, 7; 3:7, 15; 4:7; 5:6; 6:14; 7:21; 8:8 [twice], 9, 10, 13; 10:16; 12:26).[36] With all that in view, Hebrews most definitely gives the impression of a careful literary composition with a concentric overall structure.[37]

2.3. *The* Haphtarah *of Hebrews:* Jer *31:31–34*

As was stated in 1.5, early *haphtaroth* were in the range of three to five verses. And moreover, since in the PTC prophetic readings from Jeremiah were much less frequent than readings from Isaiah, Heb 8:8–12 (partially repeated in Heb 10:16–17) in the middle part of the homily must catch one's attention. Not only are the four verses of Jer 31:31–34 the longest quotation from the LXX in the New Testament, but covenant renewal as a central theme in the overall textual landscape of Hebrews has gained increasing recognition in

---

"'Verhärtet eure Herzen nicht': Der Hebräer, eine Synagogenhomilie zu *Tischa be-Aw*" (Diss. theol., University of Basel, 2004), 93–102.

[35] That Jesus "taught" (διδάσκω) his sermon in the synagogue can be found in Matt 4:23; 9:35; 13:54; Mark 1:21; 6:2; Luke 4:15; 6:6; 13:10; John 6:59; 18:20.

[36] Likewise, other synagogue homilies in the New Testament draw heavily upon the Hebrew Bible. See Luke 4:18–27; John 6:26–59; Acts 13:16–41; 17:2–3.

[37] For a more detailed treatment of the literary composition, see Gelardini, "'Verhärtet eure Herzen nicht,'" 169–334 (especially chs. 8.2.1, 8.3.1, 8.4.1, 8.5.1, and 8.6.1).

Hebrews scholarship in recent years. In this context, I would like to mention the commentary of Harold W. Attridge[38] and the monographs by John Dunnill[39] and Knut Backhaus.[40]

A closer look at reconstructed and extant lectionary lists of the PTC testifies to several variant readings from Jer 31, namely, the oldest, Jer 31:31–34 (which forms its own paragraph in the *BHS*),[41] then Jer 31:32–39,[42] but also Jer 31:33–40 (cf. Table 2).[43] All variants contain the same theme: God's desire to renew his covenant with Israel after having rejected them because they broke the covenant by sinning. Verses 35–40 speak of the rebuilding of the "city" (of Jerusalem), which shall never be destroyed thereafter.

2.4. *The* Sidrah *of Hebrews: Exod 31:18–32:35*

If Hebrews contains the *haphtarah* of Jer 31:31–34 literally quoted in the central part, the next task is to identify the *sidrah*. It was previously stated that the *sidrah* would be found in the introduction, which would refer to it in midrashic manner and end by quoting the initial verse of the *sidrah*. Another clue is given by the fact that the *sidrah* should be similar or complementary to the quoted *haphtarah*.

Reconstructions of the PTC to discover which Torah portion would have been paired with Jer 31 point towards the narration of the golden calf in Exod 32–34. Jacob Mann makes clear in his monumental monograph that in regard to these two chapters "shifting of *sedarim*" took place,[44] possibly because of the partially harsh content in Exod 32–33. Tradition is hence aware of at least two variants: a multiply-testified and older reading from Exod 31:18(–32:35?) and a

---

[38] Harold W. Attridge, *The Epistle to the Hebrews: A Commentary on the Epistle to the Hebrews* (Hermeneia; Philadelphia: Fortress, 1989).

[39] John Dunnill, *Covenant and Sacrifice in the Letter to the Hebrews* (SNTSMS 75; Cambridge: Cambridge University Press, 1992).

[40] Knut Backhaus, *Der Neue Bund und das Werden der Kirche: Die Diatheke-Deutung des Hebräerbriefs im Rahmen der frühchristlichen Theologiegeschichte* (rev. and abridged Habil. theol., Münster, 1994; NTAbh.NF 29; Münster: Assendorff, 1996).

[41] Wacholder, "Prolegomenon," LVII.

[42] Perrot, "Reading of the Bible," in *Mikra* (ed. Mulder and Sysling), 1:142.

[43] Editorial Staff, "Triennial Cycle," 15:1387–1388. Neither Wachholder nor Perrot mention an additional *haphtarah* reading from 1 Kgs 18:27–39.

[44] Jacob Mann, *The Palestinian Triennial Cycle: Genesis and Exodus with a Hebrew Section containing Manuscript Material of Midrashim to these Books* (vol. 1 of *The Bible as Read and Preached in the Old Synagogue: A Study in the Cycles of the Readings from Torah and Prophets, as well as from Psalms and in the Structure of Midrashic Homilies*; LBS; New York: Ktav, 1971; repr. of 1940 edition with new Prolegomenon), 510–530.

reading from Exod 34:27(–35?; cf. Table 2). As has been shown for the *haphtarah*, the material in Exod 31:18–34:35 all belongs to the same story: The narration gives account of the idolatry with the golden calf, the consequent punishment of the sons (and daughters), Moses' intercession, and finally the renewed covenant mediated through him. It is obvious that the *haphtarah* from Jer 31:31–34 (covenant renewal) and a possible *sidrah* from the chapters Exod 31:18–32:35 (breaking of the covenant) do indeed complement each other.

The basic theme of Heb 1–2 is the comparison of the son Jesus to the angels, where the superiority of the former over the latter is emphasized. Hebrews scholarship has been puzzled by this introductory theme, because it does not seems to fit well with the rest of the homily. Yet the motive of the angel's presence as a punitive measure by God is an important *topos* in the account of the idolatry with the golden calf (Exod 32:34; 33:2–3), and stays very much an important motive in numerous rabbinic retellings of that same narrative (e.g., *Pesiq. Rab.* 10:6, 9). The angel's presence signifies God's absence; it is the reminder of God's wrath in the aftermath of Israel's construction of the golden calf. Like Moses in the Exodus account, Jesus in Hebrews is able to change God's wrathful intentions, which are based on the covenant and carried out through punishing angels.[45] The author seems to want to appease the audience regarding the deadly threat that could endanger them (Heb 2:2–3), by assuring them that the Messiah sent at the end of times is superior to the angels. Heb 1–2 contains, as expected, many quotations from the book of Psalms.

In Heb 3–6 we find an explicit quotation (Ps 95:7–11, in Heb 3:7–11) and several lengthy interpretations of the Kadesh-barnea account in Num 13–14. This narrative recounts God's rejection of the Exodus generation and hence the irreversible end of the Sinai covenant. One may argue, then, that Heb 1–6, as the introduction

---

[45] "When they made the golden calf, the angels came bringing accusations against them. Then it was that Moses said: *For I was in dread of the [angels of] anger and hot displeasure* (Deut 9:19 [cf. Heb 12:21!]). It was then also that Moses rose up forthwith, girded his loins with prayer and speaking in defense of Israel, sought mercy of the Holy One, blessed be He.... Moses meant: Master of the universe, I know that they deserve death, in keeping with what thou didst say to me: *He that sacrificeth unto the gods ... shall be utterly destroyed* (Exod 22:19). Nevertheless, I beseech Thee, deliver them from the destroying angels. Remember the merit of the Fathers: ..." (*Pesiq. Rab.* 10:9, Braude).

of the homily, presents a condensed account (just two narrative stages: the gain of Israel's covenantal status at the beginning [Sinai] and its loss at the end [Kadesh-barnea]) of the history of this generation that failed through sin by "turning away from the living God" (Heb 3:12: τῷ ἀποστῆναι ἀπὸ θεοῦ ζῶντος). Sin or sins are mentioned 29 times in Hebrews,[46] while the harsh threats and the announcement of judgment[47] support the earnest mood. Important within these chapters is the theme of the Sabbath rest in Heb 4:1–11. Again, its recurrence seems puzzling at first sight, but once it becomes clear that Heb 4:4 does not quote Gen 2:2 but Exod 31:17b, one may be surprised to find that the Sabbath rest is the covenant sign between God and the sons (and daughters) of Israel. To honor the Sabbath means to honor God the creator, but to ignore the creator equals the kind of idolatry reported in the next chapter. That is why disrespect towards the Sabbath rest—at least in the text—requires the death penalty (Exod 31:12–17). Therefore Heb 4:4 quotes the beginning of the *sidrah*, which is not referred to literally but, as has been shown, midrashically. Consequently, I believe, we are given good reasons to perceive Exod 31:18–32:35 as the *sidrah* and Jer 31:31–34 as the *haphtarah*. These readings are not only the basis but also the hermeneutical key to this homily. The book of Hebrews may well constitute the first literary evidence of this pair of readings, which has only been known before from reconstructions of the ancient PTC employing later evidence.

2.5. *The Basis of Hebrews: The Palestinian Triennial Cycle*

If the identified *sidrah* and *haphtarah* in Hebrews are indeed part of an early form of the PTC, then these readings, as any other readings, fall into a certain season of the liturgical cycle. The PTC—so it is mostly assumed—began with the month Nisan,[48] because the biblical account in Exod 12:2 states that God decreed the month of the Exodus would be the "first," and hence that month was retrojectively perceived as the beginning of the history of the people of Israel. Moreover, each book of the Torah began on one of the four

---

[46] Heb 1:3; 2:17; 3:13, 17; 4:15; 5:1, 3; (6:6); 7:26, 27; 8:12; 9:26, 28 (twice); 10:2, 3, 4, 6, 8, 11, 12, 17, 18, 26 (twice); 11:25; 12:1, 3, 4; 13:11.

[47] Heb 4:12–13; 9:27; 10:26–31; 12:23, 25–29; 13:4.

[48] Editorial Staff, "Triennial Cycle," 15:1389. The article notes that Jacob Mann believed the beginning of the PTC to be in the month Tishri.

New Years mentioned in *m. Roš Haš.* 1:1.⁴⁹ Tables 1–3, drawn from the *Encyclopaedia Judaica*, provide a reconstruction of the PTC. As may be seen from Table 2, the readings of Hebrews fall into the first week of the fifth month, the month of Av. This month is prominent for containing the most important day of fast in Jewish tradition, the ninth day of Av, in Hebrew *Tisha be-Av*. This day of fast, the "day of fast of the fifth [month]," is known from Zech 8:19 and later references in the Mishnah (*m. Roš Haš.* 1:3), the Tosefta (*t. Taʿan.* 4:6) and the Talmudim (*b. Taʿan.* 12a; *y. Taʿan.* 12a). They all speak as if *Tisha be-Av* was observed back in the time of the Second Temple.

Tisha be-Av commemorates and mourns over the sins of Israel and the covenant curse that followed upon them. According to an early source in the Mishnah (*m. Taʿan.* 4:6; cf. also *b. Taʿan.* 29a), making reference to Num 14:29(–35), it was on *Tisha be-Av* that God decreed that the desert generation was not to enter the promised land, because of its sins (the first being the idolatry at Sinai and the last being at Kadesh-barnea). As was argued in 2.4, the Kadesh-barnea narration is given in Heb 3–6. Numbers 14:29 is quoted literally in Heb 3:17 and midrashically treated in Heb 3:7–19 and 4:1–13. Hence not only the reconstructed PTC but also the Mishnah, and Hebrews even before, connect Exod 32–34 and Num 13–14 with *Tisha be-Av*.

The narration in Exod 32–34 speaks of two ascensions of Moses. The first began on Sivan 1—so rabbinic tradition says—when Moses stayed forty days in God's presence, as the biblical account tells us (Exod 24:18). In knowledge of Israel's idolatry in the camp, God sends Moses down (Exod 32:7). Moses descends and ascends on the same day a second time in order to plead for atonement for this idolatry of the people. Moses returns again after forty days (Exod 34:28), according to rabbinic tradition on Av 29 (*S. ʿOlam Rab.* 6). Between the first and the second covenant therefore lay 80 days. To state an intricate matter simply, these 80 days from Sivan 1 to Av 29 seem to have been shifted at some point from Tammuz 17, when Moses supposedly smashed the tablets, to Tishri 10. Tishri 10 is the commemoration (and celebration) of Yom Kippur, the day when God forgave the first sin of his covenant people, the idolatry with

---

⁴⁹ Editorial Staff, "Triennial Cycle," 15:1386: Genesis began on Nisan 1 of the first year; Exodus began on Shevat 15 of the first year; Leviticus began on Tishri 1 of the second year; Numbers began on Shevat 15 of the second year; and Deuteronomy began on Elul 1 of the third year.

the golden calf, and all other sins of Israel in consequence. These eighty days, in the form of the Ten Special Sabbaths (= 80 days), received great attention in Jewish liturgy. The three Sabbaths from Tammuz 17 to *Tisha be-Av* (21 days) conventionally had exhortative sermons, whereas comforting sermons were required for the seven Sabbaths from *Tisha be-Av* to Yom Kippur on Tishri 10 (59 days). Sermons, homiletic Midrashim, from this liturgical season are preserved in the corpora *Pesiqta de Rab Kahana* and *Pesiqta Rabbati*. It is important to understand at this point that theologically speaking *Tisha be-Av* and Yom Kippur do presuppose each other, the one is mirrored in the other, which may explain why only these two days in the liturgical year require the most rigorous fasting. On the one hand, then, the fast day (*Tisha be-Av*) firstly commemorates the sins but looks hopefully to their forgiveness promised at Yom Kippur. On the other hand, the feast day (Yom Kippur) predominantly rejoices over the forgiveness but at the same time warns against committing new sins.

Upon returning to Hebrews, we encounter this very polarity. If Heb 1–6 puts great emphasis on sin, the mood in the central part, Heb 7–10, changes considerably. The feast day of Yom Kippur is even mentioned in Heb 9:7, and a deeper analysis of these chapters makes clear that Jesus functions here as the sin offering of Yom Kippur, by means of which—so the author promises—he will attain atonement for his people. But not only that, Jesus functions also as an inauguration sacrifice for the new covenant. More puzzling, though, remains the question of why Jesus is compared to the high priest; I believe the *sidrah* can help to decipher this puzzle. Theologically speaking, Jesus does exactly what Moses did in Exod 32–34. In rabbinic tradition Moses is frequently viewed as high priest in the time when the cult was not erected yet. His atoning intercession during his second ascension is, so to speak, the first Yom Kippur, the proto-Day of Atonement before liturgy existed. That is the reason why Jesus is compared to a high priest. Practically speaking, if the addressees of Hebrews did read the *sidrah* from Exod 31:18–32:35, only one week later they would have heard Exod 33:1–34:35 with its comforting content. Hence it makes sense if our author wraps his harsh exhortation into hopeful words about forgiveness, which is read about in the next week and yearned for at Yom Kippur. It is interesting that not only in the New Testament but also in rabbinic tradition the lowest point in the liturgical year, *Tisha be-Av*, yielded the most powerful messianic concepts, the birth of the Messiah and his victorious deeds (cf. e.g., Heb 1:5–14; 10:37; *y. Ber.* 2:4). Consequently, Heb 10–13 speaks of the discipline of the sons (and daughters). This discipline is bestowed on the penitent regardless of the atonement, as may be learned from Exod 32–34.

The homily ends on an uplifting note, in which the sons (and daughters) are assured they have regained access to the inherited land (an access lost on *Tisha be-Av* due to the breaking of the covenant), which is a logical consequence of the covenant renewal. That this land is the heavenly one may have historical reasons. According to the Mishnah (*m. Ta'an.* 4:6; cf. also *b. Ta'an.* 29a), *Tisha be-Av* commemorates not only the prohibition to enter the land but also the destruction of the First *and* the Second Temple; later too, the conquering of the last stronghold of the Bar Kochba revolt, the city Bethar, and also the erection of a heathen temple in Jerusalem by Hadrian and the renaming of the city as *Aelia Capitolina*. The day of fast at *Tisha be-Av* became the most important day of mourning in Jewish Tradition and ever since has been a symbol of persecution and misfortune of Jews. The author of Hebrews may be speaking to Jewish slaves in Rome, exiled in the aftermath of the second Jewish War; that may be why he could not promise the return to the material city of Jerusalem and was left only with the possibility of promising the heavenly one, which in Jewish conceptuality exists exactly above the terrestrial one.

Now that it has been shown that Hebrews is closely linked with *Tisha be-Av*, it is possible to pose a second thesis: Hebrews is one of the oldest pieces of literary evidence that combines the *sidrah* from Exod 31:18–32:35 and the *haphtarah* Jer 31:31–34 with *Tisha be-Av*.[50] This may not least be evidence that the PTC—most likely in an early form—was indeed already in operation, as Levine claims, at the end of the first and/or beginning of the second century CE.

---

[50] Elbogen, *Jüdische Gottesdienst*, 164; Jacobs, "Reading of Torah," 15:1251–1252; Leo Trepp, *Der jüdische Gottesdienst: Gestalt und Entwicklung* (Stuttgart: Kohlhammer, 1992), 174. The Mishnah (*m. Meg.* 4:6; cf. also *b. Meg.* 31b) decreed for fast days the special readings from Lev 26 and/or Deut 28 (cf. Heb 6:7–8). The Tosefta introduced Deut 4:25–40, which warns against idolatry, and kept Lev 26 (*b. Meg.* 31b). Another change—or return to the original custom—occurred at the time of the *geonim* (seventh century CE). Since the decreed passages in the Mishnah were chosen in connection with drought, the *geonim* thought Exod 32:11–14 and Exod 34:1–10 would suit fast days more appropriately. The readings became—besides the *megillat Ekha*—in the morning Deut 4:25–40 with Jer 8:13–9:23 and in the afternoon Exod 32:11–14 and 34:1–10 (or Exod 34:1–19) with Isa 55:6–56:8.

Conclusion

I have tried to show in this article that Hebrews is an ancient synagogue homily of the type *petichta* with a consequent *Sitz im Leben* within the Sabbath gathering. As a homily, Hebrews functions as interpretation, teaching, and application of the *sidrah* from Exod 31:18–32:35 (breaking of the covenant) and the *haphtarah* from Jer 31:31–34 (covenant renewal). The *sidrah* in the introduction of the homily is on the one hand not quoted but referred to in midrashic manner, yet it quotes—as it should—the last verse prior to (or first verse of) the *sidrah*, namely Exod 31:17b in Heb 4:4. As expected, the complementary *haphtarah* is quoted explicitly in the central part of the homily. The fact that these readings appear so central and serve to structure the homily does justice to the obvious importance and extraordinary quantity of quotations from the LXX in Hebrews. The reconstructed readings are part of the PTC in early form, and they hint at the most important day of fast in Jewish tradition, *Tisha be-Av*. This suggestion is confirmed when the central quotations and the theological concepts in Hebrews are compared with extra-biblical information on *Tisha be-Av*.

Dr. theol. Gabriella Gelardini
Wissenschaftliche Oberassistentin am Lehrstuhl für Neues Testament
Universität Basel, Theologische Fakultät
Nadelberg 10, CH-4051 Basel, Switzerland
gabriella.gelardini@unibas.ch

First Year

Sidrah	Haphtarah	Sidrah	Haphtarah	Sidrah	Haphtarah
Nisan		Iyyar		Sivan	
Gen 1:1	Isa 42:5	Gen 6:9	Isa 54:9–10	Gen 12:1	Josh 24:3–18
Gen 2:4	(not extant)	Gen 8:1	Hab 3:1–5	Gen 14:1	Isa 41:2–14; 1 Kgs 10:9
Gen 3:24	(not extant)	Gen 8:15	Isa 42:7–21	Gen 15:1	Zeph 3:9–19; Isa 1:1–17
Gen 5:1	Isa 30:8–15	Gen 9:18	Isa 49:9–13	Gen 16:1	Isa 64:1
		Gen 11:1	(not extant)		
Av		Elul		Tishri	
Gen 22:1	Isa 33:7–22	Gen 26:11	Isa 65:23–66:8	Gen 30:21	1 Sam 1:11
Gen 23:1	1 Kgs 1:1	Gen 27:1	Isa 46:3–6	Gen 31:3	Jer 30:10–16; Mic 6:3–7:20
Gen 24:1	Judg 19:20	Gen 27:28	Mic 1:1; 5:7–13	Gen 32:4	Obad 1:1
Gen 24:42	Isa 12:3–14:2	Gen 28:10	Hos 12:13	Gen 33:18	Nah 1:12–2:5
Gen 25:1	2 Sam 5:17–6:1	Gen 29:31	Isa 60:15		
Kislev		Tevet		Shevat	
Gen 40:23	Amos 1:3–15; 2:6	Gen 43:24	Jer 42:12–17; 43:12–14; 1 Kgs 3:15	Gen 49:27	Zech 14:1; Mic 2:12
Gen 41:1	Isa 29:8	Gen 44:18	Josh 14:6; Ezek 37:10	Exod 1:1	Isa 27:6; Ezek 16:1; 20
Gen 41:38	Isa 11:2–9	Gen 47:28; 48:1	1 Kgs 13:14	Exod 3:1	Isa 40:11; 2 Kgs 20:8
Gen 42:18	Isa 50:10–52:11	Gen 47:28; 48:1	1 Kgs 2:1	Exod 4:14	Isa 55:12
		Gen 49:1	Isa 43:2	Exod 6:2	Judg 13:2
Adar		Tammuz		Heshvan	
Exod 7:18	Joel 3:3	Gen 17:1	Isa 63:10–11	Gen 35:9	Isa 43:1–7
		Gen 18:1	Isa 33:17–34:12; 2 Kgs 4	Gen 37:1	Jer 38:8
Exod 8:16	Isa 34:11	Gen 19:1	Isa 17:14–18:7	Gen 38:1	Isa 37:31–37
Exod 10:1	Isa 19; Jer 4:6; 1 Sam 6:6	Gen 20:1	Isa 61:9–10	Gen 39:1	Isa 52:3–9
Exod 12:13	Jer 46:13–28	Gen 21:1	1 Sam 2:21–28		

Table 2

Second Year

Sidrah	Haphtarah	Sidrah	Haphtarah	Sidrah	Haphtarah
Nisan		**Iyyar**		**Sivan**	
Exod 12:29	Isa 21:11	Exod 16:25	Isa 58:23	Exod 24:1	Isa 60:17–61:9
Exod 13:1	Isa 46:3	Exod 18:1	Isa 6; 61:6–10	Exod 25:1	Isa 66
Exod 13:21	Isa 45:24	Exod 21:1	Jer 34:1	Exod 26:31	Ezek 16:10–19
Exod 15:21	Isa 49:10	Exod 22:26	Isa 49:3	Exod 27:20	Hos 14:7
					Ezek 43:10
				Exod 29:1	Isa 61:6
Av		**Elul**		**Tammuz**	
Exod 34:27	**Jer 31:33–40; 1 Kgs 18:27–39**	Lev 1:1	Isa 43:21; Jer. 21:19; Mic 6:9–7:8	Exod 30:1	Mal 1:11–2:7
Exod 37:1	1 Kgs 8:8–22	Lev 3:1	Ezek 44:11; 20:41	Exod 30:12	2 Kgs 12:5
Exod 38:21	Jer 30:18	Lev 4:1	Ezek 18:4–17	Exod 31:1	Isa 43:7–21
Exod 39:1	Isa 33:20–34:8; 1 Kgs 7:13	Lev 5:1	Zech 5:3–6:19	Exod 32:14	2 Sam 22:10–51
		Lev 6:1	Jer 7:21		
		Tishri		**Heshvan**	
		Lev 6:12	Mal 3:9	Lev 13:29	2 Kgs 5
		Lev 8:1	Ezek 43:27	Lev 14:1	2 Kgs 7:8
		Lev 9:1	1 Kgs 8:56–58	Lev 15:1	(not extant)
		Lev 12:1	Isa 66:7	Lev 16:1	Ezek 44:1
Kislev		**Tevet**			
Lev 17:1	(not extant)	Lev 22:1	(not extant)		
Lev 18:1	Ezek 22:1	Lev 24:1	(not extant); Jer 36:6; Ezek 34		
Lev 19:1	Amos 9:7	Lev 25:1	Isa 24:2		
Lev 21:1	Ezek 44:25	Lev 25:39			
Shevat		**Adar**			
Lev 26:3	Jer 16:19; Ezek 12:20	Num 4:17	1 Sam 6:10		
Num 1:1	Hos 2:1	Num 4:21	Judg 13:2–25		
Num 2:14	(not extant)	Num 5:11	Hos 4:14		
Num 3:14	Isa 43:9	Num 6:1	Judg 13:2		

Table 3

Third Year

Sidrah	Haphtarah	Sidrah	Haphtarah	Sidrah	Haphtarah	Sidrah	Haphtarah
	Nisan		Iyyar		Sivan		Tammuz
Num 6:22	(not extant)	Num 12:1	—	Num 17:16	Ezek 44:15	Num 23:2	(not extant)
Num 8:1	Zech 4:14	Num 13:1	Josh 2:1; Judg 18:7	Num 18:25	Ezek 44:29	Num 25:10	Mal 2:5
Num 9:22	(not extant)	Num 14:1	—	Num 20:14		Num 26:52	Josh 17:4
Num 11:1	(not extant)	Num 15:1	—	Num 22:2	Mic 5:6	Num 28:1	Ezek 45:12
		Num 16:1	1 Sam 11				
	Av		Elul		Tishri		Heshvan
Num 30:1	Jer 4:2	Deut 1:1	Jer 30:4; Amos 2:9	Deut 5:1	(not extant)	Deut 10:1	2 Kgs 13:23
Num 32:1	Jer 2	Deut 2:1	(not extant)	Deut 6:4	1 Kgs 10:39	Deut 11:26	Isa 54:11–55:6
Num 33:1	(not extant)	Deut 3:23	Jer 32:16	Deut 8:1	Jer 9:22–24	Deut 12:20	Jer 23:9
Num 34:1	Ezek 45:1	Deut 4:1	(not extant)	Deut 9:1	Jer 2:1; 2 Kgs 8:30	Deut 15:7	Isa 61:1–2
	Josh 21:41						
Num 35:9	Josh 20:1						
	Kislev		Tevet		Shevat		Adar
Deut 17:14	1 Sam 8:1	Deut 21:10	Isa 54:1–10	Deut 29:9	Isa 55:6–58:8; Mic 7:18–20	Deut 33:1	Josh 1:1–18
Deut 17:24	1 Sam 10:24	(not extant)	(not extant)	Deut 31:1	Jer 12:15	Deut 34:1	(not extant)
Deut 18:1	Jer 29:8	(not extant)	(not extant)	Deut 31:14	Judg 2:7	Shekalim	
Deut 20:10	Josh 24:1	Deut 26:1	Isa 60:1–22	Deut 32:1	Ezek 17:22	Zakhor	
						Parah	
						Ha-Hodesh	

PART TWO

SOCIOLOGY, ETHICS, AND RHETORIC IN HEBREWS

PORTRAYING THE TEMPLE IN STONE AND TEXT: THE ARCH OF TITUS AND THE EPISTLE TO THE HEBREWS*

Ellen Bradshaw Aitken

The Epistle to the Hebrews has attracted a variety of interpretive approaches, including readings that are predominantly structural, theological, literary, ethical, or sacramental. Seldom, however, does one find readings that explicitly explore Hebrews in political or ideological terms. This is a result in part of the lack of easily identifiable historical references in the text.[1] It is also a result of the difficulty both of assigning anything but a fairly broad range of dates for the composition of Hebrews and of locating its geographical provenance. Thus Hebrews floats, as it were, unanchored in place and time, lending itself to readings that are less dependent upon place and time than are political and ideological approaches.[2]

---

* This is a revised version of a paper that was delivered at a conference held on 24–25 February 2001 at the University of South Florida, and subsequently published in *Religious Texts and Material Contexts* (ed. Jacob Neusner and James F. Strange; Studies in Ancient Judaism; Lanham: University Press of America, 2001), 73–88. It was subsequently reprinted with its concluding section in *Sewanee Theological Review* 45 (2002): 135–151. I thank both publishers for permission to reprint the article here.

[1] Hebrews seldom refers to the historical experience of its audience; an exception is Heb 10:32–34, "But recall those earlier days when, after you had been enlightened, you endured a hard struggle with sufferings, sometimes being publicly exposed to abuse and persecution, and sometimes being partners with those so treated. For you had compassion for those who were in prison, and you cheerfully accepted the plundering of your possessions, knowing that you yourselves possessed something better and more lasting" (NRSV). On the relevance of this passage for the dating of Hebrews, see below.

[2] We might compare the development of political readings of parts of the Pauline corpus, which are facilitated by the relative precision possible in dating these letters. See, for example, Dieter Georgi, *Theocracy in Paul's Praxis and Theology* (trans. David E. Green; Minneapolis: Fortress, 1991); Helmut Koester, "From Paul's Eschatology to the Apocalyptic Schemata of 2 Thessalonians," in *The Thessalonian Correspondence* (ed. Raymond F. Collins; Louvain: Peeters, 1990), 441–458, reprinted as "Imperial Ideology and Paul's Eschatology in 1 Thessalonians," in *Paul and Empire: Religion and Power in Roman Imperial Society* (ed. Richard A. Horsley; Harrisburg, Penn.: Trinity Press International, 1997), 158–166; and Neil Elliott, *Liberating Paul: The*

It is my contention in this essay, however, that it is possible to correlate certain aspects of the Christology and the community ethic found in Hebrews with events in Roman imperial rule, and particularly its expression in imperial propaganda as it is manifested in monuments and ritual. This correlation invites an interpretation of Hebrews in political terms. In order to do so, however, it is necessary to provide the text with a provisional anchor in time and space, that is, by proceeding on the hypothesis that Hebrews was composed in the city of Rome in the 70s or early 80s of the first century CE. Moreover, if the correlation is convincing, it can become the basis for establishing the plausibility of this hypothesis about the compositional date and provenance of Hebrews.

More specifically, I am arguing here that Hebrews should be read as one response to the imperial ideology expressed in the events and monuments surrounding the triumph of Vespasian and Titus, a triumph bestowed upon them by the Roman Senate for their victory in the First Jewish War and the destruction of Jerusalem in 70 CE. To anticipate my conclusions, Hebrews makes use of some of the elements of the triumph—both the customary rites of the triumph and the key elements of the Flavian triumph—in order to articulate resistance to imperial rule and ideology. It does so by depicting to whom the "real" triumph belongs and where the "real" temple is. In addition, it does so by promoting an ethic for the community, its inscribed audience, an ethic that is consonant with the identity of the true triumphant ruler and that values solidarity with those who are perceived to be suffering under Flavian rule.

My presuppositions in making this argument include the following: First, Hebrews is a highly multivalent text that contains numerous interwoven ways of constructing and defining the identity and ethic of its audience, as is not uncommon in texts that are homiletical in character.[3] Thus, within a broad view, the reading of Hebrews

---

Justice of God and the Politics of the Apostle (Maryknoll, N.Y.: Orbis, 1994). David A. deSilva's recent commentary, *Perseverance in Gratitude: A Social-Rhetorical Commentary on the Epistle "to the Hebrews"* (Grand Rapids: Eerdmans, 2000), provides an explicitly *social* interpretation of Hebrews in that he uses the categories of honor and shame as markers of social status. Although he speaks of the reproach, loss of honor, lowered economic status experienced by Hebrews' audience as a result of their refusal to participate in Roman religions, and their rejection of their neighbors' values, he assumes this situation as common to all Christian groups and thus does not relate it to a historical, political situation specific to the audience of Hebrews.

[3] On the homiletic character of Hebrews, see Lawrence Wills, "The Form of the

presented here is one that works together with others, for example, a recognition of the way in which the story of the journey through the wilderness toward the Jordan River is used to constitute the audience[4] or interpretations that emphasize the eschatological dimension of its worldview and theology.[5] Second, Hebrews is ultimately a parenetic text, aimed at shaping the community's way of life.[6] Third, I presuppose that there can be multiple rhetorical sites for developing political resistance, that such sites do not need to be explicitly political, and that a political ideology can be developed through scriptural interpretation, cultic reflection, allegory, and hymnody, as well as through visual art, coinage, architecture, and religious festivals.[7]

The Date and Provenance of Hebrews

A brief overview of the main arguments about the compositional date of Hebrews is in order. A date after 60 CE is supported by the

---

Sermon in Hellenistic Judaism and Early Christianity," *HTR* 77 (1984): 280–283; C. Clifton Black, "The Rhetorical Form of the Hellenistic Jewish and Early Christian Sermon: A Response to Lawrence Wills [*HTR* 77 (1984): 277–299]," *HTR* 81 (1988): 1–18; Harold W. Attridge, "Paraenesis in a homily (λόγος παρακλήσεως)," *Semeia* 50 (1990): 211–226. See also George W. MacRae, "Heavenly Temple and Eschatology in the Letter to the Hebrews," *Semeia* 12 (1978): 179–199. Hebrews characterizes itself as a λόγος τῆς παρακλήσεως ("word of exhortation") at 13:22; see Harold W. Attridge, *The Epistle to the Hebrews* (Philadelphia: Fortress, 1989), 14, 408, who points out that this designation is used in Acts 13:15 for Paul's synagogue address in Pisidian Antioch. More recently, David deSilva accepts the position that Hebrews is a sermon, but one that makes significant use of the conventions of hellenistic epideictic rhetoric; see deSilva, *Perseverance in Gratitude*, 58, 514.

[4] See Ernst Käsemann, *The Wandering People of God: An Investigation of the Letter to the Hebrews* (trans. Roy A. Harrisville and Irving L. Sandberg; Minneapolis: Augsburg, 1984); Ellen Bradshaw Aitken, *Jesus' Death in Early Christian Memory: The Poetics of the Passion* (NTOA 53; Göttingen: Vandenhoeck & Ruprecht, 2004), 130–164.

[5] See, for example, MacRae, "Heavenly Temple"; C. K. Barrett, "The Eschatology of the Epistle to the Hebrews," in *The Background of the New Testament and Its Eschatology: C. H. Dodd Festschrift* (ed. W. D. Davies and David Daube; Cambridge: Cambridge University Press, 1954), 363–393; Jean Cambier, "Eschatologie ou hellénisme dans l'Épître aux Hébreux: Une étude sur μένειν et l'exhortation final de l'épître," *Salesianum* 11 (1949): 62–86.

[6] The alternation of exposition and exhortation in Hebrews is widely recognized and informs most attempts to outline the structure of Hebrews; see the discussion in Attridge, *Hebrews*, 14–21. Attridge also identifies (p. 21) the two types of exhortation found in the text, "let us hold fast" and "let us approach" (both found in Heb 4:14–16). On the pastoral dimension of Hebrews, see Otto Kuss, "Der Verfasser des Hebräerbriefes als Seelsorger," *TTZ* 67 (1958): 1–12, 65–80.

[7] See James C. Scott, *Domination and the Arts of Resistance: Hidden Transcripts* (New Haven: Yale University Press, 1990).

indications that the audience have been believers for some time (Heb 5:12) and that they are dependent upon others who "heard the Lord" (Heb 2:3); earlier dates are generally tied to untenable hypotheses about Paul, Apollos, Aquila, or Priscilla as the author.[8] A date following the Neronian persecutions in Rome in 64 CE is suggested by the references to past persecution of the community (Heb 10:32–34; 12:4).[9] Arguments for a *terminus ad quem* of 96 CE depend upon accepting a secure dating of *1 Clement*, with its use of the text of Hebrews, to 96 CE. Harold W. Attridge, questioning such a certain date for *1 Clement* and preferring to place it broadly between 90 and 120 CE, opts for dating Hebrews before 100 CE because of the reference to Timothy in the postscript of Hebrews (Heb 13:23). Attridge thus concludes with a date range for Hebrews of 60–100 CE, with the possibility of a date in the 70s or 80s because of the theological and literary affinities with other Christian texts of this period.[10]

The destruction of the Jerusalem temple has occasionally been used in arguments about compositional date: the lack of any mention of the destruction of the temple in a text so concerned with the rituals of the temple, along with the use of the present tense for the temple activities, has been taken to indicate a date before 70 CE.[11] Against this position, I agree with Attridge and Erich Grässer that Hebrews is concerned not with the Herodian temple per se but with

---

[8] For a summary of arguments about authorship, see Attridge, *Hebrews*, 1–6; Erich Grässer, *An die Hebräer* (3 vols.; EKKNT 17; Zürich: Benziger and Neukirchen-Vluyn: Neukirchener, 1990–1997), 1:19–22; Frederick F. Bruce, "'To the Hebrews': A Document of Roman Christianity," *ANRW* 25.4:3496–3499; deSilva, *Perseverance in Gratitude*, 23–39; Cynthia Briggs Kittredge, "Hebrews," in *Searching the Scriptures*, vol. 2: *A Feminist Commentary* (ed. Elisabeth Schüssler Fiorenza; New York: Crossroad, 1993), 430–434.

[9] See Attridge, *Hebrews*, 298–299, particularly on how the language of these verses recalls Tacitus's description (*Annales* 15.44) of the persecution of Christians in Rome under Nero in 64 CE. The reference is admittedly ambiguous, however, and others, opting for an earlier date, have taken it as a reference to the expulsion of the Jews from Rome under Claudius in 49 CE; see William Manson, *The Epistle to the Hebrews: An Historical and Theological Reconsideration* (London: Hodder and Stoughton, 1951), 159–161; Bruce, "'To the Hebrews,'" 3519.

[10] Attridge, *Hebrews*, 9. Grässer (*An die Hebräer*, 1:25), following the same lines of argumentation, prefers a date in the 80s or 90s since he sees indications of increased pressure on the Christian community, a situation that he relates to the reign of Domitian (81–96 CE).

[11] See, for example, Bruce, "'To the Hebrews,'" 3514; Albert Vanhoye, *Situation du Christ: Hébreux 1–2* (LD 58; Paris: Cerf, 1969), 50; August Strobel, *Der Brief an die Hebräer* (NTD 9/2; Göttingen: Vandenhoeck & Ruprecht, 1975), 83; and most recently, deSilva, *Perseverance in Gratitude*, 20–21.

the desert tabernacle, and moreover uses the tabernacle cult as a foundation for the Christology and parenesis of the text.[12] The destruction of the Herodian temple is thus not an expressed element in this exposition and therefore cannot be determinative of the date of Hebrews. It is possible to observe, moreover, that this debate centers on the *destruction* or loss of the temple per se rather than on the display and celebration of that destruction as part of the imperial propaganda of Vespasian, Titus, and Domitian.

The position that Hebrews was composed for an audience in Rome enjoys a broad consensus, and I shall not fully rehearse the arguments here.[13] I would note, however, that arguments that dissent from this view nonetheless connect Hebrews with Rome in some fashion, usually locating the author in a Roman context.[14] Any attempts to locate Hebrews geographically must contend with the phrase "those from Italy greet you" (Heb 13:24, ἀσπάζονται ὑμᾶς οἱ ἀπὸ τῆς Ἰταλίας), which may equally designate a group within Italy (including Rome) or a group abroad sending greetings back to their home community.[15]

The strong homiletical character of Hebrews also has implications for the discussion of the provenance and destination of the text. Even

---

[12] Attridge, *Hebrews*, 8; Grässer, *An die Hebräer*, 1:25.

[13] Key elements in arguing for a Roman provenance for Hebrews include its use by *1 Clement*, especially 36.2–6 but also elsewhere; see Attridge, *Hebrews*, 6–7; and Donald A. Hagner, *The Use of the Old and New Testaments in Clement of Rome* (NovTSup 34; Leiden: Brill, 1973). Peter Lampe is cautious about accepting Hebrews as a text of Roman Christianity and thus does not discuss it at any length in his study of earliest Christianity in Rome; see Peter Lampe, *Die stadtrömischen Christen in den ersten beiden Jahrhunderten: Untersuchungen zur Sozialgeschichte* (WUNT 2/18; Tübingen: Mohr Siebeck, 1987), 60–61. Bruce, although dating Hebrews to the reign of Nero, takes it as a text written most probably to a community in Rome ("'To the Hebrews,'" 3517–3519). The position that Hebrews was written to a Jewish-Christian house-church in Rome was put forward more than a century ago by Theodor Zahn, *Introduction to the New Testament* (trans. John Moore Trout et al.; 3 vols.; New York: Charles Scribner's Sons, 1909 [3d German ed. 1897–1899]), 2.345–351. Adolf von Harnack followed Zahn's arguments, arguing, however, not for a Jewish-Christian group as the addressees, but rather for the house-church associated with Priscilla and Aquila, and suggesting that Priscilla was the main author of Hebrews, with the help of Aquila; see Adolf von Harnack, "Probabilia über die Adresse und den Verfasser des Hebräerbriefs," *ZNW* 1 (1900): 16–41.

[14] Thus, Hugh W. Montefiore in *The Epistle to the Hebrews* (New York: Harper, 1964), 9–11, argues that Hebrews was written to the Corinthian church by Apollos, from Ephesus, but carrying the greetings of the Roman community after the death of Paul.

[15] See Attridge, *Hebrews*, 10.

though Hebrews is unlikely to be a transcript of a sermon, it certainly uses considerable material from a homiletical context, material that may have developed within a Roman Christian environment. We might then reasonably suppose that this material was reworked into an elegant and coherent piece of rhetoric both for internal use and for sending to other communities. We should therefore expect ample resonance between the themes, motifs, and arguments of Hebrews and the experience of Christians in the city of Rome. Moreover, Hebrews lacks a thoroughgoing epistolary character, and we see little distance between the situation of the inscribed author or authors and the inscribed audience; both are located in much the same rhetorical context, a context that can be connected in a number of ways with Christianity in the city of Rome.[16] It is therefore appropriate to read Hebrews in the context of public life in the city of Rome, and provisionally, for the purposes of this argument, sometime in the 70s and 80s—that is, during the reigns of Vespasian, Titus, and the early years of Domitian.

The Flavian Triumph in Rome

The celebration of the Roman victory in Judea, culminating in the destruction of Jerusalem, has been characterized as the "Flavian Actium." In other words, just as the Battle of Actium in 31 BCE provided one of the chief ideological foundations for Augustan rule, so too did the Flavians employ the Judean victory as the chief propagandistic tool for promoting their consolidation of imperial rule, following the civil wars of 69 CE—the year of the four emperors—as an assertion of imperial order out of factionalism.[17] The Judean war, of course, provided the political and military ground out of which the general

---

[16] A consistent historical-rhetorical reading of Hebrews has yet to be done. Such a reading would evaluate the inscribed rhetorical situation (including the inscribed author and audience) before reconstructing the historical situation of the text. On such an approach, see Elisabeth Schüssler Fiorenza, *Rhetoric and Ethic: The Politics of Biblical Studies* (Minneapolis: Fortress, 1999), esp. 105–128.

[17] See Gilbert Charles-Picard, *Les trophées romains. Contribution à l'histoire de la religion et de l'art triomphal de Rome* (BEFAR 187; Paris: Boccard, 1957), 343–344, 359–360, who argues that Jerusalem became the "Flavian Actium." See also Michael Pfanner, *Der Titusbogen* (Beiträge zur Erschliessung hellenistischer und kaiserzeitlicher Skulptur und Architektur; Mainz: Phillip von Zabern, 1983), 101, on the use of this victory in Flavian propaganda and on the specific association of the triumph and the apotheosis of Titus.

Vespasian was acclaimed as *imperator* by the legions under his control in 69 and from which he began his cautious journey back to Rome in 70.[18] Following Titus's capture of Jerusalem and the Roman Senate's voting of a triumph for Vespasian and Titus in 71, the subjugation of Judea stood at the center of Flavian propaganda. That is, the Flavian rulers exploited the one-time event of the triumph as the defining point for the public display of their rule.[19] Although the coin issues depicting *Judaea Capta* or *Judaea Devicta* would have spread across the empire,[20] most of the public display was in the city of Rome itself.[21] We may enumerate the chief ceremonial and monumental occasions of this display: in 71, the celebration of the triumph with prayers, procession, executions, and sacrifices; Vespasian's building of the Temple of Peace, dedicated in 75, next to the Roman Forum and in which were housed the spoils from the Jerusalem temple (Josephus, *J.W.* 7.158–161); in 81 or shortly thereafter, following Titus's death,[22] the erection of the Arch of Titus at the highest point

---

[18] Fergus Millar, *The Roman Near East 31 BC–AD 337* (Cambridge, Mass.: Harvard University Press, 1993), 73–74.

[19] On the increased political dimension of the triumph in the principate, see Michael McCormick, *Eternal Victory: Triumphal Rulership in Late Antiquity, Byzantium, and the Early Medieval West* (Cambridge: Cambridge University Press, 1986), 20. McCormick also points out that by such vehicles as monuments, vestments, coinage, titles, and religious rites, an emperor could amplify the victory celebrated in the triumph (21). On the relationship between triumphs and other Roman *pompae*, see Harriet I. Flower, *Ancestor Masks and Aristocratic Power in Roman Culture* (Oxford: Clarendon, 1996), 107–109. Flower argues that both the triumphal procession and the funeral procession were "overtly political in content, even and especially in representing relationships with the gods" (109). In reading the triumphal rite as political, my work is also informed by that of Simon R. F. Price, *Rituals and Power: The Roman Imperial Cult in Asia Minor* (Cambridge: Cambridge University Press, 1984).

[20] See, among others, Harold Mattingly, *Coins of the Roman Empire in the British Museum* (6 vols.; London: The British Museum, 1923–1962), 2:115–117. The first issue dates from 71 CE and appears to have been issued in preparation for the triumph; the coins continued through 73 and were revived in 77–78, as well as under Titus. See D. Barag, "The Palestinian *Judaea Capta* Coins of Vespasian and Titus and the Era on the Coins of Agrippa II Minted under the Flavians," *Numismatic Chronicle* 138 (1978): 14–23; Colin M. Kraay, "The *Judaea Capta* sestertii of Vespasian," *Israel Numismatic Journal* 3 (1963): 45–46; Mattingly, *Coins*, 2:xlv–xlvi. E. Mary Smallwood, *The Jews under Roman Rule from Pompey to Diocletian* (Leiden: Brill, 1976), 330 n. 164; and McCormick, *Eternal Victory*, 26–27.

[21] Smallwood, *Jews under Roman Rule*, 329.

[22] Titus died in September 81; coins from 81–82 depict him as *divus* (see Mattingly, *Coins*, vol. 2, plate 69, 9; and Peter N. Schulten, *Die Typologie der römischen Konsekrationsprägungen* [Frankfurt a. M.: Numismatischer Verlag Schulten, 1979], 66–67), thus establishing a *terminus post quem* for the arch. Pfanner (*Der Titusbogen*, 91–92) argues for a date very early in the reign of Domitian as the most likely time for the erection of the arch.

of the Via Sacra;[23] and apparently another, earlier arch in the Circus Maximus, erected during the lifetime of Titus, probably circa 80,[24] which made explicit mention in its dedicatory inscription of Titus's conquest of Judea and Jerusalem, "following the precepts of his father."[25] The inscription on this earlier arch highlights an important dimension of the Flavian ideology, namely, the celebration of succession from victorious father to victorious son, precisely that dimension of rule which was missing in the Julian-Claudian period and most notably in the year of the four emperors (69 CE), during which the disputes over succession led to civil war.[26]

The Arch of Titus on the Via Sacra, as is well known, depicts the triumphal procession, including, on one of the large passageway reliefs (north), Titus and Vespasian in a four-horse chariot, accompanied by lictors, and on the facing relief (south), the weighty spoils from the Temple—a menorah (lampstand) and the table of the shewbread, to which are attached two vessels and two trumpets[27]—which

---

[23] On the primary function of the triumphal arch from the first century CE onward as an instrument of imperial propaganda for advertising imperial events and honors, see Pfanner, *Der Titusbogen*, 97.

[24] This arch has not been found but may be one of at least four triumphal arches, known from coins, reliefs, and mosaics, in the Circus Maximus, and perhaps the triple arch depicted on the Forma Urbis Romae (the Marble Plan); on this hypothesis, see Pfanner, *Der Titusbogen*, 98. Lawrence Richardson (*A Topographic Dictionary of Ancient Rome* [Baltimore: Johns Hopkins University Press, 1992], 30) accepts this location and suggests that it was most likely located at the rounded end of the Circus Maximus.

[25] *CIL* 6:944; Hans U. Instinsky, "Der Ruhm des Titus," *Philologus* 97 (1948): 370–371. The text of the inscription reads: *Senatus Populusque Romanus Imp. Tito Caesari Divi Vespasiani F. Vespanian(o) Augusto Pontif. Max. Trib. Pot. X Imp. XVII (C)os VIII PP Principi Suo quod praeceptis patr(is) consiliisq(ue) et auspiciis gentem Iudaeorum domuit et urbem Hierusolymam omnibus ante se ducibus regibus gentibus aut frustra petitam aut omnino intemptatam delevit.* See Pfanner, *Der Titusbogen*, 98.

[26] This dimension is also apparent in the various literary descriptions of the triumph. Josephus (*J.W.* 7.121) remarks that, although the Senate had voted a triumph each to Vespasian and Titus, they nonetheless decided to celebrate a common triumph. Suetonius (*Lives of the Caesars* 8.6) mentions that Titus shared in his father's triumph. Cassius Dio, writing around the beginning of the third century CE, emphasizes the importance of the succession in his account of Vespasian's acclamation and the celebration of the triumph. According to Cassius Dio (*Roman History*, epitome of Book 65.12), upon his acclamation Vespasian is so overcome by emotion that he is able only to say, "My successor shall be my son or no one at all" (ἐμὲ μὲν υἱὸς διαδέξεται, ἢ οὐδεὶς ἄλλος).

[27] For a discussion specifically of the spoils from the Jerusalem temple, see Leon Yarden, *The Spoils of Jerusalem on the Arch of Titus: A Re-investigation* (SSIR 8/16; Stockholm: Paul Åströms, 1991).

are carried in the procession, along with depictions of the battles and signs with the names of the conquered cities and towns. The center of the arch's coffered ceiling shows the apotheosis of Titus. This arch is the visual depiction of the triumph celebrated some ten years earlier.[28]

We have extensive knowledge about the celebration of this triumph, thanks to Josephus's detailed account of it in his *Jewish War* (7.123–162), combined with the relative conservatism of this aspect of Rome's ritual life.[29] It is possible to identify the key elements:[30] the triumph begins outside the city boundary of Rome (the *pomerium*) in the Campus Martius, where the triumphators, Vespasian and Titus, have spent the night (*J.W.* 7.123). The triumphators are crowned with laurel, clad in purple, given the scepter to hold, and acclaimed (*J.W.* 7.124–126). Following prayers and breakfast, the triumphators and the procession enter the city through a gate, the Porta Triumphalis,[31] at which a sacrifice is made (*J.W.* 7.127–130). The lengthy procession customarily included the captives and the

---

[28] The dedicatory inscription on this arch is simpler than that on the arch in the Circus Maximus; it reads: *Senatus Populusque Romanus Divo Tito Divi Vespasiani F. Vespasiano Augusto*. Pfanner argues (in *Der Titusbogen*) that the straightforward message of this inscription emphasizes the divinization of Titus over the celebration of the Judean victory per se, although the depiction of the triumph on the arch functions ideologically to support the Senate's divinization of the emperor.

[29] The fifth-century Christian historian Paulus Orosius provides a much shorter description of the same triumph in *Historiae* 7.9. His account is notable for his emphasis on the display of father and son as co-triumphators. "Vespasian and Titus, the emperors, entered the City celebrating a magnificent triumph over the Jews. This was a fair sight and one hitherto unknown to all mortals among the three hundred and twenty triumphs which had taken place from the founding of the City until that time, namely, father and son riding in one triumphal chariot, bringing back a most glorious victory over those who had offended the Father and the Son" (from Paulus Orosius, *The Seven Books of History against the Pagans* [trans. Roy J. Deferrari; Washington, D.C.: Catholic University of America Press, 1964], 303). Josephus does not make mention of a single chariot, although his description is ambiguous on this point, "behind them Vespasian drove first, and Titus followed, but Domitian rode alongside" (μεθ' ἃ Οὐεσπασιανὸς ἤλαυνε πρῶτος καὶ Τίτος εἴπετο, Δομετιανὸς δὲ παρίππευεν, *J.W.* 7.152).

[30] A detailed discussion of the history and elements of the triumph, along with references to the relevant ancient testimonia, can be found in W. Ehlers, "Triumphus," *RE* 30 (1939): 493–511; see also Hendrik S. Versnel, *Triumphus: An Inquiry into the Origin, Development, and Meaning of the Roman Triumph* (Leiden: Brill, 1970); and more recently Ernst Kunzl, *Der römische Triumph: Siegesfeiern im antiken Rom* (Munich: Beck, 1988).

[31] On the importance of the *entry* into the city and its similarity to the Greek rite of εἰσέλασις, the privilege granted to Olympic victors of a triumphal return to their native town, see Versnel, *Triumphus*, 154–163.

spoils taken in the war, as well as vignettes of the war (*J.W.* 7.139–147), with the triumphators, clothed as Jupiter Maximus Optimus, at the end, followed by their freedpersons.[32] Prominent in the Flavian triumph were, of course, the sacred objects from the Jerusalem temple (*J.W.* 7.148–151), along with seven hundred "choice" prisoners of war, bound and in submission (*J.W.* 7.118, 137–138). The concluding phase of the triumph begins with the execution of the most prominent of the prisoners of war, in this case the general Simon bar Giora (*J.W.* 7.153–155),[33] followed by the sacrifices and the dedication of the laurel crown to the Capitoline gods in the temple of Jupiter Capitolinus (*J.W.* 7.153, 156).[34] Although the procession was the most visible, public aspect of the triumph, historians of religion point out that the triumph was at its heart concerned with the return of the general or emperor to the temple of the Roman gods and with acclaiming the epiphany of the god in the person of the triumphator.[35] In other words, the apotheosis of Titus depicted on the ceiling of the arch had already been displayed—in his lifetime—on the day of the triumph. The Arch celebrates his consecration.[36] We

---

[32] Versnel, *Triumphus*, 95.

[33] See also Otto Michel, "Studien zu Josephus: Simon Bar Giora," *NTS* 14 (1968): 407–408.

[34] See Inez Scott Ryberg, *Rites of the State Religion in Roman Art* (MAAR 22; Rome: American Academy, 1955), 141. Ryberg's reading of the triumph attempts to find the "essential elements" of the triumph's significance; thus she identifies the sacrifices and the dedication of the crown as, to paraphrase, what really matters, even though other parts of the triumph may be more visible and memorable. I would eschew such an approach and recognize instead that the performance of the triumph as a whole does matter; the Capitoline sacrifices may indeed be the culmination of the rites, but as such they participate with the elements within the patterns, structures, and sequences of the ritual.

[35] See Versnel, *Triumphus*, 83. Versnel's consideration of the triumph includes an examination of two opposing arguments, namely, whether the triumphator was seen as Jupiter or as an ancient Roman king. He concludes that the vesture of the triumphator with the *ornatus Iovis*, the *corona Etrusca*, and red lead, along with the acclamation *triumphe*, characterize the triumphator as the representative of Jupiter, but inasmuch as some of these aspects, notably the *ornatus Iovis*, were originally associated with the king, the royal and the divine are merged in the triumphator (92).

[36] Pfanner (in *Der Titusbogen*, 99) stresses that the arch's iconographic program not only honors a divinized emperor, but also "grounds and demonstrates his divinity." The arch can thus be described as a "consecration monument" ("*Konsekrationsmonument*"). According to this reading the lower registers depict Titus's earthly triumph as the foundation of his divine position. The ceiling coffer with the apotheosis of Titus is thus the heavenly consummation of this earthly triumph, supported by the portrayal of the guarantees of this status: the personified figures of the *virtus*, *honos*, and *victoria* of the Augusti. A reference in Cassiodorus (*Variae* 10.30.1) sug-

can recognize, in light of these monuments, that the triumph was probably one of the most prominent features in the religio-political landscape of Flavian Rome.[37]

The Epistle to the Hebrews in Light of the Flavian Triumph

The depiction of the Son, Jesus, in the Epistle to the Hebrews, is expressed chiefly in the words of the psalms. Nevertheless, it makes use of many of the motifs that we find in the Roman triumph, especially as it was celebrated by the Flavians. First, the principal themes of Heb 1 and 2 are the return of the Son, Jesus, to the heavenly realm, to his throne on the right hand of the Father, where he shares in the reign of the Father. The Son is said to have a scepter (Heb 1:8) and to be "crowned" with glory and honor (Heb 2:7). Moreover, all his enemies are "under [his] feet" (Heb 1:13) and all things are subject to him (Heb 2:8, ὑποτάσσω, precisely the word used for subjugated nations and prisoners). Through the use of Pss 2, 8, and 110, Hebrews brings to the forefront of its depiction of Jesus issues of sonship, succession, and rule[38]—issues central to Flavian propaganda.

---

gests, moreover, the possibility that the arch was crowned with a pair of elephants or, more likely, a quadriga drawn by elephants. Pfanner interprets this feature as showing the heavenly triumph of Titus, carried into heaven on the quadriga, and corresponding to the quadriga drawn by horses in his earthly triumph. See Pfanner, *Der Titusbogen*, 3, 99.

[37] The building of the Colosseum, close to the Forum and the Via Sacra, should now also be counted among the ways in which the Flavian victory in the First Jewish War was displayed in the city of Rome. A recently deciphered inscription from the Colosseum declares that the emperor (first Vespasian, then corrected to Titus, probably after Vespasian's death) "ordered the new amphitheater to be built from the spoils of war" (*ex mani[i]bus*), that is, the booty belonging to the victorious general. The spoils in this case are most likely those from the First Jewish War, including the riches of the Jerusalem temple. See Géza Alföldy, "Eine Bauinschrift aus dem Colosseum," *ZPE* 109 (1995): 195–226. An English summary and discussion of Alföldy's work may be found in Louis Feldman, "Financing the Colosseum," *BAR* 27 (July/August 2001): 20–31, 60–61. Feldman mentions the tradition, not attested in any known text, that Jewish prisoners-of-war actually built the Colosseum (60). According to Josephus (*J.W.* 6.420), ninety-seven thousand prisoners-of-war were taken by the Roman army in the war; many of these would have been transported to Rome, and it is quite reasonable to suppose that they formed part of the labor force for the extensive Flavian building program in Rome, including the erection of the Colosseum. We should also bear in mind that those ninety-seven thousand prisoners-of-war may have included some "Christians" whom the Roman army would be unlikely to distinguish from "Jews."

[38] On the importance to the triumph of holding the *imperium*, see Versnel, *Triumphus*, 185–194. On these themes in Hebrews, see Kenneth Schenck, "Keeping His

Moreover, this depiction includes elements of the triumph: the crown, scepter, glory and honor,[39] the visible subjugation of enemies, and the triumphant journey of return to the temple (in this case the heavenly temple, as will become clear in Heb 9:11–12). Jesus is, in my view, depicted in Hebrews as the triumphator in procession to the temple. The text displays the apotheosis of Jesus rather than the apotheosis of Titus, but both are portrayed as the son who rightfully rules alongside his father in victory.

Second, in Hebrews the Son is also the ultimate high priest (Heb 4:14–5:10), offering himself. We may recall that in the Roman triumph the triumphator is also the sacrificer, the priest of Jupiter Capitolinus, who makes the concluding sacrifice of the triumph.[40] Like Jesus in Hebrews, Titus was both son and priest, but Hebrews fills this image with allusions to a story of Jesus' death and his offering of himself (Heb 5:7–10; 9:12, 26; 10:1–18; 13:12–13).[41] I would suggest here that Hebrews is critiquing the ideology of divine rule expressed in the triumphal sacrifices, but doing so indirectly by means

---

Appointment: Creation and Enthronement in Hebrews," *JSNT* 66 (1997): 91–117, who argues that the focus of sonship in Hebrews is on the Son's enthronement in heaven, where he fulfills his divine appointment.

[39] That the triumph and its associated monuments honor the emperors is without doubt. A more specific connection may be suggested by the presence of the figure of *Honos* (i.e., personified honor) accompanying Titus's chariot on the inner relief of the Arch of Titus. This figure, however, is also interpreted as the Genius of the Roman people; see Ryberg, *Rites of the State Religion*, 147; Pfanner (in *Der Titusbogen*, 69–70) discusses the identification closely, concluding that the figure is more likely to be *Honos*. On the increased tendency to include allegorical and personified figures in monumental art at the end of the first century CE, see Ryberg, *Rites of the State Religion*, 97.

[40] Ryberg (*Rites of the State Religion*, 141) argues that at the heart of the triumph lies the repayment of vows made to Jupiter Capitolinus made prior to the general's departure on military campaign. Thus the concluding sacrifice, amid all the opportunities of display and glorification, is the performance of these vows, the returning to the gods of what was promised. Hebrews emphasizes that Jesus offers himself in accordance with God's will; by placing the quotation of Ps 40:6–8 on the lips of Jesus, the author of Hebrews at 10:7 portrays Jesus as saying, "'See, God, I have come to do your will, O God' (in the scroll of the book it is written of me)" (NRSV). Despite some differences, both the Roman triumph and Hebrews understand the sacrifice as fulfilling the demands of the relationship with the divine.

[41] On traditions of Jesus' passion in Hebrews, see Martin Dibelius, "Gethsemane," in Dibelius, *Botschaft und Geschichte*, vol. 1: *Zur Evangelienforschung* (ed. Günther Bornkamm; Tübingen: Mohr Siebeck, 1953), 258–271; August Strobel, "Die Psalmengrundlage der Gethsemane-Parallele. Hebr 5:7ff.," *ZNW* 45 (1954): 256; Paul Andriessen, "Agonisse de la mort dans l'Épître aux Hébreux," *NRTh* 96 (1974): 2986–2991; Helmut Koester, "'Outside the Camp': Hebrews 13.9–14," *HTR* 55 (1962): 300; and Aitken, *Jesus' Death*, 130–164.

of typological reflection on the Yom Kippur rituals and the inadequacy of the high priests in the earthly sanctuary. Thus the typological argument about Levitical sacrifices becomes the rhetorical site for resistance to the Roman imperial ideology.

Third, the monumental and ritual expressions of the Flavian triumph all feature the spoils from the Jerusalem temple. These, as much as the glory of the son, become the vehicle of the ideology.[42] Josephus enumerates them as they were carried in procession: they "consisted of a golden table, many talents in weight, and a lampstand, likewise made of gold [he then depicts it in detail] ... after these, and last of all the spoils, was carried a copy of the Jewish Law" (*J.W.* 7.148–150 [Thackeray, LCL]). Hebrews 9:2–5 likewise goes into great detail about the furnishings of the sanctuary. Hebrews speaks of the "table," the "bread of the presence," the golden altar of incense, the ark of the covenant "overlaid on all sides with gold," the golden urn holding the manna, Aaron's rod, the tables of the covenant, and the cherubim of glory overshadowing the mercy seat. It is important to note that Hebrews does not utilize these items in the typological exposition that follows; they are, as it were, extraneous to the immediate argument but may serve some larger rhetorical purpose. Hebrews includes many more items than does Josephus and may draw upon a traditional list,[43] but all of the items on Josephus's list (table, lampstand, and copy of the law) are included; the lampstand and the table of the shewbread depicted on the Arch of Titus are mentioned both in Hebrews and by Josephus. There is, moreover, similarity in diction, not least the emphasis on gold. In view of other motifs of the triumph in Hebrews, I would suggest that the list of articles from the sanctuary is specifically included in Heb 9 because of the prominence of the Temple spoils from Jerusalem in the display of Flavian ideology. Hebrews is thus rhetorically displaying the items within its own triumphal statement.

Like the Flavians, Hebrews makes use of the "sanctuary" of Israel to promote its message of true rule. Hebrews does so by turning to

---

[42] Ryberg (*Rites of the State Religion*, 146), surveying the iconography associated with triumphs, posits that the Arch of Titus is unusual in that it does not portray the triumphator's sacrificing, a scene that might be expected as the companion relief to the triumphal procession. She suggests that the depiction of the golden objects from the Jerusalem temple was chosen instead because of the great interest that they attracted in Rome.

[43] See the discussion in Attridge, *Hebrews*, 232–238.

the wilderness tabernacle (perhaps precisely because the Jerusalem temple is no longer standing) and making it the earthly shadow of the heavenly realities, pointing out its inadequacies, and showing its abolition (Heb 10:9) through the self-offering of Jesus. We may thus be more precise and say that Hebrews makes use of both the earthly sanctuary and the heavenly sanctuary (the true one) to promote its message of true and proper rule, just as the Flavians made use of both the Jerusalem temple and the Capitoline temple to promote theirs.[44] Thus, one of the many strategies of Hebrews is to take the elements of the imperial triumph and place them in the service of its Christology. This Christology, following the opening chapters of Hebrews, is ultimately one of divine rule, in which the enthroned Son shares in the reign of the Father in the heavens, with his enemies subject to him (Heb 1:13). In the Roman triumph, the triumphator's freedpersons followed him in procession; so too in Hebrews, those whom Jesus has liberated from being held in slavery their whole lives by "the fear of death" (Heb 2:15) are to follow after Jesus in his victorious journey.[45] Thus Jesus in Hebrews is both "the one who leads the way" (Heb 2:10; 12:2, ἀρχηγός)[46] and "forerunner" (Heb 6:20, πρόδρομος) for the community of freedpersons, as they too enter "into his rest" (Heb 4:1) and into the heavenly realm.

The inscribed audience of Hebrews, moreover, is receiving a "kingdom that cannot be shaken" (Heb 12:28, βασιλεία ἀσάλευτος). The explicit ethic for community is, in addition, one of solidarity with those who are exposed to abuse, torture, persecution, imprisonment, and dispossession of property. This ethic is first held up to the community as how they have indeed behaved in "those earlier days": exposed to abuse and persecution, becoming partners (κοινωνοί) with those so treated, and "having compassion (συνεπαθήσατε) on those in prison" (Heb 10:32–34). They are, furthermore, explicitly exhorted to maintain that same ethical solidarity in the present: "Remember

---

[44] The transfer of the Jerusalem temple tax into the *fiscus Judaicus*, paid to the Capitoline temple and gods, implies that, as a result of Roman victory, proper tribute is due not to the god of the Jerusalem temple but instead to the Capitoline gods.

[45] Harold W. Attridge, "Liberating Death's Captives: Reconsideration of an Early Christian Myth," in *Gnosticism and the Early Christian World: In Honor of James M. Robinson* (ed. James E. Goehring et al.; Sonoma, Calif.: Polebridge, 1990), 103–115.

[46] On ἀρχηγός, see Paul-Gerhard Müller, *ΧΡΙΣΤΟΣ ΑΡΧΗΓΟΣ: Der religionsgeschichtliche und theologische Hintergrund einer neutestamentlichen Christusprädikation* (EHS.T 28; Bern: Lang, 1973).

those who are in prison, as though you were in prison with them; those who are being tortured, as though you yourselves were being tortured" (Heb 13:3).⁴⁷ That is, the community that belongs to the reign of Jesus and is receiving an unshakable kingdom is here exhorted to be one with those in Rome (and presumably elsewhere) who are the objects of imperial persecution.⁴⁸ They are indeed to expose themselves to the same risks.

I would suggest that this ethic of solidarity may in part be a response to a perception of increased threat on the part of the Christian and Jewish communities in Rome⁴⁹—a perception that may have been fueled by the public display of *Judaea Capta*, as well as by the large number of Judean, Galilean, and Samaritan enslaved prisoners-of-war in Rome following the war.⁵⁰ It is difficult to know

---

⁴⁷ I cite here the translation of the NRSV; the Greek emphasizes participation in the suffering of others: μιμνῄσκεσθε τῶν δεσμίων ὡς συνδεδεμένοι, τῶν κακουχουμένων ὡς καὶ αὐτοὶ ὄντες ἐν σώματι. "The language expresses the solidarity that the whole community is to feel with those who are conspicuously persecuted" (Attridge, *Hebrews*, 386).

⁴⁸ In discussing Roman prisons and the practice of visiting prisoners, Craig A. Wansink suggests (*Chained in Christ: The Experience and Rhetoric of Paul's Imprisonments* [JSNTSup 130; Sheffield: Sheffield Academic Press, 1996], 80) that "association with the imprisoned drew suspicion to oneself, and this often led to one's death"; see, for example, Dio Chrysostom *Achilles (Or. 58)* 3.7; 11.5–6; Philostratus *Life of Apollonius* 4.46; Tacitus *Annales* 6.5.9.

⁴⁹ A full consideration of the religious profile of Jewish and Christian groups in Rome in the second half of the first century is not possible here. Given the indications of multiple synagogues and house-churches in Rome in this period, along with the rich range of theological expression among Christians by the middle of the second century, it is reasonable to assume a great deal of diversity of practice and belief among Jews and Christians. We should not, moreover, assume sharp divisions between Jews and Christians in Rome; rather, it is better to think of a variety of ways in which people may have identified their religious and social affiliations, including some groups who might be characterized, albeit imprecisely, as Jewish-Christian. Simon R. F. Price has recently discussed the question of pluralism and socio-religious identity in a lecture, "Religious Pluralism in the Roman World: Pagans, Jews, and Christians," at the Annual Meeting of the Society of Biblical Literature, Nashville, Tennessee, November 2000. Price argues for the importance of recognizing clusters of religious markers in any given case, rather than placing the evidence in impermeable categories of religious identity, e.g., Jewish *or* Christian; Isis *or* Mithras. On the Jewish and Christian communities in Rome, see, *inter alia*, George La Piana, *Foreign Groups in Rome During the First Centuries of the Empire* (Cambridge, Mass.: Harvard University Press, 1927); Harry J. Leon, *The Jews of Ancient Rome* (Philadelphia: Jewish Publication Society, 1960); Lampe, *Die Stadtrömischen Christen*; Karl P. Donfried and Peter Richardson, eds., *Jews and Christians in First-Century Rome* (Grand Rapids: Eerdmans, 1998). Harnack's discussion of Hebrews in the context of multiple house-churches in Rome is also of interest in this regard; see Harnack, "Probabilia über die Adresse und den Verfasser des Hebräerbriefs."

⁵⁰ See Smallwood, *Jews under Roman Rule*, 519.

how this display and this changing population affected Christians and Jews in Rome; there is little evidence, if any. Hebrews, however, may indeed contain some indications of the impact in its development of both an ideology of true divine rule held by the Father and Son and an ethic of solidarity with those who suffered under imperial rule. That is, in responding to a perception of increased threat and in resisting the public display of imperial rule expressed in the triumph, Hebrews develops its own triumphal scheme and writes its audience into the triumphal procession as the freedpersons of the victorious ruler, enthroned in heaven. Hebrews does not do so directly but rather through the typological and allegorical interpretation of scripture, particularly the psalms of divine rule, the story of the wilderness journey to the promised land, and the cultic prescriptions for worship in the wilderness tabernacle. It thus employs scriptural interpretation as a rhetorical site for developing a religio-political critique and the articulation of an ethic appropriate to that critique.

In conclusion, I would return to the question of assigning a date for the composition of Hebrews. The argument presented here suggests that Hebrews fits well into the period when the ideology of the Flavian triumph flourished, not only in the ceremony of the triumph itself, but in its continued promulgation in the city of Rome through a series of monuments, that is, in the period between 71 and 81 CE. A more precise date, namely, shortly after the death of Titus in 81 and the building of the Arch of Titus on the Via Sacra, celebrating his apotheosis, may be suggested by the emphasis in Hebrews on the enthronement of the Son in heaven as the culmination of his triumph. This argument depends on the strength of the correlation between two distinct constructions of political theology, one preserved in the text of Hebrews, the other preserved in the rituals and monuments associated with the Flavian triumph. As a response to these articulations of the political theology of the Flavian emperors, as they were experienced in the city of Rome, Hebrews creates its own political theology out of the building materials available in its immediate civic context. The scriptures of Israel and the traditions available to this early Christian community then provide the means to fill out this depiction of Jesus as triumphator and divine ruler enthroned in heaven, but as a triumphator whose journey is marked by suffering, struggle, and solidarity with those in need.

Concluding Pastoral Reflections

The persuasive strategies of the rhetoric of Hebrews aim at shaping a community's understanding of itself and its actions in light of an understanding of Jesus' triumphal journey back to the heavenly sanctuary. As we have seen, the community of the baptized is to take and keep their place in the triumphant procession, as the freedpersons of the victorious ruler, freed from the power of death (Heb 2:15). This is a stance of solidarity—in the first place, with Jesus, and in the second place, with those in the community (and perhaps outside) who are suffering abuse, torture, deprivation of property, and imprisonment. Thus, the lofty Christology and cosmology of Hebrews are directed not at a spiritualized existence but at an ethic and a religious identity. It is, moreover, a specifically anti-individualist ethic inasmuch as the community members are to maintain solidarity with one another. This solidarity is perhaps most challenging when it requires crossing over into the situation of another and when that crossing over involves becoming a partner or participant in the experience of suffering. This radical act of literal compassion, or "suffering with," pushes beyond the model of "ministry to" someone in need. It requires profound risk and the shifting of one's own identity (or the identity of the gathered community) so that entering into what a culture defines as shameful becomes a place of ultimate honor, contrary to all earthly appearances. It is, in Hebrews' terms, to live and act according to hope, that is, according to the reality and identity made possible for the people of God through Jesus' suffering shame, abuse, and death.

Hebrews' use of the theology of the Roman triumph is, moreover, an act of resistance and an act of appropriating the religio-political strategies of the oppressor for the community's own ends. In proclaiming an alternative, "true" triumph and victor, it is likely that Hebrews thus empowers those who are dispossessed. This is important to bear in mind since often Christian triumphalism has been adopted by those wielding political power in order to reinforce their opposition to an enemy, as seen in the use of triumphal theology over Jews or against Islam. Such a misuse of Jesus' triumph neglects the ethic of entering fully into the suffering of others, of bearing the abuse that the other bears, and of becoming an outsider to the familiar and comfortable. Hebrews asks us to consider instead what proclamations of victory require our resistance in the present day.

Ellen Bradshaw Aitken, Th.D.
Associate Professor of Early Christian History and Literature
McGill University, Faculty of Religious Studies
Birks Building, 3520 University Street
Montreal, Quebec, H3A 2A7, Canada
ellen.aitken@mcgill.ca

HOW TO ENTERTAIN ANGELS:
ETHICS IN THE EPISTLE TO THE HEBREWS*

Knut Backhaus

> A *religious* question is either a life-and-death-question or it is (*empty*) talk. This language game—you may say—is played with life-and-death-questions only. Just as the word "ouch!" has no meaning—except as a cry of pain.
>
> Ludwig Wittgenstein[1]

1. *Under Discussion*

1.1. *"Self-Referential and Trivial": Disproportion Between Theology and Ethics*

The theological mountain is in labor—but what is born is a moral mouse! It is this impression one may get reading the Epistle to the Hebrews in order to piece together its instructions into an ethical whole. On the one hand, there is widespread agreement that the demanding concept of this λόγος τῆς παρακλήσεως (Heb 13:22) aims from the outset at a moral purpose. This view is strengthened by the key passages Heb 4:14–16; 10:19–25; and 13:20–21, which have the form of an exhortative appeal,[2] and by the paraenetic tendency

---

* This paper was originally written in German: Knut Backhaus, "Auf Ehre und Gewissen! Die Ethik des Hebräerbriefs," in *Ausharren in der Verheissung: Studien zum Hebräerbrief* (ed. Rainer Kampling; SBS; Stuttgart: Katholisches Bibelwerk, forthcoming). As a rule, I quote Hebrews from the translation in Harold W. Attridge's commentary. I am very grateful to my Munich colleague Professor Alexander J. M. Wedderburn for having critically checked my English or, as he perhaps would prefer to say, my Scottish.

[1] Ludwig Wittgenstein, *Denkbewegungen: Tagebücher 1930–1932, 1936–1937* (part 1, *Normalisierte Fassung*; ed. Ilse Somavilla; Innsbruck: Haymon, 1997), n. 203.

[2] The *propositio* Heb 4:14–16 concludes the first major section and leads up to the *argumentatio* (Heb 4:14[5:1]–10:18); Heb 10:19–25 opens the third major section, which is directly orientated towards exhortation. Thus both of these passages frame the christological central section. In the form of a concluding prayer, Heb 13:20–21 recapitulates the paraenesis of Hebrews. For structural and rhetorical analysis of Hebrews, see Knut Backhaus, *Der Neue Bund und das Werden der Kirche:*

of the particular pericopes³ as well as of the overall structure.⁴ It seems clear that the author tries to master a serious crisis of his addressees by providing an elaborate Christology that may give guidance and motivation for a Christian ethos.

There is, however, some embarrassment as far as the particular form of such an ethos developed in Hebrews is concerned. The exhortations of the first and second major sections (Heb 1:1–4:13; 4:14–10:18) mostly urge the community⁵ in a self-referential manner to adopt the *homologia* worked out in the epistle.⁶ Nevertheless, readers today are far from being impressed by the specific instructions eventually offered in the last major section, especially in Heb 13: Let us do good works (Heb 10:24)! Attend Sunday service (Heb 10:25)! Let the marital bed be undefiled (Heb 13:4)! Respect the church authorities (Heb 13:7, 17)! Keep to orthodox doctrine (Heb 13:9)!

To arrive at exhortations of this kind, it may seem, the intellectual level of the Epistle of Jude would suffice. Further, when ethics is seen as not only the desired result but the starting-point of the christological reflection,⁷ it is hard to avoid the impression that Hebrews imposes on the massive base of doctrinal exposition the statue of an ethical dwarf in heroic bearing.⁸

Die Diatheke-Deutung des Hebräerbriefs im Rahmen der frühchristlichen Theologiegeschichte (NTAbh 29; Münster: Aschendorff, 1996), 47–64.

³ On the interrelationship between expository and exhortatory sections, see Hans-Friedrich Weiss, *Der Brief an die Hebräer* (KEK 13; Göttingen: Vandenhoeck & Ruprecht, 1991), 42–51; and recently George H. Guthrie, *The Structure of Hebrews: A Text-Linguistic Analysis* (NovTSup 73; Leiden: Brill, 1994), esp. 112–147.

⁴ Analogous to the *peroratio* of deliberative rhetoric, the last major section, in particular the final chapter, Heb 13, responds *directly* to the pragmatic situation of the addressees, thereby differing distinctively from the first major sections.

⁵ In my understanding the "community" of Hebrews is a relatively autonomous group with its own educational status within urban Roman Christianity; for discussion, see Weiss, *Hebräer*, 75; Knut Backhaus, "Der Hebräerbrief und die Paulus-Schule," *BZ* 37 (1993): 183–208, esp. 196–204.

⁶ On ὁμολογία in Hebrews, see Heinrich Zimmermann, *Das Bekenntnis der Hoffnung: Tradition und Redaktion im Hebräerbrief* (BBB 47; Cologne: Hanstein, 1977), 44–52; Franz Laub, *Bekenntnis und Auslegung: Die paränetische Funktion der Christologie im Hebräerbrief* (BU 15; Regensburg: Friedrich Pustet, 1980), esp. 9–50.

⁷ So Floyd V. Filson, *"Yesterday": A Study of Hebrews in the Light of Chapter 13* (SBT 4; London: SCM, 1967), 25–26, 82; Jukka Thurén, *Das Lobopfer der Hebräer: Studien zum Aufbau und Anliegen von Hebräerbrief 13* (Åbo: Akademi, 1973), 246–247; Barnabas Lindars, *The Theology of the Letter to the Hebrews* (Cambridge: Cambridge University Press, 1991), 101.

⁸ See William Wrede, *Das literarische Rätsel des Hebräerbriefs* (FRLANT 8; Göttingen: Vandenhoeck & Ruprecht, 1906), 16–20; Richard Perdelwitz, "Das literarische Problem des Hebräerbriefs," *ZNW* 11 (1910): 59–78 and 105–123, here 61.

Thus it is not difficult to understand that, on the other hand, the excess weight of theory arouses doubts about the author's paracletical purpose: "Pastoral care, to be sure, is the only business he does not manage."[9] The epistle is said to be more interested in speculation than in ethics and to develop a general conception that obviously exceeds the needs of any paraenetical purpose.[10] Several scholars even challenge the integrity of the awkward ch. 13 (esp. vv. 22–25), which they suppose to have been appended in order to suggest Pauline authorship to the readers.[11]

1.2. *"Separationist and Esoteric": Disproportion Between Universal Claim and Group Ethic*

It rarely happens that the exhortation of Hebrews is made the subject of special studies, except as a case of theological criticism. It was Rudolf Bultmann's skeptical judgment that has set the standard: poorly immunized against legalism, the ethics of Hebrews abandons the indicative foundation of the moral imperative. The baptized are transposed into the heavenly realms on the basis of the sanctification performed by Christ, with no explanation of the desecularization they have to acquire under their own steam (cf. Heb 13:13–14). In the epistle's expository effort Bultmann cannot help seeing a typological delight in speculation, and he does not expect the author, who may enjoy his interpretation, to reveal its use to us.[12]

As a characteristic example of the prevalent tendency to attach importance to the ethical program of Hebrews chiefly for the

---

[9] Hans-Martin Schenke, "Erwägungen zum Rätsel des Hebräerbriefes," in *Neues Testament und christliche Existenz: Festschrift für Herbert Braun zum 70. Geburtstag am 4. Mai 1973* (ed. Hans Dieter Betz and Luise Schottroff; Tübingen: Mohr Siebeck, 1973), 421–437, here 422; see also Hans-Martin Schenke and Karl Martin Fischer, *Einleitung in die Schriften des Neuen Testaments* (2 vols.; Gütersloh: Gütersloher Verlagshaus), 1978/1979, 2:259–263.

[10] Philipp Vielhauer, *Geschichte der urchristlichen Literatur* (Berlin: de Gruyter, 1981), 243; Helmut Feld, *Der Hebräerbrief* (EdF 228; Darmstadt: Wissenschaftliche Buchgesellschaft, 1985), 61–62.

[11] For discussion, see Thurén, *Lobopfer der Hebräer*, 49–55; Harold W. Attridge, *The Epistle to the Hebrews* (Hermeneia; Philadelphia: Fortress, 1989), 384–385; Erich Grässer, *An die Hebräer* (3 vols.; EKKNT 17; Zürich: Benziger and Neukirchen-Vluyn: Neukirchener, 1990–1997), 3:343–345; Backhaus, "Paulus-Schule," 192–196; and A. J. M. Wedderburn, "The 'Letter' to the Hebrews and Its Thirteenth Chapter," *NTS* 50 (2004): 390–405.

[12] Rudolf Bultmann, *Theologie des Neuen Testaments* (ed. Otto Merk; 9th ed.; Tübingen: Mohr Siebeck, 1984), 113–114, 517–519.

sake of *Sachkritik*,[13] let me outline Wolfgang Schenk's extensive essay (1985).[14]

The semiotic analysis starts from the exhortation Heb 13:16; this choice is justified by both the contextual function of the segment and its representative meaning. With sound arguments Schenk qualifies the first noun in the prohibition Heb 13:16a, τῆς δὲ εὐποιΐας καὶ κοινωνίας μὴ ἐπιλανθάνεσθε, as "charity," in the sense of an institutionalized project of social aid (73–74), and the second one as an active demonstration of fraternal fellowship (74–75). In conjunction with its parallel in Heb 13:1–2a, this instruction proves to be part of a stabilizing paraenetical process that aims at cohesion within the community as well as solidarity between different Christian communities (cf. Heb 10:33–34; 11:36). Thus, in comparison with Paul (cf. Gal 6:10), inclusive love of neighbor is reduced to love of brethren reserved for Christian associates. Schenk concludes that, in contrast to the communities of the apostolic age, "the mystic conventicle addressed in Hebrews" regards itself as a "new cultic club" in an esoteric way (78).[15]

The following causal clause, τοιαύταις γὰρ θυσίαις εὐαρεστεῖται ὁ θεός, both in its passive construction and in placing "God" at the end, draws the readers' attention to human conduct before God, so that Schenk offers us the translation: "For it is God who finds satisfaction in such 'sacrifices.'" It is at this point that Schenk feels uneasy with the Christian spirit of this notion of God being deeply influenced by the *tremendum* of the "Old Testament-numinous" way of thinking, which he also finds in the "terrors of the New Covenant" developed in the whole epistle (cf. 85–87) and which in his opinion reduces the newness of the universalistic approach which takes Easter as its starting-point. This theological shortcoming leads to a separationist ethical approach "that is no longer capable of considering the Christian community as vanguard of God's new world" (89). Under the influence

---

[13] So emphatically Jack T. Sanders, *Ethics in the New Testament: Change and Development* (Philadelphia: Fortress, 1975), 106–110; Siegfried Schulz, *Neutestamentliche Ethik* (Zürich: Theologischer Verlag, 1987), 632–640; more cautiously Wolfgang Schrage, *Ethik des Neuen Testaments* (2d ed.; GNT 4; Göttingen: Vandenhoeck & Ruprecht, 1989), 325–329.

[14] Wolfgang Schenk, "Die Paränese Hebr 13,16 im Kontext des Hebräerbriefes: Eine Fallstudie semiotisch-orientierter Textinterpretation und Sachkritik," *ST* 39 (1985): 73–106.

[15] For similar views, see Richard Völkl, *Christ und Welt nach dem Neuen Testament* (Würzburg: Echter, 1961), 358–359; Schulz, *Neutestamentliche Ethik*, 638–640; Schrage, *Ethik des Neuen Testaments*, 329.

of its ethics of gratitude inspired by Stoic philosophy (cf. 12:28) the epistle fails to maintain a sense of mission *ad extra*. It is an ideology limited to the present time and obedience towards the authorities that replaces both hope as "passion for what is possible" and prophetic searching for a community of the risen Lord (90–92). Thus the community of the readers settles down contemplating its existence as a family of priestly mystics gathered round the high priest, and securing its ethics by means of sacrificial imagery. By demanding a permanent attitude of προσέρχεσθαι Hebrews aspires to "some vision of 'sober-minded ecstasy' that lets the readers fathom the mystery elaborated by itself" (93; cf. 92–97). In Schenk's view the crucial point, then, of the "separationist ecclesiology and ethics" of Hebrews is the "fear of not being on the right side" (89).

There is little reason to object to this understanding as far as the descriptive analysis of the text is concerned. What I do not hold to be legitimate, however, is that Schenk, following a general trend, stops trying to understand the text at this point and switches over immediately to *Sachkritik*. He concludes that the segment Heb 13:16 as well as the ethical passages of Hebrews in general, marked by esoteric group consciousness, at best may serve as an instructive example to illustrate the weight and profile of the theology of the Apostle Paul (cf. Gal 6:6–10; Rom 12) (97–98).

1.3. *The Problems at Issue*

Let us summarize the objections raised against the ethical program of Hebrews in the form of questions that do not suggest normative theological claims but historical investigation of the social setting and theological shape of our epistle:

(1) What is the relationship between the ethical exhortations of Hebrews and its general theological conception? In this regard both the self-referential character (esp. Heb 1–12) and the pragmatic triviality (esp. Heb 13) of the epistle are subjects of critical discussion.

(2) Why are the ethical exhortations of Hebrews restricted to the boundaries of the Christian community? In this regard we have to pay attention to the impression of a separationist and esoteric theology.

We will do justice to the exegetical points at issue if we not only answer the historical questions but also explain in what way they are intimately related to each other. In short: What, from an ethical point of view, does it mean within the context of a Christian community when the addressees hold the belief that Jesus has become far superior to the angels, that he has entered with his own blood through the veil into the sanctuary, that he intercedes on behalf of his people as the high priest according to the order of Melchizedek? What we are going to ask, therefore, is the only *sachkritische* question which in the field of ethics really gets at the point at issue: "Don't tell me what you believe in, tell me what *changes* because you believe in it!" (as Bertolt Brecht would have asked us). To summarize, in what way does the *auctor ad Hebraeos*, beyond doubt a *virtuoso* of faith, change the ethos of his addressees?

2. Interpretation

2.1. The Semantic Features

First of all we have to examine the semantic features of Hebrews as far as they are part of the paraenesis,[16] taking the form of an imperative, cohortative, or a functional equivalent (participial or δεῖ-construction, etc.) or directly supporting the paraenesis.

(a) The first strand, which marks the paraenetical train of thought, consists of *cognitive instructions* providing the (re-)organization of religious knowledge. In this regard the impression of the self-referential character of Hebrews is confirmed, for it is the epistle itself that furnishes the readers with the organizing principles by working out the Christian *homologia*. These paraenetical clauses are often connected with the theological passages by means of causal conjunctions.

There is a significantly frequent use of instructions concerning orientation by virtue of acquired religious knowledge,[17] conscious acquirement of such knowledge,[18] stability defined by confession,[19] and mutual

---

[16] By the text type "paraenesis," I understand a communicative act, for the purpose for providing counsel, that habitualizes and motivates individual or communitarian practice on the basis of the evidence of an instruction and within the framework of an authoritative relationship; for details, see Wiard Popkes, *Paränese und Neues Testament* (SBS 168; Stuttgart: Katholisches Bibelwerk, 1996), 13–52.

[17] "Therefore (διὰ τοῦτο), it is necessary for us to pay attention (προσέχειν) all the more to what has been heard" (Heb 2:1); see Heb 12:25; 13:7.

[18] "Wherefore (ὅθεν), holy brethren, partakers of a heavenly calling, consider (κατανοήσατε) the apostle and high priest of our confession (ὁμολογία), Jesus" (Heb 3:1); see Heb 7:4; 12:2–3.

[19] "Let us hold fast to the confession (ὁμολογία) of hope unwavering" (Heb 10:23); see Heb 3:6, 14; 4:14; 6:4–6, 18–19; 10:28–29, 32.

control of loyal practice of faith.[20] The standard "possessive" expression ἔχομεν has a similar purpose, though it is not directly in the form of an exhortative appeal. It serves to affirm the knowledge of the religious perspective and way of life: "We *have* (viz. in the form of the *homologia* we have acquired) a high priest (Heb 4:14–15; 8:1; cf. 10:21), strong encouragement (Heb 6:18), an anchor for the soul (Heb 6:19), boldness for entrance into the sanctuary (Heb 10:19), a greater and abiding possession (cf. Heb 10:34), a great reward (cf. Heb 10:35), a cloud of witnesses (Heb 12:1), an altar (Heb 13:10)."

It is in this context, i.e., the organization of the knowledge and practice of faith, that the *exempla*, which are characteristic of the ethical concept of Hebrews, ought to be seen. Thus the widespread opinion that Hebrews reveals a clearly discernible ethics of imitation should be put more precisely in so far as the author introduces models to follow only in order to illustrate the right attitude of faith. The epistle does not deal with examples of virtues or acts of morality nor does it appeal to its readers to imitate some special realization of faith. What it calls for is positive or negative *exempla* of a proper endurance in the faith that one has once espoused or an endurance that is required, in order to hold out with the necessary patience and hope to that which is promised imperturbable by rival interpretations of the world; in short, *exempla* of *stabilitas fidei*.

> The absolute paradigm is Jesus, who has shared in the temptations of his people (Heb 2:18; 4:15), who, with prayer, learned obedience through what he suffered (Heb 5:7–9), and who, after having endured cross, shame, and hostility "for the sake of the joy which lay before him" (cf. Heb 12:1–3), stands before "us," who are running with patience "the race which lies before us," as τῆς πίστεως ἀρχηγὸς καὶ τελειωτής.[21] Further, the "cloud of witnesses" (Heb 11:1–40) serves as

---

[20] "Let us have consideration (κατανοῶμεν) for one another with an aim of provoking love and good works" (Heb 10:24); see Heb 3:12–13; 10:25; 12:15.

[21] See Anselm Schulz, *Nachfolgen und Nachahmen: Studien über das Verhältnis der neutestamentlichen Jüngerschaft zur urchristlichen Vorbildethik* (SANT 6; Munich: Kösel, 1962), 293–298; Graham Hughes, *Hebrews and Hermeneutics: The Epistle to the Hebrews as a New Testament Example of Biblical Interpretation* (SNTSMS 36; Cambridge: Cambridge University Press, 1979), 75–100; Franz Laub, "'Schaut auf Jesus' (Hebr 3,1): Die Bedeutung des irdischen Jesus für den Glauben nach dem Hebräerbrief," in *Vom Urchristentum zu Jesus: Festschrift für Joachim Gnilka* (ed. Hubert Frankemölle and Karl Kertelge; Freiburg i. Br.: Herder, 1989), 417–432; Thomas Söding, "Zuversicht und Geduld im Schauen auf Jesus: Zum Glaubensbegriff des Hebräerbriefes," *ZNW* 82 (1991): 214–241, esp. 228–234; David A. deSilva, *Despising Shame: Honor Discourse and Community Maintenance in the Epistle to the Hebrews* (SBLDS 152; Atlanta: Scholars Press, 1995), 165–178.

a paradigmatic catalog to shape the pilgrimage of the faithful Christian people towards the promised land. Worthy of imitation, moreover, is the consistency of faith shown by the departed leaders of the community (Heb 13:7). The author wants his addressees to be "imitators (μιμηταί) of those who through faith and perseverance inherited the promises." Besides Esau (cf. Heb 12:15–17), it is the wandering generation of the desert that serves as a negative example of deafness, apathy, and apostasy (cf. Heb 3:7–4:11).

These instructions serve to transform the readers' perspective (permanently).[22] It is the christological *homologia* that serves as the organizing center of the transformed view: the heavenly high priest is, so to speak, the sun in the interpretative universe arranging all the particular aspects of religious knowledge in its ethical orbits so that the plausibilities of the dominant culture, into which the addressees are in danger of relapsing,[23] lose their attraction.

(b) The second strand, which is concentrated in particular in the main paraenetical passages, links instructions to dynamic verbs. This semantic field overlaps with the cognitive one in so far as it describes an inward movement, that is to say, an orientation, aimed at the system of Christian knowledge developed in Hebrews.[24]

In this respect the compounds προσέρχεσθαι (Heb 4:16; 10:22; 11:6; cf. 7:19, 25) and εἰσέρχεσθαι (Heb 4:1, 3, 11; cf. 6:20; 10:19) are of decisive relevance. Approaching or entering are depicted as leading to different destinations: the throne of grace, eternal Sabbath rest, the heavenly sanctuary. What connects these images is the motif of the accessibility of God's presence in the sacred space of the crucified Lord.[25] "Approaching" as well as "entering," therefore,

---

[22] In some passages Hebrews indicates the circumstances when the new perspective was first acquired, e.g., as far as the history of mission (Heb 2:3–4), catechetical aspects (Heb 5:11–6:2), or the biography of the community (Heb 10:32–34) are concerned.

[23] In my view, the paraenetical instructions in their convergence show clearly that the widely discussed "relapse" is related not to the ancestral religion of former Jews but to the social home reality of the (pagan) Roman milieu; for discussion, see Backhaus, *Der Neue Bund*, 264–282.

[24] Remarkably, the adjective used to indicate the attitude of the readers, νωθρός, is related to both the cognitive process of hearing (Heb 5:11) and the whole movement of faithful existence (Heb 6:12).

[25] On the soteriological thrust of these dynamics, see Laub, *Bekenntnis und Auslegung*, 265–272; John M. Scholer, *Proleptic Priests: Priesthood in the Epistle to the Hebrews*

describe the Christian experience of reality, in so far as the usual way of seeing the world is transcended in the direction of God.

The readers are stimulated to a consistent practice of faith not only by imagery from the sphere of athletics and battle (Heb 12:1, 4, 12–14)[26] but also with reference to the semantic fields of ways and wandering (cf. Heb 2:1; 3:7–4:11; 10:20; 11:8–10, 13–16, 27; 12:18–24; 13:13–14) concentrated in the idea of the socially homeless pilgrim people of God. The Christians form God's "cultic community on the move,"[27] whose whole existence may be summarized in the statements of the goal in Heb 9:14 and Heb 12:28: λατρεύειν, that is, "to worship amid the everyday world."[28]

The purpose of these dynamic instructions is once more the redefinition of competing realities. The addressees are led into their own cognitive world, whose ways are unequivocally defined by the *homologia*. This *eisodos* into the sacred space (Heb 10:19) corresponds to the *exodus* from the space of the urban dominant culture (Heb 13:13; cf. 11:8, 27, 29).[29]

(JSNTSup 49; Sheffield: Sheffield Academic Press, 1991), 91–149 (προσέρχεσθαι), 150–184 (εἰσέρχεσθαι); Hermut Löhr, *Umkehr und Sünde im Hebräerbrief* (BZNW 73; Berlin: de Gruyter, 1994), 250–285; Wilhelm Thüsing, "'Lasst uns hinzutreten...' (Hebr 10,22): Zur Frage nach dem Sinn der Kulttheologie im Hebräerbrief," in idem, *Studien zur neutestamentlichen Theologie* (WUNT 82; ed. Thomas Söding; Tübingen: Mohr Siebeck, 1995), 184–200; Knut Backhaus, "Per Christum in Deum: Zur theozentrischen Funktion der Christologie im Hebräerbrief," in *Der lebendige Gott: Studien zur Theologie des Neuen Testaments: Festschrift für Wilhelm Thüsing zum 75. Geburtstag* (ed. Thomas Söding; NTAbh 31; Münster: Aschendorff, 1996), 258–284.

[26] See David A. deSilva, *Perseverance in Gratitude: A Socio-Rhetorical Commentary on the Epistle "to the Hebrews"* (Grand Rapids: Eerdmans, 2000), 361–364.

[27] William G. Johnsson, "The Pilgrimage Motif in the Book of Hebrews," *JBL* 97 (1978): 239–251, here 249.

[28] See Ernst Käsemann, *Das wandernde Gottesvolk: Eine Untersuchung zum Hebräerbrief* (4th ed.; FRLANT 55; Göttingen: Vandenhoeck & Ruprecht, 1961); Johnsson, "Pilgrimage Motif"; Erich Grässer, "Das wandernde Gottesvolk: Zum Basismotiv des Hebräerbriefes," in idem, *Aufbruch und Verheissung: Gesammelte Aufsätze zum Hebräerbrief* (ed. Martin Evang and Otto Merk; BZNW 65; Berlin: de Gruyter, 1992), 231–250; Markus Bockmuehl, "The Church in Hebrews," in *A Vision for the Church: Studies in Early Christian Ecclesiology in Honor of J. P. M. Sweet* (ed. Markus Bockmuehl and Michael B. Thompson; Edinburgh: T&T Clark, 1997), 133–151, esp. 140–143; deSilva, *Perseverance*, 70–71, 394–395; Iutisone Salevao, *Legitimation in the Letter to the Hebrews: The Construction and Maintenance of a Symbolic Universe* (JSNTSup 219; Sheffield: Sheffield Academic Press, 2002), 296–305.

[29] See Harold W. Attridge, "Paraenesis in a Homily (λόγος παρακλήσεως): The Possible Location of, and Socialization in, the 'Epistle to the Hebrews,'" *Semeia* 50 (1990): 211–226, here 221–223.

So again an inward counter-world is established or worked out, in which the readers may take up—in Martin Heidegger's sense—"ethos," that is, "an abode, a dwelling-place. The noun designates the open space in which one lives."[30] This sort of living, to be sure, must be put into effect. The problem Hebrews primarily deals with is not that the addressees do not know what they should do but that they do not do what they should know.[31] Cognition, therefore, must gain an active dimension, that is to say, an aspect of movement.

(c) Proceeding now from the exhortations to the imagery that structures the epistle we at once notice the affinity: the imagery is primarily shaped in cultic or sociomorphic style. In its soteriological center the epistle outlines, with a delight in typological details, the symbolic counter-world of the heavenly sanctuary. Thereby it pursues the intention to show to God's pilgrim people the "new and living way" from the "pro-fanum" through the veil into God's most holy presence, from the transitory sphere to the eternal one, from the earthly world of shadows to the divine light (cf. Heb 8:1–10:25; esp. Heb 9:6–14; 10:19–22).[32]

The images for salvation are often taken from the political or social order so that the contrast between the homeland of faith and the earthly realities may come to light. The goal of the Christians is the promised land (cf. Heb 11:9), the *polis* with foundations whose maker and fashioner is God (Heb 11:10), the better, that is, heavenly fatherland (Heb 11:14, 16), the city of the living God, the heavenly Jerusalem, the assembly of the firstborn who are enrolled in heaven (Heb 12:22–23),[33] the unshakable kingdom (Heb 12:28), the city which remains and which is to come (cf. Heb 13:14).

---

[30] Martin Heidegger, "Brief über den Humanismus," in idem, *Wegmarken* (vol. 9; Frankfurt a. M.: Vittorio Klostermann, 1976), 313–364, here 354, 354–357.

[31] See Frank J. Matera, "Moral Exhortation: The Relation between Moral Exhortation and Doctrinal Exposition in the Letter to the Hebrews," *TJT* 10 (1994): 169–182, here 170–171; on lethargy as the ethical crux of Hebrews, see Thomas E. Schmidt, "Moral Lethargy and the Epistle to the Hebrews," *WTJ* 54 (1992): 167–173.

[32] On the "theology of access," see Marie E. Isaacs, *Sacred Space: An Approach to the Theology of the Epistle to the Hebrews* (JSNTSup 73; Sheffield: Sheffield Academic Press, 1992).

[33] On the political background of this image, see Attridge, *Hebrews*, 375; Weiss, *Hebräer*, 678–680; deSilva, *Perseverance*, 466–467.

Thus, it is the dynamism of change in the readers' view and (inward) position that characterizes the overall argumentation of Hebrews. The experience of this earthbound life and the participation in heavenly reality confront one another. While worldly experience is fading away, the pilgrim's path is illuminated by the kindly light of heaven. Hebrews, to be sure, does not call upon its readers to *withdraw from the world* but it pleads for *superiority to the world*.[34] When God's reality alone is absolute, then the faithful wandering through this life will pass through things of relative importance only. Christians will not abandon this world but they will learn to deal with it with greater detachment.[35]

2.2. *The Customary Paraenesis*

2.2.1. *Group-Ethical Orientation*

Throughout our exploration of the semantic features of the paraenesis of Hebrews it became evident that the impression of a certain self-referential character of the epistle's ethics is justified: Hebrews does not deal with general love of one's neighbor or enemy nor the church's world mission. Rather, it aims at introducing its readers deeper into the "mystery" which it itself has unfolded. Nevertheless, in the same way it became evident, too, that this "mystery" serves as the (intended) referential system providing the standards for the addressees' ethical orientation in general. The customary paraenesis[36] is meant to safeguard the basic social conditions of this referential system.

In my view, the approach of social history will do more justice to the ethics of Hebrews than criticism based on theological aesthetics. Before we examine whether the admonitions of Hebrews may spread out in all directions with a seemingly Pauline impetus, so that the community finds itself to be the "vanguard of God's new world,"

---

[34] See the chapter on Hebrews in Völkl, *Christ und Welt*, 350–360: "Das Ethos der Wanderer."

[35] For more detail, see Knut Backhaus, "Das Land der Verheissung: Die Heimat der Glaubenden im Hebräerbrief," *NTS* 47 (2001): 171–188.

[36] The adjective "customary" does not indicate any contrast with "topical" but emphasizes the conventional character of the exhortations. It is paraenetical convention that serves social habitualization and so it is of topical relevance to Christian communities in the making. For discussion, see Weiss, *Hebräer*, 72–74.

let us take a closer look at how such a vanguard might in concrete terms be formed.

In a sense, it is not unfair to suggest that Hebrews is driven by "fear of not being on the right side," for in the inevitable decision between the formative church and the dominant culture threatening its self-definition, the epistle urges its readers to opt for the right side and to realize it by means of social organization.[37] The crucial question, then, is whether the exhortations fulfill their purpose to construct and secure the symbolic counter-world that may direct and strengthen the cognitive self-affirmation of Christians confronted with the claims of pagan society. From this point of view, triviality does not seem to be a surprising feature of ethical instruction. After all, the sense of a proposition in religious and ethical speech is gained from the concrete, that is, socially embedded, form of life of the one who speaks.

Viewed from the perspective of individual ethics, in the judgment of many interpreters the exhortations of Heb 13 are lacking any recognizable plan. If we, however, take into consideration their group-ethical function, a clear purpose is revealed. This purpose is not inspired by pleasure in literary composition, to be sure, but by the deliberate intention to establish Christian community within the social world of the first century.

The *transitus* Heb 12:28–29 indicates the subject of the following chapter. In Heb 13, vv. 1–5a then deal with the social stabilization of the community, while vv. 7–17, framed by the instruction on the "authority of the leaders," primarily regulate the organization of knowledge. The "inserted" and at-first-sight incoherent passage Heb 13:5b–6 defines Christian "courage" as the decision for the "right side." It is exactly this idea which is worked out in the cohortative vv. 13–14, in which the ethics of Hebrews is summarized from a theocentric point of view. Throughout twelve chapters the readers, repeatedly called to change their usual perspective, have been prepared for such a theocentric definition of Christian ethos. Now they learn in the closing paraenesis which everyday factors may work to

---

[37] On the social function of "line drawing" between right and wrong sides, see Bruce J. Malina, *The New Testament World: Insights from Cultural Anthropology* (3d ed.; Louisville: Westminster John Knox, 2001), 27–30.

ground and to secure the normative referential system of a Christian community model.

2.2.2. Social Stabilization (Heb 10:24–25a; 13:1–6)

(a) *Heb 10:24–25a*: There is only one explicit admonition prior to ch. 13, and it is programmatically set into the prelude of the *peroratio*:

> Let us have consideration for one another (κατανοῶμεν ἀλλήλους) with an aim of provoking love and good works (εἰς παροξυσμὸν ἀγάπης καὶ καλῶν ἔργων), not forsaking our own assembly (ἐπισυναγωγή), as is the custom of some, but encouraging (one another) (παρακαλοῦντες). (Heb 10:24–25a)

This exhortation aims at the community's cohesion: first, by means of mutual control ("take consideration for one another"), promoting ("provoking") a practice of *agape* that performs "services for the saints," and motivation of "good works" that may build up the community (cf. Heb 6:10);[38] secondly, by means of regular attendance at the community's worship, which is the only way of consolidating the cognitive system of a religious minority in the long run;[39] and thirdly, by means of the triad "consolation, support, admonition," which Hebrews lets us hear in the verb παρακαλέω (cf. Heb 3:13; 13:19, 22). In short, the author pleads for cohesion by means of assembling, practical building up of an in-group, and affirmation of a corresponding self-awareness. The Christian community (re-)establishes itself as a social reality.

What these verses present *in nuce* is explicated in Heb 13. Although it may seem as if the instructions do not follow a clear direction they are arranged most purposefully in three ways: they deal with modes of social obligation within the community; the several ways of Christian practice they postulate seem to be threatened; and they complement each other so that the coherent shape of a socially efficient minority behavior is visible.

---

[38] The noun ἀγάπη is used in Hebrews only at 10:24 and 6:10, and in both cases the noun ἔργον refers to human action with a positive connotation.

[39] On the interdependence between loyal attendance at worship and *stabilitas fidei*, see Grässer, *An die Hebräer*, 3:26–30.

(b) *Heb 13:1*: "Let brotherly love (φιλαδελφία) remain." The opening verse presents the *cantus firmus* of the epistle's paraenetical catalog. The community regards itself as a fraternal association forming "fictive kinship."[40] Hence it provides the emotionally anchored solidarity, the conformity of interests, and those particular ethical rights and duties of mutual support which were obligatory family values in the Mediterranean society of the first century.[41] This self-definition, to be sure, is common Christian heritage, but by reflecting on the motif of the *syngeneia* of the faithful with their high priest (cf. Heb 2:10–18) Hebrews gives christological substantiation to it.

By "converting" to the "right side," Lucian of Samosata (ca. 120–180 CE) states, Christians become "brethren." How such a familial ethos marked the community's everyday life, Lucian satirically illustrates by telling the story of the charlatan Peregrinus, who has climbed the ladder fast among Christians and is eventually put in prison by the public authorities. Several exhortations of Heb 13, and most of all the reversal of significant values, are reflected and elucidated in this pagan observation of early Christian σπουδή (*Peregr.* 12–13; cf. Heb 4:11; 6:11).

> From the very break of day aged widows and orphan children could be seen waiting near the prison, while their officials even slept inside with him after bribing the guards. Then multifarious meals were brought in, and sacred books of theirs were read, and excellent Peregrinus—for he still went by this name—was called by them "the new Socrates." Indeed, people came even from the cities in Asia, sent by the Christians at their common expense, to succor and defend and encourage him (παραμυθησόμενοι). They show incredible speed whenever such public action is taken; in short, they lavish it all. So it was then in the case of Peregrinus; much money came to him from them by reason of his imprisonment, and he procured not a little revenue from it. The poor wretches have convinced themselves, first and foremost, that they are going to be immortal and live for all time, in consequence of which they despise death (καταφρονοῦσιν; cf. Heb 12:2) and even willingly give themselves up to the authorities, most of them. Furthermore, their

---

[40] See deSilva, *Perseverance*, 485–486; on the biblical background, Geoffrey W. Grogan, "The Old Testament Concept of Solidarity in Hebrews," *TynBul* 49 (1998): 159–173.

[41] On the ideal and the reality of family in the Roman empire of the first century, see Keith R. Bradley, *Discovering the Roman Family: Studies in Roman Social History* (New York: Oxford University Press, 1991); Halvor Moxnes, ed., *Constructing Early Christian Families: Family as Social Reality and Metaphor* (London: Routledge, 1997); Malina, *New Testament World*, 134–160.

first lawgiver persuaded them that they are all brothers of one another after they have transgressed once for all by denying the Greek gods and by worshipping that crucified sophist himself and living according to his laws (κατὰ τοὺς ἐκείνου νόμους βιῶσιν). Therefore they despise (καταφρονοῦσιν) all things indiscriminately and consider them common property, receiving such doctrines traditionally without any definite evidence. So if any charlatan and trickster, able to profit by occasions, comes among them, he quickly acquires sudden wealth by imposing upon simple folk. (Harmon, LCL, with slight variations)

(c) *Heb 13:2*: "Do not forget hospitality, for through this some have inadvertently entertained angels." From φιλαδελφία the view turns to φιλαξενία. This basic attitude of urban communities met the demands of a most lively culture of traveling and communication that was characteristic of early Christianity, thereby advancing the Christians' empire-wide interconnection to a remarkable degree (cf. Rom 12:13; *Peregr.* 16). Alluding to scriptural, Jewish, and pagan narratives about the inadvertent accommodation of "divine guests" (e.g., Gen 18–19; Ovid, *Metam.* 8.620–724) the brief causal clause extends the familial relationship to the community of heaven:[42] those who are socially marginalized experience close solidarity and partake in the boundless family of faith.

(d) *Heb 13:3*: "Remember those who are in bonds, as if bound with them, and those who are ill-treated, as if you yourselves were in (their) body." The tendency to marginalize cognitive minorities or to put them under pressure to become assimilated may, if need be, assume the form of imprisonment or public violence (cf. Heb 11:36–38). Looking back on some persecution in the past, the passage Heb 10:32–34 provides the nearest comment on this admonition. The scene is similar to that drawn by Lucian: formerly the addressees have shown themselves as sharers with those who were imprisoned, and the seizure of their possessions they accepted "with joy." The stronger the pressure the out-group exerts, the closer must the solidarity of the in-group be.

---

[42] For discussion, see Grässer, *An die Hebräer*, 3:349–352. On the history of the motif, see Daniela Flückiger-Guggenheim, *Göttliche Gäste: Die Einkehr von Göttern und Heroen in der griechischen Mythologie* (Bern: Peter Lang, 1984); on the social value of hospitality, see Bruce J. Malina, "Hospitality," in *Handbook of Biblical Social Values* (ed. John J. Pilch and Bruce J. Malina; 2d ed.; Peabody: Hendrickson, 2000), 115–118.

(e) *Heb 13:4*: "Let marriage be esteemed (τίμιος) among all and let the marital bed be undefiled, for God judges fornicators and adulterers." Once more we will hardly do justice to the group-ethical train of thought if we interpret this appeal for the appreciation of marriage "among all" with regard to private morality only[43] or reduce its meaning to the history of ideas as being "a consequence of Jewish-Christian sexual radicalism."[44] Rather, what is at stake here, put forward by means of conventional language, is the insight that the *intimate* decision for living in marriage is of extensive *public* relevance. Matrimonial stability after the model of Jewish monogamy forms an essential condition for a community that differs in lifestyle from the dominant pagan culture and whose normative system is not endangered by the promiscuity of its members. Such a community may hand down its interpretative standards to the following generation without being directly influenced by the traditions of out-groups, and, not least, its appreciation of familial values in the "ecclesiola" of one's own household supports the familial self-affirmation of the community in general.

(f) *Heb 13:5a*: "Let your conduct be unmercenary and be content with what you have." As Lucian has shown in satirical exaggeration, it was a distinctive feature of an early Christian community that "all" was considered "common property." The moderation of the faithful and their consequent readiness to give financial support to their group, its economic system, and its social network have often been named among those factors that made the Christian model of life an attractive one in the Mediterranean society of the first centuries.[45] Nevertheless, the experience of "up and out" was a most serious problem to the third generation: wherever the church lives at the bottom of contemporary culture, those who climb up the ladder in society are in danger of leaving the church. Therefore this admonition is not aimed at individual modesty only but at the estab-

---

[43] So Harald Hegermann, *Der Brief an die Hebräer* (THKNT 16; Berlin: Evangelische Verlagsanstalt, 1988), 269 (sanctification); Grässer, *An die Hebräer*, 3:353–357 ("private life").

[44] So Kurt Niedermimmer, *Askese und Martyrium: Über Ehe, Ehescheidung und Eheverzicht in den Anfängen des christlichen Glaubens* (FRLANT 113; Göttingen: Vandenhoeck & Ruprecht, 1975), 162–163.

[45] See Douglas E. Oakman, "Self-Sufficiency," in *Social Values*, 181–183.

lishment of a community that proves itself socially viable and ready for competition.

(g) *Heb 13:5b–6*: While the exhortations are designed to establish the conditions required to strengthen the social plausibility of the symbolic universe in which the Christian minority lived, the causal clauses look loosely affixed and lack, as it seems, any plan: an allusion to possible experience of the transcendent world (v. 2b); an appeal to self-consciousness (cf. v. 3b); a fierce warning of judgment (v. 4b). The motive the author names at the close, however, unifies what has been said before: God is unswervingly on the side of those who believe in him and proves himself the only normative court, so that in comparison with him any human opinion turns out to be of limited importance. It is this theological self-affirmation that gives courage to Christians to show indifference to the majority opinion in the dominant culture:

> For he himself has said, "I will not abandon you, nor will I forsake you" [Deut 31:6, 8]. So we should take courage and say, "The Lord is my helper, and I shall not fear; what will any human being do to me?" [Ps 117:6 LXX] (Heb 13:5b–6)

2.2.3. *Organization of Knowledge (Heb 13:7–17)*

(a) *Heb 13:7, 17 (cf. Heb 13:18, 24)*: Early Christian communities were essentially places for imparting religious knowledge. This had an attractive effect on those who had been socialized in pagan culture, for neither the established nor the popular religions provided any social or ethical knowledge that might give direction in times of growing confusion.[46]

Thus the significance of the ἡγούμενοι[47] is intelligible. The framework of the paraenetical catalog that treats of the Christian stock of knowledge presents them as bearers of cognitive competence and moral authority. Acceptance of a new code of behavior depends fundamentally on the reference-persons whom the subjects of a social group allow to determine binding standards of orientation. The role

---

[46] See Jochen Bleicken, *Verfassungs- und Sozialgeschichte des Römischen Kaiserreiches* (vol. 2; 3d ed.; Paderborn: Schöningh, 1994), 118–121.
[47] On this noun, see Laub, *Bekenntnis und Auslegung*, 47–50; Erich Grässer, "Die Gemeindevorsteher im Hebräerbrief," in *Aufbruch und Verheissung*, 213–230.

of such "significant others" (George H. Mead) in the process of second socialization grows even more important where one's whole perception of reality undergoes a religious transformation.

Verse 7 calls for *anamnesis* that may establish tradition and for *mimesis* that may stabilize values by imitating those leaders of the founding generation who have laid down the foundations of Christian self-definition. It emphasizes their competence in the field of faith, in terms of how they proclaimed the word of salvation or accepted its consequences in an exemplary manner (ἀναστροφή).[48] Verse 17 directly stratifies the community, referring to "obedience" and "subordination" based on an ethics of responsibility. Accountable to God for those entrusted to them, the leaders represent the one who is the "significant other" per se. Verse 18 strengthens the author's own claim to significance by alluding to his exemplary and attractive manner of conduct (ἀναστρέφεσθαι); v. 24 links the author and the body of leaders. The personal constellation arranged in this way secures the form of interaction that is necessary for the affirmation of knowledge and values.

(b) *Heb 13:8–10*: Starting with Christ as the reference-person with regard to Christian continuity and identity (v. 8), the *auctor ad Hebraeos* warns the addressees in a rather general way against the temptation of being carried off "by diverse and strange teachings." He contrasts the Christian treasure, the "altar" as the cultic symbol of immediate access to God, with the useless foods of earthbound worship (vv. 9–10).[49] Only the reality of salvation that may be reached in the Christian community will give entrance into the divine counter-world. Indeed, "the altar," that is to say, a coherent doctrine developed from the christological center, was of no little importance to the attractiveness of early Christianity. Unlike the competing cults, which seldom got beyond a few speculations, Christian theology, deeply rooted in religious practice, was able to elaborate a symbolic world that might be experienced as home of the homeless.[50]

---

[48] For discussion, see Attridge, *Hebrews*, 391–392; Grässer, *An die Hebräer*, 3:367–370.
[49] For discussion, see Attridge, *Hebrews*, 393–397; Grässer, *An die Hebräer*, 3:372–382; Marie E. Isaacs, "Hebrews 13.9–16 Revisited," *NTS* 43 (1997), 268–264 esp. 273–284.
[50] See Bleicken, *Verfassungs- und Sozialgeschichte*, 176–177.

(c) *Heb 13:11–14*: Inspired by the axiomatic thinking of platonizing metaphysics, the cultic typology of Hebrews localizes this homeland "outside the camp."[51] Here we are entering the center of the epistle's paraenesis. Four times ἐξ- designates the place of Jesus and his sacrificial saving death, the basic movement of those who follow him, and, indirectly, the place of the city which is to come. The entrance into the divine presence, the imitation of Christ, and the search for the eternal homeland assume the form of an exodus from urban Roman culture (ἐξερχώμεθα), thereby leading to the social stigmatization of the "wandering people" (τὸν ὀνειδισμὸν αὐτοῦ φέροντες). The fate of those who find themselves marginalized reveals their christological and ecclesiological status: the community is παροικία amidst the world. The history of this idea may scarcely be overestimated.[52] The call for social exodus shows an illuminating parallel to the appeal of John the Seer (Rev 18:4), who urges the people of God to come out from the sinful city (ἐξέλθατε).[53] Both authors plead for an attitude that refuses any integration into the dominant culture.

---

[51] On the metaphysical aspects here, see James W. Thompson, *The Beginnings of Christian Philosophy: The Epistle to the Hebrews* (CBQMS 13; Washington: Catholic Biblical Association, 1982), 141–151.

[52] On the motif of "wandering between the worlds," see Erich Grässer, "'Wir haben hier keine bleibende Stadt' (Hebr 13,14): Erwägungen zur christlichen Existenz zwischen den Zeiten," in *Aufbruch und Verheissung*, 251–264; Kurt Niedwimmer, "Vom Glauben der Pilger: Erwägungen zu Hebr 11,8–10 und 13–16," in *Zur Aktualität des Alten Testaments: Festschrift für Georg Sauer zum 65. Geburtstag* (ed. Siegfried Kreuzer and Kurt Lüthi; Frankfurt a. M.: Peter Lang, 1992), 121–131; with special emphasis on the *polis*, Michael Theobald, "'Wir haben hier keine bleibende Stadt, sondern suchen die zukünftige' (Hebr 13,14). Die Stadt als Ort der frühen christlichen Gemeinde," *TGl* 78 (1988): 16–40.

[53] In the view of Hans-Josef Klauck ("Das Sendschreiben nach Pergamon und der Kaiserkult in der Johannesoffenbarung," in idem, *Alte Welt und neuer Glaube: Beiträge zur Religionsgeschichte, Forschungsgeschichte und Theologie des Neuen Testaments* [NTOA 29; Freiburg i. Ue.: Universitätsverlag and Göttingen: Vandenhoeck & Ruprecht, 1994], 115–143, here 137–141), this appeal summarizes the purpose of Revelation; see Knut Backhaus, "Die Vision vom ganz Anderen: Geschichtlicher Ort und theologische Mitte der Johannes-Offenbarung," in *Theologie als Vision: Studien zur Johannes-Offenbarung* (ed. Knut Backhaus; SBS 191; Stuttgart: Katholisches Bibelwerk, 2001), 10–53, here 25–30. Insightfully, deSilva, *Despising Shame*, 315–317: "Despite its eloquence, its cultured, literary Greek, Hebrews is less interested in making a place for Christianity within Greco-Roman society than Luke or even Paul." It is hard to see how Sanders (*Ethics in the New Testament*, 110) might give reasons from the text for his judgment that the ethics of Hebrews is congruent with "good citizenship." Even less convincing is the suggestion by Richard W. Johnson (*Going Outside the Camp: The Sociological Function of the Levitical Critique in the Epistle to the Hebrews* [JSNTSup 209; Sheffield: Sheffield Academic Press, 2001], 146–153) that Hebrews aims at "world mission."

The *auctor ad Hebraeos*, however, gives this refusal the less aggressive note of a hopeful, worshiping *eisodos* into the sacred space of Christ's counter-world (ἐξερχώμεθα πρὸς αὐτόν!).

(d) *Heb 13:15–16*: It is in this sense that the sacrificial imagery for ethical behavior in the frame of the double instruction v. 15a and v. 16b returns to the basic interpretative system that underlies the central part of Hebrews. The calling for prayers of praise and confession, beneficence and fellowship (vv. 15b–16a) once again aims at both the cognitive and the practical construction of Christian reality. Rooted in God's prior activity, such realization is considered to be thankful re-action (cf. Heb 12:28).[54] The common world of early Christians—their worshiping, their self-awareness as described in the *homologia*, their solidarity under pressure, and their practical *koinonia* in everyday life—takes part in the great drama between heaven and earth performed by the Son and high priest Jesus Christ. While the dominant culture will remain captured in a self-referential system, what opens above the marginalized existence of the undistinguished Christian minority is the heavenly reality. And it is at this very point where the imperative is literally rooted in the indicative: Δι' αὐτοῦ . . .

3. Sociological Considerations

3.1. Legitimation of the Christian Model

The interpretation of the paraenetical passages of Hebrews allows us to give an answer to our opening questions:

Ad (1): The general theological conception of Hebrews legitimates the referential system that safeguards and determines both the perception of reality and the self-understanding of the community. The ethical exhortations aim at the segmentation of Christian identity by providing the basic social conditions for this referential system. So the general theological conception as well as the particular ethical instructions serve the same purpose, i.e., the systematic and practical conceptualization of an interpretative sphere that protects the self-definition of the community from the cognitive majority and the

---

[54] On thankfulness as a basic feature of the patron-client relationship in the Mediterranean society of the first century, see deSilva, *Perseverance*, 474–476.

pressure of cultural assimilation and enables the individual to internalize specifically Christian standards of practice.

Ad (2): The ethical exhortations of Hebrews recommend the efficient self-organization of an in-group in a crisis of interpretation and motivation produced by the experience of being socially stigmatized. What is required in this liminal phase between society and community is first of all a concentration upon the internal realm of one's own cognitive group.[55] Marginalization gains a dignity of its own by being regarded as entrance into God's sacred space so that a symbolic universe may be established that no longer depends on what is plausible in the view of the dominant culture.

So, to ask Brecht's question again, what is changed by the ethics of Hebrews? It is the referential system, the social self-definition, and the practical horizon of faith. In short, the faithful are "changed."

"Furthermore, their first lawgiver persuaded them that they are all brothers of one another after they have transgressed once for all by denying the Greek gods and by worshipping that crucified sophist himself and living according to his laws." Let us consider Lucian's satirical comment from the point of view of the sociology of knowledge.[56]

The interpretation above has revealed how Hebrews works out structures of legitimation in order to establish and safeguard an autonomous sub-universe of both referential and social interrelationships that provide the individual Christians with an order of meaning. It is this cognitive, normative, and emotional orientation that is of ethical relevance, either directly in the biographical process of the second socialization or indirectly by means of habitualization and institutionalization.[57] It goes without saying that Hebrews relativizes

---

[55] See Popkes, *Paränese*, 42–44.

[56] For the following reflections, see Peter L. Berger and Thomas Luckmann, *The Social Construction of Reality: A Treatise in the Sociology of Knowledge* (London: Penguin, 1991), esp. 97–146, 157–166. This treatise may in part be read as a sociological comment on the ethics of Hebrews. Therefore the recent monograph by Salevao (*Legitimation*, esp. 170–249) enters a very important field, though I seriously doubt if it takes the right way by reaffirming the classical relapse theory. For critical discussion of the sociology of knowledge approach, see ibid., 11–94; Attridge, "Paraenesis," 217–221 (reserved); deSilva, *Perseverance*, 7–16; recently, with a problematic interpretative framework, Johnson, *Going Outside the Camp*; in general, Leo G. Perdue, "The Social Character of Paraenesis and Paraenetic Literature," *Semeia* 50 (1990): 5–39.

[57] Legitimation and socialization should not be considered as different functions of paraenesis. Rather, the difference lies in the point of view: legitimation provides

the significant values of the dominant culture in this way so that in the view of those responsible for the definition of society this different sub-universe will be separationist and esoteric.

This explains why the reasons Hebrews puts forward in support of the ethical exhortations seem to be loosely and unsystematically connected. The author is less concerned to give ethics a logically coherent foundation than to give those who are going to practice the ethics an inward homeland secured by multiple reference: harsh sanction[58] against conversion to the competing system, arousing both *metus* and *spes* in order to give emotional support to social boundaries (cf. Heb 6:4–8 and 6:9; 10:26–31 and 10:39);[59] allusions to the experience of transcendence and group solidarity; references to scripture; historical insights and moral examples; imagery of athletics and battle. The symbolic world of the theological exposition and the paraenetically stimulated practice prove to be interdependent: Practice that seems to be trivial at first sight turns out to be profound from the perspective of eternity; social functions that serve group maintenance obtain points of orientation and motivation; the "significant others" substantiate and limit their claims in view of the "Son and high priest" or God as the "significant other" per se; the individual death may be integrated within a meaningful reality (cf. Heb 2:15); history is ordered in a cohesive unity that includes the cognitive "ancestors," present collective experience, and the hoped-for reality of the generation that is to come, so that the individual may transcend the finitude of isolated existence (cf. Heb 11:1–12:2); "an inferior ontological status, and thereby a not-to-be-taken-seriously cognitive status,"[60] is assigned to competitive definitions of reality (cf. e.g., Heb 7:11–28; 8:1–13). Religious "alternation"[61] as a comprehensive form

---

the relevant social segment with a conceptual machinery of objective reality; and (second) socialization arranges the subjective internalization of this reality and the role-specific activity it demands. On the social setting of the community of Hebrews, see the important insights of Craig R. Koester, *Hebrews* (AB 36; New York: Doubleday, 2001), 64–79.

[58] The violence of this defensive procedure seems to be proportional to the seriousness with which the threat caused by the alternative reality was felt; cf. Berger and Luckmann, *Social Construction*, 104–105, 175–176.

[59] On the problem of sin, which is not systematically developed in Hebrews, see Löhr, *Umkehr und Sünde*, 11–135; on the "impossibility of second penitence" see ibid., 215–235; from a sociological point of view, Salevao, *Legitimation*, 250–338.

[60] Berger and Luckmann, *Social Construction*, 132.

[61] See Berger and Luckmann, *Social Construction*, 176–182.

of second socialization rebounds on the individual's home reality by reshaping familial ethos and rearranges knowledge of world and history within the new system of reference (cf. Heb 5:11–6:3).[62] This extensive counter-definition of reality is summed up in the way Hebrews reorganizes the ethical patterns of social acceptance.

3.2. *Transformation of Social Acceptance*

Individuals as well as groups that are, by religious conversion, widely disconnected from the dominant plausibility structure will develop their own value system, which may be considered as an elaborate counter-world of the home reality that has been abandoned. From an external point of view, those values may seem subversive, but within the community they strengthen both self-awareness and immunity to social ostracism and to the rejection of their own identity concept by the dominant culture.

Lucian (*Peregr.* 12–13) remarks that having been thrown into prison gave Peregrinus "no little reputation" (οὐ μικρὸν αὐτῷ ἀξίωμα περιεποίησεν), while the Christians "despised" property and death (καταφρονέω). This observation draws our attention to a basic revaluation of ἀξίωμα that is mirrored in the ethics of Hebrews. Fixing public worth and social acceptance, the pivotal values "honor" and "shame" are the core determinants in the group life of Mediterranean culture in the first century.[63] It is this value system that Hebrews consistently redefines.[64]

Thus the epistle focuses on the minority status of Christians. In previous persecution they were "made a public spectacle through reproaches and afflictions" (ὀνειδισμοῖς τε καὶ θλίψεσιν θεατριζόμενοι) because of their "illumination" (φωτισθέντες) or they shared the fate of those who were treated in this way (Heb 10:32–33). "Shame"

---

[62] On the instruction presupposed in Heb 5:11–6:3, see Thompson, *Beginnings*, 17–40; Löhr, *Umkehr und Sünde*, 164–187; Wilhelm Thüsing, "'Milch' und 'feste Speise' (1Kor 3,1f und Hebr 5,11–6,3): Elementarkatechese und theologische Vertiefung in neutestamentlicher Sicht," in *Studien*, 23–56.

[63] See David A. deSilva, *The Hope of Glory: Honor Discourse and New Testament Interpretation* (Collegeville: Liturgical Press, 1999); Joseph Plevnik, "Honor/ Shame," in *Social Values*, 106–115; Malina, *New Testament World*, 27–57; a more (and probably too) skeptical view is taken by F. Gerald Downing, "'Honor' among Exegetes," *CBQ* 61 (1999): 53–73.

[64] For details, see the instructive monograph by deSilva, *Despising Shame*, esp. 145–208; summarized in David A. deSilva, "Despising Shame: A Cultural-Anthropological Investigation of the Epistle to the Hebrews," *JBL* 113 (1994): 439–461.

proves to be an identity marker of being a Christian: Moses, a prototype of faith, already deemed the "shame of Christ" to be "wealth greater than the treasures of Egypt," therefore leaving the land of exile like one seeing Him who is unseen (Heb 11:24–27). The call for social exodus at Heb 13:13–14 is specified by a participle that depicts the Christians bearing the "shame" of Jesus (τὸν ὀνειδισμὸν αὐτοῦ φέροντες), because with him they find both the *polis* that remains and their real "civic pride." The initiator and perfecter of faith, Christ, is the example of being a Christian because he has endured the cross despising (καταφρονέω) shame and disregarding all the hostility to himself "on the part of sinners" (cf. Heb 12:2–3).

It is at this point that Hebrews refers to the totally different, viz. heavenly, system of values: all the splendor of power is transposed to the cross, which has to all appearances been the place of ultimate humiliation.[65] The *mors turpissima crucis* is revealed as an act of enthronement to the right hand of God, and here the central passages present Jesus to the readers (Heb 1:3, 8; 4:16; 8:1; 10:12–13) as being superior to the angelic retinue (Heb 1:5–14) and crowned with glory (δόξα) and honor (τιμή) (Heb 2:7, 9; cf. 3:3; 5:4–5; 13:21). When those who belong to him follow him, they will obtain their own *doxa* (Heb 2:10), for he will not be ashamed (ἐπαισχύνεται) to call them "brethren" (Heb 2:11), thereby changing them into "partakers of a heavenly calling" (Heb 3:1).

Thus Hebrews redefines the standards that provide social acknowledgement (ἀξίωμα) and so transforms the values that give orientation to ethical practice. The "court of reputation"[66] for those who "approach" is no longer the plausibility structure of the urban majority but God as the founder of the better or heavenly homeland (cf. Heb 11:8–16).

In ironical reversal of the conventional standards, God is not ashamed (ἐπαισχύνεται) to be called the God of those who believe in him (Heb 11:16), and the world is not worthy of those it considers to be marginal (Heb 11:38). Public opinion loses any relevance as

---

[65] See Otto Kuss, "Der theologische Grundgedanke des Hebräerbriefes: Zur Deutung des Todes Jesu im Neuen Testament," in idem, *Auslegung und Verkündigung* (vol. 1; Regensburg: Friedrich Pustet, 1963), 281–328, here 305–320.

[66] For this term, see Julian Pitt-Rivers, "Honour and Social Status," in *Honour and Shame: The Values of Mediterranean Society* (ed. John G. Peristiany; London: Weidenfeld and Nicolson, 1965), 19–77, here 21–39, esp. 27; for the relevance of this term to Hebrews in detail, see deSilva, *Despising Shame*, 276–313.

an ethical court, because the only court Christians allow is that of heaven (cf. Heb 13:5b–6). It is in this light that the concentration on God's reward, which is a characteristic of Hebrews and which is so often criticized,[67] should be seen: Hebrews does not aim at human reward, but acknowledgement *sub specie aeterni*.[68] It is not the Christians who are contemptible, but their shame (cf. Heb 12:2).

> The counter-definition of reality and the resultant devaluation of public opinion may find special support in the Platonic way of thought shared by Hebrews (cf. Plato, *Crito* 44c; 46c–47d; *Gorg.* 526d–527e).[69] There is an illuminating parallel in the first contact between Platonizing philosophy and Roman *pietas* in the *Somnium Scipionis* dealing with the very subject of true reward. Glory among people (*ista hominum gloria*), Scipio Africanus maior tells his grandson from his eternal point of view, is of little value compared to infinity: "If you will only look on high and contemplate this eternal home and resting place, you will no longer attend to the gossip of the vulgar herd or put your trust in human rewards for your exploits. Virtue herself, by her own charms, should lead you on to true glory (*ad verum decus*). Let what others say of you be their own concern; whatever it is, they will say it in any case. But all their talk is limited to those narrow regions which you look upon, nor will any man's reputation endure very long, for what men say dies with them and is blotted out with the forgetfulness of posterity." To this Aemilianus responds: "If indeed a path to heaven (*limes ad caeli aditum*), as it were, is open to those who have served their country well, henceforth I will redouble my efforts, spurred on by so splendid a reward (*tanto praemio exposito*)!" (Cicero, *Resp.* 6:23/25–6:24/26; Keyes, LCL).[70]

Faith according to Hebrews is Christian loyalty towards this invisible universe, a loyalty based on the "things unseen" that have been proved (Heb 11:1). The internalized standard this "court of reputation" applies is the Christian's συνείδησις (Heb 9:9, 14; 10:2, 22;

---

[67] Völkl, *Christ und Welt*, 358–359; Herbert Braun, "Die Gewinnung der Gewissheit in dem Hebräerbrief," *TLZ* 96 (1971): 321–330, here 322–323, 330; Schulz, *Neutestamentliche Ethik*, 633–635; Schrage, *Ethik des Neuen Testaments*, 326–327.

[68] A sociological approach may show that the motif of reward has a function of its own in the Roman patron-client relationship; see in detail deSilva, *Despising Shame*, 209–275, 304–307; deSilva, *Perseverance*, 59–64.

[69] See deSilva, *Despising Shame*, 82–86, 320.

[70] For interpretation, see Karl Büchner, *M. Tullius Cicero: De re publica: Kommentar* (Heidelberg: Winter, 1984), 435–508, esp. 484–502; on our passage also Michael von Albrecht, *Meister römischer Prosa von Cato bis Apuleius* (2d ed.; Heidelberg: Lambert Schneider, 1983), 127–137.

13:18).⁷¹ It is conscience that marks the inner commitment to the value system once accepted; "purified" and "perfected," it leads the individual as well as the community into God's immediate presence.⁷² It is not a moral change only that is at stake here, but the comprehensive orientation of mind, heart, and practice according to God's sanctity, a fundamental renewal within the magnetic field of a heaven that has been opened by Christ, although under the weighty conditions of everyday fidelity.⁷³ The ethics of Hebrews turns the religious question into a question of life, a point of honor, and a matter for conscience.

Peter L. Berger entitled his classic treatise on the sociology of religious knowledge *A Rumor of Angels*. He was inspired by a verse from the final paraenesis of Hebrews, which has so often been a subject of exegetical criticism: "Do not forget hospitality, for through this some have inadvertently entertained angels" (Heb 13:2).⁷⁴ Berger shows that the consciousness of secularism, as any other plausibility structure, is no absolute taken-for-granted certitude. The consistent relativizers will in the end of all relativizing relativize their own thinking. The way, therefore, is open to set out to explore those rumors of angels and to follow them up to their source.

---

⁷¹ On συνείδησις in Hebrews, see Grässer, *An die Hebräer*, 2:136–139; deSilva, *Perseverance*, 300–301; on conscience being an inward court in Philo, see Walther Völker, *Fortschritt und Vollendung bei Philo von Alexandrien: Eine Studie zur Geschichte der Frömmigkeit* (TU 49/1; Leipzig: Hinrichs, 1938), 95–105; Christian Maurer, "σύνοιδα, συνείδησις," *TWNT* 7 (1964): 897–918, here 910–912; David Winston, "Philo's Ethical Theory," *ANRW* 21.1: 372–416, here 389–391.

⁷² On the complex term τελείωσις, which must not be reduced to a concept of moral development, see David Peterson, *Hebrews and Perfection: An Examination of the Concept of Perfection in the "Epistle to the Hebrews"* (SNTSMS 47; Cambridge: Cambridge University Press, 1982), esp. 126–167; Scholer, *Proleptic Priests*, 185–200; Löhr, *Umkehr und Sünde*, 276–285; deSilva, *Perseverance*, 194–204. On perfection in Philo, see Völker, *Fortschritt und Vollendung*, esp. 318–350; for comparison with Hebrews, see Charles E. Carlston, "The Vocabulary of Perfection in Philo and Hebrews," in *Unity and Diversity in New Testament Theology: Essays in Honor of George E. Ladd* (ed. Robert A. Guelich; Grand Rapids: Eerdmans, 1978), 133–160.

⁷³ See also Horst Nitschke, "Das Ethos des wandernden Gottesvolks: Erwägungen zu Hebr. 13 und zu den Möglichkeiten evangelischer Ethik," *MPTh* 46 (1957): 179–183, esp. 179–180. A sensitive observation is contributed by Thomas G. Long, "Bold in the Presence of God," *Int* 52 (1998): 53–69, here 63: "Every event in the visible world, every experience, every seemingly tangible reality is attached to a cord of words that leads behind the curtain, and only there, in what cannot be seen, is the truth. That is why 'we must pay greater attention to what we have heard...' (2:1)."

⁷⁴ Peter L. Berger, *A Rumor of Angels: Modern Society and the Rediscovery of the Supernatural* (Garden City: Doubleday, 1970), 95.

In Berger's view, this endeavor will start with basic human experience that leads to an inductive theology revealing "in, with, and under" religious projection the crucial dimension of transcendence. Wherever the construction of reality is oriented in the light of a symbolic universe that is not a room closed to the world outside but has open windows for the realization of transcendence, everyday life will burst its limits and its truly "other" reality will be rediscovered. The moral challenge of the moment is not dispelled in this way. On the contrary, each human gesture in the everyday dramas of life, however meaningless it may seem, becomes infinitely meaningful and gains an immeasurable ethical relevance. In the midst of human affairs we "entertain angels," keepers of transcendence in a disenchanted world. The theological mountain is in labor—and what is born is an ethical universe.

Prof. Dr. theol. Knut Backhaus
Lehrstuhl für neutestamentliche Exegese und biblische Hermeneutik
Ludwig-Maximilians-Universität München
Katholisch-Theologische Fakultät
Geschwister-Scholl-Platz 1, D-80539 München, Germany
knut.backhaus@kaththeol.uni-muenchen.de

THE INTERSECTION OF ALIEN STATUS AND CULTIC DISCOURSE IN THE EPISTLE TO THE HEBREWS

Benjamin Dunning

1. *Introduction*

What made Mormons different? In his innovative study, *Religious Outsiders and the Making of Americans*, R. Laurence Moore examines the motif of outsiderhood as a self-designation for religious groups in 19th- and 20th-century America. Of particular interest is his chapter on the early days of the Church of Jesus Christ of Latter-Day Saints and the hostile polemic surrounding the group. Here Moore poses a simple but critical query: *why* did "most everyone who wrote about Joseph Smith's church [in the 19th century], and above all this included the Mormons themselves, [assert] that Mormons were not like other Americans"?[1] What exactly was so different about this group? Perhaps even more to the point, what made Mormon difference so significant in 19th-century America?

Potential "objective" answers to this question may seem straightforward: polygamy, perceived "sectarian" behavior, theological innovations, and so on. Yet when we take into account the movement's birth in "an era fecund in religious inventiveness," the issue becomes decidedly more complex.[2] As Moore perceptively points out,

---

[1] R. Laurence Moore, *Religious Outsiders and the Making of Americans* (Oxford: Oxford University Press, 1986), 27.

[2] Moore, *Religious Outsiders*, 29. We should note that polygamy was not practiced by a large majority of 19th-century Mormons and did not become a significant part of polemical literature against the group until over a decade after its founding. As Moore notes, "Interestingly, other American religious groups that adopted distinct sexual practices and followed them consistently, the Shakers and the Oneida 'perfectionists,' for example, were far less persecuted than the Mormons. In assembling a historical reality, one need not abandon the reasonable proposition that the practice of plural marriage constituted one difference between Mormons and other Americans. The problem is that this difference took on rather greater significance, and led to far greater conflict, than any objective difference in value system would have warranted." As for other "peculiarities of the Mormon faith," the early Mormon position contained significant theological novelty but "was generally in line with other liberalizing trends that provoked religious controversy [but *not* scandalized

"a generation that read almost daily about the claims of various men and women to new religious revelation might have been expected to greet Joseph Smith's Book of Mormon more calmly than one vociferous part of it did."[3] The question this raises for the study of the Latter-Day Saints is this: how can one account for the historical and cultural *significance* of perceived Mormon difference?

In light of this dilemma, Moore concludes that any attempt to mount an "objective" case for Mormon difference proves unhelpful and is best abandoned. Instead, he contends:[4]

> Mormons were different because they *said* they were different and because their claims ... prompted others to agree and to treat them as such. The notion of Mormon difference, that is, was a deliberate invention elaborated over time ... [By declaring their outsider status,] they built a usable social identity for themselves. (italics added)

Moore thus highlights the role that a discourse of outsiderhood played in forming communal religious identity against the backdrop of a disorienting array of religious options in 19th-century America. To put it bluntly, the early Mormon community put this discourse to work in order to construct and maintain their distinctive religious identity in a confusingly pluralistic universe.

Indeed, recent scholarship has examined the ways in which the very category of "otherness" functions not to demarcate essentialized difference but rather to define social *relationships* in a particular way—i.e., to accomplish a social function in a given cultural context with respect to that which is marked as "other." As Jonathan Z. Smith has pointed out, the issue at stake is not really difference but rather proximity: how a group marks out its own sense of self over and against those who are too much like it. In Smith's memorable phrase, "'Otherness,' whether of Scotsmen or lice, is a preeminently political matter."[5] By inventing themselves as the outsiders with respect to American culture, the early Mormons were in fact able to construct a powerful notion of *insiderness*—one that served both to define/protect the boundaries of community identity and also to reinforce

---

outcry] in the 19th century. Theologically, in fact, Mormonism was in its beginnings a dull affair." See Moore, *Religious Outsiders*, 28–30.

[3] Moore, *Religious Outsiders*, 29.

[4] Moore, *Religious Outsiders*, 31, 46.

[5] Jonathan Z. Smith, "What a Difference a Difference Makes," in *"To See Ourselves As Others See Us": Christians, Jews, "Others" in Late Antiquity* (ed. Jacob Neusner and Ernest S. Frerichs; Chico, Calif.: Scholars Press, 1985), 10.

communal solidarity against the threat of the overly proximate in 19th-century America.

If we turn now to another dizzyingly diverse socio-religious world, that of Greco-Roman antiquity, might we see tantalizing textual traces of a similar dynamic at work in a set of burgeoning socio-religious movements commonly lumped under the rubric of "early Christianity"? Particularly noteworthy is the use of what I will label "alien rhetoric"—the early Christian appeal to language of sojourning, foreignness and alien status as a means of self-designation.[6] Although this motif is used extensively in several early Christian texts, I will focus here on its deployment in the Epistle to the Hebrews.[7] I will pay particular attention to how this language functions strategically to construct a "usable social identity" for a socio-religious movement seeking to define itself not simply vis-à-vis a singular other such as "Judaism" (itself a reified scholarly construct), but rather with respect to the vast range of social, philosophical, and cultic identities and practices that proliferated in the Roman world. In other words, even as the Latter-Day Saints made use of a discourse of outsiderhood to invent and maintain a certain type of communal identity, so also early Christians were able, in a vastly different cultural context, to utilize the language of alien status to achieve similar ends.

---

[6] "Rhetoric" is used here in the more general sense (that is, the use of language for persuasive means) rather than the narrower sense of ancient rhetoric. For a discussion of ancient rhetorical categories in relationship to Hebrews and other ancient literature, see David A. deSilva, *Perseverance in Gratitude: A Socio-Rhetorical Commentary on the Epistle "to the Hebrews"* (Grand Rapids: Eerdmans, 2000), 39–58.

[7] For broader studies of the stranger and alien motif in early Christianity, see Reinhard Feldmeier, "The 'Nation' of Strangers: Social Contempt and its Theological Interpretation in Ancient Judaism and Early Christianity," in *Ethnicity and the Bible* (ed. M. G. Brett; Leiden: Brill, 1996); Eckhard Plümacher, *Identitätsverlust und Identitätsgewinn: Studien zum Verhältnis von kaiserzeitlicher Stadt und frühem Christentum* (BibS(N) 11; Neukirchen-Vluyn: Neukirchener, 1987). Also note that the scholarly focus on this motif in early Christianity has centered around discussion of 1 Peter. See in particular John H. Elliott, *A Home for the Homeless: A Sociological Exegesis of 1 Peter, its Situation and Strategy* (Philadelphia: Fortress, 1981); Reinhard Feldmeier, *Die Christen als Fremde: Die Metapher der Fremde in der antiken Welt, im Urchristentum und im 1. Petrusbrief* (Tübingen: Mohr Siebeck, 1992). For a catalogue of relevant references in the patristic literature through the third century, see J. Roldanus, "Références patristiques au 'chrétien-étranger' dans les trois premiers siècles," *CBP* 1 (1987): 27–52.

2. From Abraham to "Us": Alien Rhetoric as Paraenetic Strategy in Hebrews

In terms of the larger thematic and theological concerns of Hebrews as a whole, Ernst Käsemann was the first scholar to draw attention to the wandering people of God as a key motif for understanding the text in its entirety: "Faith thus becomes a confident wandering ... in every age faith's wandering must be a march through a zone of conflict and death, and it is clearly shown in the example of Jesus ... God's people traverse [this zone] for the sake of the Word."[8] While Käsemann is no doubt correct about the importance of this theme for understanding Hebrews, his study does not examine in depth the sub-theme that emerges in Heb 11—the explicit use of alien rhetoric, i.e., the language of sojourning, strangeness, foreignness, and alien status:

> By faith Abraham obeyed, when he was called to go forth to a place which he was going to receive as an inheritance; and he went out, not knowing where he was going. By faith he sojourned in the land of the promise, as in a foreign land, dwelling in tents along with Isaac and Jacob, those fellow-heirs of the same promise. For he was waiting expectantly for the city having foundations whose artisan and builder is God.... In faith, all these people died, not having received the promises. But they saw them and greeted them from a distance. And they confessed that they were strangers and sojourners on the earth. For those who say such things make it clear that they are seeking a homeland. And if they were reminiscing about that [land] from which they had departed, they would have had a time to return. But as it stands, they long for a better [homeland], that is, a heavenly one. Therefore God is not ashamed to be called their God; for he has prepared a city for them. (Heb 11:8–10, 13–16)[9]

In this pericope, Hebrews carefully constructs the character of Abraham as "the *paroikos* 'par excellence.'"[10] By designating Abraham as a

---

[8] Ernst Käsemann, *The Wandering People of God: An Investigation of the Letter to the Hebrews* (trans. Roy A. Harrisville and Irving L. Sandberg; Minneapolis: Augsburg, 1984), 44. Note also William G. Johnsson's study, which builds on Käsemann's work, examining the (closely-related) pilgrimage motif in Hebrews through exegesis of the relevant texts. See William G. Johnsson, "The Pilgrimage Motif in the Book of Hebrews," *JBL* 97 (1978): 239–251.

[9] Translations from Hebrews and other ancient sources are my own.

[10] P. J. Arowele, "The Pilgrim People of God—An African's Reflections on the Motif of Sojourn in the Epistle to the Hebrews," *AJT* 4 (1990): 441. For a thorough examination of the meaning and use of πάροικος in Greco-Roman antiquity, see Elliott's discussion with respect to 1 Peter in John H. Elliott, *1 Peter: A New*

πάροικος or "resident alien," the text is making a characterization that resonates with the LXX.[11] Yet simply appealing to the LXX connection does little to illuminate the *function* of Abraham as πάροικος in the Hebrews pericope.[12] Indeed the story of Abraham the sojourner, while clearly associated with the Septuagint, could be used in a variety of ways in antiquity, often ones that explicitly downplayed its sojourner/alien aspect.

For example, Philo characterizes Abraham's arrival in the land of promise as "just like having come back from a foreign land to his own country" (καθάπερ ἀπὸ τῆς ξένης εἰς τὴν οἰκείαν ἐπανιών).[13] Similarly, in *Jewish Antiquities*, Josephus only mentions that Abraham "settled" (κατῴκησε, 1.154; cf. also 1.157) in Canaan.[14] In Reinhard Feldmeier's analysis,[15]

Translation with Introduction and Commentary (AB 37b; New York: Doubleday, 2000), 476–483; Elliott, *Home for the Homeless*, 24–49. These discussions pay particular attention to Hellenistic sources from Asia Minor, the LXX and New Testament texts. Elliott draws on this impressive array of sources to argue that the vast majority of the term's occurrences reflect a political-legal sense of "being or living as a resident alien in a foreign environment or away from home." See Elliott, *Home for the Homeless*, 35. Thus Elliott argues that πάροικος and its cognates function generally and in 1 Peter as technical terms for a legal status based on a lack of citizenship, irrespective of religious considerations. Note however, that while Elliott is adamant that the use of sojourning language in 1 Peter signifies the technical social status of its audiences, he allows for its metaphorical usage in Hebrews, citing its "Platonic cosmological perspective." See Elliott, *Home for the Homeless*, 55. Be that as it may, pinning down a singular and monological "meaning" for πάροικος or any other relevant alien terminology is less helpful for this project, given our concern with the *function* of this rhetoric in a particular text.

[11] Notably Gen 17:8, in which God explicitly promises to give to Abraham and his descendants the land of Canaan where Abraham currently sojourns as a resident alien (καὶ δώσω σοι καὶ τῷ σπέρματί σου μετὰ σὲ τὴν γῆν, ἣν παροικεῖς, πᾶσαν τὴν γῆν Χανααν). Also Gen 23:4, in which Abraham exclaims to the Hittites, "I am a resident alien and sojourner among you" (Πάροικος καὶ παρεπίδημος ἐγώ εἰμι μεθ' ὑμῶν).

[12] Here I follow post-structuralist critiques of a general source/origin orientation towards textual analysis, well expressed by Michel Foucault in his problematizing of "the notion of influence, which provides a support—of too magical a kind to be very amenable to analysis—for the facts of transmission and communication; which refers to an apparently causal process (but with neither rigorous delimitation nor theoretical definition) the phenomena of resemblance or repetition." Michel Foucault, *The Archaeology of Knowledge and the Discourse on Language* (trans. A. M. Sheridan Smith; New York: Pantheon, 1972), 21.

[13] Philo, *Abr.* 62.

[14] We should not overplay this point, given that κατοικέω is the same verb used in Heb 11:9 to refer to Abraham, Isaac and Jacob dwelling in tents in the land of promise. However, when each passage is looked at in context (especially given the reference to a transient dwelling place such as a tent in the case of Hebrews), the contrast seems clear.

[15] Feldmeier, "'Nation' of Strangers," 247–248.

> Quite deliberately, then, *living in the land as situation of fulfilled promise is contrasted with the existence as strangers*. The corollary of this is that in its own land Israel is not a sojourner at all, but a full citizen, designated as such by God. This connection is so close that even the foreignness of the patriarchs, so frequently emphasized in the book of Genesis, is suppressed and the text is emended accordingly ... Thus Josephus also plays down the foreignness of Abraham, and instead emphasizes that he *lived in the land, left it to his descendants, and possessed it*.

Even in an early Christian context such as *1 Clem.* 10, we can see a use of the Abraham story that makes similar choices, highlighting Abraham's faithful obedience (*1 Clem.* 10.1–2, 7) and his future inheritance of the land (*1 Clem.* 10.4) but not his sojourning status at any point during the narrative. Thus, in our analysis of the Abraham narrative in Heb 11, we need to examine not just its connection to the Septuagint, but also what is at stake in the specific ways in which the pericope builds its own distinctive narrative using the cultural material at its disposal.

In this particular telling, Abraham is introduced as an exemplar of faithful submission: having been called, he obeyed and went out by faith, even though he was ignorant of where he was going (Heb 11:8, Πίστει καλούμενος Ἀβραάμ ὑπήκουσεν ἐξελθεῖν εἰς τόπον ὃν ἤμελλεν λαμβάνειν εἰς κληρονομίαν, καὶ ἐξῆλθεν μὴ ἐπιστάμενος ποῦ ἔρχεται). Thus the discussion from the outset is couched not only in terms of faith (the motif that serves as an anaphoric structuring device throughout the chapter) but also of Abraham's *obedience*. As an act of ὑπακοή, Abraham enters into the new status and identity which the text is about to explicate.

In Heb 11:9, the explicit construction of Abraham as alien begins in earnest. The patriarch's faithful obedience to God's call is characterized in terms of sojourning—living in the land divinely promised to him as though it were foreign (Πίστει παρῴκησεν εἰς γῆν τῆς ἐπαγγελίας ὡς ἀλλοτρίαν). At this point, however, the text makes clear that the sojourning motif has a larger function than simply to describe the particular character of Abraham. Accordingly, Hebrews spreads its net a little wider, designating not only Abraham but also Isaac and Jacob as those who dwelled in tents, evoking imagery of nomadic transience (ἐν σκηναῖς κατοικήσας μετὰ Ἰσαὰκ καὶ Ἰακώβ); Isaac and Jacob are included not simply as fellow tent-dwellers but also as fellow-heirs (τῶν συγκληρονόμων τῆς ἐπαγγελίας τῆς αὐτῆς). With the addition of these two figures to the motif, the *social* function of the sojourning motif comes into view. The implications are communal, constructing an identity for a multigenerational group of people (Abraham, Isaac and Jacob), not simply the Abraham figure.[16]

Of course on one level, all the heroes in the catalogue of Heb 11 have larger communal implications. As David A. deSilva points out, the example list "is calculated to rouse emulation by praising the figures of the past who have attained honorable memory."[17] Hearers of the text are meant to identify with the individuals being listed and emulate their positive character traits. Thus figures such as Abel, Enoch, and Noah all display characteristics of faithfulness (righteous "sacrifice," belief in God's existence, condemnation for the world, etc., Heb 11:4–5, 7) that the audience of the text as a whole is supposed to imitate—through the actions of the *individuals* who comprise that audience.

We see a similar dynamic at work in another early Christian catalogue of heroes, found in chapters 9–13 of *1 Clement* (ca. 93–97 CE). Here the text's readers are instructed to look intently upon those who have perfectly rendered service to God's magnificent glory (*1. Clem.* 9.2, ἀτενίσωμεν εἰς τοὺς τελείως λειτουργήσαντας τῇ μεγαλοπρεπεῖ δόξῃ αὐτοῦ [Ehrman, LCL]). *1 Clement* then takes its readers on an excursion into this "looking intently," reminding us that Enoch was found righteous in obedience (*1. Clem.* 9.3, ὃς ἐν ὑπακοῇ δίκαιος εὑρεθείς), Noah faithful through his service (*1. Clem.* 9.4, πιστὸς εὑρεθεὶς διὰ τῆς λειτουργίας αὐτοῦ), and Abraham faithful in his obedience (*1. Clem.* 10.1, πιστὸς εὑρέθη ἐν τῷ αὐτὸν ὑπήκοον γενέσθαι). A bit further on, it informs us, through essentially synonymous expressions, that on account of faith/piety and hospitality, Abraham was given a son (*1. Clem.* 10.7, διὰ πίστιν καὶ φιλοξενίαν) and both Lot and Rahab were saved (*1. Clem.* 11.1, διὰ φιλοξενίαν καὶ εὐσέβειαν; *1. Clem.* 12.1, διὰ πίστιν καὶ φιλοξενίαν).

It is clear that these descriptions in *1 Clement* function not just to convey information about each particular character but also to draw out individual paraenetic implications for the text's readers. This

---

[16] Note also that this move continues to shape the patriarchal sojourning narrative to Hebrews' particular ends. Contrast this to the assertion of Gen 37:1, for example, that Jacob settled in the land in which his father sojourned (κατῴκει δὲ Ιακωβ ἐν τῇ γῇ, οὗ παρῴκησεν ὁ πατὴρ αὐτοῦ).

[17] deSilva, *Perseverance*, 380.

broader thrust is made explicit in *1 Clem.* 11.1 with the more general application of Lot's deliverance: "On account of his hospitality and piety, Lot was saved out of Sodom, when the entire region was judged by fire and sulfur; when he did so, the Master made clear that he does not forsake those who hope in him, but consigns to punishment and torment those who have other allegiance" (Διὰ φιλοξενίαν καὶ εὐσέβειαν Λὼτ ἐσώθη ἐκ Σοδόμων, τῆς περιχώρου πάσης κριθείσης διὰ πυρὸς καὶ θείου, πρόδηλον ποιήσας ὁ δεσπότης, ὅτι τοὺς ἐλπίζοντας ἐπ' αὐτὸν οὐκ ἐγκαταλείπει, τοὺς δὲ ἑτεροκλινεῖς ὑπάρχοντας εἰς κόλασιν καὶ αἰκισμὸν τίθησιν). Thus these examples are not simply descriptive or of passing narrative interest, but also have contemporary theological and paraenetic relevance for the text's readers.

On the other hand, the comparison with *1 Clement* helps us to see an additional hermeneutical move that Heb 11 is making in the Abraham pericope. Both texts set out a series of historical exemplars whose laudable actions are intended for practical appropriation by readers, both individually and communally. However, in contrast to *1 Clem.* 9–13, Heb 11 also places an explicit emphasis on community, constructing a discourse of common identity.[18] Here Pamela M. Eisenbaum has drawn attention to another function of what she terms "a multi-dimensional hero list": "to explain and legitimate the existence of the community which is being addressed, by grounding the members of that community in a significant genealogical history."[19]

Consequently, it is not just the figure of Abraham, or even Abraham, Isaac, and Jacob who are in view. Rather, the patriarchs function as representatives of a much broader vision of lineage—one that allows for the application of the sojourning motif (and also the promise of the eschatological city introduced in Heb 11:10) beyond these three figures to the audience who will claim this sacred history as their own. Indeed, opening up the sojourning motif in this way

---

[18] Here I reluctantly resort to reference to a "community" as a stylistic convention in order to highlight the social and collective implications of the rhetorical strategy found in the text. This should in no way be equated with the standard move so common within New Testament scholarship to imagine distinct and reified communities each represented and reflected by a particular text—i.e., I am not positing a "Hebrews Christianity" or even a singular "Hebrews community." Rather, I am using the term "community" with a view to the rhetoric's function for communal identity formation, a usage that allows for the fluidity of multiple audiences and reading contexts.

[19] Pamela M. Eisenbaum, *The Jewish Heroes of Christian History: Hebrews 11 in Literary Context* (SBLDS 156; Atlanta: Scholars Press, 1997), 87.

appears to be pivotal to the text's purposes in employing it at all, given that this move necessarily interrupts the flow of the narrative by introducing Isaac prior to the announcement of his miraculous birth in Heb 11:11.[20] As Eisenbaum aptly summarizes, Abraham functions as an ideal example for what the text wants to convey: "separation and marginalization... The audience is part of this trajectory by implication."[21]

This conclusion is confirmed and reinforced by what follows: a series of interpretive moves that broaden the scope of Abraham's outsider status even further. Thus Heb 11:12 contrasts the one man, Abraham (ἑνός), to those begotten by him: "just as the stars of heaven in number and innumerable as the sand along the shore of the sea" (καθὼς τὰ ἄστρα τοῦ οὐρανοῦ τῷ πλήθει καὶ ὡς ἡ ἄμμος ἡ παρὰ τὸ χεῖλος τῆς θαλάσσης ἡ ἀναρίθμητος). The reference to οὗτοι πάντες or "all these ones" who have died in faith in Heb 11:13 continues this broadening function.

The precise referent of this phrase is a matter of scholarly debate. On the one hand, Harold W. Attridge is most likely correct in his contention that οὗτοι πάντες refers principally to the three patriarchs, rather than all the heroes mentioned thus far (he notes that the οὗτοι πάντες logically could not include Enoch, who did not see death, Heb 11:5, τοῦ μὴ ἰδεῖν θάνατον).[22] On the other hand, however, we ought to consider the possibility of some sort of link between the οὗτοι πάντες and the line of Abraham's descendants referenced in Heb 11:12. While the overall structure of Heb 11 (with its emphasis on individuals acting in faith) and the fact that the innumerable descendants are only described as an objective result of Abraham's faith (not subjects of their own action) make it unlikely that the descendants are meant to be the direct referent of οὗτοι πάντες, the immediate proximity of verses 12 and 13 leaves space for readers to make a loose interpretive connection between the two. Therefore, the οὗτοι πάντες can function as a rhetorical encouragement for readers (appropriating a place in this lineage as "Abraham's descendants")

---

[20] The well-known debate over the textual problems of Heb 11:11 falls beyond the scope of this inquiry.

[21] Eisenbaum, *Jewish Heroes*, 161.

[22] See Harold W. Attridge, *The Epistle to the Hebrews* (Hermeneia; Philadelphia: Fortress, 1989), 329. Note Eisenbaum's counterargument that οὗτοι πάντες refers to all the heroes mentioned up to this point; see Eisenbaum, *Jewish Heroes*, 160-161.

to see themselves and their own community in the reinforcement of identity that is to follow.

Thus the text moves on to disclose that the οὗτοι πάντες are those who died without having received the promises. Indeed they only saw them and greeted them from a distance (Heb 11:13, μὴ λαβόντες τὰς ἐπαγγελίας ἀλλὰ πόρρωθεν αὐτὰς ἰδόντες καὶ ἀσπασάμενοι). As Attridge points out, Hebrews has already made the claim in Heb 6:15 that Abraham did in fact obtain a promise (καὶ οὕτως μακροθυμήσας ἐπέτυχεν τῆς ἐπαγγελίας).[23] But this promise refers to the birth of Isaac, a fact acknowledged by Heb 11:11–12 as well. Instead a different promise is in view, the promise of land as put forth in Heb 11:9. Yet in Heb 11:13, the connotations of the sojourning motif serve to shift the focus away from the specific piece of territory known as Canaan towards a broader concept of eschatological homeland (πατρίς), mentioned explicitly in Heb 11:14: "For those who say such things make it clear that they are seeking a homeland" (οἱ γὰρ τοιαῦτα λέγοντες ἐμφανίζουσιν ὅτι πατρίδα ἐπιζητοῦσιν). Of course, this πατρίς is not yet possessed. Rather the οὗτοι πάντες confess that they are strangers and sojourners on the earth (Heb 11:13, καὶ ὁμολογήσαντες ὅτι ξένοι καὶ παρεπίδημοί εἰσιν ἐπὶ τῆς γῆς). The audience of Hebrews is meant to appropriate this communal identity.

In the larger strategy of the text, this call to take on an identity of otherness not only resonates with but also transforms earlier paraenesis and identity-constructing moves that have been made. For example, Hebrews calls its audience in chapters 3 and 4 not to be like the generation whose corpses fell in the wilderness (Heb 3:17, τὰ κῶλα ἔπεσεν ἐν τῇ ἐρήμῳ). Readers are given strict warnings not to harden their hearts (Heb 3:8, 15, μὴ σκληρύνητε τὰς καρδίας ὑμῶν) and to fear lest anyone seem to have fallen short while the promise of entering God's rest still remains (Heb 4:1, φοβηθῶμεν οὖν, μήποτε καταλειπομένης ἐπαγγελίας εἰσελθεῖν εἰς τὴν κατάπαυσιν αὐτοῦ δοκῇ τις ἐξ ὑμῶν ὑστερηκέναι). In Heb 4:11 the text offers a strong thrust of exhortation: "Let us hasten then to enter into that rest, in order that no one might fall in the same pattern of disobedience" (Σπουδάσωμεν οὖν εἰσελθεῖν εἰς ἐκείνην τὴν κατάπαυσιν, ἵνα μὴ ἐν τῷ αὐτῷ τις ὑποδείγματι πέσῃ τῆς ἀπειθείας). Thus the wilderness generation serves as a foil against which the text may more

---

[23] Attridge, *Hebrews*, 329.

effectively urge a different agenda for the community: to hold fast to their confession (Heb 4:14, κρατῶμεν τῆς ὁμολογίας; Heb 10:23, κατέχωμεν τὴν ὁμολογίαν; cf. also Heb 3:1) and enter God's rest.

But what are the contents of this confession? The three references given above offer little elucidation. Here again we come to a question that has provoked much scholarly discussion. According to Alfred Seeberg, the ὁμολογία ought to be understood as a fixed and standardized verbal confession of the community.[24] Käsemann is slightly more cautious, but does argue that "the ὁμολογία of Hebrews not only denotes the primitive Christian liturgy of the community, *but that in addition the Christology of Hebrews represents a detailed exposition and interpretation of the community's liturgical* ὁμολογία."[25] Attridge suggests a profession of faith that "took place within liturgical contexts with some formula or formulas... Given the prominence of the title 'son' in Hebrews, it is likely that the community's confession of Jesus as Son of God was involved."[26]

Of course definitive answers to this question remain historically inaccessible.[27] But irrespective of our conclusions on this issue, we ought to take note of the function of ὁμολογέω within the sojourning motif at Heb 11:13. Here the οὗτοι πάντες (that is, Abraham, Isaac, and Jacob—and, by extension, the audience of Hebrews) *confess* that they are strangers and sojourners on the earth. This is not to push Attridge's theory so far as to posit a liturgical formula within Hebrews' community that involved identification of the community as strangers and sojourners (although the possibility should not be ruled out). Rather, it is to suggest that the use of confession language in Heb 11:13 resonates backwards to the earlier uses of ὁμολογία in the text, allowing the audience to reimagine the contents of their confession in light of their identity as strangers and sojourners on the earth.

Thus holding fast (Heb 4:14, κρατῶμεν; Heb 10:23, κατέχωμεν) now becomes not simply about dogged perseverance in the face of

---

[24] Alfred Seeberg, *Der Brief an die Hebräer* (Leipzig: Quelle u. Meyer, 1912), 32.
[25] Käsemann, *Wandering*, 171. Emphasis original.
[26] Attridge, *Hebrews*, 108. See also Craig R. Koester, *Hebrews: A New Translation with Introduction and Commentary* (AB 36; New York: Doubleday, 2001), 126–127.
[27] Although of the three hypotheses, Attridge's seems most defensible, especially given Hebrews' concluding reference to "the fruit of lips that confess his name" (Heb 13:15, καρπὸν χειλέων ὁμολογούντων τῷ ὀνόματι αὐτοῦ).

perceived oppression or continued assent to certain christological propositions but also about embracing a certain understanding of social identity—choosing to identify with a community that classifies itself as outsiders. According to Craig R. Koester, the text uses the earlier calls to hold fast in order to "bolster commitments by affirming the confession that gave the group its identity."[28] Consequently, by linking the language of confession to the motif of sojourning, Hebrews is able to utilize this carefully engineered construction of its audience's marginal status as a powerful means of promoting solidarity (even as the Latter-Day Saints used their outsider status to construct a strong sense of "insiderness").

In a similar way, the various metaphors of entrance used earlier in the text are also transformed. The construction of Hebrews' audience as a community of strangers and sojourners serves to reposition them as a group in relation to the text's previous metaphors. Indeed, within the metaphorical space set up by Heb 3 and 4, the community stands on the edge of the eschatological promised land, and their window of opportunity for entrance into God's rest remains (see Heb 4:1, 6). They are called to approach the throne of grace with boldness (Heb 4:16, προσερχώμεθα οὖν μετὰ παρρησίας τῷ θρόνῳ τῆς χάριτος), possessors of a hope that enters inside the curtain (Heb 6:19, εἰσερχομένην εἰς τὸ ἐσώτερον τοῦ καταπετάσματος). In fact, the audience not only possesses this *hope*, but they have actually obtained an entrance into the sanctuary for themselves through the blood of Jesus (Heb 10:19, τὴν εἴσοδον τῶν ἁγίων ἐν τῷ αἵματι Ἰησοῦ).

Yet ironically enough, due to the text's deployment of the sojourning motif, "entrance" is now to be understood through solidarity with a community of outsiders. By verbally appropriating a self-designation as strangers and sojourners (i.e., the transformed notion of confession that we see in Heb 11:14: οἱ γὰρ τοιαῦτα λέγοντες), Abraham, Isaac, and Jacob, along with the community that they represent rhetorically, "make it clear that they seek a homeland" (Heb 11:14, ἐμφανίζουσιν ὅτι πατρίδα ἐπιζητοῦσιν). The text maintains that this "sojourner status" is one that is voluntarily assumed. Indeed, if these people had been reminiscing about the land from which they went out, they would have had opportunity to return (Heb 11:15, εἰ μὲν ἐκείνης ἐμνημόνευον ἀφ' ἧς ἐξέβησαν, εἶχον ἂν

---

[28] Koester, *Hebrews*, 293.

καιρὸν ἀνακάμψαι). But the strangers and sojourners do not seek to return.[29] The paradox implied through such a construction of their communal identity is that only as outsiders will they obtain the entrance that they seek: a better homeland, a heavenly one (Heb 11:16, κρείττονος . . . ἐπουρανίου).

Thus there is a place of "true citizenship" for Christians, a locale in which their insider status is recognized and assured. The text will partially clarify the eschatological details of how entrance to this heavenly homeland is gained in what follows (see below). However, the rhetorical emphasis remains on the outsider position of Christians in the present moment—insider status defined in alien terms. With this paradox in place, the explicit use of alien rhetoric draws to a close, via an appeal designed to reinforce and encourage solidarity: God is not ashamed to be called these people's God for he has prepared a city for them (Heb 11:16, διὸ οὐκ ἐπαισχύνεται αὐτοὺς ὁ θεὸς θεὸς ἐπικαλεῖσθαι αὐτῶν· ἡτοίμασεν γὰρ αὐτοῖς πόλιν).

3. A Hermeneutical Turn: Heb 13:13 and Ancient Cultic Discourse

Although the overt use of alien language ends here,[30] the motif continues to reverberate as a subtext throughout the rest of Heb 11 (and also the remainder of the text). Overall Eisenbaum has convincingly argued that outsiderness is "the most fundamental characteristic of the heroes of Hebrews."[31] This can be seen in multiple ways. Moses is constructed as a hero who chose outsider status (Heb 11:25–26, μᾶλλον ἑλόμενος συγκακουχεῖσθαι τῷ λαῷ τοῦ θεοῦ . . . τὸν ὀνειδισμὸν τοῦ Χριστοῦ) over the pleasures of a symbolic "citizenship" (i.e., the treasures of Egypt, τῶν Αἰγύπτου θησαυρῶν) because he was looking ahead to his reward (τὴν μισθαποδοσίαν).[32] Similarly, the finale of Heb 11 crescendos to a feverish pitch as it depicts the sufferings of the faithful and culminates in a vivid and evocative description of marginalization: "they went around in sheepskins, in

---

[29] Note the contrast between the nuance of Heb 11:15 and that of a Platonic-Philonic trajectory in which emphasis is placed on the return of the sojourning soul to the heavenly homeland from which it set out.
[30] With the exception of Heb 13:2—see discussion below.
[31] Eisenbaum, *Jewish Heroes*, 184.
[32] Here "reward" functions analogously to the various "entrance" metaphors already utilized—i.e., one gains it through solidarity with the text's constructed margins.

goat skins, in need, afflicted, ill-treated—of these people the world was not worthy—wandering about in deserts and mountains and caves and holes in the ground" (Heb 11:37–38, περιῆλθον ἐν μηλωταῖς, ἐν αἰγείοις δέρμασιν, ὑστερούμενοι, θλιβόμενοι, κακουχούμενοι, ὧν οὐκ ἦν ἄξιος ὁ κόσμος, ἐπὶ ἐρημίαις πλανώμενοι καὶ ὄρεσιν καὶ σπηλαίοις καὶ ταῖς ὀπαῖς τῆς γῆς).

Here again the solidarity of the current audience with those who have chosen this outsider status is reiterated. The heroes of Heb 11 do not achieve their entrance. As the chapter closes, they have not received the promise (Heb 11:39, οὐκ ἐκομίσαντο τὴν ἐπαγγελίαν). The text implies to its audience that God's better thing (Heb 11:40, κρεῖττόν τι) very much depends on them, because without their solidarity, this community of past "strangers and sojourners" will not be made perfect (Heb 11:40, ἵνα μὴ χωρὶς ἡμῶν τελειωθῶσιν). Hebrews' readers are called to put aside every impediment and easily besetting sin (Heb 12:1, ὄγκον ἀποθέμενοι πάντα καὶ τὴν εὐπερίστατον ἁμαρτίαν), to run the race set before them (Heb 12:1, τρέχωμεν τὸν προκείμενον ἡμῖν ἀγῶνα), and to look to Jesus in order not to grow weary (Heb 12:2–3, ἀφορῶντες εἰς τὸν τῆς πίστεως ἀρχηγὸν καὶ τελειωτὴν Ἰησοῦν ... ἵνα μὴ κάμητε). Only through these steps of identification with those sojourners who have gone before—a deliberate positioning of the Christian self as other—will entrance be obtained for all.

Thus in chapter 12, Hebrews moves back into spatial metaphors, contrasting what the community has not approached—that which can be touched and a kindled fire and darkness and gloom and storm (Heb 12:18, ψηλαφωμένῳ καὶ κεκαυμένῳ πυρὶ καὶ γνόφῳ καὶ ζόφῳ καὶ θυέλλῃ)—with what they have approached: Mount Zion and a city of the living God, heavenly Jerusalem (Heb 12:22, Σιὼν ὄρει καὶ πόλει θεοῦ ζῶντος, Ἰερουσαλὴμ ἐπουρανίῳ).[33] Here again the language of entrance is not far from view. But what is the way of this approach? How does the audience come to the heavenly mountain and the πόλις of the living God?

We do not receive an answer to this question until the final chapter of the text:[34]

---

[33] This appeal to a πόλις resonates with the notion of a "true citizenship" that seems implicit in the discussion found in Heb 11:16.

[34] The contention of some scholars that Heb 13 is a secondary addition remains unconvincing, especially given key aspects of literary unity such as will be examined below. For a brief overview, see Attridge, *Hebrews*, 384–385.

Do not be carried away by various strange teachings; for it is good that the heart be made firm by grace, not by foods, which have not benefited those who conduct themselves [in this way]. We have an altar from which those who serve in the tent do not have authority to eat. For the bodies of animals whose blood is brought into the sanctuary as a sin offering by the high priest are burned outside the camp. Therefore Jesus also suffered outside the gate in order that he might sanctify the people through his own blood. *Consequently, let us go to him outside the camp,* bearing his reproach. For here we do not have an enduring city; rather we seek after that city which is to come. Through him let us always offer up a sacrifice of praise to God; this is the fruit of lips which confess his name. Do not neglect well-doing and fellowship; for God is delighted with such sacrifices. (Heb 13:9–16, italics added)

Here Hebrews takes a key hermeneutical turn: the call to go to Jesus outside the camp, bearing his reproach (Heb 13:13, ἔξω τῆς παρεμβολῆς τὸν ὀνειδισμὸν αὐτοῦ φέροντες) serves as the overt lens through which all the previous paraenesis of the text is refracted. That is to say, Heb 13:13 functions hermeneutically to transform the text's paraenesis. How is the audience to hold fast, approach, and enter? These are metaphors steeped in the language of insider status—yet they must now be appropriated through identification with the margins (i.e., by going to Jesus outside the camp). The text's final word on drawing near does not emphasize joining Jesus in the heavenly sanctuary (Heb 9:24) but rather joining him in identification with alterity and reproach. It is the strangers and sojourners who will experience entrance into the city that is to come.[35]

Yet at the same time, this crucial hermeneutical move takes place in a specific *context*—a larger discussion that makes extensive use of cultic imagery (Heb 13:9–16). Here the text plays with the LXX's conceptual categories of the Levitical cult, drawing a strong contrast between Levitical cultic practice and the sacrifice of Jesus. Thus Attridge characterizes Heb 13:11 ("For the bodies of animals whose blood is brought into the sanctuary as a sin offering by the high priest are burned outside the camp," ὧν γὰρ εἰσφέρεται ζῴων τὸ αἷμα περὶ ἁμαρτίας εἰς τὰ ἅγια διὰ τοῦ ἀρχιερέως, τούτων τὰ σώματα κατακαίεται ἔξω τῆς παρεμβολῆς) as a "generalizing paraphrase" of the portion of the Yom Kippur ritual described in Lev 16:27–28:[36]

---

[35] Feldmeier's evaluation of a similar paradox with respect to 1 Peter seems apposite here as well: "The terms for foreignness, clearly negative from their origin, when revalued and preserved as a specific expression of Christian identity... gain positive, even elitist overtones." See Feldmeier, "'Nation' of Strangers," 258.
[36] Attridge, *Hebrews*, 397.

καὶ τὸν μόσχον τὸν περὶ τῆς ἁμαρτίας καὶ τὸν χίμαρον τὸν περὶ τῆς ἁμαρτίας, ὧν τὸ αἷμα εἰσηνέχθη ἐξιλάσασθαι ἐν τῷ ἁγίῳ, ἐξοίσουσιν αὐτὰ ἔξω τῆς παρεμβολῆς καὶ κατακαύσουσιν αὐτὰ ἐν πυρί, καὶ τὰ δέρματα αὐτῶν καὶ τὰ κρέα αὐτῶν καὶ τὴν κόπρον αὐτῶν· ὁ δὲ κατακαίων αὐτὰ πλυνεῖ τὰ ἱμάτια καὶ λούσεται τὸ σῶμα αὐτοῦ ὕδατι καὶ μετὰ ταῦτα εἰσελεύσεται εἰς τὴν παρεμβολήν

So the young bull of the sin offering and the goat of the sin offering, whose blood was brought in to be an appeasement in the sanctuary, will be brought outside the camp and they will be burned in the fire, even their skin and their meat and their dung. The one who burns them will wash his clothes and bathe his body with water and after these things, he will come into the camp.

Helmut Koester's work on Heb 13 clearly demonstrates the way in which this textual contrast operates:[37]

> Leviticus: Whoever performs the burning *outside the camp is unclean.*
> Hebrews: Jesus suffered *outside the gate* in order to *sanctify* the people.
> Leviticus: After being *sanctified* he may *enter the camp* again.
> Hebrews: Let us *go out* to him *outside of the camp* to bear his *reproach.*

Formulated in this way, we can see how Hebrews reworks elements of the Levitical tradition to highlight the *cleansing* function of Jesus' sacrifice—thereby shifting the role of the space ἔξω τῆς παρεμβολῆς. In this reading of the Levitical mandate, ἔξω τῆς παρεμβολῆς is transformed: what was once a place which created a need for cleansing prior to one's return inside has now become the site of the sacrifice that actually brings about the people's purification.

Scholars have understood the significance of this reinterpretation of Levitical tradition in a number of ways. One option is to read this passage as an allegory, privileging otherworldliness (i.e., soul over body), and often associated with Philo.[38] Thus James Moffatt argues that this text "makes a broad appeal for an unworldly religious fellowship, such as is alone in keeping with the χάρις of God in Jesus our Lord."[39] The other major alternative is to interpret the appeal to join Jesus ἔξω τῆς παρεμβολῆς as a call to leave Judaism. According to this argument, as F. F. Bruce maintains, "the 'camp' stands for

---

[37] Helmut Koester, "'*Outside The Camp*': Hebrews 13.9–14," *HTR* 55 (1962): 300.
[38] Cf. Philo, *Ebr.* 100; *Gig.* 54; *Leg.* 2.54–55; *Det.* 160.
[39] James Moffatt, *A Critical and Exegetical Commentary on the Epistle to the Hebrews* (New York: Scribner's, 1924), 235. See also, as representative: Herbert Braun, *An die Hebräer* (HNT 14; Tübingen: Mohr Siebeck, 1984), 467; Gerd Theissen, *Untersuchungen zum Hebräerbrief* (StNT 2; Gütersloh: Mohn, 1969), 104.

the established fellowship and ordinances of Judaism. To abandon them, with all their sacred associations inherited from remote antiquity, was a hard thing, but it was a necessary thing."[40]

Helmut Koester has argued against both these interpretive trajectories, suggesting that the contrast is not Philonic or anti-Jewish but rather an "anticultic antithesis": "And since the refuge in sacred places and cultic performances is abolished for those people who stay 'outside the camp' with Jesus, the sacrifices of God are rather thanksgiving and charity (Hebrews 13, 15–16)."[41] As Attridge observes, the connection between strange teachings and food in Heb 13:9 (διδαχαῖς ποικίλαις καὶ ξέναις μὴ παραφέρεσθε· καλὸν γὰρ χάριτι βεβαιοῦσθαι τὴν καρδίαν, οὐ βρώμασιν ἐν οἷς οὐκ ὠφελήθησαν οἱ περιπατοῦντες) is most likely inspired by some sort of cultic dining.[42] This would certainly seem to be sound textual support for Koester's position. However, even if Koester is correct that the contrast being articulated in Heb 13:9–16 places its primary emphasis on the generally anti-cultic rather than the specifically anti-Jewish or the Philonic, this interpretive solution does not necessarily exhaust the potential function of cultic discourse in the text.

Thus as we think about possible readers and audiences for Hebrews in the late first century, we ought to analyze the rhetorical strategy of Heb 13:9–16 not only in terms of the text's intended emphasis (Philonic otherworldliness, anti-Jewish, anti-cultic, etc.) but also in terms of the larger fields of connotation/contestation at play in the Roman Empire—fields in which an *audience* might locate this particular use of cultic discourse as it could be put to work for the larger purposes of early Christian identity formation. (Indeed it is not simply my personal methodological orientation that necessitates this move to readers and multiple interpretive possibilities; rather, the possibility of various interpretations seems to be an actual part of the text's strategy, characterized by Attridge in terms of its "deliberate ambiguity."[43]) To put it simply, what sorts of work could

---

[40] F. F. Bruce, *The Epistle to the Hebrews* (NICNT; Grand Rapids: Eerdmans, 1964), 403. Other representative examples include Floyd V. Filson, *'Yesterday': A Study of Hebrews in the Light of Chapter 13* (Naperville, Ill.: Alec R. Allenson, 1967), 60–65; Philip E. Hughes, *A Commentary on the Epistle to the Hebrews* (Grand Rapids: Eerdmans, 1977), 580.

[41] Koester, "'Outside,'" 303.

[42] See the full discussion in Attridge, *Hebrews*, 394–396.

[43] Attridge, *Hebrews*, 396.

discussions of cult do in ancient projects of identity construction?

Here an analogous example from Roman antiquity proves illustrative. Cultic practice and discourse were ubiquitous in the Roman world, "intertwined with every group, each level of a city's social existence."[44] Particularly relevant for our purposes is the discourse surrounding cults labeled as *"foreign"*—that is, in some way exterior with respect to a perceived normative center of so-called "Romanness" across the empire. On the one hand, the marker stones of the *pomerium* (the sacred boundary of the city of Rome) provided a physical boundary that helped to construct and maintain a "definitional myth": foreign cultic practice could not take place inside the city's sacred boundary.[45] Yet on the other hand, the temple of Magna Mater, a cult that represented the quintessentially "foreign," could be incorporated within the *pomerium* such that the exotic castrated *galli* became, in Mary Beard's apt phrase, "the Roman emperor's closest neighbors" on the Palatine Hill.[46]

In trying to understand the relationship between cult and outsider status with reference to Magna Mater (and foreign cults more generally), scholars have typically posited two possible solutions: either the Romans gradually domesticated foreign cults (thereby eradicating their foreignness), or they were simply ignorant of the truly foreign nature of these cults prior to incorporation.[47] In response to

---

[44] Robin L. Fox, *Pagans and Christians* (San Francisco: HarperCollins, 1986), 89.

[45] Here Beard et al. offer the example of Augustus "banning Egyptian rites within the *pomerium*—so 'restoring' (or maybe 'inventing') a principle that the worship of foreign gods should not occur within the sacred boundary of Rome"; Mary Beard et al., *Religions of Rome* (2 vols.; Cambridge: Cambridge University Press, 1998), 1:180. We also ought to note that the Roman *coloniae* in the first and second centuries CE modeled their own religious institutions on those of the capital, including the establishment of a sacred boundary. See Beard et al., *Religions of Rome*, 1:328–329. Thus the connotative significance of the *pomerium* would have extended far beyond the city of Rome itself.

[46] Mary Beard, "The Roman and the Foreign: The Cult of the 'Great Mother' In Imperial Rome," in *Shamanism, History and the State* (ed. Nicholas Thomas and Caroline Humphrey; Ann Arbor: University of Michigan Press, 1994), 181.

[47] For the former option, see the approach in Cyril Bailey, *Phases in the Religion of Ancient Rome* (Westport, Conn.: Greenwood, 1972), 183. The latter position is well expressed by Maarten J. Vermaseren: "The Romans had brought their ancestral Goddess [i.e., 'ancestral' in light of Rome's traditional connection to Troy] to the new country and provided her with proper accommodation, only then to discover how widely and profoundly their own attitude differed from the Asian mentality. They were shocked by the Eastern rites, with their loud ululations and wild dances, with their entrancing rhythms, which by pipe and tambourine whipped up the people into ecstasies of bloody self-flagellation and self-injury." Maarten J. Vermaseren,

this dichotomy, Mary Beard has argued convincingly that these conflicting aspects of discourse surrounding Roman attitudes towards "foreign" cults (evidenced by both archeological remains and texts) should not be primarily understood in terms of either option, but rather in terms of *unresolved tension*. Thus Beard sees foreign cultic discourse as a rhetorical site for struggles of identity formation; in this case, on "the nature of 'Roman-ness': on what it was to be Roman and on what could count as Roman religious experience [during the first centuries of the Common Era]—in the context of a huge and ethnically diverse empire."[48]

As we turn back to the use of cultic imagery in Heb 13:9–16, I wish to be explicit about the purpose of this example, clarifying exactly what I am trying to do (and not to do). The point is not to compare Magna Mater (or any other so-called "mystery religion") to early Christianity. It is not to draw an explicit historical parallel between the insider/outsider boundary of the *pomerium* and the placing of Jesus and Hebrews' audience outside an insider/outsider boundary in Heb 13:13.[49] Nor does this analogy necessitate following current scholarly trends to locate Hebrews in the city of Rome.[50] Indeed, while I am quite sympathetic to this position, locating the text any more specifically than in the Roman Empire in the late first century CE is irrelevant to the point I seek to make here.

Instead, I wish to highlight how Beard's creative approach to a scholarly dichotomy that posits gradual domestication or ignorance of a cult's foreign nature as the *only* two options proves illuminating to the binary opposition between literal anti-Jewish/anti-cultic antithesis and allegorical Philonic otherworldliness so often used to interpret Heb 13:9–16. That is to say, we do not necessarily have to read the contrast in this passage between the Levitical cult and the sacrifice of Jesus as either definitively anti-cultic *or* definitively allegorical/symbolic (with respect to the soul in the world) and nothing

---

Cybele and Attis: The Myth and the Cult (trans. A. M. H. Lemmers; London: Thames and Hudson, 1977), 96. See also: Franz Cumont, *The Oriental Religions in Roman Paganism* (New York: Dover, 1956), 51–53; John Ferguson, *The Religions of the Roman Empire* (Ithaca: Cornell University Press, 1970), 27; Howard H. Scullard, *Festivals and Ceremonies of the Roman Republic* (Ithaca: Cornell University Press, 1981), 21.

[48] Beard, "Roman and the Foreign," 166.

[49] Although this parallel remains a tantalizing possibility whose further exploration might prove illuminating.

[50] See discussion in Attridge, *Hebrews*, 9–13.

more. Rather we ought to note how the text picks up the *same* two motifs which Beard highlights with reference to Magna Mater—cultic discourse and outsider status—and uses their intersection in a different way.

Whereas Roman literary elites used the foreign cult of Cybele as a rhetorical site for working out the nature of "Roman-ness," leaving the issue of the cult's foreignness in unresolved tension, Heb 13 is definitive on the issue of outsider status, calling its audience to actively take on an alien or "foreign" identity by going to Jesus outside the camp; at the same time, it allows the question of cultic practice to remain in unresolved tension. On the one hand, then, the text offers an objection to teachings in some sense connected to food in Heb 13:9, as well as apparently metaphorical interpretations of "sacrifices" in Heb 13:15–16. However, on the other hand, it gives an ambiguous but nonetheless decidedly *positive* characterization of the Christians' altar (θυσιαστήριον) in Heb 13:10.[51] Thus cultic discourse in this pericope functions as a rhetorical site for working out a certain notion of "Christian-ness"—a conception of early Christian identity whose accent falls on embracing outsider status—rather than a clear and unambiguous stance on a certain type of Christian cultic practice (or lack thereof).

Therefore, the appeal to cultic imagery in Heb 13:9–16 does not necessarily function solely to allegorize or polemicize against cultic practice. Rather it places the text's critical project of identity formation in a larger connotative cultural context, one that would not have been limited to the scriptures of Israel for any given early Christian audience (despite the fact that Heb 13:9–16 relies heavily on the language and categories of Levitical tradition found in the LXX). As noted above, cultic practice and discourse were to be found everywhere in the ancient Mediterranean. Due to this ubiquity, across the Roman Empire, "religion was, and remained, good to think with," as Mary Beard points out.[52] Thus the intersection of ancient discourses on cult and foreign/alien/outsider status provided a site for diverse groups—not only elites interacting with Magna Mater in Rome but also early Christians—to construct and solidify boundaries

---

[51] Suggestions for the referent of this θυσιαστήριον have included the Eucharist, the cross (or Christ's death), and the heavenly sanctuary of Heb 8–9. See discussion in Koester, *Hebrews*, 568–569.

[52] Beard et al., *Religions of Rome*, 1:166.

of communal identity amidst the disorienting heterogeneity of the Roman world.

In Heb 13:9–16, then, we see the culmination of a project of identity construction that enters this larger conversation (at least from the reference-point of potential ancient audiences), while still making use of rhetoric and images associated with the Levitical tradition. The result, as discussed above, is a metaphorical movement to the periphery, effected in the life of the community through embracing a self-identification of alien status. One goes to Jesus outside the camp by appropriating an identity of communal "other-ness" (vis-à-vis not simply "Judaism" but amidst the much broader diversity and fluidity of socio-religious identities available in antiquity), and then re-interpreting and implementing the exhortations of the text from that "marginal" position. These exhortations include not just the paraenetic metaphors discussed above (urging the audience to enter and draw near), but also the very concrete directives found in Heb 13:1–7. Therefore the call to go "outside the camp" does not simply orient the readers towards an otherworldly city; rather, the concern extends to matters of tangible everyday life.

Seemingly traditional directives—exhortations to hospitality, care for prisoners, marital purity, finances, and imitating community leadership—are transformed by the call to go outside the camp. That is to say, these directives (read in the light of Heb 13:13) serve to constitute communal behavior in such a way as to reinforce the audience's radical sense of itself at the margins of society, while at the same time advocating a not particularly radical course of conduct—certainly not one that undermines broader social stability in any significant way.[53] As Helmut Koester has pointed out, "for Hebrews, 'outside the camp' is identical with the worldliness of the world itself."[54]

Indeed, nothing in these exhortations indicates radical or subversive engagement with the larger society. Rather, our analysis of the alien rhetoric in Hebrews has shown the function of this rhetoric to construct a *usable social identity* (to borrow Moore's phrase) for early Christian communities. The discourse of alien identity found in

---

[53] Much could be said that falls beyond the limited scope of this article in terms of detailed exegesis of these directives. But in general, it seems best to group the various paraenetic directives of Heb 13:1–9 loosely under the kind of common wisdom and values found in Greco-Roman, Jewish and early Christian moralists. See the approach in Attridge, *Hebrews*, 386–388.

[54] Koester, "'*Outside*,'" 302.

Hebrews performed a specific function with respect to identity formation for the communities that put it to work: it allowed certain groups of early Christians to conceptualize and maintain their own distinctive insider status within the vast cultural field of cultic identities in the Roman Empire, while at the same time leaving the issue of actual cultic practice in unresolved tension.[55] This was done paradoxically by using a rhetoric of outsiderness, rooted in a collective memory of Abraham and other great heroes of the faith. Thus concrete directives for communal behavior could be read through the lens of this alien status, thereby promoting and reinforcing the community's understanding of its own distinctiveness within the larger Roman society, and simultaneously maintaining its connection to Hebrew epic and its affirmation of traditional mores.

Benjamin Dunning
Ph.D. Candidate
Harvard University, Graduate School of Arts and Sciences
Committee on the Study of Religion
12 Quincy Street, Cambridge, Mass. 02138, U.S.A.
dunning@fas.harvard.edu

---

[55] Here I hope to have distanced myself from other scholarly treatments of this motif in early Christianity that understand the use of alien rhetoric singularly as a secondary response to a primary historical given—whether that be the socio-legal status of a community, a way of making meaning out of society's persecution, or even the failure of the *parousia*. See for example Arowele, "Pilgrim People," 438–55; Elliott, *Home for the Homeless*; Feldmeier, "'Nation' of Strangers," 247–270.

REFLECTIONS OF RHETORICAL TERMINOLOGY IN HEBREWS

Hermut Löhr[1]

1. *Introductory Remarks*

Rhetorical analysis of New Testament texts has gained renewed interest in the last two or three decades. For the letters of the Apostle Paul, the studies of Hans Dieter Betz on Galatians[2] and Folker Siegert on Rom 9–11[3] remain the starting points of a new era of research, which can be subsumed under the heading of "rhetorical criticism."

In this context it is noteworthy that the names mentioned represent *different* approaches to the subject: whereas Betz re-introduced the use of the categories of classical Greek and Roman rhetoric and epistolography into historical-critical exegesis of the New Testament writings, Siegert's inspiring book is mainly interested in the analysis of argumentation and relies on the so-called *nouvelle rhétorique* initiated by Chaïm Perelman and Lucie Olbrechts-Tyteca.[4] But, as Carl J. Classen has correctly pointed out in several articles,[5] rhetorical criticism is of course not an invention of twentieth-century exegesis. It picks up and modifies older traditions and interests of biblical studies. One noteworthy name, which should be cited in this context for the sake of example, is that of Philipp Melanchthon.[6] Many more could be adduced.

---

[1] I thank my brother Winrich A. Löhr for revising a first draft of this paper.

[2] Hans Dieter Betz, "The Literary Composition and Function of Paul's Letter to the Galatians," *NTS* 21 (1975): 353–379; idem, *Galatians: A Commentary on Paul's Letter to the Churches in Galatia* (Hermeneia; Philadelphia: Fortress, 1979).

[3] Folker Siegert, *Argumentation bei Paulus, gezeigt an Röm 9–11* (WUNT 34; Tübingen: Mohr Siebeck, 1985).

[4] Cf. Chaïm Perelman, *La nouvelle rhétorique* (Paris: Presses universitaires de France, 1958); Chaïm Perelman and Lucie Olbrechts-Tyteca, *Rhétorique et philosophie: pour une théorie de l'argumentation en philosophie* (Paris: Presses universitaires de France, 1952).

[5] Classen's major contributions to the subject are conveniently gathered in Carl J. Classen, *Rhetorical Criticism of the New Testament* (WUNT 128; Tübingen: Mohr Siebeck, 2000).

[6] Philipp Melanchthon, *Römerbrief-Kommentar 1532* (ed. Rolf Schäfer; vol. 5 of *Melanchthons Werke in Auswahl*, ed. Robert Stupperich; Gütersloh: Gütersloher Verlagshaus Gerd Mohn, 1965).

Since the re-appearance of rhetorical criticism on the agenda of biblical studies, traditional Greek and Roman rhetorical categories have also made their way into the exegesis of Hebrews. Barnabas Lindars, for example, in a paper presented at the 1988 SNTS meeting, described Hebrews as a piece of deliberative rhetoric.[7] In the following year, Walter G. Übelacker was innovative in combining different approaches to describe the genre and intention of Hebrews, among them rhetorical criticism and some aspects of the *nouvelle rhétorique*.[8] Four years later, Thomas Olbricht tried to show in an article that the comparative argumentation of Hebrews can be described with the Aristotelian category of *auxesis*.[9] Although chiefly concerned with discourse analysis, David A. deSilva, in a dissertation published in 1995, is strongly interested in the rhetorical aspects of Hebrews.[10] Recent commentaries on Hebrews, such as those of William L. Lane[11] and Craig R. Koester,[12] devote some pages to the results of rhetorical criticism on our text. The most recent German-language commentary on Hebrews, by Martin Karrer, is more fundamentally based on a rhetorical analysis of the text.[13] But we could mention more and earlier titles, which—without using the heading of rhetorical criticism—were very well aware of the rhetorical skill and techniques used in Hebrews.[14]

---

[7] Barnabas Lindars, "The Rhetorical Structure of Hebrews," *NTS* 35 (1989): 383. Without discussing Lindars' arguments, Harold W. Attridge (*The Epistle to the Hebrews: A Commentary on the Epistle to the Hebrews* [Hermeneia; Philadelphia: Fortress, 1989], 14) labels Hebrews as "clearly an epideictic oration."

[8] Walter G. Übelacker, *Der Hebräerbrief als Appell: I. Untersuchungen zu* exordium, narratio *und* postscriptum *(Hebr 1–2 und 13,22–25)* (ConBNT 21; Lund: Almqvist & Wiksell, 1989).

[9] Thomas H. Olbricht, "Hebrews as Amplification," in *Rhetoric and the New Testament: Essays from the 1992 Heidelberg Conference* (ed. Stanley E. Porter and Thomas H. Olbricht, JSNTSup 90, Sheffield: Sheffield Academic Press, 1993), 375–387. Like Attridge (*Hebrews*, 14), Olbricht considers Hebrews to be an example of epideictic rhetoric. More specifically, he sees structural analogies between Hebrews and funeral speeches in antiquity (378–381).

[10] David A. deSilva, *Despising Shame: Honor Discourse and Community Maintenance in the Epistle to the Hebrews* (SBLDS 152, Atlanta: Scholars Press, 1995). Cf. also his recent commentary: idem, *Perseverance in Gratitude: A Socio-Rhetorical Commentary on the Epistle "to the Hebrews"* (Grand Rapids: Eerdmans, 2000).

[11] William L. Lane, *Hebrews 1–8* (WBC 47a; Dallas: Word Books, 1991), lxxv–lxxx.

[12] Craig R. Koester, *Hebrews: A New Translation with Introduction and Commentary* (AB 36; New York: Doubleday, 2001), 87–92, 92–96 for language and style, also revealing some aspects of the structure of argumentation.

[13] Martin Karrer, *Der Brief an die Hebräer: Kapitel 1,1–5,10* (ÖTK 20/1; Gütersloh: Gütersloher Verlagshaus; Würzburg: Echter, 2002).

[14] Some indications of older attempts to find a rhetorical structure in Hebrews

The categories used in the rhetorical criticism of the New Testament are basically *descriptive* ones. As Classen pointed out in an article originally published in German in 1991, the self-limitation of Betz, who refers exclusively to the categories and terminology of *classical* rhetoric, is therefore not cogent. *Any* attempt and *any* terminology, whether recent or old, may be useful for describing the strategy and the rhetorical means of a given text. This is the reason why, in my view, Siegert's more open approach to Paul is also more illuminating than Betz's, when it comes to simply understanding the text and grasping its techniques. Though there are certainly unresolved questions, to learn about the structure of the text and its argumentative strategies we can refer to a number of thorough, though often controversial, exegetical works.

Nevertheless, there is a good *historical* reason to retain the categories and terminology of classical rhetoric for contemporary critical exegesis: it could and should be asked whether the authors of our texts made *conscious* use of the current rhetorical conventions or handbooks, or if they simply used rhetorical devices without being aware of conventions or the norms of rhetorical theory. To decide on this question, the use of rhetorical *termini technici* would be a sound argument in favor of the former assumption. Whereas this task has convincingly been carried out for Paul by Classen,[15] we still lack, as far as I can see, a similar systematic investigation into the Epistle to the Hebrews. The following observations try to show the fruitfulness of this approach for the understanding of Hebrews.

My argument here is a cumulative one. As is true for all other New Testament or other early Christian writings, Hebrews is not a rhetorical handbook. So we cannot expect a technical use of rhetorical terminology in the strict sense. We will not come across definitions or discussions focusing on rhetoric and its categories. The phrases and expressions I have selected can certainly be understood without any reference to the language of rhetoric. But taken together they might provoke—and indeed they did provoke in me—the impression that our author could have used them consciously, being well aware of their rhetorical background. This is why I speak of "reflections"

---

are given by Hans-Friedrich Weiss, *Der Brief an die Hebräer* (KEK 13; Göttingen: Vandenhoeck & Ruprecht, 1991), 50–51 n. 32.

[15] Carl J. Classen, "Paul and the Terminology of Ancient Greek Rhetoric," in Classen, *Rhetorical Criticism*, 29–44.

of rhetorical language. If this result could generally be accepted, it would give us some insight into the cultural knowledge of our unknown author.

2. Reflections of Rhetorical Terminology

As a first example, I cite Heb 8:1:[16]

> Κεφάλαιον δὲ ἐπὶ τοῖς λεγομένοις, τοιοῦτον ἔχομεν ἀρχιερέα, ὃς ἐκάθισεν ἐν δεξιᾷ τοῦ θρόνου τῆς μεγαλωσύνης ἐν τοῖς οὐρανοῖς.
>
> The main point among the things mentioned: we have such a high priest, who has taken his seat at the right hand of the throne of the Majesty in the heavens.

With this phrase, the text sums up arguments of the preceding chapters, especially of Heb 7, on the heavenly high priest. At the same time it announces a new subject, that of the two tents, further developed in Heb 9. It is the expression κεφάλαιον δὲ ἐπὶ τοῖς λεγομένοις which signals the textual function of the following lines as a sum of the things said (note: λεγομένοις, not γεγραμμένοις!) before. Searching κεφάλαιον in the current dictionaries[17] informs us about similar expressions with a comparable textual function in Greek literature from Plato onwards. So in the present context κεφάλαιον could be certainly a current and non-technical word. In the New Testament, it occurs only twice, in Hebrews and in Acts 22:28, in a totally non-argumentative context.

But there is more. While Classen—in his article mentioned above—has amply demonstrated the obvious rhetorical implications of the verb ἀνακεφαλαιοῦν in Rom 13:9,[18] we could add that the common *terminus* κεφάλαιον itself is also used in rhetorical handbooks, especially for a series of arguments in deliberative speech. From Isocrates and Anaximenes of Lampsakos onward the rhetors reflected on these

---

[16] All citations from the New Testament are taken from: Barbara Aland and Kurt Aland et al., eds., *Novum Testamentum Graece* (27th ed.; Stuttgart: Deutsche Bibelgesellschaft, 1993). All translations—including those from non-biblical sources—are mine.

[17] Cf. e.g., Walter Bauer, *Griechisch-deutsches Wörterbuch zu den Schriften des Neuen Testaments und der frühchristlichen Literatur* (ed. Kurt Aland and Barbara Aland; 6th rev. ed.; Berlin: de Gruyter, 1988), 874; LSJ, 944.

[18] Classen, "Terminology," 30.

main arguments.¹⁹ Anaximenes himself enumerates δίκαιον, νόμιμον, συμφέρον, καλόν, ἡδύ, and ῥᾴδιον.²⁰ Later on, these arguments bore different names; e.g., they were called the τέλη by Aristotle (*Rhet.* 1.3.5 [1358b]) and the τελικὰ κεφάλαια by Hermogenes of Tarsus (born ca. 161 CE).²¹

For the rhetor Theodorus (first century BCE), cited by Quintilian, *Inst.* 3.6.2 (cf. 3.11.3 and 3.11.27), the *caput, ad quod referantur omnia*, is the κεφάλαιον γενικώτατον, the fundamental question in a given law case. Κεφάλαιον thus replaces the more common *terminus technicus* στάσις (Latin *status*) in the language of rhetoric.

With this in mind as we turn back to the context of Heb 8, we can note that the verses that follow are not just a summary of things already said, but provide the starting point of a new argument. So here κεφάλαιον might not mean "the sum" or "the gist," but "the main argument." Considering the possibility of a technical use of the word can lead us to a new interpretation in its actual textual context.

In the same context we come across the expression ἀναγκαῖον ("necessary"). Hebrews 8:3 explains why every high priest needs a sacrifice: this is ἀναγκαῖον, because it is the function of the high priest to offer goods and sacrifices:

Πᾶς γὰρ ἀρχιερεὺς εἰς τὸ προσφέρειν δῶρά τε καὶ θυσίας καθίσταται· ὅθεν ἀναγκαῖον ἔχειν τι καὶ τοῦτον ὃ προσενέγκῃ.

For every high priest is appointed to offer gifts and sacrifices. Therefore it is necessary that he has something to offer.

---

¹⁹ For more detailed information, cf. Joseph Martin, *Antike Rhetorik: Technik und Methode* (HAW 2/3; Munich: Beck, 1974), 169–170. Still most useful for this and other rhetorical *termini* in antiquity are: Johann C. G. Ernesti, *Lexicon Technologiae Latinorum Rhetoricae* (Leipzig, 1797; 2d repr., Hildesheim: Georg Olms, 1983) and idem, *Lexicon Technologiae Graecorum Rhetoricae* (Leipzig, 1795; 2d repr., Hildesheim: Georg Olms, 1983).
²⁰ Anaximenes, *Rhet.* 1.4 (1421b, 23–27); cf. Anaximenes, *Ars Rhetorica: Quae vulgo fertur Aristotelis ad Alexandrum* (ed. Manfred Fuhrmann; Leipzig: B. G. Teubner, 1966), 6, lines 1–5.
²¹ In *Progymnasmata* 6, Hermogenes enumerates νόμιμον, δίκαιον, σύμφερον, δύνατον, and πρέπον (Leonard Spengel, *Rhetores Graeci* [3 vols.; Leipzig: B. G. Teubner, 1853–1856], 2:119), whereas in *Staseis* 7 (Spengel, *Rhetores Graeci*, 2:164–166), he discusses νόμιμον, δίκαιον, σύμφερον, δύνατον, ἔνδοξον, and ἐκβησόμενον. Other enumerations of the τελικὰ κεφάλαια are cited by Heinrich Lausberg, *Handbuch der literarischen Rhetorik: Eine Grundlegung der Literaturwissenschaft* (2 vols.; Munich: Max Hueber, 1960), vol. 1 § 375.

Again the argumentation can be understood without reference to rhetoric, but the use of the expression adds argumentative force: it is not just a *fact*, but a *necessity*, that is expressed. One can ask what sort of necessity is expressed here. Harold W. Attridge sees in the syntagma "the logical language of necessity,"[22] while Erich Grässer goes a step further in speaking of "(theo-)logische Denknotwendigkeit,"[23] which is an apt interpretative label, but not a historical rhetorical category. The language of necessity is, as most commentators do not fail to note, also present in Heb 7:12, 27 and 9:16, 23, passages which in fact evoke different categories of necessity. Taking together ἀνάγκη and ἀναγκαῖος, the words are used in the New Testament most often in Hebrews, i.e., five times, against four times in 1 Corinthians and four times in 2 Corinthians.[24]

Can this repeated use be further explained within the framework of ancient rhetoric? Indeed it can. For chronological reasons, perhaps less important for our argumentation is the fact that the ἀναγκαῖον figures in a list of the afore-mentioned τελικὰ κεφάλαια given in the *Progymnasmata* of Nikolaos of Myra from the fifth century CE:[25]

> ἔστι δὲ ταῦτα τὸ συμφέρον, τὸ δίκαιον, τὸ νόμιμον, τὸ δυνατόν, τὸ ἔνδοξον, τὸ ἀναγκαῖον, τὸ ῥᾴδιον.
>
> They (i.e., the τελικὰ κεφάλαια) are the useful, the just, the lawful, the possible, the glorious, the necessary, the easy.

Not as an argument in deliberative speech, but in the context of poetics, the ἀναγκαῖον, understood as a natural necessity, takes us back to Aristotle. In *Poet.* 9.1 (1451a), Aristotle defines the task of the poet:

> φανερὸν δὲ ἐκ τῶν εἰρημένων καὶ ὅτι οὐ τὸ τὰ γενόμενα λέγειν, τοῦτο ποιητοῦ ἔργον ἐστίν, ἀλλ' οἷα ἂν γένοιτο καὶ τὰ δυνατὰ κατὰ τὸ εἰκὸς ἢ τὸ ἀναγκαῖον. (Halliwell, LCL)
>
> From what was said, it is obvious that it is not the task of the poet to say what happened, but what could happen or what is possible according to conformity or necessity.

---

[22] Attridge, *Hebrews*, 218.
[23] Erich Grässer, *An die Hebräer* (3 vols.; EKKNT 17; Zürich: Benziger and Neukirchen-Vluyn: Neukirchener, 1990–1997), 2:85. In note 70 on the same page he rejects Hans Windisch's opinion that it is the law that stands behind this necessity.
[24] ἀνάγκη: 1 Cor 7:26, 37; 9:16; 2 Cor 6:4; 9:7; 12:10; Heb 7:12, 27; 9:16, 23. ἀναγκαῖος: 1 Cor 12:22; 2 Cor 9:5; Heb 8:3.
[25] Spengel, *Rhetores Graeci*, 3:475–476.

In *Rhet.* 1.4.2 (1359a), Aristotle excludes the ἀναγκαῖον together with the ἀδύνατον from the deliberative speech:

ὅσα δὲ ἐξ ἀνάγκης ἢ ἐστὶν ἢ ἔσται ἢ ἀδύνατον εἶναι ἢ γενέσθαι, περὶ δὲ τούτων οὐκ ἔστι συμβουλή. (Freese, LCL)

Everything which of necessity either is or will be, or which is impossible to be or to become—those things are outside the scope of deliberation.

In this concept of deliberative rhetoric, the category of ἀναγκαῖον plays the role of a boundary marker between the themes and arguments within the scope of consideration, and those without. For P. Rutilius Lupus, a Roman rhetor flourishing in the first century CE, and cited and criticized by Quintilian in *Inst.* 9.3.99, the ἀναγκαῖον figures even among the *figurae verborum*:[26]

'Ἀναγκαῖον. *hoc schema tunc prodest atque omnis eius utilitas in eo est, cum volumus ostendere necessitudinem aut naturae aut temporis aut alicuius personae.*

The necessary. This state is then useful, and all its usefulness is there, when we want to show the necessity of nature or time or of some person.

Another possible reflection of rhetorical terminology in Hebrews is the verb πρέπειν, which is used two times in Hebrews, in Heb 2:10 and 7:26. In Heb 2:10 it refers to the suffering of the Son of God. In Heb 7:26 the accent is a more soteriological one: it was "fitting" for *us* to have such a high priest. The commentaries note pagan Hellenistic theology and philosophy as the background to this idea of appropriateness, citing in this respect the fundamental study of Max Pohlenz on the expression τὸ πρέπον.[27] Whereas Pohlenz himself devoted many pages to the use of πρέπον in rhetoric[28]—work which for a long time seemingly went unnoticed by scholarly debate on our epistle—Alan C. Mitchell proposed for the first time[29] the

---

[26] P. Rutilius Lupus, *Schemata Dianoeas et lexeos: Saggio introduttivo, testo e traduzione* (ed. Giuseppina Barabino; Pubblicazioni dell'Istituto di filologia classica e medioevale dell'Università di Genova 27; Genova: Istituto di filologia classica e medioevale, 1967), 176, lines 1–3.

[27] Max Pohlenz, "Τὸ πρέπον: Ein Beitrag zur Geschichte des griechischen Geistes," in idem, *Kleine Schriften I* (ed. Heinrich Dörrie; Hildesheim: Georg Olms, 1965), 100–139.

[28] Pohlenz, "Beitrag," 105–117.

[29] Mitchell himself refers in a footnote to James Moffatt, *A Critical and Exegetical Commentary on the Epistle to the Hebrews* (ICC 14; Edinburgh: T&T Clark, 1924), 29, who refers *inter alia* to Aristotle, *Eth. nic.* 4.2.2 (1122a).

interpretation of πρέπειν in Hebrews with the help of rhetorical terminology.[30] According to Mitchell, the author of Hebrews connects the rhetorical and stylistic category of πρέπον with his theological assumptions. Since according to Heb 2:3 God has spoken to humankind through the Son, the christological and soteriological event can be described in rhetorical categories. Seductive as this theological interpretation might be, for me it remains somewhat doubtful whether the concept of soteriology as *communication* between God and mankind is really present in the passages cited. Nevertheless Mitchell's essay points, in my opinion, in the right direction. The use of πρέπειν in the argumentation of Hebrews indeed links theological considerations with rhetorical terminology. As in the case of κεφάλαιον and ἀναγκαῖον, we are again referred to the field of argumentation: πρέπον figures among the "main arguments" of the *genus deliberativum*.[31] Hermogenes writes in his *Progymnasmata* 11:[32]

> διαιροῦνται δὲ αἱ θέσεις τοῖς τελικοῖς λεγομένοις κεφαλαίοις, τῷ δικαίῳ, τῷ συμφέροντι, τῷ δυνατῷ, τῷ πρέποντι.
>
> The fundamental questions are divided according to the so-called final main arguments, the just, the useful, the possible, the appropriate.

And for Quintilian, the *decor* of a *person* cited as example is one of the arguments in a deliberative speech (*Inst.* 3.8.35; cf. 10.1.27 and 10.1.71), thus introducing an ethical concept into rhetoric:[33]

> *Sed personam saepius decoris gratia intuemur, quae et in nobis et in iis, qui deliberant, spectanda est.*
>
> But more often it is for the sake of appropriateness that we consider a personality, which is to be regarded by us as by those who are deliberating.

The next example to be discussed here was in fact the starting point of my reflections on rhetorical terminology in Hebrews. In my monograph, *Umkehr und Sünde im Hebräerbrief*,[34] I studied among other texts

---

[30] Alan C. Mitchell, "The Use of πρέπειν and Rhetorical Propriety in Hebrews 2:10," *CBQ* 54 (1992): 681–701.

[31] Examples are given by Lausberg, *Handbuch*, vol. 1 § 375.

[32] Spengel, *Rhetores Graeci*, 2:18.

[33] Marcus Fabius Quintilianus, *Institutiones Oratoriae: Ausbildung des Redners. Zwölf Bücher* (ed. and trans. Helmut Rahn; 2 vols.; 2d ed.; Texte zur Forschung 2–3; Darmstadt: Wissenschaftliche Buchgesellschaft, 1988), 1:372.

[34] Hermut Löhr, *Umkehr und Sünde im Hebräerbrief* (BZNW 73, Berlin: de Gruyter, 1994).

the famous passage Heb 6:4–8, a text which denies the possibility of a second repentance or conversion (the Greek expression used in the text is μετάνοια) within the wider context of the theological thinking of our letter. The sharp ἀδύνατον ("impossible") at the beginning of verse 4 was interpreted synchronically in the context of the arguments and examples of the following verses, in comparison with the other occurrences in Hebrews (Heb 6:18; 10:4; 11:6), but also on a metatextual level in the horizon of textual pragmatics.

As I realized only later, ἀδύνατον plays a certain role in rhetoric, more exactly in the theory of argumentation. A hint in this direction was already given by Siegert,[35] who, however, did not mention its significance for the interpretation of Hebrews. Whereas τὸ δυνατόν belongs again to the κεφάλαια of argumentation (as noted above) and appears in Quintilian, *Inst.* 3.8.25, even as a Greek *terminus technicus*,[36] Aristotle in his rhetoric already provides us with a reflection on δυνατόν and ἀδύνατον in the context of the common topics of the three *genera* of speech. According to Aristotle, the *topos* of the possible is most appropriate for deliberative rhetoric (*Rhet.* 2.18.5 [1392a]). Unfortunately Aristotle restricts himself to enumerating several examples of logical and natural possibility, whereas for the ἀδύνατον he only concludes:

> περὶ δὲ ἀδυνάτου δῆλον ὅτι ἐκ τῶν ἐναντίων τοῖς εἰρημένοις ὑπάρχει.
> (Aristotle, *Rhet.* 2.19.15 [1392b]; Freese, LCL)
>
> Concerning the "impossible" it is obvious that it consists of the things contrary to those said.

And, as is expressed in *Rhet.* 1.4.3 (1359a),[37] the impossible (like the ἀναγκαῖον, discussed above) cannot figure among the objects of deliberation. Despite failing to develop further the category of ἀδύνατον, Aristotle gives us some proof that ἀδύνατον is part of the reflection and language of rhetoric. The distinction of the possible and the

---

[35] Siegert, *Argumentation*, 60.
[36] Quintilian, *Inst.* 3.8.25: *melius igitur, qui tertiam partem duxerunt* δυνατόν, *quod nostri possibile nominant: quae ut dura videatur appellatio, tamen sola est* (Rahn, *Institutiones Oratoriae*, 1:368). In the sentence before, Quintilian argues against the *necessarium* as a third part of deliberative arguments. He writes: *itaque mihi ne consilium quidem videtur, ubi necessitas est, non magis quam ubi constat quid fieri non posse: omnis enim deliberatio de dubiis est* (Rahn, *Institutiones Oratoriae*, 1:368).
[37] Cf. also Anaximenes, *Rhet.* 1.12 (1422a, 20–21): ἀναγκαῖα δὲ τὰ μὴ ἐφ' ἡμῖν ὄντα πράττειν, ἀλλ' ὡς ἐξ ἀνάγκης θείας ἢ ἀνθρωπίνης οὕτως ὄντα (Fuhrmann, *Ars Rhetorica*, 7, lines 14–15).

impossible is fundamental for each orator, as Aristotle stresses in *Rhet.* 1.3.8 (1359a):

> ἀναγκαῖον καὶ τῷ συμβουλεύοντι καὶ τῷ δικαζομένῳ καὶ τῷ ἐπιδεικτικῷ ἔχειν προτάσεις περὶ δυνατοῦ καὶ ἀδυνάτου, καὶ εἰ γέγονεν ἢ μή, καὶ εἰ ἔσται ἢ μή. (Freese, LCL)
>
> It is necessary for the one who gives advice and for the one who argues in court and the one who exhibits something to have propositions concerning the possible and the impossible, and as to whether something happened or not, or will happen or not.

If the author of Hebrews actually has in mind this rhetorical usage of the language of necessity, we do not need—according to the author's intent—to search in or behind the text for hidden reasons for the sharp "impossible" in Heb 6:4. The passage Heb 6:4–8 makes explicit the limits of the *deliberatio*: "impossible" is not only a second conversion, but also further argumentation on this point. The text marks the limits of the theological and pastoral discourse.

An investigation into the use of rhetorical terminology in Hebrews would be fairly incomplete without taking account of the text's self-designation[38] as λόγος τῆς παρακλήσεως in Heb 13:22, which some have thought to be a technical expression for a homily in a Jewish-Christian milieu:[39]

> Παρακαλῶ δὲ ὑμᾶς, ἀδελφοί, ἀνέχεσθε τοῦ λόγου τῆς παρακλήσεως, καὶ γὰρ διὰ βραχέων ἐπέστειλα ὑμῖν.
>
> I urge you, brethren, to hold on to the word of admonition, for I have written to you (only) briefly.

The expression λόγος τῆς παρακλήσεως is comparatively rare in Greek literature, and it does not seem to be a clear-cut designation of some oral or written genre. Nevertheless in Acts 13:15, it is used in the mouth of the ἀρχισυνάγωγοι of Pisidian Antioch in the sense of an oral discourse or a sermon. In 1 Macc 10:24, on the contrary, the same expression refers to a written text (the letter of King Demetrios

---

[38] That the expression λόγος τῆς παρακλήσεως (Heb 13:22) refers to the written text (and not to some oral message or ideal *kerygma*) is made obvious by the reference to the letter at the end of the same verse.

[39] After Hartwig Thyen, *Der Stil der Jüdisch-Hellenistischen Homilie* (FRLANT 47; Göttingen: Vandenhoeck & Ruprecht, 1955), 16–18, who does not seem to regard the expression λόγος τῆς παρακλήσεως to be technical, cf. Lawrence Wills, "The Form of the Sermon in Hellenistic Judaism and Early Christianity," *HTR* 77 (1984): 277–299.

I Soter to the Jews in the ensuing verses), though it is not clear whether the expression itself (the plural λόγους παρακλήσεως is used) has the form of the letter in view. Other non-technical occurrences include Diodorus of Sicily, *Bibl. hist.* 15.16.2 and Dio Chrysostom, *1 Regn.* 9.4 (again the plural is used). Thus the use of λόγος τῆς παρακλήσεως in Hebrews is *no* evidence for rhetorical language.[40]

3. Conclusions

"Praxis precedes theory." With this statement, Carl J. Classen[41] justly describes the limits of using categories of ancient rhetoric for the interpretation of given texts. The use of rhetorical techniques is more often than not independent of the use of the classical handbooks by the authors. Rhetorical skill could and can be acquired in different ways: by education, by hearing or reading outstanding examples of speech or literature, or by following the precepts of this or that handbook. The same is true of the *termini* used. In general, the language of rhetorical theory and advice does not only consist of *termini technici*. Influences of theological, philosophical, or everyday language can be noticed everywhere in the handbooks. Especially in the field of argumentation, rhetorical theory only states in a more systematic form what common sense had already formulated with the same words, though not in a fixed order.

In our investigation of Hebrews we did not come across a word or term that makes sense only as a *terminus technicus* of rhetorical language. Nor is there any direct and unambiguous evidence for the use of rhetorical handbooks by the author of Hebrews. What does strike the reader of Hebrews, however, is the use of words and phrases that stress an argument by citing (pseudo-)logic[42] or other necessity, possibility, or appropriateness. The fact that some (not all) of these expressions and phrases reappear in rhetorical theory could

---

[40] The use of προσέχειν in Heb 2:1 is for Karrer (*Hebräer*, 151) a trace of the *genos dikanikon*, although he interprets the context of Heb 2:1–4 as deliberative rhetoric. For προσοχή cf. Martin, *Antike Rhetorik*, 66, 70 n. 99.

[41] Cf. Classen, "Terminology," 29 n. 3.

[42] For this aspect of the argumentation in Hebrews, cf. the older attempt of Wilhelm C. Linss, "Logical Terminology in the Epistle to the Hebrews," *CTM* 37 (1966): 365–369. In n. 2 on p. 365, Linss refers to a dissertation by W. A. Jennrich, "Rhetorical Style in the New Testament: Romans and Hebrews" (Ph.D. diss., Washington University, St. Louis, 1947), which was not accessible to me.

certainly be accidental or due to the existence of common-sense *universalia*. But the same fact could also provide us with a valuable historical argument: our author, whose rhetorical skill was clearly recognized even before the new era of rhetorical criticism, might reveal by his terminology some traces of rhetorical knowledge and formation, especially in the sphere of argumentation. So the impression of a very logical, rational, and even modern kind of argumentation in Hebrews, which is repeatedly expressed in the secondary literature, can be modified and corrected by studying classical rhetoric. At the same time the expressions employed by the author point to the field of deliberative rhetoric, thus confirming the assumption that Hebrews is an early Christian literary example of the *genus deliberativum*.

Prof. Dr. theol. Hermut Löhr
Professor für Neues Testament
Friedrich-Schiller-Universität Jena, Theologische Fakultät
Fürstengraben 6, D-07737 Jena, Germany
hermut.loehr@uni-jena.de

PART THREE

TEXTUAL-HISTORICAL, COMPARATIVE, AND
INTERTEXTUAL APPROACHES TO HEBREWS

LOCATING HEBREWS WITHIN THE LITERARY LANDSCAPE OF CHRISTIAN ORIGINS

Pamela M. Eisenbaum

The so-called "Epistle to the Hebrews" is almost certainly the most mysterious text to have been preserved in the NT canon. The author's identity, the provenance, the addressees, and the date and occasion for writing are all widely disputed. Interestingly, modern scholarship mimics ancient scholarship in this regard; the fathers also vigorously debated these questions until Augustine and Jerome finally settled the question by declaring the text Pauline and canonical.[1] Although one might be able to identify a "majority view" on some of these issues, that "majority view" coincides with, and is better designated, the "traditional view" held by church authorities since the fifth century. Most scholars actively working on Hebrews today would readily admit, I think, that there is no modern scholarly consensus about the specific context of Hebrews. Indeed, many scholars, myself included, have expressed resignation about ever possessing knowledge about Hebrews' chronological, geographical, and social situation, unless, perchance, some miraculous new evidence appears. Thus we often make and hear calls for recognizing the limits of our evidence and laying aside those questions about the text's context. The best we can hope for is to interpret Hebrews on its own terms, "as a distinctive Christian writing."[2] This attitude toward Hebrews has left this rich document largely in isolation from other Christian literature and from the whole history of Christian origins. While I appreciate the humility in recognizing the limits of historical evidence,

---

[1] For Augustine, see *Doctr. chr.* 2.8.12–13; *Civ.* 10.5; 16.22. For Jerome, see *Epist.* 129.7. Helpful discussions of how Hebrews achieved canonical status can be found in William H. P. Hatch, "The Position of Hebrews in the Canon of the New Testament," *HTR* 29 (1936): 133–151; Otto Michel, *Der Brief an die Hebräer* (KEK 13; Göttingen: Vandenhoeck & Ruprecht, 1966), 37–39; and Craig R. Koester, *Hebrews: A New Translation with Introduction and Commentary* (AB 36; New York: Doubleday, 2001), 24–27.

[2] Cynthia Briggs Kittredge, "The Letter to the Hebrews," in *The New Oxford Annotated Bible* (ed. Michael D. Coogan; 3rd ed.; New York: Oxford, 2001), 369NT.

such an attitude makes Hebrews only more mysterious, and thus more frustrating to interpret.

Although I have discovered no new pieces of evidence, I wish to appeal to a new *kind* of evidence in order to take up these seemingly intractable questions about Hebrews. Perhaps the word "framework" would capture better what I intend to do in the following paper than does "evidence," since the evidence to which I will appeal is not new so much as simply neglected by most contemporary scholars of Hebrews. Recently, several important, synthetic scholarly works have appeared that reframe not only how we think about Christian origins and post-biblical Judaism, but how we think about Jewish-Christian relations and the construction of Jewish and/or Christian identity in the first four centuries within the wider context of the Greco-Roman world. Such scholarship has made me newly aware of the biases embedded in the questions we pose, especially when it comes to the "context of Hebrews." More specifically, new scholarly paradigms are emerging that have emboldened me to tackle the contextual questions about Hebrews that I once thought unanswerable. With the exception of the question of provenance, I will make new suggestions about the authorship, occasion, addressees, and date of Hebrews. Before moving to my proposals for describing the context of Hebrews, I first wish to explain briefly what I mean by "context."

Text and Context

For most of the history of modern biblical scholarship, scholars have been preoccupied with questions concerning the origin of a given document, or passage, or saying, etc., because they believed that knowledge of a text's origins leads to knowledge of its meaning. Thus, when scholars look for information about a text's context, they typically turn to literary and historical evidence that is generally considered prior to, or contemporary with, the document under investigation. Put another way, scholars tend "to look behind the text" to see how it came into being in the first place. The "afterlife" of the text is generally not considered very useful in determining a text's origins. The one possible exception is text-criticism, but because the traditional goal of text-criticism has been to establish the *Urtext*, interpreters have typically used text-criticism merely to *look through* a manuscript of the 3rd, 4th, or 5th century so as to (re)construct a first-century original. Once scholarly confidence is established that one has the original text or nearly original text, then establishing the "context" becomes a matter of identifying the specific social and rhetorical situation that engendered that first-century text.[3]

To be sure, I count myself among those biblical scholars interested in the origins of texts, and I make claims about the origins of Hebrews in this essay. However, I think scholars have often confused questions concerning the origin of a text with the method needed to pursue those questions, by assuming they need to work backwards from the point of the text's composition. The first problem with this assumption is that in many cases it is logically untenable. Hebrews is a case in point. Not only is the date disputed, the chronological range of possibility covers a large swath of time (the *terminus a quo* is sometime after the death of Jesus, while the *terminus ad quem* is the first citation of Hebrews by a later author, but even this is more complicated than at first it may seem).[4] Under these circumstances, how can there be reasonable certainty about what other documents are prior and thus influential to the production of Hebrews, except to go backwards to texts assuredly preceding the *terminus a quo*? Perhaps this explains why scholars have spent more time comparing Hebrews to Hellenistic Jewish writers like Philo or apocalyptic texts and the Dead Sea Scrolls than to early Christian literature, leaving Hebrews in isolation from the literary landscape of early Christian texts. As Craig R. Koester has wittily commented in regard to this issue, "In the history of early Christian theology, Hebrews sometimes is thought to be like Melchizedek, without father, mother or genealogy (Heb 7:3)."[5]

---

[3] In a remarkable shift, however, some prominent text-critics today have put the once-sacred quest for the original text aside and begun to use their skills to pursue other kinds of questions. I will be appealing to some of their work below. Two overviews of this shift in text-criticism can be found in Bart D. Ehrman, "The Text as Window: New Testament Manuscripts and the Social History of Early Christianity," in *The Text of the New Testament in Contemporary Research: Essays on the Status Quaestionis* (ed. Bart D. Ehrman and Michael W. Holmes; Grand Rapids: Eerdmans, 1995), 361–379; and Eldon J. Epp, "The Multivalence of the Term 'Original Text' in New Testament Textual Criticism," *HTR* 92 (1999): 245–281.

[4] Although a majority of scholars recognize *1 Clement* as dependent on Hebrews, the traditional dating of 96 CE for *1 Clement* has been rightly called into question. A few have suggested a date as late as 140, though the current tendency is to date it within the first quarter of the second century. For discussion, see Harold W. Attridge, *The Epistle to the Hebrews* (Hermeneia; Philadelphia: Fortress, 1989), 6–8.

[5] Koester, *Hebrews*, 58. Koester's commentary is something of an exception to

The second problem with the scholarly search for origins is that the literary post-history of a text does, in fact, influence interpreters in their interpretation of a text, but it is often unconscious and uncritical. Because Hebrews is part of the NT canon, and because most NT texts are dated to the first century, scholars have tended to assume that Hebrews is a first-century text. At the very least, the burden of proof has rested on those who wish to date it later than the first century. In other words, the very presence of Hebrews in the canon unconsciously biases scholars toward a first-century date, in spite of the fact that scholars are well aware that Hebrews' canonical authority was questioned up to the fifth century. Later in this paper I will not only argue for a second-century date, but more importantly I hope to demonstrate there is virtually no evidence tying Hebrews to the first century. Thus the burden of proof needs to shift to those who wish to uphold its location in the first century. To be sure, scholars believe they have evidence for a first-century date and have created arguments to support it, but I suspect that scholars would never have found such "evidence" if Hebrews were not presently in the canon. Similarly, the ascription "To the Hebrews" biases scholars toward thinking the text is directed toward Jewish-Christians or Christians attracted to Judaism, even as the same scholars acknowledge the superscription is a later accretion—that is to say, not a part of the "original" text. Indeed, there is precious little within the body of Hebrews itself to indicate that the addressees are in danger of "back-sliding into Judaism."[6]

The point I wish to make is primarily methodological: the textual history of Hebrews has been under-utilized in the interpretation of the text, and I hope to begin to correct the situation by appealing to what we know about the uses of literary texts in early Christianity and the motivation for their production. As Harry Gamble has pointed out, NT scholars for a long time downplayed the literary culture of early Christianity, with the result that "The failure to con-

---

the rule: he makes considerable effort to connect Hebrews to other early Christian literature. Most commentators will list a few points of similarity or dissimilarity with other texts, most often 1 Peter, but this information is rarely used to contextualize Hebrews.

[6] Barnabas Lindars sums up the traditional view that "Hebrews is written to a group of Jewish converts who are in danger of relapsing into Judaism" (*The Theology of the Letter to the Hebrews* [Cambridge: Cambridge University Press, 1991], 4). The traditional view still has many defenders; one of the most articulate is Lindars himself.

sider the extent to which the physical medium of the written word contributes to its meaning—how its outward aspects inform the way a text is approached and read—perpetuates a largely abstract, often unhistorical, and even anachronistic conception of early Christian literature and its transmission."[7]

It seems to me that Gamble's critique is particularly apt for Hebrews. Although scholarly reconstructions of the social situation of Hebrews abound, there is virtually no specific information about the social context given in the text itself. Reconstructions of Hebrews' social context or rhetorical situation therefore remain extremely tenuous. Thus I intend to focus on another kind of contextual evidence. The most concrete contextual information we possess about Hebrews derives from its literary context—that is, its genre, its affinity to or dissimilarity with other texts, and its textual history. Using this kind of information, one can begin to identify what function a text like Hebrews could have played in the literary culture of early Christianity.[8]

Authorship

While virtually all modern scholars have abandoned the notion of Pauline authorship and wisely recognize the futility of identifying the author with a specific person known from the pages of history, scholars generally do not ponder why Hebrews might have circulated anonymously.[9] As for myself, I no longer find the question of the author's identity interesting, but I am curious about *why* the author

---

[7] Gamble, *Books and Readers in the Early Church: A History of Early Christian Texts* (New Haven: Yale University Press, 1995), 42. Cf. Stanley K. Stowers, who offers a similar critique and attempts to correct it in his reading of Romans (*A Rereading of Romans: Justice, Jews, and Gentiles* [New Haven: Yale University Press, 1990]; see esp. 6–22).

[8] One of the reasons this kind of literary contextualization has not been pursued more vigorously is because of the long-established assumption that early Christian culture was not "literary." Even though form-criticism has given way in recent years to more holistic readings of biblical texts (for the most part), many assumptions of form-criticism still prevail, especially that early Christians were fairly simple folk and that the literature that now comprises the NT represents either collections of oral material or was occasioned by very specific situations and thus literary forms were considered largely incidental to content. In this way, bibliographic and literary characteristics were perceived to be unrelated to the "generative circumstances" of early Christian documents. See the discussion by Gamble, *Books and Readers*, 10–20.

[9] According to Attridge, the last person to defend Pauline authorship was William Leonard in 1939 (*Hebrews*, 2).

chose not to write in his (or her)[10] own name, nor use a pseudonym. Pursuing the question of authorship this way is useful, I think, and can best be addressed by first turning to the textual history of Hebrews.

Early Greek manuscripts of Hebrews indicate that the text of Hebrews circulated within Pauline letter collections. While different forms of the *corpus Paulinum* circulated, and some versions did not include Hebrews, there is no evidence that Hebrews circulated with other collections of Christian writings (for instance, with documents that come to be known as the Catholic Epistles).[11] Neither is there evidence that Hebrews circulated independently, as was the case, for example, with Revelation and some of the Catholic Epistles, as well as some of the writings of the Apostolic Fathers.[12] Hebrews appears

---

[10] Since we do not know the identity of the author, we cannot discern the gender of the author with any certainty. However, I will use the male pronoun when referring to the author for two reasons: (1) as a matter of convenience; and (2) because the author projects a male perspective; see Heb 11:32.

[11] In addition to the evidence of majuscules, Hebrews has been identified in eight papyri: $\mathfrak{P}^{12}$; $\mathfrak{P}^{13}$; $\mathfrak{P}^{17}$; $\mathfrak{P}^{46}$; $\mathfrak{P}^{79}$; $\mathfrak{P}^{89}$; $\mathfrak{P}^{114}$; $\mathfrak{P}^{116}$. ($\mathfrak{P}^{116}$ was recently published by Amphilochios Papsthomas, "A New Testimony to the Letter to the Hebrews," *Tyche* 16 (2001): 107–110.) Six of the eight manuscripts have been identified as portions of now lost codices. ($\mathfrak{P}^{12}$ and $\mathfrak{P}^{13}$ appear to be from scrolls, but any significance that might be attached to this observation is minimized by their being opisthographs.) With the exception of $\mathfrak{P}^{46}$, the famed Chester Beatty codex of the Pauline epistles which contains the entirety of Hebrews, these papyri are very fragmentary and preserve Hebrews alone. This statistic is not unusual, however, since 98 of our current 116 NT papyri preserve only a single NT text. In the case of the five fragmentary texts originating from codices, scholars tend to assume the contents would have included texts in addition to Hebrews, though almost all these texts are too fragmentary to determine this with certainty and there is no way to determine what these other texts were. But from everything else known about the textual transmission of Hebrews, it is reasonable to assume it was bound with other Paulines. I am grateful to Eldon J. Epp for helping me to acquire an up-to-date list of early witnesses to Hebrews, and especially for alerting me to the publication of $\mathfrak{P}^{116}$. See also Eldon J. Epp, "The Codex and Literacy in Early Christianity and at Oxyrhynchus: Issues Raised by Harry Y. Gamble's *Books and Readers in the Early Church*," *CRBR* 10 (1997): 15–37 (with "Appended Note 2 on Additional Newly Published Oxyrhynchus Papyri of the New Testament," which Prof. Epp was kind enough to send me, now in a reprint of the article in idem, *Perspectives on New Testament Textual Criticism: Collected Essays, 1962–2004* [NovTSup 116; Leiden: Brill, 2005], 548–550); idem, "Issues in the Interrelation of New Testament Textual Criticism and Canon," in *The Canon Debate: On the Origins and Formation of the Bible* (ed. Lee M. McDonald and James A. Sanders; Peabody, Mass.: Hendrickson, 2002), 485–515, esp. 488–489, and 503–507.

[12] Epp, "Issues in Textual Criticism and Canon," 492. See also Gamble, "The New Testament Canon: Recent Research and the Status Quaestionis," in *The Canon Debate: On the Origins and Formation of the Bible* (ed. Lee M. McDonald and James A. Sanders; Peabody, Mass.: Hendrickson, 2002), 267–294, esp. 287–288.

in all the great majuscules of the fourth and fifth century, and, as Eldon J. Epp rightly observes, "Hebrews' place in the canon was firm by the end of the fourth century"—indeed much firmer than Revelation.[13] Its position varies, but two positions are most common in Greek manuscripts: between 2 Thessalonians and the Pastorals; or after Philemon at the end of the collection.[14] The logic of the first sequence appears to lie in the distinction between letters to churches or communities and letters to individuals.[15] The rationale for the second sequence is likely the dispute about Pauline authorship, or at least the recognition that the document was anonymous. $\mathfrak{P}^{46}$ places Hebrews after Romans, which may seem idiosyncratic, but Hebrews holds this position in nine minuscules as well, and there is some evidence that early on there existed a four-part Pauline letter collection that included Romans, Hebrews, 1 Corinthians, and Ephesians.[16] Moreover, second-century writers who demonstrate knowledge of Hebrews also demonstrate knowledge of other Pauline letters, and sometimes of a letter collection.[17] In short, ancient Christian readers consistently associated Hebrews either with Paul or the *corpus Paulinum*, even as patristic literati recognized the problem of assigning Hebrews to Paul. Since manuscripts of Hebrews attest to

---

[13] Epp, "Issues in Textual Criticism and Canon," 502.

[14] See Kurt Aland, "Die Entstehung des Corpus Paulinum," in *Neutestamentliche Entwürfe* (ed. Kurt Aland; Munich: Kaiser, 1979), 302–350; David Trobisch, *Paul's Letter Collection: Tracing the Origins* (Philadelphia: Fortress, 1994), 10–21; as well as discussions by Epp, "Issues in Textual Criticism," 503–508; and Gamble, "New Testament Canon," 282–286.

[15] Although Gamble is not convinced that Hebrews was present in early collections of Paul's letters, he, like most others, recognizes the catholicizing tendency evident in the transmission of the Pauline letter collection ("New Testament Canon," 285; *Books and Readers*, 98–100). Nils Dahl pioneered this line of thought in "The Particularity of the Pauline Epistles as a Problem in the Ancient Church," in *Neotestamentica et Patristica: Eine Freundesgabe, Herrn Professor Dr. O. Cullmann zu seinem 60. Geburtstag überreicht* (NovTSup 6; Leiden: Brill, 1962), 261–271.

[16] See David Trobisch, *Die Entstehung der Paulusbriefsammlung: Studien zu den Anfängen christlicher Publizistik* (NTOA 10; Göttingen: Vandenhoeck & Ruprecht, 1989). A simplified version of Trobisch's argument concerning the four-letter collection appears in *Paul's Letter Collection*. It should also be noted that while Hebrews follows 2 Thessalonians in Codex Vaticanus, there exist chapter enumerations indicating that Hebrews should—or originally did—follow Galatians.

[17] A letter collection seems to be implied by the reference to "all his letters" in 2 Pet 3:15. Knowledge of multiple Pauline letters is also evident in *1 Clement*, Ignatius, and Polycarp. A thorough discussion can be found in Andreas Lindemann, *Paulus im ältesten Christentum: Das Bild des Apostels und die Rezeption der paulinischen Theologie in der frühchristlichen Literatur bis Markion* (BHT 58; Tübingen: Mohr Siebeck, 1979).

the document's having circulated without claiming Pauline authorship for itself (the way, say, Ephesians does) the question then arises: Why did readers, hearers, or scribes ever associate Hebrews with Paul in the first place?

This question is rarely posed. Rather, scholars assume the author was of the "Pauline school" and view the text as theologically resonant with Pauline views.[18] That there are similarities between Paul's letters and Hebrews can hardly be denied. At the same time, however, there are many dissimilarities, most glaringly of style—so much so that it is hard to imagine that hearing Hebrews read aloud would have reminded the listeners of Paul. Moreover, one can also point to similarities between Hebrews and 1 Peter (as many scholars have), but the textual history of Hebrews does not indicate a connection between Hebrews and the figure of Peter.[19] Thus doctrinal similarity seems unlikely as the motivating factor for placing Hebrews within the Pauline letter collection or ascribing Hebrews to Paul.[20] As for a personal connection between the writer of Hebrews and Paul or a Pauline congregation, it is certainly possible, perhaps even likely, but such a connection only intensifies the mystery of anonymity: why did the author of Hebrews not write pseudonymously in Paul's name, like others whose writings became part of the Pauline letter collection? Conversely, if the author was a leading member within a Christian community, why did he not use his own name, as did Ignatius of Antioch and Polycarp of Smyrna?[21]

---

[18] See, for example, David A. deSilva, who confidently asserts, "The author of Hebrews, in sum, is a member of the Pauline mission whose task it is to nurture and preserve the work started by the apostolic leader" (*Perseverance in Gratitude: A Socio-Rhetorical Commentary on the Epistle "to the Hebrews"* [Grand Rapids: Eerdmans, 2000], 39).

[19] A. Welch argued that Peter was the author, but, like most arguments identifying a particular individual as the author of Hebrews, this never caught on (*The Authorship of the Epistle to the Hebrews* [Edinburgh: Anderson & Ferrier, 1898]). Most of the proposed authors of Hebrews, however—other than Paul himself—have been Paul's associates.

[20] Cf. Hatch ("Position of Hebrews," 133–134) who argued that Hebrews was placed after Romans in $\mathfrak{P}^{46}$ because of theological similarities.

[21] Of course, Hebrews is not the only document in early Christianity to have circulated anonymously. But it does seem to be the only one connected to the Pauline school to have been anonymous. Cf. *1 Clement*, which begins with a salutation but does not name any individuals as senders, only "the church of God in Rome." Other letters of the second century, e.g., *Martyrdom of Polycarp* and *Letter of the Churches in Vienne and Lyons*, identify churches rather than individuals as their authors.

I propose three possible answers: (1) if Hebrews was originally a letter sent to a community by an author at some remove from it, whoever first inserted Hebrews into the *corpus Paulinum* omitted the address because it was not authored by Paul and/or because the author's name was of no significance; (2) if the text was originally designed as a speech composed for presentation to a local congregation, rather than as a letter, there would not have been a formal address to record the name of the speaker/writer and the text was simply preserved this way; (3) the author deliberately concealed his identity for some reason. Since certitude is unattainable, I will venture to move only from the possible to the probable.

The first option seems unlikely. Since there is no textual evidence that there ever was an epistolary salutation at the beginning of Hebrews, I consider it unlikely that Hebrews was originally composed as a letter. I realize that such a claim makes the last few verses of Hebrews (13:18–25) harder to explain, but these are the *only* verses that make Hebrews look like a letter at all. There are few points of direct address in the second person, and the author for the most part subsumes his individual voice into the collective "we."[22] If one accepts that Hebrews was not originally intended to be a letter, then the author, sometime after composing Hebrews, sent his composition to another community and added the final verses as a personal note, or perhaps he added the final verses to make the text look like a letter, particularly a Pauline letter. The latter is more probable than the former because if the author wished to send his treatise to another community, he would not have sent the original but made a copy, and the copy would in all likelihood have included an address, for which there is no trace in the textual tradition.[23]

Because there is a growing scholarly consensus that Hebrews was originally composed as a speech or, to use the author's own words, an "exhortation," the second explanation would appear more plausible than the first. There is also scholarly consensus that Hebrews reflects the work of a highly skilled writer. If Hebrews was originally a speech (which the author or a scribal editor later sent to one or

---

[22] Cf. deSilva, who perceives a distinct personality in Hebrews (*Perseverance in Gratitude*, 25).

[23] In regard to the likelihood of authors keeping copies of letters, see E. Randolph Richards, "The Codex and the Early Collection of Paul's Letters," *BBR* 8 (1998): 151–166; and Gamble, *Books and Readers*, 100–101.

more communities) then the document's anonymity must be explained as a literary accident: the author's identity was somehow lost by scribes who neglected to preserve it. But this, too, seems to me unlikely. Too many issues are left unresolved if the anonymity-as-accident theory is accepted. For example, there exists no evidence of variants of the superscription, "To the Hebrews." Although such superscriptions were added after a document became part of a collection, the consistency of the title "To the Hebrews" is striking, given that nothing in the document mentions "Hebrews" or "Jews." Moreover, titles of speeches normally refer to their subject matter, not their audience (cf. Melito's *De Pascha*, or Plutarch's *De Superstitione*).[24] Yet by raising these objections I do not mean to imply that Hebrews originally was a letter. But neither do I think it was a speech or sermon intended for a specific occasion or occasioned by a single event.

Hebrews was obviously written to be read aloud—its literary style, especially appealing to the ear, makes that clear—thus, in terms of modern genre typologies, Hebrews is a "speech." But I want to propose that the author of Hebrews was motivated by an *issue* rather than an occasion, and, further, that he was inspired by other Christian literature, most importantly, the letters of Paul, known to him as a corpus. This two-part proposal helps explain the title as well as the mixed message about whether the document was originally a letter or speech. I suggest that Hebrews was composed by an educated and theologically reflective person who wished to clarify and perhaps unify competing christological claims. The author is much more concerned about the subject of which he writes, namely a systematic understanding of Christology, than about the behavior or well-being of his audience. This theoretical focus distinguishes Hebrews not only from the authentic letters of Paul, but from the pseudonymous letters as well (with the possible exception of Ephesians). The cumulative effect of this evidence is that it is likely that the author was motivated by a theological issue rather than problems of practice in a particular community.[25] This observation alone, however,

---

[24] Comparing titles of Plutarch's various texts within the *Moralia* collection is instructive: some texts were obviously originally composed as letters, e.g., *Gamika Parangelmata* (*Advice to Bride and Groom*), which retains the address "From Plutarch to Pollianus and Eurydice, health and prosperity."

[25] See Eisenbaum, "The Virtue of Suffering, the Necessity of Discipline, and the Pursuit of Perfection in Hebrews," in *Asceticism in the New Testament* (ed. Leif Vaage and Vincent Wimbush; New York: Routledge, 1999), 331–353, esp. 331–332.

does not explain why no subject-related title was ever associated with Hebrews (such as "On the High Priesthood of Christ").

The superscription is best explained if someone (probably not the author but a scribal editor) first put the document into circulation as a part of the Pauline letter collection, so that the title "To the Hebrews" was consistently part of the exemplar scribes used to copy Hebrews. David Trobisch has argued that the four-letter edition of the *corpus Paulinum* mentioned earlier, which included Romans, Hebrews, 1 Corinthians, and Ephesians, came into existence in Paul's lifetime. That this collection belongs to such an early date strikes me as implausible, but because Trobisch argues that these four letters were intentionally compiled and edited as a group so as to provide a catholic edition for general circulation, it does seem likely that, among the many permutations of the Pauline letter collection, this four-letter edition circulated relatively early.[26] Gamble, who believes the earliest identifiable edition of the *corpus Paulinum* is a seven-letter edition, nevertheless relies on a similar argument, namely that this seven-letter edition was driven by the need to mitigate the particularity of the Pauline letters.[27]

My point is that in all likelihood whoever first supplied the superscription "To the Hebrews" was familiar with a catholicized *corpus Paulinum* in which it was not self-evident that Paul's letters were addressed to specific Christian communities. Let us take Paul's letter to the Romans, for example: since the designation "Romans" can be taken in several ways (e.g., the citizens of the Roman Empire generally, Roman imperial authorities, people living in the City of Rome, etc.), the person who wished to insert Hebrews into the *corpus Paulinum* would not necessarily understand *pros romaious* as reflective of an address to a specific group of believers.[28] Furthermore, Galatia

---

[26] Trobisch, *Die Enstehung der Paulusbriefsammlung*, 82–110; cf. Gamble ("New Testament Canon," 285–286), who critiques the ascription of the four-letter collection to the first century. See also Aland on the complexity and variety of Pauline letter collections ("Die Entstehung des Corpus Paulinum").

[27] Gamble, *Books and Readers*, 59–61; and Dahl, "The Origin of the Earliest Prologues to the Pauline Letters," *Semeia* 12 (1978): 233–277. This corpus actually consisted of ten letters, but was presented as "Paul's letters to the seven churches" (counting certain pairings of correspondence as "one" letter), as a way to give it catholic appeal. The ten letters were 1 and 2 Corinthians, Romans, Ephesians, 1 and 2 Thessalonians, Galatians, Philippians, Colossians, and Philemon—Philemon being counted together with Colossians.

[28] In addition, there is abundant evidence that Romans circulated in a departicularized form; see Gamble, *The Textual History of the Letter to the Romans* (Grand Rapids: Eerdmans, 1977).

was understood to be a province, Corinth a city, while the letter to the Ephesians was likely not addressed to people in Ephesus anyway but simply "to the holy ones who are also faithful in Christ Jesus."[29] In other words, whoever titled Hebrews "To the Hebrews" may not have understood that Pauline letter titles normally matched the particular Christian communities to whom they were originally addressed. (Perhaps he thought the letters were addressed to *kinds* of people?) Thus either the author or the scribal editor who inserted Hebrews into the Pauline letter collection named the document "To the Hebrews" partly in imitation of Pauline letter-titles (as he understood them) and partly because he thought it aptly related to the text's contents as envisioned within the *corpus Paulinum*.[30]

If Hebrews was only published as part of the Pauline letter collection, then the anonymity of Hebrews is explained by the scribal editor's desire to blend the text into the Pauline letter collection. Presumably the editor thought the work would gain credibility by its association with Paul, but the editor did not need to insert Paul's name into the text by creating a phony salutation with a phony address; Hebrews' presence in the collection was enough. Indeed, once a collection of Paul's letters began to circulate with Hebrews included, Hebrews was perceived to be connected to Paul (or his followers), even when its authorship was doubted, as by Origen and Chrysostom.[31] In sum, the author or scribal editor deliberately concealed his identity as an *implicit* form of pseudonymity.[32]

Date

I agree with the majority of scholars that *1 Clement* betrays knowledge of Hebrews. Since the date of *1 Clement* is not fixed, the *terminus ad quem* for Hebrews can be as late as the first quarter of the

---

[29] Gamble, *Books and Readers*, 98.

[30] As Gamble says of those responsible for developing the *corpus Paulinum* in the second century: "they were shaped by ideas about the number of letters or addressees and about the order of the letters and that had distinctive textual complexions" (*Books and Readers*, 100).

[31] Cf. Gamble's comments on Ignatius's letters, which became widely known and influential only as a corpus (*Books and Readers*, 110–111).

[32] Cf. the comment of Erich Grässer: "... weil die Anonymität vom Hebräerbriefautor *gewollt* ist." (*An Die Hebräer* [3 vols.; EKKNT 17; Zürich: Benziger and Neukirchen-Vluyn: Neukirchener, 1990–1997], 1:17; emphasis in original).

second century. The *terminus a quo* is harder to fix. The most important question in this regard—and the one that constitutes the biggest debate in studies of Hebrews—is whether the text was written before or after the destruction of the temple in Jerusalem in 70 CE. There are two common arguments in favor of dating Hebrews prior to 70: that the author speaks of the sacrificial cult as if it were a present reality; and that he would have been compelled to mention the destruction of the temple—had it already taken place—in order to demonstrate his supersessionist view of the new covenant in Christ. The first argument is unconvincing because many other ancient authors, Jewish and Christian, speak of the temple and sacrifice in the present tense long after the temple has been destroyed.[33] The second argument, however, is not as easily dismissed and requires more consideration.

The author of Hebrews, more so than any other NT author, argues strongly for the "obsolescence" of Judaism, or at least the end of the "old covenant" (Heb 8:13; 10:9). If this is the point of which he wishes to persuade his audience, what better proof than God's destruction of the temple, which put a decisive end to the priestly establishment in Jerusalem and the practice of cultic sacrifice? The omission must mean, so the argument goes, that the author writes the text prior to the destruction of Jerusalem and probably prior to the Jewish War with Rome.

While this argument is by no means implausible, its flaws are significant. First, the author of Hebrews never actually uses the word "temple." He speaks only of the "tabernacle," which encased the presence of God and was carried by the Israelites in the wilderness. Indeed, the author gives no impression of having experiential knowledge of the temple cult. All the information conveyed in Hebrews about the cult derives from the biblical text, primarily Exodus and Leviticus. Second, the argument that Hebrews is written prior to the temple's destruction is usually predicated on the assumption that the addressees are retreating from their commitment to Christ and moving back toward traditional Judaism and, if this is the case, then the author's neglecting to mention the fall of the temple seems peculiar. But, as I intend to show subsequently, if the addressees are not from Jewish backgrounds, but are Gentile, or of mixed origins, then the

---

[33] See, e.g., Josephus, *C. Ap.* 2.77; *1 Clem.* 40; and *Diogn.* 3.

omission in Hebrews of this cataclysmic event in recent Jewish history does not seem so surprising. The omission is even less surprising if the author is not writing to people in Jerusalem, but rather to those who have no direct experience of the tragedy. Third, it is possible to stand the argument on its head, so to speak. The author's conviction that the cult is obsolete may be derived from its already having disappeared as a result of the war. In other words, the author has reached his conclusions precisely because his ruminations about these matters happen in a world that is devoid of Jewish cultic institutions. In this case, the author does not feel compelled to mention the destruction because it is a fact he and his constituents take for granted. Thus the argument for a pre-70 date begs some of the questions it attempts to answer. Because it constitutes an argument from silence, the author's failure to mention the fate of the temple can never be a decisive indicator for dating Hebrews.

Similarly, the numerous attempts to date Hebrews by relying on references to persecution found in the text have not worked. Because they are not historically specific, they can be interpreted in various ways. While the abuse is reportedly serious—the audience has been plundered of its possessions (Heb 10:34)—they have not suffered to the point of shedding blood (Heb 12:4). Among scholars who support a Roman context for Hebrews, several see these remarks as indicative of a time before the Neronian persecution in 64. However, if the intended audience was located in the surrounding environs, but not necessarily within the city itself, they may not have experienced the same incendiary death suffered by the urban Christians in Rome. Moreover, if Hebrews were written well after the Neronian persecution (in the 90's?), the generation to which the author writes might not have experienced that persecution first-hand. Like the destruction of the Jerusalem temple, Nero's burning of Christians in Rome cannot be used as a marker for either an early or a late date.

Ultimately, there is no way to disguise the lack of concrete data pointing to a specific historical moment. This realization has led Attridge to say that a date cannot be pinned down beyond the range of 60–100 CE.[34] While it is difficult to argue with absolute conviction, my view is that a date sometime early in the second century (or very late in the first) is much more likely than an earlier date. I have three reasons for this view.

---

[34] Attridge, *Hebrews*, 9.

First and most simply, the author of Hebrews places some distance between the time of Jesus and his own audience. As he says in Heb 2:3, "how can we escape if we neglect so great a salvation, which was from the beginning spoken through the Lord, confirmed for us by those who heard him."[35] "Confirmed for us by those who heard him" indicates that the writer of Hebrews is at least one generation removed from Jesus and his first followers. I say "at least" because "confirmed for us by those who heard him" does not necessarily mean that such teachings were passed directly from the apostles to the community addressed by Hebrews.[36] Early Christians believed that faithful disciples could reliably transmit teachings orally, such that it was as good as receiving the information from the Lord himself. In any case, the author and audience cannot be placed within the first community of disciples.

More importantly, when the author says "confirmed" (ἐβεβαιώθη), he is not likely referring to casual oral communication, but to more official, or officially recognized, types of testimony that validated what was previously spoken.[37] The βεβαιόω word-group is used several times by the author of Hebrews. The RSV and NRSV rendering of this verb in Heb 2:3 as "attested," however, does not reflect its usual range of meaning. The Greek word generally means to confirm, establish, secure, or guarantee, hence my translation of "confirmed."[38] Indeed, in Heb 2:2, the author uses the related adjective βέβαιος; there it is traditionally rendered as "valid," as in, "if the message declared through angels was valid." In Heb 2:3 the author clearly means to convey that what was first spoken by the Lord was somehow confirmed or established or perhaps even that it was ratified or made efficacious.[39] The mention of "signs and wonders" in the following verse may well refer to the powers granted to the apostles as "proof" of Jesus' authenticity. Together, the two verses read:

> [H]ow can we escape if we neglect so great a salvation, which was from the beginning spoken through the Lord, confirmed for us by those who heard him, while God at the same time bore witness by

---

[35] Translations of Hebrews are mine, based on the NRSV.
[36] Heb 2:3 has sometimes been used to argue that the audience cannot be more than one generation removed from Jesus. See, e.g., William L. Lane, *Hebrews* (2 vols.; WBC 47; Dallas: Word Books, 1991), 1:lviii.
[37] Attridge, *Hebrews*, 67.
[38] "βεβαιόω," BDAG 172–173.
[39] Cf. the author's use of the verb βεβαιόω in Heb 9:17.

signs and wonders and various miracles, and by allotments of the holy spirit, according to his will. (Heb 2:3–4)

"Signs and wonders" frequently refers to the powers of the apostles as described in the book of Acts.[40] Paul uses the expression in the same way;[41] signs and wonders confirm the authenticity of an apostle. It may even be that the author of Hebrews is referring specifically to Pentecost, which followed almost immediately upon Jesus' ascension, since he includes the phrase "allotments of the Holy Spirit," but this cannot be determined with certainty. Nevertheless, the author of Hebrews almost surely refers to the apostles (at least those people who are widely recognized as legitimate purveyors of the gospel message) in Heb 2:3, and his use of the verb βεβαιόω, "confirm," communicates his belief that the apostles' teaching was not merely the passing on of the message but its establishment as a divine constitution.

The author uses the same terminology in Heb 9:17 in reference to a will "taking effect" (βεβαία) when the person who wrote it dies. That the term in Heb 2:3 connotes something like "taking effect" or "being instituted" is further implied by the parallelism between Heb 2:2 and 2:3. Just as "the message declared through angels became valid (βέβαιος)," which is the author's way of saying that the word of God formerly spoken by the prophets—or the "old covenant," as he now thinks of it—was officially instituted, presumably in the form of Torah, so now what was spoken by the Lord has been "confirmed"; it has become a newly effectuated covenant. Such a view seems more plausibly located later, rather than earlier, in the first century. Moreover, this terminology may indicate that the author understands the new covenant to have taken written form already, and it is from such texts that the Lord has spoken.

My second reason for dating Hebrews late builds on the first: I strongly suspect that the writer of Hebrews knows other early Christian writings, including one or more written gospels. My reasons for making the suggestion about the author's access to written gospels depends on the presence of some important details about Jesus' life that appear

---

[40] The expression "signs and wonders" occurs several times in Acts: Acts 2:22, 43; 4:30; 5:12; 6:8, 7:36; 14:3; 15:12. In the gospel literature it appears only in John 4:48.

[41] In the Pauline literature, the expression appears in Rom 15:19; 2 Cor 12:12; and 2 Thess 2:9.

in Hebrews. Admittedly, direct literary dependence is very difficult to prove, and I will not attempt it here. However, I think a reasonably strong case can be made that Hebrews knows either a written gospel or at least a gospel tradition that post-dates the destruction of the temple:[42]

> [W]hich (hope) we have as an anchor of the soul, steady and firm and reaching into the interior of the veil (καταπετάσματος), where Jesus has entered as a forerunner for us, having become High Priest forever according to the order of Melchizedek. (Heb 6:19–20)

> Therefore, brothers and sisters, we have confidence for (gaining) entrance into the Holy Place by the blood of Jesus, which (entrance) he offered to us as a new and life-giving way through the veil (καταπετάσματος), that is, his flesh. (Heb 10:19–20)

The only other NT writers who use the term καταπέτασμα are Mark, Matthew, and Luke. The latter two derive their usage from Mark, for the mention of the veil comes at the same point in the gospel story in all three, at the moment of the crucifixion.[43] For Hebrews, and presumably for the gospel writers, it refers to the entry point the priest passed through on Yom Kippur to enter the "Holy of Holies."[44] Although Hebrews does not describe the *tearing* of the curtain, the connection between gaining entry into the inner sanctum of the temple and Jesus' death is striking. It is difficult to imagine that Jesus' crucifixion would have been linked to entry into the inner sanctum as an independent theological tradition or that such a theological interpretation would have naturally come to mind prior to the destruction of the temple. Thus I suggest that these two passages in Hebrews and their resonance with the tearing of the curtain in the synoptic gospels provide strong evidence for a post-destruction date for Hebrews.

My third reason for dating Hebrews relatively late is its affinity to writings of the second century. Christians of the second century begin to write in a more elevated style and to write for broader audiences. They also write treatises that pursue a sustained line of

---

[42] Although I will not attempt to make a case for them here, other details of Jesus' life connected to gospel tradition appear in Heb 2:14–18 (the temptation story) and Heb 5:7 (Gethsemane).

[43] Mark 15:38; Matt 27:51; Luke 23:44.

[44] It is clear that καταπέτασμα refers to the veil that divides the inner sanctum from the rest of the tabernacle; see Attridge, *Hebrews*, 184–185, 284.

argumentation about a theological issue; most first-century Christian documents do not follow such a form. While certainly there were real-life circumstances that influenced the writer of Hebrews to compose his brilliant essay on Christology, it might also be the case that the author is partly motivated by the very existence of other Christian literature that is in circulation. In other words, he is inspired to write because he has been inspired by other Christian writings, perhaps because he recognizes that they hold the power to influence others.

It is clear that the influence of the Pauline letter collection on subsequent Christian writers from the late first century onwards can hardly be overstated. Even before there were standardized collections, it is evident that letters were passed on to others beyond those to whom they were originally sent. It is likely that the practice of sharing letters initiates the trajectory of catholicizing, and the formation of the *corpus Paulinum* is almost surely a result of the desire to universalize the Pauline letters.[45] The tendency to address Christian audiences broadly increases significantly in second-century writings. Thus, when the author of *1 Clement* wrote to the Corinthian church to chastise them about deposing leaders they should not have deposed, he need not have written the 65 chapters that now comprise the document. His lengthy disquisitions about the harmony of all creation, his exhortative discussions of obedience, humility, and other virtues that promote peace and harmony—all of which he bolsters with countless examples from scripture—are indications that his purpose is not merely to fix the situation at Corinth, but to address Christians at large on the subject of church unity and to construct arguments that would earn the respect of any others who happen to come upon his letter.

As Gamble has said of such apostolic writings, "From a literary standpoint all these documents are less pieces of occasional correspondence than they are theological essays in letter form."[46] In my view, Hebrews is the quintessential example of the "theological essay" of which Gamble speaks, and thus its genre makes more sense within the context of the early second century. This does not mean that it was not originally "occasioned" by more particular social circum-

---

[45] A similar tendency can be observed in the way several of the Catholic Epistles address their audiences: James: "to the twelve tribes in the dispersion"; 1 Peter: "to the exiles of the dispersion"; 2 Peter: "to those who have obtained faith."

[46] Gamble, *Books and Readers*, 106.

stances, but I do not think the text of Hebrews provides enough information to enable us to reconstruct these circumstances. The circumstances of Hebrews that are most readily identifiable are literary and bibliographic and thus pertain to its publication and circulation, not its initial production.

Addressees

Scholars have advocated many different locations for Hebrews. My own view is that Hebrews has some connection to Rome, but since it has been notoriously difficult for scholars to reach any agreement about Hebrews' point of origin or the locale of the addressees, I do not wish to defend the connection to Rome now. Rather, I will focus on the two issues that continue to preoccupy most commentators on Hebrews: whether Hebrews was directed to a specific audience or a general or ideal audience; and the background or ethnic make-up of its addressees.

First to the matter of whether Hebrews is written for a specific audience. It seems to me that lack of geographic references (with the exception of "those from Italy" in the postscript) and inability of scholars to reach agreement among the countless proposed possibilities, indicate that, in fact, the text is devoid of the information needed to identify the addressees' geographic location. Thus I understand Hebrews as directed to an ideal audience imagined by the author. To the extent that audiences are always projections by an author,[47] understanding Hebrews as written not to a single community but rather to a more broadly understood body of Christians does more justice to the text of Hebrews than narrowing its implied audience to a single place at a single moment. Furthermore, there is so little specificity of any kind relating to the social situation that lies behind Hebrews that it seems not merely accidental. In another words, Hebrews is *suspiciously* lacking in information related to questions of who, what, where, when, etc. Although the first public reading of Hebrews must have taken place at a particular time in a particular place, this moment in history, and thus the social situation, is not recoverable. Hebrews—whether originally composed in

---

[47] As Attridge says, "In some respects, as contemporary literary critics point out, the audience as we know it is the creation of the text" (*Hebrews*, 9 n. 66).

order to be part of the Pauline letter collection or later edited so as to fit into that collection—was "published" and became known as part of a collection, not as an independent writing. The very reason such collections were formed was to facilitate broad circulation. Thus the encoded audience of Hebrews is a Christian audience broadly conceived.

Now to the second issue: the ethnic background or religious leanings of the addressees. Many interpreters, even when they are resigned about pinning down the specific geographic or chronological context, attempt to understand the social circumstances of the audience, particularly with regard to their religious or ethnic backgrounds, practices, and beliefs. Put another way, scholars attempt to reconstruct what problems or conditions existed among the addressees and then these problems or conditions are understood to have prompted the author of Hebrews to respond.[48]

Since I do not think we possess the data to describe the social circumstances that gave rise to the composing of Hebrews, I do not think we can describe the social background(s) of the real-life individuals and communities to whom Hebrews was addressed. However, when I say Hebrews is addressed to a general audience, I do not mean anyone and everyone the author can possibly imagine; I mean that the audience was deliberately conceived to include Christians more generally, and perhaps Jews or God-fearers who might well be persuaded by the author's argument about the nature and significance of Christ. The question thus remains: who are the implied or ideal readers and what seems to be at stake in the argument the author constructs?

More often than not, the traditional view of the addressees of Hebrews as either Jewish-Christians or Judaizing Christians still prevails, although recently more commentators seem amenable to the idea that Hebrews is addressed to a Gentile or mixed audience.[49] Others have astutely pointed out that not only is the ethnic background of the addressees elusive, but its determination contributes

---

[48] Lindars, in *Theology of the Letter to the Hebrews*, is one example of a scholar who offers a considerably detailed reconstruction of the events that prompted the writing of Hebrews; another (though very different) is Ernst Käsemann, *The Wandering People of God: An Investigation of the Letter to the Hebrews* (trans. Roy A. Harrisville; Minneapolis: Augsburg, 1984).

[49] See my discussion in *The Jewish Heroes of Christian History: Hebrews 11 in Literary Context* (SBLDS 156; Atlanta: Scholars Press, 1997), 7–11.

little to the understanding of Hebrews, since the author is most concerned to address their identity as Christians, encouraging them not to flag in their Christian commitment.[50] One reason for the question's insolubility is that we have tended to operate with general assumptions about religious, ethnic, and political identity in antiquity that are anachronistic; particularly anachronistic have been our assumptions about what constitutes "Judaism" and "Christianity" in the first few centuries of the Common Era, both at the communal and individual level. Recent works dealing with Jewish-Christian relations in antiquity as well as the nature of religious identity among Jews and Christians in the first four centuries are, I suspect, just beginning to reveal how problematic our categories are for understanding how an ancient Jew or Christian constructed their religious identity.[51] Most relevant to the matter at hand is the questioning of the so-called "parting of the ways"—the separation of Judaism and Christianity, which used to be regarded as largely accomplished by the turn of the second century—so that those scholars who have worked most extensively on ancient Jewish-Christian relations think such separation came about much more slowly and unevenly and that perhaps we should not speak of separate and distinct communal identities until the fourth or fifth century.

Let me move from these broad historiographical generalizations to more specific observations about the late first and early second century and the implications for locating Hebrews socially and chronologically. There were three wars between Romans and Jews during this time. The significance of the war of 66–70, resulting in the destruction of the Second Temple, need not be recounted in detail. We know less about the Diaspora war of 115–117 when the Jews of Egypt, Cyprus, and Cyrenaica rebelled, but most scholars seem to think it resulted in the decimation of Egyptian Jewry.[52] The third war, the Bar Kochba revolt of 132–135, resulted in the de-Judaization

---

[50] Koester, *Hebrews*, 46–48.

[51] See, for example, the recent collection of essays in *The Ways that Never Parted: Jews and Christians in Late Antiquity and the Early Middle Ages* (ed. Adam H. Becker and Annette Yoshiko Reed; Tübingen: Mohr Siebeck, 2003); and Judith M. Lieu, "'The Parting of the Ways': Theological Construct or Historical Reality?" in *Neither Jew nor Greek: Constructing Early Christianity* (London: T&T Clark, 2002), 11–29; repr. from *JSNT* 56 (1994): 101–119.

[52] See Shaye J. D. Cohen, *From the Maccabees to the Mishnah* (Philadelphia: Westminster/John Knox, 1987), 17.

of Jerusalem, which was reconstituted as Aelia Capitolina, and the renaming as Palestina of the region once known as Judea. In short, the late first and early second century may stand as the worst period of Jewish-Roman relations. Certainly, it was a time of ongoing conflict and persecution. Furthermore, as Seth Schwartz has recently argued, material and literary remains seem to indicate that Jewish society in Palestine barely existed at all, and, presumably, any sense of Jewish identity that individuals possessed might have amounted to no more than a vague memory.[53] After three wars, countless Jews were no doubt sold into slavery and were detached from their usual connections of support.

The second century also provides the first direct evidence of Roman persecution of Christians *qua* Christians, in Pliny's letter to Trajan and in the letters of Ignatius.[54] It remains unclear to what extent and by what criteria Romans began to differentiate between Christians and Jews, but I suspect that many Christians, especially during the first revolt, were victims of Rome's revenge on rebellious Jews. The fact that the gospels were composed in the wake of the temple's destruction indicates how significant the destruction of the temple was to Christians as well as Jews. But by the early second century, the letters of Ignatius and Pliny's letter to Trajan provide evidence that Christians were persecuted for being Christians. Thus martyrdom and resistance to Rome, especially resistance to participation in the idolatrous imperial cult, were something that Jews and Christians shared in common during this period.

If one grants that Hebrews was written after the destruction of the temple, it is difficult to imagine that the recipients of Hebrews would have been attracted to Judaism because of the security and status it enjoyed in the Roman world. Yet the assumption that the addressees are either Jewish Christians or Judaizing Christians, together with the references to persecution, has led the majority of commentators to hold this view (with minor variations and permutations). While the author is clearly steeped in knowledge of the LXX and is focused on the relationship of Jesus' sacrifice to the Israelite cultic practices surrounding the tabernacle, there is nothing in Hebrews that indicates the addressees practice some form of Judaism. The

---

[53] Seth Schwartz, *Imperialism and Jewish Society: 200 BCE to 640 CE* (Princeton: Princeton University Press, 2001).

[54] Nero's persecution of Christians in 64 is recorded later by Tacitus.

references in Heb 6:2 and 9:10 to ablutions are not only *not* distinctly Christian, they are not distinctly Jewish; perhaps that is why the author calls them *various* ablutions (Heb 9:10). As with the practice of blood sacrifice itself, these are practices that pious Jews and Gentiles would not find strange, but would associate instinctively with religious piety. The same could be said about the mention of "food and drink" in Heb 9:10 and "foods" in Heb 13:9 ("be strengthened by grace, not by foods, which have not benefited their adherents"). That the author has in mind an audience who might believe in the religious power of certain eating practices (cultic meals, festival meals, or foods associated with magic) or abstention from certain foods at certain times does not necessarily point to the observance of *kashrut*. Although the author mentions these items within discussions about the meaning of scripture, and thus one might infer the audience follows the practices prescribed in scripture, the author's rhetoric hardly indicates that the addressees were engaged in specific practices to which the author objects and because of which he writes. What is more likely is that the author is expounding scripture for the edification of his audience, whom he sees as not adequately knowledgeable of "the oracles of God." His mention of foods or ablutions is couched in such a way that a Jew or a Gentile would understand that such religious practices are unimportant; they are a matter of teachings, not of actual practice. He is more forceful in his accusations of sluggishness and their failing to meet together, so that commentators take these comments as indicators of the situation of the audience. In the case of sluggishness, this seems to me a classic rhetorical move designed to "rev people up" and thus offers little historical information. As Attridge says, their failing to meet is the most concrete datum about the audience there is.[55] Yet it is not clear that there are specific ritual meetings they are failing to attend; the issue is simply that they do not meet as often as they should. The need to meet is not made clear, though one can infer that if people do *not* meet together, the extent to which they form a community is in doubt.

My point is that the "situation" that most likely inspired the author of Hebrews, other than his devotion to the study of scripture and theological reflection itself, is indeed religious identity, but this identity is not one form of Christianity over against another, nor is it

---

[55] Attridge, *Hebrews*, 12.

even the attempt to construct a Christian identity over against Jewish identity (*in spite of* its seeming supersessionist theology). Indeed, Hebrews is noticeably lacking in the polemics that characterize the gospels and Paul's letters. Those writings often give the impression that those who make up the body of Christ are not associated with or do not understand themselves as part of the Jewish community. Christian polemics against Jews pick up again in the mid-second century, with the writings of Barnabas, Melito, Justin, Tertullian and others. As Judith M. Lieu has observed, there seems to be a hiatus in the rancor in the early second century.[56] The authors of 1 Peter, *1 Clement*, and other works known only in fragments from Eusebius are not concerned to construct a rhetoric of difference between Judaism and Christianity. Many scholars have recognized and articulated the similarities between 1 Peter, Hebrews, and *1 Clement*, but they are usually accounted for on the grounds of all belonging to Roman Christianity and/or literary dependence or oral tradition. I want to suggest that the resonances add up to something more.

These texts have the following in common: knowledge or experience of persecution coupled with repeated exhortations to endure by following the example of Jesus; an emphasis on the blood of Christ; and an understanding of the believers as aliens and sojourners in this world. Moreover, all these writers demonstrate that they are learned in the scriptures, and through exposition they explicate the relationship between the past as preserved in scripture and the current world in which they live. But from the standpoint of Jewish-Christian relations, as well as relations between Jews and Christians on the one hand and pagan Rome on the other, the similarities of these documents indicate that the shared experience of persecution during this time may have led to a greater sense of commonality among Jews and Christians, or, at the very least, little awareness of any significant differences. Whereas once I would have lumped Hebrews together with Barnabas because of its supersessionist theology, I now see Hebrews' "supersessionism" as possibly a desperate attempt to construct anew a religious heritage that seems to have all but disappeared. It is in some ways neither Judaism nor Christianity

---

[56] Judith M. Lieu, *Image and Reality: The Jews in the World of the Christians in the Second Century* (Edinburgh: T&T Clark, 1996), 4.

and in other ways it represents both—a unique form of Judeo-Christian religiosity that perhaps existed briefly when Rome was the common enemy of Jews and believers in Jesus and before the rhetoric of Christian and Jewish leaders could construct firm boundaries between Judaism and Christianity.

Pamela M. Eisenbaum, Ph.D.
Associate Professor of Biblical Studies and Christian Origins
Iliff School of Theology
2201 S. University Boulevard, Denver, Colo. 80210-4798, U.S.A.
peisenbaum@iliff.edu

HEBREWS AND THE HERITAGE OF PAUL

Dieter Georgi[1]

Since my student days I have been made increasingly aware of how much images can influence understanding. I learned that this was even stronger in the case of common as well as unconscious images. One of the images it has not been easy to shake off since my very first days of study at the university in Mainz is the term "school"—in my case, the "Bultmann-school." As a student of Ernst Käsemann and of Eduard Schweizer I was automatically counted among the "Bultmannschüler." This was further reinforced when I was employed as assistant of Günther Bornkamm, my "Doktorvater," as we call that in Germany, since he was another "Schüler" of Rudolf Bultmann. By association, any direct or indirect "Schüler" of Bultmann was considered as belonging to the same unitary school, even though I learned that Käsemann, Schweizer, and Bornkamm could easily disagree with each other and with Bultmann, and I with them.

My association with this "school" remained in later years, when I, succeeding Helmut Koester, became involved in the organization of the "Arbeitskreis Alte Marburger." This was the name of the annual meeting of the former students of Bultmann, with Bultmann himself present each time. Despite the fact that the participants of these meetings were identified as "Bultmannschüler," one of my interesting experiences was that more than half of the participants would deny that they belonged to a "Bultmann-Schule."

The question therefore was: is this actually a school or is it not? And if it is, what does it mean to be a member of a school? In my own personal case as well as in that of a good number of fellow students who regularly had teachers from different "schools," the issue could become confused quite easily: for example, was I not part of the so-called "Barth-Schule" as well? Despite all the variations

---

[1] Due to a serious ailment I was unable to deliver the following paper. I am grateful to Harold W. Attridge, himself the author of an imposing and fascinating commentary on Hebrews. He stepped in and read the paper and did so without hesitation.

and confusions existing in the practical reality of these so-called "schools," my experience has been that people possess very definite hermeneutical associations when they use the metaphor and image of "school." So, despite having studied with different teachers and in different universities, and despite my own long and varied international teaching career, I have regularly been called a "Bultmannian" to this day.

The concept of "school" is not a new one, and closer study reveals that the ancient and best-known "schools" already anticipate to a high degree the personal experiences I spoke about. For example, the "Socratic school" as a whole does not represent a unity but rather a very extensive variety. The teachings of the different branches of this "school" were not uniform.

The term "school" usually requires one head who is revered by several students. It requires a stringent curriculum, continued even after the founder of the school and his original students have died.

You might think that I have lost Hebrews from sight. On the contrary. In any discussion of Hebrews, the term "school" as in "Pauline school" quickly comes into the picture, usually poorly defined. Out of my own self-interest as an alleged member of a modern "school," I find it proper to approach the problem of the succession of generations in a typological as well as a historical sense. The title I gave to my opening lecture in Heidelberg was "Das Problem der *Generationenfolge* im Urchristentum." Here Hebrews played a major role. The common debate then revolved around the issue of Pauline authorship and the Roman Catholic claim of Pauline authenticity of Hebrews. But this debate obviously has little interpretative weight. Much more significant is the question of whether there was such a thing as a "Pauline school." Or was there not rather a succession of generations, each with its own independence?

An important point of enlightenment with respect to the nature and role of Hebrews came for me from the book of Günther Zuntz, *The Text of the Epistles: A Disquisition upon the Corpus Paulinum.*[2] The book had a strong impact on me and inspired me further.

The first challenge of the book was the opposition to the com-

---

[2] Günther Zuntz, *The Text of the Epistles: A Disquisition upon the Corpus Paulinum* (The Schweich Lectures of the British Academy, 1946; London: Oxford University Press, 1953).

mon separation of textual criticism and other methodological steps in exegesis. I know that it is very difficult to move beyond the common division of methods, especially to give up on the isolation of textual criticism. But the arguments of Zuntz made it obvious that the interplay of textual criticism and exegesis is not only important for autographs, but is to be taken into account in the case of later copyists and their collections too.

As regards the first challenge, it means that in many cases variants are not merely differences in copying of texts but the consequence of revisionary activity. This includes conscious decisions about exclusion and inclusion of documents. If Zuntz is correct in his analysis that the early Pauline papyrus 𝔓⁴⁶ shows signs of textual-critical skill and even the presence of revisionary activity, and if there is any inkling that the person who copied or is represented by 𝔓⁴⁶ had redactional interests in this collection, then why not try to push the "who was it?" question of 𝔓⁴⁶ much further: was there not only revisionary activity involved, but independent thinking about the impact of Paul?

This brings up another issue, namely, whether Hebrews in its original form interprets the Epistle to the Romans. The direct relationship of Hebrews and Paul found in 𝔓⁴⁶ enhances the thesis of my teacher William Manson that Hebrews interprets Paul, in particular Romans.[3]

Manson lists a limited number of quite important terms and ideas in Hebrews: righteousness, justification, and Christology. He adds martyrdom, a concept usually considered marginal. Nevertheless it occurs in key places, like Paul's discussion of apostleship and in traditional formulae like Rom 3:24–26 and parallels.[4]

---

[3] William Manson, *The Epistle to the Hebrews. An Historical and Theological Reconsideration* (2d ed.; London: Hodder & Stoughton, 1953).

[4] In Rom 3:24–26 and 5:9, Paul is reinterpreting martyrological traditions. In Rom 3:24–26, the martyrological dimension is signified by the use of the term ἱλαστήριον, which is found in 4 Macc 17:22 in a martyrological sense and means there the saving effect of the death of the martyrs (in the plural). In these two passages in Romans, the term αἷμα appears. It is so rare in Paul (only four times altogether) that the existence of a tradition seems to be an obvious option. The saving event is brought about by the innocent death of a certain individual (plural or singular). The concept of the death of a martyr is found in the tradition of the Lord's Supper in 1 Cor 10:16 and in 11:27. The notion of a tradition here appears obvious because Paul again has the death of an individual in view. Rom 8 speaks of martyrdom too, supported by the term ἀπολύτρωσις, a word that is also rare for Paul (Rom 3:24).

Another challenge is Zuntz's placement of Hebrews as $\mathfrak{P}^{46}$ does, and the resulting consequences. Contrary to the usual order of Paul's letters, $\mathfrak{P}^{46}$ and Zuntz place Hebrews after the Epistle to the Romans. This positioning is not found in any other manuscript. It follows that the canon of the Pauline writings is later than Hebrews. The very fact that the positioning of Hebrews is not supported by any other manuscript and is unique in the Church speaks for an early date of this text.

So far the discussion has made it obvious that $\mathfrak{P}^{46}$ is older than all other manuscripts which we have. I propose that the collection of the other letters going under the name of Paul was collected at the earliest at the end of the second century. In the second generation, the other Pauline writings were collected and interpreted with all probability under the guidance of Hebrews. A third generation reverses the order of the writings of Paul to our present form, with Hebrews at the end. The curious consequence of this development is that the least Catholic letter and its tradition is claimed as authentic by the Roman Catholic church.

I suggest that the composition as we have it in $\mathfrak{P}^{46}$ gives us decisive hermeneutical keys and the clue that a learned writer of the Hellenistic-Roman age, influenced by Jewish training, was involved.

Zuntz gives the Gnosis-issue a direction that would move it beyond the usual misunderstanding as "Weltanschauung" and into a primarily hermeneutical dimension. This would easily go together with a certain learnedness which was typical for Gnostics. Zuntz is right.

So the first two chapters of Hebrews demonstrate a close interplay of biblical exegesis and mythical presupposition and projection and are quite significant, especially if read in the succession $\mathfrak{P}^{46}$ offers.

Manson is right when he addresses major issues of the Pauline epistles, particularly controversial ones, as arising from the attempt by the followers of Jesus to put their relationship with the Jews on a different level. Manson also brings the concept of martyrdom into the discussion.

On the basis of the tradition behind $\mathfrak{P}^{46}$ one can argue that Hebrews redirects the understanding of righteousness, justification, and Christology as presented by Paul in Romans, so that they no longer function as points of polemics against or division from Jewish tradition, but rather provide a common basis. The writer of the original copy of Hebrews, by his conscious integration of Jewish martyrdom-theology, interprets πίστις as "trust" rather than as "faith/belief."

The usual argument that Hebrews is written rather late is merely an unfounded hypothesis. A dating of Hebrews during the time of Domitian makes more sense because at that time we definitely have Christian martyrs. My hypothesis therefore is that the author of Hebrews writes his tractate under Domitian, putting behind him the experience of Jewish and "Christian" martyrdoms, at a time when the question of whether church and synagogue should separate was still undecided. They are definitely not separated yet. But both have to deal with the catastrophe of the first Jewish War and the question whether the Pharisaic-rabbinic tradition was the only proper representation and continuation of pre-70 Judaism. The church was undecided on that matter. Matthew, for instance, was of the opinion that the Pharisaic-rabbinic direction was the right one. It only needed Jesus, the Christ turned into wisdom, as the basic authority.

Hebrews builds on the majority of Judaism, that of the Diaspora. After the destruction of the temple, Diaspora Judaism had lost its center. The majority of the Diaspora Jews were not interested in following the Pharisaic rabbis, and the majority of the Diaspora synagogue had questioned the cultic reality, importance, and functions of the temple long before its destruction. In fact, they had replaced it by a more or less spiritualized understanding. The Christology of Hebrews plays a major role in this change, with Melchizedek as a rather decisive figure. It appears to be the intention of Hebrews to push not only the church but also Judaism at large into that direction as the proper understanding of the biblical tradition and of the task of God's people, not understood as anti-Jewish but as pro-Jewish. Thus the address "to the Hebrews" may originally have been demonstrating that the "newness" that Paul (and Hebrews) were talking about was biblical and not anti-Jewish segregationist. There is some polemic, particularly in Heb 13:9–11, against those who want some material aspects of cultic activity to be brought to life again, most probably something of a sacramental character. Hebrews is entirely against anything like that. In this much teaching and teachers play a role. Hebrews takes the Jewish catastrophe as a final judgment not only against any cultic endeavors, but also against the Jewish hierarchy—an aspect that is often overlooked.

Under heavy influence of Deuteronomy, Hebrews understands law most of all as parenesis. This would find some parallels in Paul's reinterpretation of the law. Following biblical models as well as the Diaspora experience, the epistle offers the liberating journey through the desert as a mode of existence for the joint venture of church and synagogue in the future. Thus Hebrews understood "his" Paul as a new offer for synagogue and church, not only for their survival but also for their flourishing in a world that seemed overcome by the powers of a demonized state.

Prof. Dr. theol. Dieter Georgi
Professor für Neues Testament (emeritus)
Johann Wolfgang Goethe-Universität Frankfurt am Main
Fachbereich 6 – Ev. Theologie, Grüneburgplatz 1
D-60629 Frankfurt am Main, Germany

PAUL AND HEBREWS: A COMPARISON OF NARRATIVE WORLDS

James C. Miller

With his[1] opening words, carefully chosen and highly stylized, the author of Hebrews begins[2] establishing the perspective within which he wants the lengthy exhortation that follows to be understood. Here, I quote only the first lines:

> Long ago God spoke to our ancestors in many and various ways by the prophets, but in these last days he has spoken to us by a Son, whom he appointed heir of all things, through whom he also created the worlds. (Heb 1:1-2)[3]

What often passes unnoticed is the thoroughgoing narrative character of this statement. Here we find events and actions, characters and characterization, all set within a temporal framework. In other words, when the author of Hebrews defines the terms framing his argument, he narrates the history of God's speaking.[4]

Although elements of narrative identified in the letters of Paul have been subject to analysis,[5] little, to my knowledge, has been done to study narrative components in Hebrews.[6] This paper makes an

---

[1] In using the male pronoun, I am making no judgment regarding the identity of the author. I merely use the pronoun for the sake of convenience. Cf. Pamela M. Eisenbaum, *The Jewish Heroes of Christian History: Hebrews 11 in Literary Context* (SBLDS 156; Atlanta: Scholars Press, 1997) 2 n. 4.

[2] Craig R. Koester contends that this setting of perspective continues through Heb 2:4. See *Hebrews* (AB 36; New York: Doubleday, 2001), 174.

[3] All quotations from Scripture are taken from the NRSV unless otherwise noted.

[4] See, for example, Otto Michel, *Der Brief an die Hebräer* (12th ed.; KEK; Göttingen: Vandenhoeck & Ruprecht, 1966), 92-93.

[5] For an overview, see Bruce W. Longenecker, "The Narrative Approach to Paul: An Early Retrospective," *Currents in Biblical Research* 1 (2002): 88-111 and idem, "Narrative Interest in the Study of Paul: Retrospective and Prospective," in *Narrative Dynamics in Paul: A Critical Assessment* (ed. Bruce W. Longenecker; Louisville: Westminster/John Knox, 2002), 3-16.

[6] For studies incorporating attention to narrative, see Harold W. Attridge, "God In Hebrews: Urging Children to Heavenly Glory," in *The Forgotten God: Perspectives in Biblical Theology. Essays in Honor of Paul J. Achtemeier* (ed. A. Andrew Das and Frank J. Matera; Louisville: Westminster/John Knox, 2002), 199-202 and Luke Timothy Johnson, "The Scriptural World of Hebrews," *Int* 57 (2003): 237-250. Iutisone

initial attempt to address this lacuna by comparing the writings of Paul and the exhortation known as "Hebrews" on the basis of the "narrative world" found in each. I do not presume that in such short space I can fully address the subject with either writer, nor can I make a thorough, detailed comparison of their writings. Rather, I seek to describe the fundamental narrative dynamics apparent in both writers and, on that basis, analyze their similarities and differences with regard to a few select issues.

After a brief explanation of terms and method, I will first construct a synthesis of the "narrative world" depicted in Hebrews. I will then turn to the same task for Paul using the seven generally accepted letters of Paul. Finally, I will make several closing observations, comparing and contrasting elements in the narrative worlds of both.

Definition and Method

Owing to the debates surrounding the definition and function of "story" or "narrative" in Paul[7] (I use the terms interchangeably in what follows), a word about methodology is in order. Once again, space does not permit a full explanation. Here, I can only highlight what guides the following investigation.[8] Two key terms or concepts require definition: narrative world and story (or narrative). In addition, I need to make clear the methodology that underlies my investigation.

Narrative World. Everyone inhabits some imaginative understanding of the world. Scholars refer to such a construct as a "symbolic world" or "symbolic universe."[9] A symbolic world is a social product that

---

Salevao's study of Hebrews also recognizes that a symbolic world contains a narrative component (*Legitimation in the Letter to the Hebrews* [JSNTSup 219; Sheffield: Sheffield Academic Press, 2002], esp. 59–60). Kenneth Schenck's *Understanding the Book of Hebrews: The Story Behind the Sermon* (Louisville: Westminster/John Knox, 2003) appeared too late for me to incorporate it into this article.

[7] See, for example, the viewpoints expressed in Longenecker, *Narrative Dynamics*.

[8] Stories may take multiple forms and perform varied functions. Furthermore, within texts, narratives may be told in full, portrayed in part, restated in nonnarrative fashion, or merely alluded to. These factors enable story to resist precise definition.

[9] The concept stems from the work of Peter L. Berger and Thomas Luckmann, *The Social Construction of Reality* (New York: Doubleday, 1966). For an astute summary and critique of Berger and Luckmann, see David G. Horrell, *The Social Ethos*

performs several vital functions in the life of an individual or group. It provides a framework for comprehending reality, so enabling a group to order and make sense of its environment. Furthermore, a symbolic world shapes a group's sense of norms, identity, and purpose. Understanding who we are is inseparable from knowing where we are in the kind of world in which we live. Thus a symbolic world is a socially created and shared set of assumptions about the way the world just "is," how it works, and our place within it.[10]

Narratives form an essential component of symbolic worlds. Stories inform answers to questions such as: Who are we? What kind of world do we live in? How did our circumstances come to be what they are, for good or ill? What kind of possibilities can our future hold?[11] Stories, in other words, help create a "world" within which a group imaginatively lives out its life.

When I speak of the "narrative world" of Hebrews (or Paul), I am asking about the stories found in that writing that portray something of the "world" imagined or created by the author.[12] In other words, what do the stories we find in Hebrews tell us about the way the world just is, how it works, and the sense of place the author imaginatively inhabits within it? Furthermore, and of crucial importance, what place do the auditors of Hebrews occupy within this world?[13]

Story. Stories involve characters, settings, and events. Fundamentally, while involving characters and taking place in settings, stories consist

---

of the Corinthian Correspondence (SNTW; Edinburgh: T&T Clark, 1996), 39–45. On the symbolic world/universe of Hebrews, see Salevao, *Legitimation*, esp. 11–94, for the theory behind the concept. Johnson, "The Scriptural World of Hebrews," examines the "world" created by Hebrews' interpretation of Scripture.

[10] J. Ross Wagner speaks of "narrative" or "story" as "the way people articulate the larger conceptions they hold concerning the cosmos and their place in it." J. Ross Wagner, *Heralds of the Good News: Isaiah and Paul "In Concert" in the Letter to the Romans* (NovTSup 101; Leiden: Brill, 2002), 29 n. 102.

[11] These questions, of course, echo those enumerated by N. T. Wright, *The New Testament and the People of God* (Fortress: Minneapolis: 1992), 123, and repeated at several points in Wright's prolific published works. Wright draws this manner of framing the matter from Brian J. Walsh and J. Richard Middleton, *The Transforming Vision* (Downers Grove: IVP, 1984), 35.

[12] We must always keep in mind that, as social creations, such worlds are dynamic, changing phenomena. Transformations may occur between Paul's early and later letters. For the sake of this investigation, I must assume a relatively stable narrative world at the broad level with which I am working in this paper.

[13] My assumption is that Hebrews and the letters of Paul function pastorally to persuade their auditors to inhabit the world created by those writings.

of meaningfully related events ordered chronologically. As such, they can be perceived as a unity. Richard B. Hays writes, "Each new event must be an intelligible—though not necessarily predictable—development of the events which precede it."[14] Thus events form a narrative when they display a *sequential* coherence.

In light of these characteristics, Robin Scroggs's observation regarding Paul becomes noteworthy. Scroggs remarks that, when reading Paul theologically, he is "surprised at the overwhelming quantity of statements that fall into the often-maligned category of salvation history." Scroggs goes on to define salvation history as follows: "Paul is conscious of being a part of an ongoing history in which God, the central actor, relates to a people with an ultimate aim."[15] In other words, here is a series of events ("ongoing history") with a sequential coherence ("an ultimate aim"). I find Scroggs's account on target not only for Paul, but for Hebrews as well. Thus Paul's letters as well as Hebrews incorporate the crucial elements of narrative.

Yet stories may be recounted in more than one way. They can be retold in narrative fashion or they can be described in a non-narrative manner in such a way that it captures the essence or overall pattern (*dianoia*) of the story. Hays has demonstrated, for example, how the phrase πίστις Ἰησοῦ Χριστοῦ in Galatians, though a non-narrative utterance, evokes a larger story of Jesus' redemptive actions.[16] Because such non-narrative descriptions remain inseparable from the narrative whose essence they describe, it is both legitimate and possible to ask about the narrative in which such a statement is rooted.[17] In what follows, I will be looking to put together narratives from the references to events, characters, and settings strewn about in largely non-narrative fashion in the letters of Paul and in Hebrews.

Method. In light of the above discussion of narrative world and story, the questions that guide this inquiry are as follows: What events

---

[14] Richard B. Hays, *The Faith of Jesus Christ* (2d ed.; Grand Rapids: Eerdmans, 2002), 194–195.
[15] Robin Scroggs, "Salvation History," in *Pauline Theology*, vol. 1, *Thessalonians, Philippians, Galatians, Philemon* (ed. Jouette M. Bassler; Minneapolis: Fortress, 1991), 215. We will return to the troubled concept of "salvation history" below.
[16] Hays, *Faith*.
[17] See Hays, *Faith*, 22–24, 28.

recounted in these writings, when arranged in chronological order, form a meaningful sequence of events? What characters take part in these events and in what settings do they occur? Which of these stories constitute leading elements of a "narrative world" in these writings?

My procedure with each author consists of portraying larger, all-encompassing narratives first. I then work to construct the key subplots within these larger stories. In addition, I examine how the appeals made to the audiences in these writings emerge from the place where these people are emplotted within the various settings, characters, and events depicted in those writings.

I contend that such a descriptive progression, moving from broad narratives to subplots within those stories, offers the best method for reconstructing a narrative world from these texts. Larger narratives provide the contexts within which the smaller stories gain their significance. Without the perspective available only through an awareness of the "big picture," the meaning of the subplots risks becoming distorted. In all of this, the tests for success are whether these reconstructions accurately reflect what we find in the writings under consideration and whether they help us make sense of the documents themselves.

One final methodological comment requires notice. I have chosen to compare Hebrews with the corpus of generally accepted Pauline letters rather than with any one letter of Paul's. Such an approach offers the advantage of a more thorough analysis of Paul. At the same time, however, it runs into problems associated with harmonizing the content of arguments addressed to differing historical circumstances. Once again, a thorough apology for the approach employed here goes beyond the scope of this article. Here I only note my cognizance of the advantages and disadvantages associated with the choice of source material for my reconstruction of Paul's narrative world.

Hebrews

Larger Narrative Elements. The most comprehensive narrative reflected in Hebrews concerns the God who spoke in the past, speaks in the present, and will once again speak in the future. The "living" God

(Heb 3:12; 9:14; 10:31; 12:22) looms over all persons and events in the sermon.[18] Its story is of a world created, upheld, called to account, and carried to its end by God "speaking."[19]

The settings of this world need to be considered from two interrelated perspectives: the spatial and the temporal. Spatial settings consist of the earth and the heavens. The latter realm is not clearly defined,[20] but is one where God, God's exalted Son, and angels dwell.[21] The earth will pass away, but heaven will endure (Heb 1:10–12; 12:26–28). When Jesus returns, the faithful will join the assembly worshiping in heaven.

The temporal setting involves two consecutive though momentarily overlapping ages.[22] The first, now passing, is being replaced during "these last days" by the age to come. This first age will end and the age to come will arrive in its fullness when Jesus returns. At that time, God's enemies will be judged, God's people will receive their salvation, and all things will be placed in submission to Jesus. For the present, these two periods of time overlap; God's Son reigns, but not everything is yet seen placed under his feet (Heb 1:13; 2:8).

One further narrative element in Hebrews warrants mention. Beginning with Abraham, to whom God promised blessing and numerous descendants, God made commitments concerning God's people.[23] Hebrews describes the future culmination of these promises variously:

---

[18] See, for example, the comments of Harold W. Attridge ("God in Hebrews," 197) regarding God as the "indispensable horizon" within which the actions of Jesus make sense in Hebrews.

[19] The opening words of the exhortation establish the significance of God speaking and the seriousness of what God speaks and has spoken (Heb 1:1–4). This theme then permeates Hebrews, closing the exhortation as well (Heb 12:25). The references are too numerous to list here.

[20] Marie E. Isaacs, *Sacred Space* (JSNTSup 73; Sheffield: JSOT Press, 1992), 205–211.

[21] On the spatial dimension in Hebrews and its relation to the temporal, the most complete discussion remains that of Isaacs, *Sacred Space*.

[22] Michel writes, "Der Hebr steht innerhalb einer christlichen Tradition, die starke Motive der Apokalyptik aufgenommen...hat." (*Hebräer*, 58). On time and eschatology in Hebrews, see esp. C. K. Barrett, "The Eschatology of the Epistle to the Hebrews," in *The Background of the New Testament and Its Eschatology* (ed. W. D. Davies and David Daube; Cambridge: Cambridge University Press, 1956), 363–393; Koester, *Hebrews*, 100–104; Mathias Rissi, *Die Theologie des Hebräerbriefs* (WUNT 41; Tübingen: Mohr Siebeck, 1987), 125–30; David A. deSilva, *Perseverance in Gratitude* (Grand Rapids: Eerdmans, 2000), 27–32.

[23] According to Craig R. Koester (*Hebrews*, 111), the word "promise" in Hebrews stands for "the word or pledge that people initially receive from God as well as for the substance they receive when God fulfills his commitment."

an "eternal inheritance" (Heb 9:15); "rest" (Heb 3:7–4:11); "perfection" (Heb 10:14; 11:40; 12:23); "(eternal) salvation" (Heb 1:14; 2:3; 5:9; 6:9; 9:28); arrival at the heavenly city (Heb 11:10); and, perhaps most importantly, "access to (the presence of) God."[24] The author depicts his auditors as sojourning in the wilderness of the world toward this goal.[25] Thus this dynamic involves both characters (auditors) and a setting (a journey in the world toward a heavenly city).

Subplots. In order to properly grasp the force of the author's exhortations, one must plot the hearers at the proper location amidst the characters, settings and events that form the subplots along this journey between promise and final fulfillment. These subplots concern attempts to address the primary obstacle impeding access to God—sin and its consequent impurity. We can identify four such stories that form substantive subplots in the argument of Hebrews: the story of the first and second covenants; the story of Jesus; the story of God's people in the past; and the story of God's people in the present.

Subplot 1: The Story of Two Covenants. God entered into a covenant relationship with Israel at Mt. Sinai, instituting a system of sacrifices in order to address the problem of impurity.[26] Under this arrangement, after first offering sacrifice for their own purification, priests

---

[24] Heb 4:16; 6:19–20a; 7:25; 12:22–24. Note the conclusion (beginning at Heb 10:19) drawn from the extensive argument (Heb 8:1–10:18) concerning the true tabernacle in which Christ's priestly service takes place: "Since we have confidence to enter the Holy Place by the blood of Jesus, by a new and living way he opened..." (my translation). Regarding the multiple conceptions of salvation, Isaacs (*Sacred Space*, 206) observes that the "various models of salvation" employed in Hebrews result in different images of heaven as "place" as well. John Dunnill (*Covenant and Sacrifice in the Letter to the Hebrews* [SNTSMS 75; Cambridge: Cambridge University Press, 1992], 134–148) also notes how Hebrews employs overlapping symbols to convey ideas of sacred time and sacred space.

[25] In the hortatory components of the sermon, note how the author weaves together references to the audience's past and to their need to persevere through present struggles toward a future destination. This dynamic, plus the explicit comparisons made between Israel in the wilderness and the auditors, creates the distinct impression that the audience is conceived of as journeying toward a heavenly destination (Heb 12:22).

[26] Isaacs states (*Sacred Space*, 91), "the sacrificial system was intended to remove the barrier of sin which hinders the worshipper's approach to God." The author's description and evaluation of the two covenants primarily runs from Heb 4:14–10:18. Because of the repeated nature of many of his points and in order not to clutter the text with references, citations of the text of Hebrews are kept to a minimum in the following paragraphs.

entered the holy of holies in the tabernacle once a year in order to make sacrifice for the people. This covenant also involved a responsive obedience on Israel's part, an obedience that entailed enduring hardships while awaiting the fulfillment of God's promised rest. In other words, the covenant required faith/faithfulness.

This covenant and its requisite means of sanctification, however, were never intended to be final. The repeated sacrifices, carried out by weak human priests in an earthly tabernacle, provided temporary, external cleansing and, thus, imperfect access to God. Furthermore, God spoke of yet another priesthood and covenant that was to come. Such a future priesthood would offer a perfect sacrifice for sin, once for all. This new covenant promised internal purification and forgiveness of sin. As a remedy for impurity, therefore, the first covenant was provisional and anticipatory.

Yet now, "in these last days," God has spoken once again, inaugurating a new covenant. This covenant remains far superior to the old in every way. Above all else, it offers an atoning sacrifice, once for all, in the heavenly tabernacle by a sinless, perfect, sympathetic, and eternal high priest—God's own son, Jesus—who now sits enthroned at God's right hand, the first to cross over into heaven. From there, in God's own presence, in the true holy of holies, he waits to assist those who will follow and join him.

This temporal and spatial setting of the two covenants provides crucial components of the narrative context for the exhortations found in the sermon. The old age is coming to a close and, as part of that development, the first covenant has been abrogated.[27] The auditors stand at the dawn of the new age with its new, superior covenant. Jesus has entered into God's presence, going to a place where the faithful will soon follow. Yet they must first navigate the time between their present setting and the next scene of the divine drama.

Subplot 2: The Journey of Jesus.[28] The story of Jesus entails a sojourn through utmost abasement to highest glory. Jesus was made like human beings in all things, enduring human suffering. Yet he remained

---

[27] Heb 7:18. According to Moulton and Milligan, ἀθέτησις was used as part of a legal formula signifying the annulment of a contract. See James H. Moulton and George Milligan, *The Vocabulary of the Greek Testament* (London: Hodder and Stoughton, 1930), 13.

[28] The key passages here are Heb 2:5–3:6; 4:14–5:10; 7:24–8:6; 9:11–10:18; 12:2–3. Once again, the sizeable number of references for each point in what follows makes it more economical to call attention to these important sections in general.

steadfastly faithful to God in the midst of this affliction. Such faithfulness ultimately entailed his presentation of his own life as a sin-offering, once for all, making Jesus the high priest and mediator of the new, much better covenant.

As a result, God raised Jesus from the dead and exalted him to God's right hand.[29] Jesus has thus entered into the most holy place, into God's own presence in heaven, by his faithful obedience blazing the path for God's people to follow. Soon all things[30] will be placed under his rule. At present, from his exalted vantage point, he lives to make intercession for God's people. Thus Jesus' journey involves faithful endurance through humility, abasement, and suffering to exaltation and honor in God's presence.

Subplot 3: The Story of God's People in the Past. In the past, with the generation that was delivered from Egypt, God's people faced the opportunity of entering God's rest (Heb 3:7–4:11). Although they had heard the good news (Heb 4:2, 6) and were poised on the edge of entering the promised land, they refused to believe. Disobedient, they died in the wilderness as a result. God still spoke, however, of a "rest" for God's people yet to come. Hence a rest, though missed by the Exodus generation, remains a possibility for God's people (Heb 4:9–11).

Yet the story of God's people in the past also portrays examples of faithfulness (Heb 6:13–15). Hebrews 11 catalogs models of such loyalty. These exemplars now stand as "witnesses," spurring God's people toward similar devotion (Heb 12:1).

Subplot 4: The Story of God's People in the Present. (In order to convey the admonitive force of the story more vividly, I will phrase the following in the first person.) Although we hope for Jesus' coming reign, when we will experience glory and honor, our experience has not matched our hopes. We are still subject to death (Heb 2:14–15). Furthermore, we have suffered shame, abuse, persecution, and loss of possessions and status (Heb 10:32–34). As a result, some of us have become weary, longing for the comfort that familiarity over

---

[29] Note that emphasis on Jesus' exaltation at God's right hand both begins and ends the body of Hebrews (Heb 1:3; 12:25 [introducing the final, climactic exhortations]).

[30] The quotation from Ps 110:1 in Heb 1:13 is used to indicate that God will make Jesus' enemies a footstool for Jesus' feet. The identity of these ἐχθροί, however, is left indefinite in Hebrews.

time has bred with the system of purification specified under the first covenant.

Yet, poised on the brink of the new age, we are in danger of following the mistake of our ancestors in the wilderness (Heb 4:11). Rather than enduring their hardships in confident assurance of better things to come, they refused to believe, drifting away from their hope. Consequently, their sojourn ended in failure and judgment. To place our hope for access to God in the mechanics of the first covenant would be to repeat their error and suffer their end.

Unlike the wilderness generation of the past, therefore, we must move on[31] through our wilderness toward greater maturity and, ultimately, enter God's rest. Like the heroes of faith in the past, who endured hardship and dishonor in hope of better things to come (Heb 11:1–12:3), we must remain faithful in our present circumstances until the end. Not only that, we must spare no effort in assisting our fellow believers on this sojourn as well (Heb 10:24–25; 13:1–17).

More precisely, we must follow the footsteps of the journey pioneered by Jesus through suffering, in the hope that we will join him in God's presence (Heb 12:1–3). Like him, we must endure suffering and shame, and with his assistance remain steadfast in our faith. Like him, we must hold fast (Heb 3:6; 4:14) to our hope of joining him in God's presence by means of his superior sacrifice for sin. In other words, like Jesus, we must run our race in such a way that we "hold our first confidence firm until the end" (Heb 3:14). Only then will we arrive at the ultimate destination of our journey, the city of the living God. There we will join the angels and the elect in the heavenly assembly in the presence of God and Jesus (Heb 12:22–24).

Salvation, therefore, remains in another time, the near future, and is located in another place, the heavenly realm.[32] Yet the identity of Jesus, his priestly work, and his presence at God's right hand[33] make such a salvation certain for those who remain faithful.

---

[31] Surveying the verbs used in the positive exhortations in Hebrews, Susanne Lehne notes that many imply movement: draw near (Heb 4:16; 10:19–25), enter (Heb 10:19–25), run (Heb 12:1–4), go forth (Heb 13:9–16). See *The New Covenant in Hebrews* (JSNTSup 44; Sheffield: JSOT Press, 1990), 105–106.

[32] Regarding the temporal and spatial aspects of salvation, once again, see Isaacs, *Sacred Space*, 218.

[33] Attridge (*Hebrews*, 36) writes, "the decisive nature of God's eschatological salvific action... is based upon two elements which determine the whole Christology of

Paul and His Stories[34]

Larger Narrative Elements. As with Hebrews, I begin with an introduction to the main actors, events and settings depicted in the narrative world of Paul's letters before describing the principal subplots. After synthesizing the material of several letters, I conclude by using Romans as a specific example of how the narrative world depicted in one letter contributes to the major exhortation of that letter.

The one creator God—sovereign, purposeful, holy, faithful and just—serves as the primary actor in Paul's world. Although God's creation has been corrupted by the entrance of sin and death, God, through Jesus Christ and the Spirit, is in the process of setting all of creation aright (Rom 8:18–21).[35] The pivotal event in this turn toward renewal is Jesus' death and resurrection. This grand narrative stretching from creation through corrupted creation to renewed creation forms the broad context within which the various subplots gain their meaning.

Adam and Jesus stand as pivotal figures within this narrative, each determining by their actions the distinct, contrasting characters of two consecutive "ages" of human history. Adam, through his one act of disobedience, introduced sin and death into human experience. Consequently, sin "reigned" over all human beings as creation itself entered into a state of bondage (Rom 5:12; 8:20–21). This

---

Hebrews, the status of Christ as the exalted Son and the sacrificial, priestly act by which he effected atonement for sin."

[34] Analyses of narrative in Paul (or "salvation history") are numerous. See Longenecker, "The Narrative Approach to Paul: An Early Retrospective"; Longenecker, *Narrative Dynamics*; and Hays, *Faith*. In addition, see the following essays in Jouette M. Bassler, *Pauline Theology*, vol. 1, *Thessalonians, Philippians, Galatians, Philemon*: N. T. Wright, "Putting Paul Together Again" (183–211); Robin Scroggs, "Salvation History" (212–226); Richard B. Hays, "Crucified with Christ" (227–246); David J. Lull, "Salvation History" (247–265). See also A. Katherine Grieb, *The Story of Romans: A Narrative Defense of God's Righteousness* (Louisville: Westminster/John Knox, 2002), who synthesizes much of the recent work of others, and J. Ross Wagner, *Heralds of the Good News*. The older works of C. H. Dodd, though not exclusively concerned with Paul, emphasize the narrative dimension of the early Christian *kerygma*. See his *According to the Scriptures* (New York: Charles Scribners' Sons, 1953) and *The Apostolic Preaching and Its Developments* (New York: Harper & Row, 1964).

[35] If a Grand Narrative exists for Paul, one may properly label it "creation history" rather than "salvation history." Cf. Edward Adams, "Paul's Story of God and Creation," in Longenecker, *Narrative Dynamics in Paul*, 38. Adams does not believe, however, that Paul's theology can be subsumed "under one all-encompassing 'story'" (ibid., 42).

period of time, inaugurated by Adam, Paul refers to as "this present evil age" (Gal 1:4). Thus Adam, sin, and death serve as central characters in Paul's world, with sin acting as a key ruler and force in the moral domain.

Jesus, through his one act of obedience, brought righteousness and life so that grace might reign (Rom 5:18, 21). Jesus' atoning death to sin and his resurrection effected the beginning of the end of the Adamic age of sin and death (Rom 3:25; 6:10). Jesus' resurrection marked the introduction of the powers of the "age to come," a time when life and peace rule. The old age will come to a complete end and the new age will arrive in its fullness when Jesus returns. At that time, *all* authorities, powers, kingdoms, and beings—whether human or suprahuman—will confess Jesus' lordship (Phil 2:11). Furthermore, all humanity and all such rulers and powers will face judgment, the dead in Christ will be raised, Jesus will hand over the kingdom to God the Father, and death will be vanquished once and for all (1 Cor 15:20–28). In effect, then, two characters, Adam and Jesus, create two distinct yet overlapping settings wherein the human dimension of the narrative plays out.

Subplots. Within these overarching events, characters, and settings we can identify several key subplots and characters in Paul's narrative world: God's people, the story of Jesus, and the story of Paul himself.

Subplot 1: God's People.[36] Long ago, God promised Abraham that God would bless all nations through him (Gal 3:6–9). God subsequently entered into a covenant with Abraham's descendants at Mt. Sinai in order to carry out that purpose through them (Rom 2:17–24).[37] Yet Israel repeatedly proved to be a stubborn and rebellious people, demonstrating that they lived under the Adamic reign of sin,

---

[36] The next several paragraphs follow Richard B. Hays, "Crucified with Christ: A Synthesis of the Theology of 1 and 2 Thessalonians, Philemon, Philippians, and Galatians," in *Pauline Theology*, vol. 1, *Thessalonians, Philippians, Galatians, Philemon*, 232–233.

[37] Paul nowhere states this point clearly, though it is present by implication in his charge that "the name of God is blasphemed among the Gentiles because of you" (Rom 2:24 [Isa 52:5]). With the exception of N. T. Wright's work, Paul's understanding of God's purposes for Israel under the Mosaic covenant remains an underdeveloped subject in Pauline studies. Wright's thesis, however, that God called Israel so that sin may be piled up in one place and dealt with there, has not received widespread approval. Without doubt, though, Wright is asking the crucial questions largely ignored by other scholars.

just like the Gentiles. They too, therefore, lived subject to God's eschatological wrath (Rom 2:17–29; 3:9, 23).

The Mosaic Law, belonging to the old age, had a temporary role. Within God's purposes, the Law was intended to serve as a guardian to discipline God's people until the appearance of the Messiah (Gal 3:19–25). Yet, because of Adamic sin, the Law actually provoked Israel to disbelief/disobedience (Rom 7:7–23). As an ineffective remedy for sin, therefore, it actually became an instrument of bondage for Israel (Gal 3:12–13; Rom 7:7–25).

Jesus' death and resurrection result in several developments for God's people. First, on the basis of faith—Jesus' faithfulness followed by human faith—God's promise to Abraham has now been fulfilled. The Gentiles are now joining Jews on an equal basis in the one, holy, eschatological people of God (Rom 15:7–12 [and OT quotations found there]; Gal 3:14). The divine purpose for the present time, therefore, consists of the formation of this people who stand joined to and in continuity with Israel, but who are also drawn from beyond it. The identity of this people is found in Jesus the Messiah rather than in Mosaic Law (Rom 10:4).

Secondly, those joined to Christ are freed from the reign of sin by the power of the Spirit (Rom 8:1–4) in order to live a new life as part of the "new creation" (Rom 6:4; 2 Cor 5:17). They have, in effect, switched "lords." Now living under the Lordship of Jesus (Rom 10:9), they belong to *ekklesiai* of the Lord's kingdom, colonies of alternative communities that bear witness to their servant-Lord (Phil 1:27; 3:20).[38] As such, they are to live "pure and blameless" lives that are "worthy of the gospel of Christ" (Phil 1:10, 27). The defining action of these people is worship of God (Rom 6:13; 12:1–2) manifested in faith/obedience patterned after that of Jesus. Thus we see the character and identity of this new people.

Thirdly, Paul and his contemporaries must still live "between the times," a time of conflict between the powers of the old age that are "passing away" (1 Cor 2:6) and the powers of the new age that are present only in part. The Spirit's power, therefore, must continually be appropriated (Rom 6:11–13; 12:2). Yet the final outcome of this conflict does not remain in doubt, since these people are part of the eschatological restoration of creation. As with the children of

---

[38] I owe this way of phrasing the matter to Michael J. Gorman, *Cruciformity: Paul's Narrative Spirituality of the Cross* (Grand Rapids: Eerdmans, 2001), 364.

Israel in the Exodus from Egypt, they are children freed from bondage and led by the Spirit (Rom 8:14–17). Yet they too must suffer while they await their inheritance (Rom 8:18–39).[39] Those "in Christ," therefore, rejoice in the hope of their salvation, a salvation to be finalized when Jesus returns.

Subplot 2: The Journey of Jesus.[40] Jesus' own story bears great significance for those united with him (Phil 2:1–11; Rom 6:1–13; 2 Cor 8:9). Though equal to God, Jesus refused to exploit his status. Rather, he willingly humbled himself, becoming human and remaining faithful to God until his death on a cross.[41] As a result, God raised Jesus from the dead and seated him as Lord at God's right hand. Jesus' story, therefore, embodies patterns of reversal (humiliation followed by exaltation), of voluntary self-humbling (including renunciation of status), of self-giving, and of obedience.[42]

This example of humble, loving service forms the basic narrative pattern for the life of the community (cf. Gal 2:20; 4:12). In embodying Jesus' self-giving manner of life (Phil 2:5), the community of God's people tells the story of how God's love was made known in Jesus. Such a lifestyle is only possible by the enablement of the Spirit, and can be characterized as "faith working through love" (Gal 5:6). Such behavior fulfills the "Law of Christ" (Gal 2:20). Thus the experiential "spirituality" of these colonies of God's kingdom should be like that of Jesus—cruciform in nature.[43]

Subplot 3: Paul. Paul's apostolic task consists of announcing the gospel, the Lordship of Jesus Christ (Rom 1:1–4), in contrast to all other false gospels.[44] In particular, Paul's calling involves making cru-

---

[39] See Sylvia C. Keesmaat, *Paul and His Story: (Re)interpreting the Exodus Tradition* (JSNTSup 181; Sheffield: Sheffield Academic Press, 1999), 96. Keesmaat details the Exodus themes prevalent in Rom 8, themes that shape the dynamics of the narrative world apparent in Paul's argument.

[40] The following three paragraphs are indebted to the overall argument of Gorman, *Cruciformity*.

[41] Jesus' death is characterized as an act of obedience (Phil 2:8; Gal 1:4; Rom 5:19), of love (Rom 5:8; Gal 2:20), and of faithfulness (Gal 2:20; 3:22; Rom 3:22, 25, 26).

[42] Gorman, *Cruciformity*, 90–91.

[43] Gorman fleshes out how this works in greater detail than is possible or necessary here. The point, for my purposes, is that Jesus' pattern of life serves as the design for Paul's communities to embody.

[44] Gorman (*Cruciformity*, 349) writes that Paul's "mission was to announce the gospel of Jesus Christ as the true Lord of all—in continuity with the God of Israel and in contrast to the counterfeit lord, the Roman emperor—and to form visible alternative communities of cruciformity animated and governed by this true Lord."

ciform communities of the one, eschatological people of God, living under Jesus' Lordship (Rom 1:5; 15:18; 16:26). For Paul, that entails going primarily to the Gentiles, incorporating them into the people of God (Rom 1:5; 15:18; 16:26) as an offering to God (Rom 15:16).[45]

Romans. As with Hebrews, Paul's instructions to his churches must be understood by plotting his auditors within these settings and in relation to the characters inhabiting this larger story and its various subplots. For example, Romans is written to various house groups of Christ-followers who are divided roughly along Jew/Gentile lines regarding matters of observance or non-observance of the Mosaic Law.[46] Paul first traces God's historic dealings with both Jews and Gentiles (Rom 1–11). He then explains how they should therefore live in a manner that honors God (Rom 12:1–15:13). Those instructions culminate with the admonition at Rom 15:7 that they, Jews and Gentiles, should accept one another in the same way Jesus embraced them. Paul supports that exhortation with quotations drawn from the Law, Prophets, and Writings, passages that all speak of Gentiles praising God.

Expressed in the first person, this is the force of the concluding exhortation as it flows from the narrative world[47] depicted in the letter: We, Jewish and Gentile followers of Jesus, live at the time Moses, David, and Isaiah foresaw. God has demonstrated his faithfulness to both Jews and Gentiles through the atoning death and resurrection of Jesus Christ. Led by the Spirit and leaving behind those aspects of our identity belonging to the Adamic age, we must embrace our call as part of God's eschatological people and, like Jesus, accept one another.

Comparisons and Contrasts: Hebrews and Paul

The differing rhetorical situations addressed by Hebrews and the undisputed Pauline writings complicate the task of making comparisons between them. Students of Paul know the difficulties created

---

[45] Each aspect of this call shapes the instructions found in his letters. Paul first and foremost seeks to shape groups of Christ-followers in a particular fashion.

[46] The following comments on Romans rest upon the argument laid out in James C. Miller, *The Obedience of Faith, the Eschatological People of God, and the Purpose of Romans* (SBLDS 177; Atlanta: Society of Biblical Literature, 2000).

[47] For a thorough analysis of the narrative elements found in Romans, see Grieb, *The Story of Romans.*

by this dynamic even when comparing Paul's own letters.[48] For this reason alone, differences between the writings rather than similarities should be expected. In what follows, therefore, I will draw attention primarily, though not exclusively, to parallels between Hebrews and Paul.

Priesthood. Having stated my intention to look for comparisons, let me begin by noting an interesting contrast. Hebrews dwells on the issue of priesthood like no other writing in the New Testament. For the writer of Hebrews, the priestly ministry of the Old Covenant no longer plays any role in the life of God's people. One true priest, the exalted Jesus, the mediator of a better covenant, now conducts the genuine sacerdotal ministry in the heavenly sanctuary.[49] Thus Jesus' ministry, specifically in its priestly dimensions, plays a vital role in Hebrews' world.

In Paul, however, the language of priestly ministry applied to Jesus remains absent altogether.[50] When Paul speaks of priestly work, he uses it to describe his own vocation (Rom 15:16) or to characterize the basic responsibility of his auditors in response to his apostolic ministry (Rom 6:13, 16, 19; esp. Rom 12:1–3).[51] In Rom 15:16, Paul portrays his calling as "the priestly service of the gospel of God" (ἱερουργοῦντα τὸ εὐαγγέλιον τοῦ θεοῦ) whose sacrifice is the Gentiles. Although Paul's language is certainly metaphorical here,[52] it never-

---

[48] The differences (and similarities) between Paul's treatment of Israel and the Law in Romans and Galatians offer a sterling example of this phenomenon. The narrative studies in Longenecker, *Narrative Dynamics*, highlight an intriguing array of comparisons/contrasts regarding specific narrative themes in these two letters.

[49] Contra John M. Scholer, *Proleptic Priests: Priesthood in the Epistle to the Hebrews* (JSNTSup 49; Sheffield: JSOT Press, 1991). Scholer argues that believers will have "access" to God, a priestly prerogative, when Jesus returns and full salvation is theirs. Thus their current priesthood is "proleptic," anticipatory of a complete priesthood to come. I contend that priesthood in Hebrews, present and future, applies to Jesus alone. Jesus' perfect priesthood guarantees the community's access to God, but having "access to God" does not makes believers priests. The "sacrifice of praise" commended in Heb 13:15 derives from the practice depicted in the Psalter where a prayer of thanks is offered, not an animal (see the references in Attridge, *Hebrews*, 400 n. 137). Thus the sacrifice encouraged here is not a priestly function.

[50] Jesus' death becomes a sacrifice of atonement (Rom 3:25; 8:3). Yet Paul never describes Jesus' ministry or actions in priestly terms.

[51] I take the "mercy" of Rom 12:1 to be the mercy by which God called Paul. Cf. Rom 12:3. On this matter, see Miller, *The Obedience of Faith*, 158–159, and Victor Paul Furnish, *Theology and Ethics in Paul* (Nashville: Abingdon, 1968), 102.

[52] This is the case when Paul uses the language of "sacrifice" elsewhere with reference to followers of Christ. Cf. not only the passages in Rom 6 and 12, but also Phil 2:17 and 4:18.

theless expresses a central element of Paul's apostolic self-understanding.[53] In other words, it captures Paul's sense of his place within his world. Given the role Jesus' priesthood plays in the world of Hebrews, it is difficult to imagine the writer of Hebrews using a priestly metaphor to describe the ministry of anyone other than Jesus.

The Story of Jesus. One of the remarkable similarities between these authors concerns the story of Jesus. In particular, we can detect strong parallels between the depiction of Jesus' "journey" in Hebrews and the stylized portrayal of Jesus found in Phil 2:6–11.[54] Both describe Jesus in human and divine terms (Heb 1:4; Phil 2:6). They depict his progression from some sort of pre-existence[55] to a human experience that entails self-humbling, faithfulness/obedience (Phil 2:7–8; Heb 3:2–6; 5:8; 12:2), and suffering to the point of death (Phil 2:8; Heb 2:9–18). This culminates in his exaltation at God's right hand, where he will exercise authority over all beings (Phil 2:9; Heb 1:4; 7:26).[56]

Furthermore, in both writers, Jesus' journey serves as a pattern for the community of believers to follow.[57] In Philippians, Paul prefaces his statements about Jesus in ch. 2 by stating that this is the

---

[53] On what this depiction says about Paul's self-understanding, see N. T. Wright, "The Letter to the Romans," *NIB*, 10:754.

[54] For narrative treatments of Phil 2:5–11, see Gorman, *Cruciformity*; Stephen E. Fowl, *The Story of Christ in the Ethics of Paul* (JSNTSup 36; Sheffield: JSOT Press, 1990), 49–101; idem, "Christology and Ethics in Philippians 2:5–11," in *Where Christology Began: Essays on Philippians 2* (ed. Ralph P. Martin and Brian J. Dodd; Louisville: Westminster/John Knox, 1998), 140–153.

[55] This is a controversial point. In Hebrews, however, Jesus is God's agent of creation (Heb 1:10). Furthermore, Jesus is the same, "yesterday, today, and forever" (Heb 13:8). In Phil 2, Jesus was in the form of God but did not exploit that status. Rather, he emptied himself, taking human form, becoming in human likeness. These phrases are riddled with translation difficulties. What, at minimum, can be maintained, however, is that Jesus possessed some sort of existence before his earthly existence. The same seems true of Hebrews. The precise nature of that "pre-existence" is never spelled out by either writer.

[56] Although resurrection is not mentioned in the Philippians passage, it is clearly implied, and plays a central role throughout Paul's writings. Resurrection receives less attention, though by no means a diminished role, in Hebrews than in Paul. Gorman (*Cruciformity*, 90–91) detects five "narrative patterns" within the Philippians passage. Although this is more detail than can be included here, I merely note that many of these patterns bear direct parallels with what we find in Hebrews. See also the analysis of this issue in L. D. Hurst, *The Epistle to the Hebrews: Its Background of Thought* (SNTSMS 65; Cambridge: Cambridge University Press, 1990), 118–119.

[57] On this point in Paul, in addition to the works by Gorman and Fowl cited above, see William S. Kurz, "Kenotic Imitation of Paul and Christ in Philippians 2 and 3," in *Discipleship in the New Testament* (ed. Fernando F. Segovia; Philadelphia: Fortress, 1985), 103–126.

mindset the Philippians are to embrace (Phil 2:5, τοῦτο φρονεῖτε ἐν ὑμῖν). He follows this exhortation and description of Jesus' actions and experience by offering Timothy (Phil 2:19–24), Epaphroditus (Phil 2:25–30), and himself (Phil 3:4–17) as examples of those who embody such a pattern of living (Phil 3:15–17). In particular, Paul calls attention to the matters of faithfulness (Phil 2:22, 29–30; 3:12–14), refusal to exploit advantages (Phil 3:4b–7), and concern for others above oneself (Phil 2:20–21, 26, 31). In addition to Philippians, we can observe the basic contours of this pattern in the story of Jesus and those "in Christ" depicted briefly in Rom 6 and then developed in greater detail beginning in Rom 12.[58]

In Hebrews, the lengthy list of those who embodied great faith begins in ch. 11 and reaches its pinnacle with the statements about Jesus in Heb 12:1–3. This progression can be obscured both by modern chapter divisions that separate this passage from ch. 11 and by the common addition of the word "our" before faith in Heb 12:2. Jesus' actions described in Heb 12:2 illustrate his faithfulness, not the community's.[59] Thus Jesus stands as the climactic example of the "great cloud of witnesses" (Heb 12:1), consideration of whom should prevent the auditors from growing weary and losing heart (Heb 12:3). Thus, in both writings, the depictions of Jesus' journey are explicitly offered as models for the community's own journey of faith.

What is notably different between Hebrews and Paul in this scheme is the role of the Holy Spirit. Although the Holy Spirit occupies a central role in Paul's depiction of how cruciform existence becomes lived out, Hebrews remains largely silent regarding the work of the Spirit on behalf of believers. In Hebrews, the Spirit does help Jesus offer himself unblemished to God (Heb 9:14). Furthermore, believers are given gifts by the Spirit (Heb 2:4) and they share in the Holy Spirit (Heb 6:4). Yet in Hebrews the Holy Spirit never occupies the same strategic role as in Paul.

Continuity/Discontinuity. Any discussion of continuity and discontinuity between the old and new orders automatically pushes to the fore controversies surrounding the issue of "salvation history." Once again, I do not pretend that I can solve these debates once and for

---

[58] Note, for example, the first exhortation specified in Rom 12:3, "not to think of yourself more highly than you ought to think."
[59] On this point, in addition to the commentaries, see Ben Witherington III, "The Influence of Galatians on Hebrews," *NTS* 37 (1991): 151.

all. I do, however, want to close with a few observations afforded by a narrative approach to the issue.

Both Paul and Hebrews posit a sharp break between covenants. It is perhaps more pronounced in Hebrews (Heb 7:18),[60] but Paul nevertheless relegates the Mosaic Law to the old age, an age now passing away (1 Cor 2:6). Furthermore, as in Hebrews, though not with the same emphasis, Paul speaks of the "new" covenant (Heb 8:7–13; 1 Cor 11:25; 2 Cor 3:6). Without question, then, in terms of covenantal salvation history, discontinuity prevails.

Yet, at the same time, both writers envision distinct continuities between old and new dispensations by placing the covenants within a larger story. Although Paul spells this out more clearly, both writers trace the identity of God's people and the promise that leads to Jesus from Abraham (Heb 2:16; 6:13; Gal 3:7–29). Furthermore, and more importantly, the covenants must be understood within the larger story of God's dealings with God's creation and God's people. Additional changes lie just ahead when, in the idiom of Hebrews, the earth will be "shaken" and God's people receive an unshakeable kingdom. Certainly there will be discontinuity between the present and that future. Yet there will be continuity as well, for *God's* word will bring it about. Viewed from this perspective, a break occurs with regard to the covenants and between major "acts" of the drama of God and creation. Yet the covenants are part of a more comprehensive, ongoing work of the one God involving creation and God's people.[61] What is needed, then, is a movement beyond a simplistic "either/or" approach to this issue. From a narrative perspective, both Paul and Hebrews require a more nuanced "both/and" description.[62]

---

[60] Both writers speak of the Mosaic covenant's annulment: Heb 7:18, ἀθέτησις; Gal 3:15, ἀθετεῖ.

[61] Thus, for example, when the experience of the wilderness generation (Heb 3:7–4:13) is used as a warning for the auditors of Hebrews, the difference between these two groups is not one of a people under different covenants or between Judaism and Christianity. Rather, "this is a contrast between generations in the ongoing history of the people of God" (Isaacs, *Sacred Space*, 80). Both generations have had "the good news announced" (εὐαγγελίζω) to them (Heb 4:2, 6).

[62] For attempts at a mediating position, at least for Paul, see Richard B. Hays, "Three Dramatic Roles: The Law in Romans 3–4," in *Paul and the Mosaic Law* (ed. James D. G. Dunn; Grand Rapids: Eerdmans, 2001), 151–164; and Bruce W. Longenecker, *The Triumph of Abraham's God* (Nashville: Abingdon, 1998).

Conclusion

By design, this study has remained sweeping and general, intended to illustrate an approach for comparing Hebrews and Paul rather than offer a definitive treatment of the subject. Much work remains to be done. Yet an exploration and comparison of the narrative worlds of these two writers holds out the promise of obtaining new insights through an unexplored means of analysis.[63]

James C. Miller, Ph.D.
Senior Lecturer
Nairobi Evangelical Graduate School of Theology
P. O. Box 24686, 00502 Karen, Nairobi, Kenya
jamiller@nbi.ispkenya.com

---

[63] For example, Salevao (*Legitimation*, 93) states that his study does not seek to "provide new information, but to enable a new way of analyzing the data we already have."

CONSTRUCTIONS AND COLLUSIONS: THE MAKING AND UNMAKING OF IDENTITY IN QOHELETH AND HEBREWS

Jennifer L. Koosed and Robert P. Seesengood

Harold W. Attridge begins his commentary on Hebrews by noting, "the Epistle... is the most elegant and sophisticated, and perhaps the most enigmatic, text of first-century Christianity."[1] Choon Leong Seow opens his commentary on Ecclesiastes by asserting, "no book in the Bible... is the subject of more controversies."[2] In many ways, Qoheleth and the Epistle to the Hebrews are similar.[3] Of particular interest to us, both texts are anonymous documents occasionally assigned to canonical figures, but only on the most ethereal data. Both Hebrews and Qoheleth provide autobiographical anecdotes that certainly could suggest authorship by Solomon or Paul, but both stop short of any certain origins.[4] There are striking parallels between

---

[1] Harold Attridge, *Hebrews* (Hermeneia; Philadelphia: Westminster, 1989), 1.

[2] Choon Leong Seow, *Ecclesiastes* (AB 18C; New York: Doubleday, 1997), ix.

[3] Structurally, both appear to have a homiletic tone and form, but they bend that form in unexpected ways: Hebrews, in its final chapters, suddenly morphs into an epistle and Qoheleth blends autobiographical exhortation with *mashal*. The rhetorical flourish and complexity of Hebrews is legendary; the language of Qoheleth is equally poignant and learned. Hebrews could be understood as an early polemic in a line of discussion that would eventually lead to the extraction of nascent Christianity from the broader Jewish discourse and theology of the first two centuries of our common era (Daniel Boyarin, *Dying for God: Martyrdom and the Making of Christianity and Judaism* [Stanford: Stanford University Press, 1999]); arguably, Hebrews is actively "remaking" an understanding of covenant, liturgy, and soteriology out of elements of Jewish ritual and text. Hebrews presents a rhetoric that is not yet "Christian" but is a very early move toward construction of a distinct "Christian" identity. Both documents use an authorial voice that assumes—demands, actually—agreement while both documents are offering fairly iconoclastic readings of Torah.

[4] Qoh 1:1: "The words of the teacher, son of David, King of Jerusalem"; Heb 13:23: "I want you to know our brother Timothy has been released." Neither text even mentions the names of their reputed authors, only significant associates. In Hebrews, a singular "I" peeps out in 13:20–21 (mated, as well, with a simple me in Heb 11:32) revealing the face of an author still frustratingly obscured. Only Timothy is named in Heb 13:23. While Qoheleth uses the autobiographical voice with abandon, the author provides notably few identifiable particulars (or biographical errors that would reveal the presence of an impostor). Only David is named as an

the rabbinic and patristic scholarship on Qoheleth and Hebrews, respectively.[5] Both books present theological problems and both have spurious traditions of multilingual variations. In both writings, the imputed authorship may be what "saved" these texts; at the very least, authorial attribution played a major role in arguments for their retention and perpetuation.

What potential is there for a "new method" of reading to illumine some of the dark corners remaining in these enigmatic and controversial texts? Historically-oriented critical approaches have certainly yielded valuable insights and impressive data. Yet the very abundance of data as well as its irreconcilable variety increasingly frustrates certainty regarding the identity of the authors of Hebrews and Qoheleth. In other words, the search for the origin has not led us to a single, sharper vision, but instead has multiplied potential authors and contexts, thereby further cluttering an already cloudy view. Readings that sever the restraints of historiography certainly alleviate some of the enigma and controversy, but an approach that disregards specific historical contexts and interpretive communities is not without shortcomings of its own. While a reader-oriented approach to Hebrews and Qoheleth would provide (and has provided) some surprising and engaging readings, can there be a way to incorporate the valued controls and stimulating boundaries created by historical inquiry with a sophisticated notion of texts, readers, and composition?[6] In the spirit of "new methods," we would apply not just a different approach to the question of authorship of Qoheleth and Hebrews, but rather an admittedly eclectic combination of approaches. Our reading will draw from insights provided by reader-response criticism, reception history, intertextuality and cultural criticism.[7] And our emphasis will be not on how reading and interpretation

---

ancestor of the writer. Both texts exhibit changing genres and voices that may indicate much is going on "off stage" that is only alluded to in the final text.

[5] On Qoheleth, see *m. Yad.* 3:5; *m. ʿEd.* 5:3; *b. Meg.* 71; *b. Šabb.* 30b; *Lev. Rab.* 28:1; *Qoh. Rab.* 1:3; 11:9; and *Num. Rab.* 161b. On Hebrews, see Eusebius, *Hist. eccl.* 2.17.12–13; 3.3.1–7; 3.38.2–3; 5.26.1; 6.14.4; 6.20.3; and 6.25.11–14.

[6] On reader-response biblical criticism—in both its positive and its negative manifestations—see Edgar V. McKnight, "Reader Response Criticism," in *To Each its Own Meaning: An Introduction to Biblical Criticism and their Applications* (ed. Steven L. McKenzie and Stephen R. Haynes; rev. ed.; Louisville: Westminster John Knox, 1999), 230–252; and The Bible and Culture Collective, *The Postmodern Bible* (New Haven: Yale University Press, 1995), 20–69.

[7] For introductions to intertextuality and cultural criticism, see Timothy K. Beal,

are moments of interaction between reader and author, but rather on how the text itself is an invested and integral party to interpretation. Far from it being a methodological experiment, we argue that such eclecticism highlights some significant aspects of how Hebrews and Qoheleth function, and, indeed, is inspired by the nature of these texts themselves.

We approach both Qoheleth and Hebrews as intertextual—not precisely in themselves, but we pursue an intertextual engagement with the reception and history of inquiry of these texts. By placing these texts and their interpretations in conversation with one another, we, as critics, are also entering into conversation, becoming ourselves sites of intertextuality—both as collaborating authors with different backgrounds and specializations and as authors engaging a reading community knit only by common interest in a single text. In noting the areas of both congruence and difference, we better recognize and understand the presence of consistent, cooperating issues in the interpretation of Qoheleth and Hebrews that reflect something basic about the nature of reading and texts. And we find one more use of our eclectic combination of methods: through them, we are able to collapse the binary divisions often installed between writer and critic, provenance and history of scholarship, text and intertext. In pursuing these inquiries together, as both colleagues and friends, we also cross the borderline sometimes erected between scholars/scholarship on the Hebrew Bible and on the New Testament. Reading in these multiple, intertextual relationships allows us to pursue a type of "ethical criticism," not in terms of simply judging a text or interpretation as right or wrong, but, in the words of Wayne C. Booth, as "fluid conversation about the qualities of the company we keep—and the company that we ourselves provide."[8]

Modern and postmodern scholarship, using (or resisting) historical and grammatical analysis, creates serious questions about the

---

"Intertextuality," and Kenneth Surin, "Culture/cultural criticism," both in *Handbook of Postmodern Biblical Interpretation* (ed. Andrew K. M. Adam; St. Louis, Miss.: Chalice, 2000), 128–130, 49–54.

[8] Wayne C. Booth, *The Company We Keep: An Ethics of Fiction* (Berkeley: University of California Press, 1988), x. For an analysis of Booth's work in biblical studies and its relationship to reader-response criticism, see *The Postmodern Bible*, 32–33. See also Adele Reinhartz, *Befriending the Beloved Disciple: A Jewish Reading of the Gospel of John* (New York: Continuum, 2001) for a book-length engagement of Booth's metaphor of the book as friend and an application of his theories of ethical criticism.

authorship imputed to Qoheleth and Hebrews by earlier, pre-modern scholarship. Despite different origins, strategies, and goals, Jewish and Christian scholarship of both texts has followed similar lines of development and addressed similar concerns. Observing this process offers an opportunity for some reflections on the making and unmaking of scholarly tradition and technique. Can we, as scholars, suspend—or even identify—the cultural, theological, and epistemological influences impinging upon our reading? Are these assumptions imposed upon or invented by the texts we read? Finally, do our "impositions" actually control these texts, or are they precisely what give these texts lasting interest? Drawing upon (deliberately?) cryptic textual references and extra-textual traditions, scholars collude with the texts of Qoheleth and Hebrews in the construction of authority, a construction that both constricts and directs generations of later interpreters and that ensures the continuing presence of a reading community.

Solomon and Qoheleth

A variety of issues in the reading of Qoheleth concerned the rabbis of the Talmud and midrash: contradictions,[9] whether or not the book "defiles the hands,"[10] and the danger of inclining a reader toward heresy.[11] What worried the rabbis has continued to worry the modern scholars: contradictions, canonization, and a seemingly unorthodox theology.[12] Like the rabbis of the Talmud, modern commentators

---

[9] "R. Judah b. R. Samuel b. Shilath said in Rav's name: The sages sought to withdraw... the book of Qoheleth because its words are mutually contradictory.... Why then did they not withdraw it? Because it begins with words of Torah and it ends with words of Torah" (*b. Šabb.* 30b) as quoted in Michael V. Fox, *A Time to Tear Down and a Time to Build Up: A Rereading of Ecclesiastes* (Grand Rapids: Eerdmans, 1999), 1.

[10] "All books in the Bible defile the hands. Song of Songs and Ecclesiastes defile the hands. Rabbi Yehuda states that Song of Songs defiles the hands and Ecclesiastes is in dispute. Rabbi Yossi states that Ecclesiastes does not defile the hands and Song of Songs is in dispute" (*m. Yad.* 3:5) as quoted in Michael J. Broyde, "Defilement of the Hands, Canonization of the Bible, and the Special Status of Esther, Ecclesiastes, and Song of Songs," *Judaism* 44/1 (1995): 67.

[11] In *Qoh. Rab.* (on verse 1:3) the verses 1:3 and 11:9 are cited as dangerous sites of potential misinterpretation—a misinterpretation that may lead the reader into heresy.

[12] Even the briefest perusal of modern commentaries reveals that all of these "problems" are always highlighted in the introductory chapters. See, for example: R. B. Y. Scott, *Proverbs, Ecclesiastes* (AB 18; Garden City, N.Y.: Doubleday, 1965);

construct theories of authorship in order to explain (away) the parts of the text that trouble them.

By the rabbinic period, Qoheleth had already been attributed to Solomon,[13] but Solomonic authorship was not enough to guarantee inclusion or retention in the canon. Solomon himself needed to be rehabilitated. The relevant Talmudic discussions are concerned with whether or not Qoheleth defiles the hands. To "defile the hands" is to be sacred scripture; the Talmudic debates indicate one of two things: either the question of canon was still open; or the canon had been set already and the discussion was over the level of divine inspiration. If the latter, the matter is one of ritual purity having to do with the absence of the Tetragrammaton.[14] No matter the exact meaning of the phrase, the judgments about Solomon's character and status are instructive. For example, in one debate, Rabbi Yehoshua finally intrudes with words from Rabbi Shimon ben Mennasiah: "Ecclesiastes does not defile the hands since it is [only] the wisdom of Solomon."[15] Solomon's wisdom may be worth revering, but it is not the same as divinely inspired text.

Seow, *Ecclesiastes*; James L. Crenshaw, *Ecclesiastes: A Commentary* (OTL; Philadelphia: Westminster, 1987); Roland E. Murphy, *Ecclesiastes* (WBC 23A; Dallas: Word Books, 1992).

[13] The Talmudic material is difficult to date with precision. The Mishnah was compiled around 200 CE but reflects older traditions. Since Rabbis Hillel and Shammai were involved in the Qoheleth debate, it appears as if Solomonic authorship was already established by the first century.

[14] Broyde, "Defilement," 66–67. The exact meaning of the debate over the defiling of hands (inclusion in canon, or being subject to rules of ritual purity) is difficult to determine because the phrase appears to be understood in both ways by the rabbinic commentators. Our uncertainty reflects their ambiguity. Adding to our current lack of clarity or consensus about when and how Qoheleth was canonized is the nature of rabbinic material. Multiple arguments are raised in order to tease out all the possible issues involved with an interpretation and its implications. Objections do not necessarily reflect the actual opinions of the rabbis, but may be best understood as a legal exercise. This is how Michael V. Fox understands the "defiling the hands" debates: "These and similar stylized discussions are homiletic devices raising difficulties to be resolved by exegetical dexterity. They are not disputes about canonicity, which was resolved much earlier" (*A Time*, 2). Broyde concludes that what is really at issue is ritual status because these three books do not contain the Tetragrammaton.

[15] *b. Meg.* 7a as quoted in Broyde, "Defilement," 67. The full passage reads: "Rabbi Yehuda says in the name of Samuel: The Book of Esther does not defile the hands. Is this to be understood to mean that Samuel rules that Esther was not written with divine inspiration? But does not Samuel himself say that Esther was written with divine inspiration; Rather [Samuel rules] that Esther was said to be read and not to be written. Let us ask: Rabbi Meir states 'Ecclesiastes does not

Although a minority opinion, ambivalence about Solomon's character continues in later interpretations of Qoheleth. For example, Rabbi David ibn Zimra (Radvaz), when asked why Qoheleth lacks the Tetragrammaton, responded that Solomon's heart was turned away from God by his many wives.[16] Solomon's predilection for foreign women tainted his good name in the book of Kings and beyond. Ambivalence about Solomon's character may also explain the absence of a Targum (Aramaic translation) or a midrash (rabbinical interpretation) on Qoheleth (or on any other wisdom literature for that matter) from the early period of rabbinical writings. Together, Solomon and Qoheleth needed to be remade to reflect rabbinic values, which in turn allowed for the proliferation of writings on Solomon and the texts presumed to be authored by him. According to Paul V. M. Flesher, the lateness of the *Targum Qoheleth* and *Qoheleth Rabbah* then can be attributed to the vast differences between sages in the wisdom and rabbinic traditions. It is only when the rabbis redefined Solomon-the-wisdom-sage as Solomon-the-Torah-sage that midrash on wisdom begins. The *Targum* "freely rewrites Qoheleth" by "substituting Torah for Wisdom."[17]

The *Targum* was redacted sometime between the seventh and twelfth centuries, and it reflects the Talmudic majority position about the theology and authorship of Qoheleth.[18] The name "Solomon" is inserted into commentary on Qoheleth, and the *Targum* argues forcefully that Qoheleth/Solomon is inspired by the holy spirit and endowed with the spirit of prophecy (*Tg. Qoh.* 1:1–2). The narrative of Solomon's life—taken from the book of Kings—is interwoven with the text of Qoheleth, thereby remaking both. Solomon is characterized as a

---

defile the hands and there is a dispute as to whether Song of Songs defiles the hands.' Rabbi Yossi states Song of Songs defiles the hands and Ecclesiastes is in dispute. Rabbi Shimon states: Ecclesiastes is one of the cases where Beit Shammai is more liberal than Beit Hillel, but Ruth, Song of Songs and Esther certainly defile the hands. This is in accordance with Rabbi Yehoshua who states: 'As learned Rabbi Shimon ben Mennasiah states: Ecclesiastes does not defile the hands since it is the wisdom of Solomon.'" See also Fox, *A Time*, 1–2. Rabbi Shimon ben Mennasiah's opinion is recorded also in the *t. Yad.* 2:14 (Broyde, "Defilement," 76, n. 40 and Fox, *A Time*, 2, n. 6), and Abba Shaul notes it in *'Abot R. Nat.* (Fox, *A Time*, 2, n. 6).

[16] Radvaz, *Response*, 2:722, as quoted in Broyde, "Defilement," 70.

[17] Paul V. M. Flesher, "The Wisdom of the Sages: Rabbinic Rewriting of Qoheleth," in *AAR/SBL Annual Meeting Abstracts* (1990): 390.

[18] Peter S. Knobel, "The Targum of Qohelet," in *The Targums of Job, Proverbs, Qohelet* (ed. Martin McNamara et al.; Collegeville, Minn.: Liturgical, 1991), 2.

penitent, exiled from his throne in Jerusalem, foreseeing the demise of his kingdom under the reign of his son Rehoboam, and advocating the Torah and the commandments as the only path to blessings in this life and the next (*Tg. Qoh.* 1:12–18).

In the same way that Jewish interpretation was standardized by the views expressed in the *Targum*, Jerome set the standard for all subsequent Christian interpretation of Qoheleth until the Reformation.[19] Solomonic authorship was already well established. Presumably drawing on the traditions already present in first-century Judaism, Origen is the first Christian commentator to identify Qoheleth with Solomon and to group Song of Songs, Proverbs, and Qoheleth together.[20] But it is Jerome's Vulgate and commentary on Ecclesiastes that directs patristic and medieval Christian understandings. Solomon is remade here as a kind of ante/i-Christ, representing the world before and without Christ, thereby demonstrating the necessity of Christ. Passages deemed difficult are spiritualized and read through Christological lenses. For example, when Qoheleth/Solomon expresses pessimistic weariness in Qoh 1:8—"the eye is not satisfied with seeing, or the ear filled with hearing"—Jerome responds that "Christ is always desiring and seeking our salvation."[21] When Qoheleth/Solomon contends that there is nothing better "than to eat and drink" (Qoh 2:24), Jerome inserts "the body and blood of the Eucharist."[22]

The first scholar, Jewish or Christian, to suggest Solomon did not write Qoheleth was Martin Luther. In *Table Talk*, he wrote, "Solomon himself did not write the book of Ecclesiastes, but it was produced by Sirach at the time of the Maccabees.... It is a sort of Talmud, compiled from many books, probably from the library of King Ptolemy Euergetes of Egypt."[23] Luther's suggestion was not picked up again for one hundred years, until the work of the Dutch philosopher Hugo Grotius. Grotius dismissed the influence of divine inspiration

---

[19] Svend Holm-Nielsen, "On the Interpretation of Qoheleth in Early Christianity," *VT* 24 (1974): 177.

[20] Murphy, *Ecclesiastes*, xlix.

[21] As quoted in Christian D. Ginsburg, *Coheleth, commonly called the book of Ecclesiastes* (1861; repr. as part of *The Song of Songs and Coheleth*, 2 vols. in 1; New York: KTAV, 1970]), 102.

[22] As quoted in Ginsburg, *Coheleth*, 102–103. See also Holm-Nielsen, "On the Interpretation," 176.

[23] Martin Luther, *Tischreden: [1531–1546]* (6 vols. of *D. Martin Luthers Werke: Kritische Gesamtausgabe*; ed. E. Kroker et al.; Weimar: Hermann Böhlaus Nachfolger, 1912), 1:207 (no. 475). Translation from George Barton, *Commentary on the Book of Ecclesiastes* (ICC; Edinburgh: T&T Clark, 1908), 21; see also Ginsburg, *Coheleth*, 113.

in the composition of the scriptures. Instead, he insisted on rigorous philological investigation and interpretation as well as the "primary sense" (historical) of the text.[24] Grotius is best known for his use of linguistic analysis to demolish arguments for Solomonic authorship. In *Annotationes in Vetus et Novum Testamentum* (1644) he writes, "I believe that the book is not the production of Solomon, but was written in the name of this king, as being led by repentance to do it. For it contains many words which cannot be found except in Ezra, Daniel, and the Chaldee paraphrasts."[25]

Once Grotius established linguistic reasons for questioning Solomonic authorship, others soon followed. First, there was only a trickle of commentators who supported Grotius' contention: Johann D. Michaelis in Germany (1751) and Bishop Robert Lowth in England (1753). In the second half of the eighteenth century, five major commentaries were published denying Solomonic authorship. After this, the trickle became a flood. In a review of nineteenth-century commentaries on Ecclesiastes, George Barton counts thirty-eight commentaries that refute Solomonic authorship, and only one which clung to it (and but one more which was non-committal). At the end of the nineteenth century, Franz Delitzsch completed what Grotius began; after a philological analysis, which set the standard for all that follow, Delitzsch famously concluded: "If the Book of Koheleth were of old Solomonic origin, then there is no history of the Hebrew language."[26]

Paul and Hebrews

In his commentary for the Anchor Bible, Craig R. Koester writes an overview of our problem that mirrors many of the ideological shifts—and even the rough sequence of those shifts—found in Qoheleth scholarship:[27]

> There have been three major shifts in the study of Hebrews. First, theological controversies in the fourth and fifth centuries concluded

---

[24] Gerald Bray, *Biblical Interpretation: Past and Present* (Downers Grove, Ill.: InterVarsity, 1996), 237.
[25] As quoted in Ginsburg, *Coheleth*, 146 and Barton, *Commentary*, 21.
[26] Franz Delitzsch, *Commentary on the Song of Songs and Ecclesiastes* (trans. M. G. Easton; Edinburgh: T&T Clark, 1877), 190.
[27] Craig R. Koester, *Hebrews* (AB 36; New York: Doubleday, 2001), 19.

several centuries of uncertainty about the status of Hebrews and led to the broad acceptance of Hebrews as canonical Scripture. Second, disputes in the sixteenth century reopened questions concerning the status of Hebrews.... Third, the late eighteenth century witnessed the emergence of historical critical readings of Hebrews that led to ongoing controversy about the book's authorship, context of composition... and place in the history of Christianity.

Much as the belief in Solomonic authorship offered both context and concern for the reading of Qoheleth, the view that Paul wrote Hebrews both provided a gloss of authority and continuity and introduced problems. Hebrews differs significantly in style and vocabulary from Paul's other writings. Further, while Hebrews' supersessionist impulses would agree with some readings of Paul (esp. of Gal 2–4 or Rom 9–10), there are concerns about anonymity which need response; Paul, simply put, confidently signed his own polemic (Gal 6:11). Even the "title" awakens concern in anyone who would read the text as a product of the "Apostle to the Gentiles."

A cursory survey of ante-Nicene patristic writers reveals an unenthusiastic consensus on Pauline authorship of Hebrews along with a determined decision to use the epistle as if it were Pauline.[28] Origen (ca. 185–ca. 254) noted Hebrews lacked Paul's "rudeness of speech" and familiar language, yet suggested the contents were certainly in agreement with Pauline theology (Eusebius, *Hist. eccl.* 6.25.11–14). Though Origen famously concludes that "God alone" knows Hebrews' author, he nevertheless argues the text is fully "Pauline" and, in quite a "post-modern" sympathetic notion of authorship, concludes Paul is the author no matter who physically wrote the words.[29]

---

[28] For much (if not most) of the following, I am particularly indebted to the first volume of Ceslas Spicq, *L'Épître aux Hébreux* (2 vols.; Paris: Gabalda, 1952–1953). According to Clement of Alexandria (at least as reported by Eusebius), Pantaenus (died ca. 200 CE) asserted that Hebrews was written by Paul, but that Paul withheld his name in deference to Jesus who had been sent to "his own," the Jews (Eusebius, *Hist. eccl.* 6.14.4). Clement concurred that Hebrews was Pauline but he supposed Paul's choice of anonymity arose more from rhetorical and persuasive desires than deference to messianic piety; Paul left off his name so that the Jews would not reject the letter, a priori, and ignore it (*Hist. eccl.* 6.14.2). Clement is quite happy quoting Hebrews as if it were by Paul (*Strom.* 5.10.62; 6.7.62) but notes there are some vocabulary and style differences between Hebrews and the other letters of the Pauline corpus. Eusebius suggests Hebrews was originally composed in Hebrew or Aramaic and then translated into Greek by Luke (*Hist. eccl.* 6.14.2).

[29] Origen cites and comments on the letter with direct attribution of the writing to Paul (*Comm. Jo.* 1.20; *Princ.* 1.5.1, etc.). Eusebius notes that there has been some dissension on the question of Pauline authorship (particularly dividing East and

In near diametric contrast to rabbinic scholarship on Qoheleth, confidence in Pauline authorship within patristic debate arises from theological motivations and assessments. The summary of debate found in Ephraem (ca. 306–373) carefully notes Hebrews' unique style, and Ephraem may be the first biblical scholar to notice or address biographical correlations in his recognition of Timothy in Heb 13:23,[30] yet the primary patristic debate over canonization and "Paulinisation" of Hebrews (and Ephraem's own conclusions) pivoted around theology and patristic constructs of Paul as Christian philosopher *par excellence* and supersessionist Apostle to the Gentiles. Even more, Ephraem (and others) suggests that those who deny Pauline origins most aggressively are motivated by Hebrews' limitations upon grace and post-baptismal reconciliation.[31] Epiphanius (ca. 315–403) is clear that Marcion and the Arians rejected Pauline composition because Hebrews failed to agree with their own theological agendas. By the time of Jerome, the patristic consensus was that only heretics seriously questioned Pauline authorship (Jerome, *Epist.* 58; Augustine, *Haer.* 89; *Ep. ad Rom. inchoata* 11.3–4 [PL 35.2095]; *Doctr. chr.* 2.8.12–13; cf. *Civ.* 10.5, which admits some openness on the question). Debates over Hebrews' author invoked assertions of theological affinity to Paul, and this affinity overrode glaring stylistic differences. Those who rejected the theology of Hebrews also questioned its Pauline origins.[32]

West and often based upon issues of style and lexicography) but that it is "obvious and plain" that the content and themes of Hebrews so closely agree with Paul's that no other author could be imaginable (*Hist. eccl.* 3.3.5). Still, however, he allows for some ambivalences of his own (*Hist. eccl.* 2.17.12). Other (roughly) fourth-century writers Methodius of Olympus and Theodore of Mopsuestia both quote Hebrews openly as Pauline (*Symp.* 5.7, which quotes Heb 10:1; *Comm. Heb.* PG 66.952). These views certainly agree with most of the manuscript evidence, which includes Hebrews along with the other thirteen Pauline epistles (though often in different locations). Consider, for example, only the extensive evidence marshaled by Spicq, *L'Épître*, and Paul Ellingworth, *The Epistle to the Hebrews* (NIGTC; Grand Rapids: Eerdmans, 1993), 8–21. To complete the Ante-Nicene treatment, we should note that Tertullian may suggest Barnabas as the author, unless he is merely misattributing his quotation in *Pud.* 20.

[30] Ephraem too suggests that Hebrews was originally composed in Hebrew or Aramaic, yet he thinks it was translated by Clement of Rome.

[31] We need not expound, of course, how attaching Hebrews to the Apostle of Grace and the explicator of salvation by faith through grace both softens Hebrews' hardness and adds an edge to any overly liberal readings of Romans, Ephesians or Galatians.

[32] Apart from a possibly mistaken ascription to Barnabas, Paul's only named competitors for authorship are Clement of Rome and Luke. Yet both Clement and

According to the tremendous survey of Ceslas Spicq, Christian opinion that Paul wrote Hebrews remained constant through the medieval period.[33] In the post-Grotius, post-Renaissance bloom of critical biblical interpretation, however, there has been a dramatic propagation of hypotheses on the authorship of Hebrews. Not satisfied with pruning Solomon from Ecclesiastes, Luther also grafted in Apollos for Hebrews, a choice popular through the eighteenth and nineteenth centuries.[34] As we have seen in Qoheleth scholarship, scholarship on Hebrews after the age of Grotius has found linguistic and stylistic variations too acute to be ignored. Most commentators on Hebrews from the last 25 years assert the data are too vague and the style too idiosyncratic for any authorship to be suggested with confidence.

When the canon of the New Testament was being formed, biblical scholarship, while well aware of stylistic concerns, suggested the theology of Hebrews could not be dissociated from Paul and asserted Pauline "authorship." Most of these scholars also argued that theological coherence and apostolicity were essential canonical qualifications. In later critical eras, when canonical debate was much less pressing, stylistic concerns became more central and certainty of Pauline authorship diminished proportionately. It may be obvious to note, but the theological needs and critical emphases of each generation of scholarship have in key ways affected the position of scholars toward authorship of Hebrews. Roughly the same may be seen behind scholarship on the Solomonic authorship of Qoheleth. Is it any surprise that, in our current high-modernist/postmodern moment, scholars express complete agnosticism and assert the irreducible complexity of the data?

The biases of scholarship which we have described are not superficial, unimportant, or antique. Precisely on the fulcrum of the nineteenth

---

Luke are also named by Eusebius (*Hist. eccl.* 6.25.14; 3.38.2) as possible translators of an originally Pauline Epistle to the Hebrews. Even when they are named as parties responsible for our final form of Hebrews, there is a decided preference to view both of these as translators and not originators. Further, neither Clement nor Luke could be said to be anything but wholly integrated into Pauline theology.

[33] However, when there was discrepant opinion, it normally was a suggestion of Lukan authorship or translation. Spicq, *L'Épître*, 1:197–219.

[34] Philip the Deacon was advocated by Ramsay and many British scholars of the nineteenth and early twentieth centuries. Modern critics have suggested Peter (due to literary congruence between 2 Peter and Hebrews), Jude (again, based on literary coherence), and Epaphras.

and twentieth centuries, Adolf von Harnack argued Hebrews was written by Priscilla in collaboration with her husband Aquila.[35] Summarizing von Harnack, Mary Rose D'Angelo writes:[36]

> Suggesting that Hebrews was written to a house-church in Rome after the death of Paul, [von Harnack] concluded that the writer was a member of that house-church and was closely associated with Timothy. Harnack also deduced that the author had to be closely enough associated with another member of the group to be able to speak as "I" or "we" interchangeably. This writer was learned and a teacher but was apologetic about using this authority to exhort others. Assuming that the name of such an author had to be found in the Acts or the Pauline corpus, Harnack concluded that this description best suits Prisca.... In Harnack's view the best explanation for the loss of the author's name was that the author was a woman. There is evidence that women's names were suppressed in the text of the New Testament, and Prisca herself was significantly demoted in some manuscripts of Acts.

Certainly, the case for Priscillian authorship is not definitive; in many ways it may not be much more than the articulation of a curious possibility—a possibility which is faced with the rather large obstacle of the masculine participle in Heb 11:32.[37] Hardly any but feminist scholars continue to advocate Priscillian authorship.[38] Yet is

---

[35] Adolf von Harnack, "Probabilia über die Adresse und den Verfasser des Hebräerbriefs." *ZNW* 1 (1900): 16–41. On Priscilla, see Acts 18:2–4, 18, 26; 2 Tim 4:19; Rom 16:3–5; 1 Cor 16:19.

[36] Mary Rose D'Angelo, "Hebrews," in *The Women's Bible Commentary* (ed. Carol A. Newsom and Sharon H. Ringe; Louisville: Westminster/John Knox, 1998), 456.

[37] We would grant that the masculine participle in Heb 11:32 is in agreement with the first-person pronoun. The obvious reason for this construction would be that the author was male. Of course, we are thus far unaware of a feminine participle extant in the (rather common) expression being employed in this verse (ἐπιλείψει με γὰρ διηγούμενον ὁ χρόνος). It does not seem impossible that we have an unconscious use of an idiomatic construction. It is also possible (though, granted, highly unlikely) that Heb 11:32 is intended to conceal the feminine origins of Hebrews or that (more possibly, but lacking supporting evidence) there has been some scribal emendation.
These not insubstantial caveats aside, we would add our own experience as differently gendered co-authors. Sentences in collaborative documents—even when written by educated and published authors—slide ambivalently from first-person singular to first-person plural. Sentences written collaboratively take on at times a unique, trans-gendered or "cross-gendered" life of their own. While we grant the problems of Heb 11:32, we do not concur with C. C. Torrey ("The Authorship and Character of the so-called 'Epistle to the Hebrews,'" *JBL* 30 [1911]: 137–56) that they are fatal.

[38] Note, most certainly, Ruth Hoppin, *Priscilla, Author of the Epistle to the Hebrews, and Other Essays* (New York: Exposition, 1969). See, additionally, the thesis of

there any better evidence to support Apollos over Priscilla and Aquila?

To whom we ascribe authorship, and why, are very culturally laden issues and are enmeshed with theological and cultural assumptions. Returning to Koester, he is certainly correct when he argues, "Biblical interpretation is the art of asking questions of texts. The way questions are posed reflects the assumptions and concerns of the interpreter and shapes the answers that are given."[39]

Constructions and Collusions

Not content to observe that the assumptions we bring as scholars are culturally and theologically driven, we are particularly intrigued by Koester's insight that the same factors affect both our answers and the very "art of asking questions." This is not a new observation for Biblical scholarship. What we find intriguing, however, is the extent and ways these texts themselves—both Hebrews and Qoheleth—strategically adopt both specificity and ambivalence in order to present themselves as fluid and malleable documents.[40]

To perpetuate themselves, texts must be read; to be read over generations, they must be specific enough to control readers but generic enough to be adapted to multiple reading communities. In his fascinating (and not completely tongue-out-of-cheek) essay, "The Selfish Text: The Bible and Memetics," Hugh S. Pyper uses insights from evolutionary biology to describe the composition, preservation, and critical engagement of texts. He writes:[41]

> Richard Dawkins' ... book *The Selfish Gene* (1976 and 1989) ... has popularized the admittedly controversial idea that human beings, indeed all living organisms, can be construed as the 'survival vehicles' for their genetic material. This claim is a variant on Samuel Butler's well-known

---

J. Massyngberde Ford that Hebrews was written by Mary (given the resonances with the apocryphal *Gospel of Mary*): J. Massyngberde Ford, "The Mother of Jesus and the Authorship of the Epistle to the Hebrews," *TBT* 82 (1975): 683–94.

[39] Koester, *Hebrews*, 19.

[40] On "specific ambiguity" and its function in texts, see Robert P. Seesengood, "Postcards from the (Canon's) Edge: The Pastoral Epistles and Derrida's *The Post Card*," in *Derrida's Bible* (ed. Yvonne Sherwood; New York: Palgrave, 2004), 49–59.

[41] Hugh S. Pyper, "The Selfish Text: The Bible and Memetics," in *Biblical Studies/Cultural Studies* (ed. J. Cheryl Exum and Stephen D. Moore; JSOTSup 266; Sheffield: Sheffield Academic Press, 1998), 70–71. Elsewhere, Pyper (quoting Dennett) argues that "a scholar is just a library's way of making more libraries"; see "The Triumph of the Lamb: Psalm 23 and Textual Fitness," *BibInt* 9 (2001): 385–392.

description of a hen as 'an egg's way of making another egg.' An organism is a gene's way of making another gene.... It is the following further adaptation of this slogan that forms the proposition that this paper will discuss: *Western Culture is the Bible's way of making more Bibles.*

Taking cues from evolutionary theories ourselves, could it be that ambivalent theology, lexical uniqueness, erratic first-person pronouns, references to other "canonical" worthies by name, and anonymity are the means for Qoheleth and Hebrews to ensure reception and retention? As critical readers, might we have been colluding with these texts in ways that perpetuate and reflect not only cultural and theological assumptions but also in ways that each text invites and performs in order to ensure survival? If this were the case, then the resolution of these questions would be the very end of the texts' adaptations and, thus, the beginning of their marginalization. As Qoheleth seductively warns, "Of making many books there is no end" (Qoh 12:12). We may be certain that subsequent generations will puzzle over our current state of the question, even as we smile at the quaint certainty of earlier scholars.

Qoheleth, through its superfluous use of "I" and repeated command to "see," and Hebrews, with its manipulative shifts to cohortative subjunctive, force the reader into submissive positions. All texts read us as we read them, but Qoheleth and Hebrews in particular are invested in the reading process; they, themselves, "read" their own traditions in ways that both defer to and subdue those traditions. Notice, for example, the way Hebrews depends upon Torah for its Christology and authority, yet the very Christology and theology it describes renders Torah superfluous, perhaps even hostile, to the full revelation of God. For Hebrews, reconciliation with God requires a sacrifice—the sacrifice of Jewish texts and the Levitical system. Hebrews cites Torah as authority for a theology that renders Torah irrelevant; Hebrews erases what it depends upon.[42] Qoheleth undermines the very values of wisdom literature even as it participates in the features of the genre. In Wisdom traditions, the created universe is liturgy, and wisdom is the awareness of its worship. But in Qoheleth, the universe comes to an end as the sun and the moon

---

[42] Jennifer L. Koosed, "Double Bind: Sacrifice in the Epistle to the Hebrews," in *A Shadow of Glory: Reading the New Testament After the Holocaust* (ed. Tod Linafelt; New York: Routledge, 2002), 89–101.

and the stars blink out (Qoh 12:2).[43] The wise are not rewarded and the fools are not punished; all go to the grave together—the righteous and the wicked, the good and the evil, the clean and the unclean, those who sacrifice and those who do not sacrifice (Qoh 9:2). Subsequent rabbinical readers not only had to tame the pessimism of the book, but also had to remake Solomon so that this Wisdom hero became a Torah hero.[44] All references to the natural world in Qoheleth became references to that which preceded and even created the natural world for the rabbis: Torah.[45]

Unlike Solomon, Paul as author of Hebrews is not rehabilitated; Paul provides a space for a supersessionist notion of early Christology that is protected from Marcionite Christology. Paul rehabilitates Hebrews. Were not Paul author of this text, Hebrews could quite easily accommodate itself to "heretical" Christologies and thus find itself excluded. Were not Paul, the apostle of grace, associated with the text, Hebrews could easily become legalistic, offering no forgiveness for the sins of the baptized. If Qoheleth canonizes Solomon, Paul sanctifies Hebrews and renders its supersessionist theology normative or "orthodox." How the critic reads the text shapes the construction of the author. How the author is imagined informs the reading of the text. And the interplay of both forms the identity of the critic.

Nearly all modern commentaries begin with questions of author, and almost all modern commentaries on Qoheleth and Hebrews

---

[43] For the apocalyptic reading of Qoh 12 see Yvonne Sherwood, "'Not with a bang but a whimper': Shrunken Eschatologies of the Twentieth Century—and the Bible," in *Apocalyptic in History and Tradition* (ed. Christopher Rowland and John Barton; Sheffield: Sheffield Academic Press, 2002), 94–116; and Timothy K. Beal, "C(ha)osmopolis: Qohelet's Last Words," in *God in the Fray: A Tribute to Walter Brueggemann* (ed. Tod Linafelt and Timothy K. Beal; Minneapolis: Fortress, 1998), 290–304.

[44] Solomon asks for wisdom rather than riches or power in 1 Kgs 3:5–13. He demonstrates this wisdom through judging in the courts between the righteous and the wicked (1 Kgs 3:16–28), and also through his discourses on the natural world (1 Kgs 4:33–34). In this way, Solomon becomes associated with Wisdom Literature (Proverbs, especially, which is conflated with 1 Kgs 4:32), which focuses on the created world rather than the Torah or Temple systems of drawing near to God.

[45] *Genesis Rabbah* begins with God looking into the Torah (as blueprint and building block) and creating the world (1:1). In *Qoheleth Rabbah*, whenever Qoheleth laments that there is nothing new under the sun, the rabbis read that there is nothing new before the sun, i.e., the Torah is before the created world and contains everything within it. Thus a pessimistic sentiment that uses and undermines wisdom categories becomes a positive statement about the enduring relevance of Torah.

leave these questions unresolved. Despite the worthy notion that we, as readers, create meanings in texts, authorship matters. Speaking personally, it changes our resistance to the supersessionist views of Hebrews if we imagine the text as the first female voice in Christianity; we can't help feeling more sympathetic, more apologetic. In our own relationship as collaborators, we find comfort and continuity in imagining Priscilla and Aquila exchanging drafts via email. If Qoheleth is a female voice (and there is no real reason to assume that it isn't) then it changes the tenor of the misogynist views expressed.

In our contemporary moment, scholars are comfortable with anonymous texts; they (we) may even prefer them. In Hebrews, the movement away from Paul and toward authorial agnosticism could of course be influenced by postmodern critiques of structures and authors. But could it also be a post-World War II response by Christian scholars to the triumphalism of Hebrews? Cutting Hebrews from authorial moorings creates an anonymous text of unknown provenance, easily left adrift in antiquity and academically related to Jewish/Christian discourse at best, while Paul, no longer needed to add legitimacy to Hebrews, can be salvaged for other purposes. Committed agnosticism on the author's identity faithfully mirrors the rhetoric of Qoheleth and Hebrews themselves. In the erasure of the author and tradition—ours and theirs—there is the erasure of authority.

Have we, in the case of these two texts, been once more co-opted and led even as we appear to be interjecting our own assumptions? Are we mastering these texts, finally relinquishing control and admitting the limits of our skill? Or are we only doing, once again, exactly what they want us to do, so as to ensure that they will be read by yet another generation?

Jennifer L. Koosed, Ph.D.
Assistant Professor of Religious Studies
Albright College
13th and Bern St., P.O. Box 15234, Reading, Pa. 19612–5234, U.S.A.
jkoosed@alb.edu

Robert P. Seesengood, Ph.D.
Adjunct Assistant Professor of Classics and Religious Studies
Drew University, Theological School
36 Madison Ave., Madison, N.J. 07940, U.S.A.
rseeseng@drew.edu

INDICES

INDEX OF MODERN AUTHORS

An "n" after a page number indicates that the reference appears only in the footnotes.

Adam, Andrew K. M. 267n
Adams, Edward 255n
Aitken, Ellen Bradshaw viii, 1, 2, 5, 131, 142n, 148
Aland, Barbara 202n
Aland, Kurt 202n, 219n, 223n
Albrecht, Michael von 173n
Alexander, Patrick H. 8
Alexander, T. Desmond 79n
Alföldy, Géza 141n
Anderson, Gary A. 43n, 45n
Andriessen, Paul 142n
Arowele, P. J. 180n, 198n
Attridge, Harold W. viii, 1, 18n, 19, 21n, 22n, 23n, 38n, 55n, 58n, 61n, 62n, 64n, 69n, 71n, 73n, 74n, 81n, 82n, 99n, 100n, 105n, 118, 133n, 134, 135n, 143n, 144n, 145n, 149n, 151n, 157n, 158n, 166n, 169n, 185, 186n, 187, 190n, 191n, 193, 195n, 197n, 200n, 204, 215n, 217n, 226, 227n, 229n, 231n, 235, 239n, 245n, 250n, 254n, 260n, 265
Aune, David E. 52n
Avraham, Gileadi 66n

Backhaus, Knut viii, 1, 2, 5, 118, 149, 150n, 151n, 156n, 157n, 159n, 167n, 175
Bailey, Cyril 194n
Barabino, Giuseppina 205n
Barag, D. 137n
Barr, James 76n
Barrett, C. K. 133n, 250n
Barth, Markus 54n
Barton, George 271n, 272n
Barton, John 279n
Bassler, Jouette M. 255n
Bauer, Walter 202n
Beal, Timothy K. 266n, 279n
Beard, Mary 194, 195, 196
Becker, Adam H. 233n
Behm, Johannes 44, 58n, 66n, 69n, 71n, 72n
Berger, Klaus 61n

Berger, Peter L. 169n, 170n, 174, 175, 246n
Bergman, Jan 43
Betz, Hans Dieter viii, 151n, 199, 201
Black, C. Clifton 133n
Bleicken, Jochen 165n, 166n
Blum, Erhard 25n
Bockmuehl, Markus 157n
Bodendorfer, Gerhard 90n
Booth, Wayne C. 267
Bornkamm, Günther 142n, 239
Boyarin, Daniel 265n
Bradley, Keith R. 162n
Braude, William G. 119n
Braun, Herbert 100n, 173n, 192n
Bray, Gerald 272n
Brecht, Bertolt 154, 169
Bremen, Katharina von 102n
Brett, M. G. 179n
Breytenbach, Cilliers 33n
Brown, John 75n, 81n
Broyde, Michael J. 268n, 269n, 270n
Bruce, F. F. 71n, 134n, 135n, 192
Buchanan, George W. 69n, 103
Büchner, Karl 173n
Bultmann, Rudolf 151, 239
Burkert, Walter 39, 45
Butler, Samuel 277

Cambier, Jean 133n
Carlston, Charles E. 174n
Charles-Picard, Gilbert 136n
Classen, Carl J. 199, 201, 202, 209
Claussen, Carsten 116n
Cohen, Shaye J. D. 233n
Collins, John J. 48n
Collins, Raymond F. 131n
Coogan, Michael D. 213n
Crenshaw, James L. 269n
Crüsemann, Frank 25n
Cullmann, Oscar 101n
Cumont, Franz 195n

INDEX OF MODERN AUTHORS

D'Angelo, Mary Rose 276
Dahl, Nils 219n, 223n
Das, A. Andrew 245n
Daube, David 133n, 250n
Davies, W. D. 133n, 250n
Dawkins, Richard 277
Deissmann, Adolf 54n
Delitzsch, Franz 272
Derrida, Jacques 13, 16
deSilva, David A. 68, 132n, 133n, 134n, 155n, 157n, 158n, 162n, 167n, 168n, 169n, 171n, 172n, 173n, 174n, 179n, 183, 200, 220n, 221n, 250n
Dibelius, Martin 91n, 142n
Dodd, Brian J. 261n
Dodd, C. H. 255n
Dohmen, Christoph 114n
Donfried, Karl P. 145n
Donner, Herbert 76n
Dörrie, Heinrich 205n
Douglas, Mary 68
Downing, F. Gerald 171n
Drexler, Josef 39n
Dunn, James D. G. 53n, 263n
Dunnill, John 68, 70n, 71n, 78n, 79n, 87n, 118, 251n
Dunning, Benjamin viii, 1, 5, 6, 177, 198

Eberhart, Christian A. viii, 1, 2, 3, 26n, 28n, 32n, 33n, 37, 38n, 39n, 45n, 47n, 48n, 58n, 64
Ego, Beate 29n
Ehlers, W. 139n
Ehrman, Bart D. 183, 215n
Eisenbaum, Pamela M. viii, 1, 2, 6, 7, 184, 185, 189, 213, 222n, 232n, 237, 245n
Elbogen, Ismar 114n, 123n
Ellingworth, Paul 69n, 71n, 73n, 74n, 84n, 274n
Elliott, John H. 179n, 180n, 181n, 198n
Elliott, Neil 131n
Ellis, E. Earle 91n, 92n, 98, 103n
Epp, Eldon J. 215n, 218n, 219
Ernesti, Johann C. G. 203n
Esler, Philip F. 68n
Evang, Martin 157n
Exum, J. Cheryl 277n

Feld, Helmut 151n
Feldman, Louis 141n

Feldmeier, Reinhard 179n, 181, 191n, 198n
Ferguson, John 195n
Filson, Floyd V. 150n, 193n
Fischer, Karl Martin 151n
Fitzmyer, Joseph A. 53n, 97n
Flesher, Paul V. M. 270
Flower, Harriet I. 137n
Flückiger-Guggenheim, Daniela 163n
Ford, J. Massyngberde 277n
Foucault, Michel 16, 181n
Fowl, Stephen E. 261n
Fox, Michael V. 268n, 269n, 270n
Fox, Robin L. 194n
Frankemölle, Hubert 102n, 155n
Frankena, Rintje 65n
Freese, John H. 205, 207, 208
Frerichs, Ernest S. 178n
Frey, Jörg 35n
Fuhrmann, Manfred 203n, 207n
Furnish, Victor Paul 260n

Gamble, Harry 216, 217, 219n, 221n, 223, 224n, 230
Gelardini, Gabriella viii, 1, 2, 4, 9, 107, 116n, 117n, 124
Georgi, Dieter viii, 1, 6, 7, 131n, 239, 244
Gerlitz, Peter 39n
Gese, Hartmut 39, 40n, 45
Ginsburg, Christian D. 271n, 272n
Girard, René 39, 45
Goehring, James E. 144n
Goldberg, Arnold 90, 93, 95, 103, 104n
Goppelt, Leonhard 98n
Gordon, Robert P. 81n
Gorman, Michael J. 257n, 258n, 261n
Grässer, Erich 19n, 25n, 100n, 134, 135n, 151n, 157n, 161n, 163n, 164n, 165n, 166n, 167n, 174n, 204, 224n
Grieb, A. Katherine 255n, 258n
Grogan, Geoffrey W. 162n
Grotius, Hugo 271, 272, 275
Guelich, Robert A. 174n
Guthrie, George H. 150n

Habermas, Jürgen 16
Hagner, Donald A. 91n, 92n, 103, 135n
Hahn, Scott W. viii, 1, 2, 3, 65, 88
Halliwell, Stephen 204

INDEX OF MODERN AUTHORS

Hanhart, Robert 76n
Hanson, Kenneth C. 108n
Harmon, Austin M. 163
Harnack, Adolf von 135n, 276
Hartenstein, Friedhelm 25n, 26n, 29n, 30n, 35n
Hatch, William H. P. 213n, 220n
Haynes, Stephen R. 266n
Hays, Richard B. 248, 255n, 256n, 263n
Hegermann, Harald 164n
Heidegger, Martin 158
Heinemann, Joseph 113n, 115n
Helyer, Larry R. 71n
Hengel, Martin 15, 16
Herr, Moshe D. 90
Holmes, Michael W. 215n
Holm-Nielsen, Svend 271n
Hoppin, Ruth 276n
Horrell, David G. 68n, 246n
Horsley, Richard A. 131n
Hossfeld, Frank-Lothar 26n
Huffmon, Herbert B. 65n
Hugenberger, Gordon P. 76n, 77n, 78, 79n, 81
Hughes, Graham 155n
Hughes, John J. 72, 73, 74, 75n, 80n
Hughes, Philip E. 193n
Humphrey, Caroline 194n
Hurst, L. D. 261n

Instinsky, Hans U. 138n
Isaacs, Marie E. 158n, 166n, 250n, 251n, 254n, 263n

Jacobs, Louis 110n
Janowski, Bernd 26n, 27n, 29n, 30n, 34n, 35n
Jenni, Ernst 33n
Jennrich, W. A. 209n
Jewett, Robert 37n, 38n, 56n, 61n
Johnson, Luke Timothy 245n, 247n
Johnson, Richard W. 167n, 169n
Johnsson, William G. 157n, 180n

Kampling, Rainer 149n
Karrer, Martin 14, 17, 103n, 200, 209n
Käsemann, Ernst 133n, 157n, 180, 187, 232n, 239
Keesmaat, Sylvia C. 258n
Kertelge, Karl 155n
Kessler, Rainer 26n
Keyes, Clinton W. 173

Kilpatrick, George D. 71n, 73n
Kittredge, Cynthia Briggs 134n, 213n
Klauck, Hans-Josef 167n
Kline, Meredith G. 65n, 79n
Knight, Douglas A. 65n
Knobel, Peter S. 270n
Koch, Klaus 27n
Koester, Craig R. 38n, 56n, 57n, 58n, 61n, 62n, 70n, 74n, 78n, 170n, 187n, 188, 196n, 200, 213n, 215, 233n, 245n, 250n, 272, 277
Koester, Helmut 131n, 142n, 192, 193, 197, 239
Koosed, Jennifer L. viii, 1, 6, 8, 265, 278n, 280
Körting, Corinna 30n
Kraay, Colin M. 137n
Kraus, Wolfgang 102n, 103n
Kreuzer, Siegfried 167n
Kroker, E. 271n
Kümmel, Werner G. 37n
Kunzl, Ernst 139n
Kurz, William S. 261n
Kuss, Otto 133n, 172n

La Piana, George 145n
Lampe, Peter 135n, 145n
Lane, William L. 37n, 61n, 67n, 72n, 73n, 75n, 80n, 200, 227n
Lang, Bernhard 43n
Laub, Franz 150n, 155n, 156n, 165n
Lausberg, Heinrich 203n, 206n
Layton, Scott 91n
Lehne, Susanne 254n
Leon, Harry J. 145n
Leonard, William 97n, 217n
Levine, Lee I. 108, 109, 110n, 111n, 112, 113n
Lieu, Judith M. 233n, 236
Lim, Timothy H. 99n
Linafelt, Tod 278n, 279n
Lindars, Barnabas 150n, 200, 216n, 232n
Lindemann, Andreas 219n
Linss, Wilhelm C. 209n
Loader, William 101
Löhr, Hermut viii, 1, 5, 6, 157n, 170n, 171n, 174n, 199, 206n, 210
Long, Thomas G. 69n, 71n, 174n
Longenecker, Bruce W. 245n, 246n, 255n, 260n, 263n
Lowth, Robert 272
Luckmann, Thomas 169n, 170n, 246n

Lull, David J. 255n
Lundquist, John M. 66n
Luther, Martin 271, 275
Lüthi, Kurt 167n

MacRae, George W. 133n
Malina, Bruce J. 68, 160n, 163n, 171n
Mann, Jacob 118, 120n
Manson, William 134n, 241, 242
Martin, Joseph 203n, 209n
Martin, Ralph P. 261n
Marx, Alfred 25n
Matera, Frank J. 158n, 245n
Mattingly, Harold 137n
Maurer, Christian 174n
McCarthy, Dennis J. 65n
McCormick, Michael 137n
McDonald, Lee M. 218n
McKenzie, Steven L. 266n
McKnight, Edgar V. 266n
McNamara, Martin 270n
Mead, George H. 166
Melanchthon, Philipp 199
Mendenhall, George E. 65
Mercado, Luis F. 92n
Merk, Otto 157n
Mettinger, Tryggve N. D. 26n
Metzger, Bruce M. 96
Michaelis, Johann D. 272
Michel, Otto 91n, 92n, 140n, 213n, 245n, 250n
Middendorp, Theophil 49n
Middleton, J. Richard 247n
Milgrom, Jacob 27n, 29n, 30n, 31n, 32n, 40, 41n, 43n, 49
Millar, Fergus 137n
Millard, Matthias 90n
Miller, James C. viii, 1, 6, 7, 8, 245, 259n, 260n, 264
Milligan, George 73n, 75n, 252n
Mitchell, Alan C. 205, 206
Moffatt, James 192, 205n
Montefiore, Hugh W. 135n
Moore, R. Laurence 177, 178, 197
Moore, Stephen D. 277n
Moulton, James H. 252n
Moxnes, Halvor 162n
Mulder, Martin J. 109n
Müller, Paul-Gerhard 144n
Murphy, Roland E. 269n, 271n

Neusner, Jacob 131n, 178n
Newsom, Carol A. 276n

Nicholson, Ernest W. 42n
Niebuhr, Karl-Wilhelm 103n
Niederwimmer, Kurt 164n, 167n
Nitschke, Horst 174n

Oakman, Douglas E. 164n
Oesch, Josef M. 111, 112n
Olbrechts-Tyteca, Lucie 199
Olbricht, Thomas 200
Osten-Sacken, Peter von der 100n
Ostmeyer, Karl-Heinrich 98n

Papsthomas, Amphilochios 218n
Perdelwitz, Richard 150n
Perdue, Leo G. 169n
Perelman, Chaïm 199
Peristiany, John G. 172n
Perrot, Charles 109n, 111, 112n, 114n, 118n
Peterson, David 174n
Pfanner, Michael 136n, 138n, 139n, 140n, 141n, 142n
Pfitzner, Victor C. 70n, 71n
Pilch, John J. 68, 163n
Pitt-Rivers, Julian 172n
Plevnik, Joseph 171n
Plümacher, Eckhard 179n
Pohlenz, Max 205
Popkes, Wiard 154n, 169n
Porter, Stanley E. 200n
Price, Simon R. F. 137n, 145n
Prigent, Pierre 51n
Pursiful, Darrell J. 75n
Pyper, Hugh S. 277

Quell, Gottfried 69n

Rahn, Helmut 206n, 207n
Reinhartz, Adele 267n
Rendtorff, Rolf 27n, 31n, 47
Richards, E. Randolph 221n
Richardson, Lawrence 138n
Richardson, Peter 145n
Riess, Richard 55n
Ringe, Sharon H. 276n
Ringgren, Helmer 43n
Rissi, Mathias 250n
Robertson, O. Palmer 78n
Rohrbaugh, Richard 68
Roldanus, J. 179n
Rowland, Christopher 279n
Rudman, Dominic 27n
Ryberg, Inez Scott 140n, 142n, 143n
Ryle, Herbert E. 97n

INDEX OF MODERN AUTHORS

Safrai, Shemuel 74n
Salevao, Iutisone 157n, 169n, 170n, 245n–246n, 247n, 264n
Sanders, Jack T. 152n, 167n
Sanders, James A. 218n
Sänger, Dieter 26n
Schenck, Kenneth 141n, 246n
Schenk, Wolfgang 152, 153
Schenke, Hans-Martin 151n
Schlier, Heinrich 53n
Schmidt, Thomas E. 158n
Scholer, John M. 156n, 174n, 260n
Schottroff, Luise 151n
Schrage, Wolfgang 152n, 173n
Schröger, Friedrich 91n, 92n, 98
Schröter, Jens 35n
Schulten, Peter N. 137n
Schulz, Anselm 155n
Schulz, Siegfried 152n
Schüssler Fiorenza, Elisabeth 134n, 136n
Schwartz, Seth 234
Schweizer, Eduard 239
Schwertner, Siegfried M. 8
Scott, James C. 133n
Scott, R. B. Y. 268n
Scroggs, Robin 248, 255n
Scullard, Howard H. 195n
Seeberg, Alfred 187
Seesengood, Robert P. viii, 1, 6, 8, 265, 277n, 280
Segovia, Fernando F. 261n
Seow, Choon Leong 265, 269n
Sherwood, Yvonne 277n, 279n
Shinan, Avigdor 113n, 114n
Siegert, Folker 199, 201, 207
Smalley, Stephen S. 52n
Smallwood, E. Mary 137n, 145n
Smend, Rudolf 76n
Smith, Jonathan Z. 178
Smith, Joseph 178
Söding, Thomas 155n, 157n
Somavilla, Ilse 149n
Spengel, Leonard 203n, 204n, 206n
Spicq, Ceslas 66n, 273n, 274n, 275
Stegemann, Ekkehard W. viii, 1, 2, 9, 13, 23
Stegemann, Wolfgang viii, 1, 2, 13, 23, 55n
Stemberger, Günter 34n, 98n, 103, 114n
Stern, Manahem 74n
Stott, John R. W. 51n

Stowers, Stanley K. 217n
Strange, James F. 131n
Strobel, August 134n, 142n
Surin, Kenneth 267n
Swetnam, James 56n, 66n, 70n, 71n, 72n, 73n
Sysling, Harry 109n

Tadmor, Hayim 65n
Taubenschlag, Rafal 74n
Taut, Konrad 99n
Teugels, Lieve 90n
Theissen, Gerd 192n
Theobald, Michael 97n, 167n
Thomas, Nicholas 194n
Thompson, James W. 167n, 171n
Thurén, Jukka 150n, 151n
Thüsing, Wilhelm 62n, 157n, 171n
Thyen, Hartwig 104n, 208n
Tönges, Elke viii, 1, 2, 4, 89, 102n, 105
Torrey, C. C. 276n
Trepp, Leo 123n
Trobisch, David 219n, 223
Troeltsch, Ernst 15
Tucker, Gene M. 65n
Turner, Victor 68

Übelacker, Walter G. 200

Vaage, Leif 222n
Vanhoye, Albert 66n, 71n, 84n, 134n
Vermaseren, Maarten J. 194n
Versnel, Hendrik S. 139n, 140n, 141n
Vielhauer, Philipp 151n
Völker, Walther 174n
Völkl, Richard 152n, 159n, 173n
Vos, Gerhardus 69n, 72n, 81n

Wacholder, Ben Zion 109n, 110n, 113n, 118n
Wagner, J. Ross 247n, 255n
Walsh, Brian J. 247n
Wansink, Craig A. 145n
Wedderburn, A. J. M. 151n
Weinfeld, Moshe 76n, 81n
Weiss, Hans-Friedrich 105, 150n, 158n, 201n
Weiss, Konrad 38n
Welch, A. 220n
Welker, Michael 34n
Westcott, Brooke F. 72n, 73n, 75n

Wick, Peter S. 91n
Wilhelm, Gernot 27n
Willi-Plein, Ina viii, 2, 3, 25, 30n, 31n, 32n, 35
Wills, Lawrence 132n, 208n
Wimbush, Vincent 222n
Windisch, Hans 91n, 92n, 101n, 104n, 204n
Winston, David 174n
Witherington, Ben 88n, 262n
Wittgenstein, Ludwig 149
Wolff, Hans J. 74n
Wrede, William 150n

Wright, N. T. 247n, 255n, 256n, 261n

Yarden, Leon 138n
Yoshiko Reed, Annette 233n
Young, Robert 16

Zahn, Theodor 135n
Zchomelidse, Nino M. 30n
Zevit, Ziony 76n
Zimmermann, Heinrich 101, 150n
Zimmermann, Ruben 98n
Zuntz, Günther 240, 241, 242

INDEX OF ANCIENT SOURCES

An "n" after a page number indicates that the reference appears only in the footnotes.

Old Testament/Hebrew Scriptures

Genesis	94, 121n	24:3–8	79
2:2	120	24:4	41
8:21a	47	24:4–11	66
14	28	24:5	41
14:17–20	92	24:7	41
15	78, 79n	24:8	41, 121
15:9–10	79	24:10	41n
17	79n	24:10a	41
17:8	181n	24:11	41n
17:10–14	79	24:11a	41
17:23–27	79	24:11b	41
18–19	163	24:18	121
21:22	76	29	41, 42, 52, 58
22:1	115	29:1	42
22:1–14	45n	29:5–6	42
22:13	79	29:7	42
22:15–18	79n, 86, 87, 88	29:20	42
22:16–17	91n	29:20–21	51
22:16–18	86	29:21	42
22:17	101	29:29	42
23:4	181n	29:36–37	42
24:1–67	76n	29:44	42
24:41	77	30:22–33	42
26:26	76	31:12–17	120
26:28	76n	31:17b	4, 120, 124
32:31^{MT} (32:30^{ET})	41, 52n	31:18–32:35	4, 118, 120, 122, 123, 124
35:22	111n		
37:1	183n	31:18–34:35	119
38	111n	32	86
49:11	51	32–33	118
		32–34	118, 121, 122, 123
Exodus	65, 119, 121n, 225	32:1–14	86
6:7	92n	32:7	121
12	52n	32:10	86
12:2	120	32:11–14	123n
12:13	52n	32:13	86
12:23	52n	32:13–14	88
19:21–24	41, 52n	32:22–24	111n
22:19	119n	32:29	86–87
24	52	32:34	119
24:1–11	41, 52n, 58	33:1–34:35	122

33:2–3	119	7:5	46n
33:20	41, 52n	7:11–27	41n
34:1–10	123n	7:38	45
34:1–19	123n	8	41, 42, 52, 58
34:27–35	119	8:7–9	42
34:28	121	8:11	42
		8:12	42
Leviticus	39, 121n, 225	8:13	42
1–7	39, 43, 45n, 87	8:21	46n
		8:23–24	42, 51
1:9	46n	8:30	42, 51
1:11	43	15:31b	41n
1:13	46n	16	3, 29, 31, 52n, 57n, 58, 87
1:17	46n		
2	44, 45, 58	16:2	30
2:1	45, 46	16:3	32
2:2	46	16:13	30
2:3	46	16:14–16	52n
2:4	45	16:16	32
2:7	45	16:16b	41n
2:9	46	16:18	52n
2:11	46n	16:20	31n
2:12	45	16:20a	52n
2:14	92n	16:21	32
2:16	46	16:23	31
3	47	16:24	31
3:5	46n	16:25	46n
3:11	46n	16:27–28	191
3:16	46n	16:28	31
4:1–5:13	45	16:29–31	31
4:5–7	47	16:32	31
4:10	46n	16:33–34	31
4:12	46n	16:34^{LXX}	34
4:16–18	47	17:11	33, 40, 41n, 52n
4:19	46n		
4:19–20a	47	17:14	41
4:20b	47	20:3	41n
4:21	46n	26	77, 83n, 123n
4:25	47	26:12	92n
4:26	46n	26:14–39	77n, 83n
4:26a	47	26:25	77n
4:26b	47		
4:30	47	Numbers	121n
4:31	46n	6:22–27	66
4:31a	47	6:24–27	111n
4:31b	47	12:7^{LXX}	28
4:34	47	13–14	119, 121
4:35	46n	14:20–23	87n
4:35a	47	14:29	121
4:35b	47	14:29–35	121
5:11–13	45, 58	19:1–11	58
6:17–21	33n	19:13	41n
6:17–23^{MT} (6:24–30^{ET})	40	19:20	41n
6:20–21	40	24:16	102

INDEX OF ANCIENT SOURCES

Deuteronomy	94, 121n, 244	1 Kings	
4:23	77n	2:23	77n
4:24	99	3:5–13	279n
4:25–40	123n	3:16–28	279n
4:26	77n	4:32	279n
4:31	76n	4:33–34	279n
7:12	76n	18:21–40	44, 46
8:18	76n	18:23	44
9:19	119n	18:24b	47
12:1–28	48	18:26	44
17:2–7	77n	18:27–39	118n
27:14–26	66	18:33	44
28	77, 83n, 123n	18:38	44, 46
28:15–68	77n, 83n		
28:26^{LXX}	84	2 Kings	
29:9	76	6:31	77n
29:10	76	11:4	76
29:11^{MT} (29:12^{ET})	76n		
29:13^{MT} (29:14^{ET})	76n	2 Chronicles	
29:19^{MT} (29:20^{ET})	77	13:22	91n
30:7	77	24:27	91n
31:6	165		
31:8	165	Ezra	
31:9–13	110n	1	113n
31:16	77n	16	113n
31:20	76n		
34:10	102	Nehemiah	108
		8:1–8	108
Joshua		8:8	108, 112n
7:11	77n	8:14–15	110n
7:15	77n		
9:15	76n	Esther	269n, 270n
9:15–20	76		
23:16	77n	Psalms	27, 29, 93, 94, 95, 114, 260n
Ruth	270n	2	141
1:17	77n	2:7	28, 91n
		8	28, 141
1 Samuel	94	8:4–6	91
2:6	56	10:7	77
2:35	94	11:5	115n
3:17	77n	14:4^{LXX}	28
14:44	77n	22	55
20:13	77n	22:23 (21:23^{LXX})	97
25:22	77n	34:15 (33:15^{LXX})	99
		39:7–9^{LXX}	60
2 Samuel	94	40:6–8	92, 142n
3:9	77n	40:7 (39:7^{LXX})	95
3:35	77n	40:7b^{MT} (40:6b^{ET})	61n
7:14	94	40:8 (39:8^{LXX})	95, 96
11:2–27	111n	45:7^{LXX}	28
13	111n	51:19^{MT} (51:17^{ET})	48, 49
19:14^{MT}	77n	59:13	77
23:2	97	69:13	115n

292 INDEX OF ANCIENT SOURCES

89:3	76n	23:10	77
90:4	29	31	20, 94, 118
94:7–11	91n	31:31–34	4, 98, 117, 118,
95 (94^{LXX})	28, 91, 94,		119, 120, 123,
	97, 100		124
95:7–11	87n, 91, 119	31:32–39	118
97:7	28	31:33	99
109:4	92	31:33–34	20
110 (109^{LXX})	94, 103, 141	31:33–40	118
110:1	253n	31:35–40	118
110:4 (109:4^{LXX})	87n, 91n, 92	34	79n
116:8	55	34:18–20	79
117:6^{LXX}	165	34:18–21	77n
		42:5	77n
Proverbs	271	51:22^{LXX}	83n

Qoheleth (Ecclesiastes)	viii, 6, 8, 265,	Lamentations (Ekhah)	115n, 121n,
	266, 267,		123n
	268, 269,		
	270, 271,	Ezekiel	
	272, 273,	9:2–3	31
	274, 275,	9:11	31
	277, 278,	10:2	31
	279, 280	16	76n
1:1	265n	16:8	76
1:8	271	17:13	76
2:24	271	17:13–19	75, 76, 77
9:2	279	17:15	84
12	279n	17:16	77
12:2	279	17:19	77
12:12	278	34:29	83n
		36:6^{LXX}	83n
Song of Songs	268n, 270n,	40:39–41	43
	271		
		Daniel	
Isaiah	113	10:6	31
24:6	77	12:1	51
26:20	95		
33:8–12	77n	Hosea	
52:5	256n	6:7	77n
53^{LXX}	83	7:13	77n
53:3	83n	8:11	77n
53:3–4	83	10:4	76n
53:4	83n	13:14	56
53:11	83n		
53:12^{LXX}	83	Habakkuk	
55:6–56:8	123n	2:3–4	95
Jeremiah	93, 113	Zechariah	
8:13–9:23	123n	8:19	121
11:10	77n		
11:16	77n	Malachi	28, 31
22:8–12	77n	2:7	31

New Testament/Christian Scriptures

Matthew	93, 229, 243	6:26–59	117n
1:23	93n	6:59	109n, 117n
2:6	93n	18:20	109n, 117n
2:15	93n	18:29	80n
2:18	93n		
2:23	93n	Acts	228, 276
4:15–16	93n	2:22	228n
4:23	109n, 117n	2:43	228n
5:9	99n	4:30	228n
5:17	94n	5:12	228n
7:12	94n	6:8	228n
8:17	93n	7:7	52n
9:35	109n, 117n	7:36	228n
11:13	94n	7:42	52n
12:18–21	93n	9:20	109n
13:35	93n	13:14	108n
13:54	109n, 117n	13:14–16	109n
21:5	93n	13:14–41	109
27:9–10	93n	13:15	94n, 112, 116, 133n, 208
27:51	229n	13:16–41	114, 117n
Mark	229	13:22	208
1:21	117n	13:42	108n
1:21–22	109n	13:44	108n
1:39	109n	14:3	228n
6:2	109n, 117n	15:12	228n
13:7–23	51	17:2	108n
15:38	229n	17:2–3	117n
		18:2–4	276n
Luke	229	18:4	108n
4:15	109n, 117n	18:18	276n
4:16	108n	18:26	276n
4:17	112	19:8	109n
4:17–20	112	24:14	94n
4:18–19	113	28:23	94n
4:18–27	117n	28:28	202
4:21–27	114		
4:31–32	109n	Romans	7, 52, 53, 217n, 219, 223, 241, 242, 260n, 274n
4:44	109n		
6:6	109n, 117n	1–11	259
13:10	109n, 117n	1:1–4	258
13:16–41	114	1:5	259
16:16	94n	2:2	53
16:29	94n	2:17–24	256
16:31	94n	2:17–29	257
23:44	229n	2:24	256n
24:27	94n	3:9	257
24:44	94n	3:21	94n
		3:22	258n
John		3:23	257
1:45	94n	3:24	241n
4:48	228n		

INDEX OF ANCIENT SOURCES

3:24–26	241	7:37	204n
3:25	256, 258n, 260n	9:16	204n
3:26	258n	10:1–22	93
5:8	258n	10:16	241n
5:9	241n	11:25	263
5:12	255	11:27	241n
5:18	256	12:22	204n
5:19	258n	15:20–28	256
5:21	256	16:19	276n
6	260n, 262		
6:1–13	258	2 Corinthians	204, 223n
6:4	257	3:6	263
6:10	256	5:17	257
6:11–13	257	6:4	204n
6:13	257, 260	8:9	258
6:16	260	9:5	204n
6:19	260	9:7	204n
7:7–23	257	12:10	204n
7:7–25	257	12:12	228n
8	241n, 258n		
8:1–4	257	Galatians	viii, 88, 199,
8:3	260n		219n, 223n, 248,
8:14–17	258		260n, 274n
8:18–21	255	1:4	256, 258n
8:18–39	258	2–4	273
8:20–21	255	2:20	258
9–10	273	3:6–9	256
9–11	199	3:6–25	88
10:4	257	3:7–29	263
10:9	257	3:12–13	257
10:12–13	95	3:14	257
10:16	95	3:15	263n
10:18	95	3:19–25	357
12	153, 260n, 262	3:22	258n
12:1	53, 57, 61, 260n	4:12	258
12:1–2	257	5:6	258
12:1–3	260	6:6–10	153
12:1–15:13	259	6:10	152
12:2	257	6:11	273
12:3	260n, 262n		
12:13	163	Ephesians	219, 220, 222,
13:9	202		223, 224, 274n
15:7	259	4:25–6:9	54
15:7–12	257	5:1	54
15:16	259, 260	5:1–2	54
15:18	259	5:2	54, 55, 57, 63
15:19	228n	5:8–9	54
16:3–5	276n		
16:26	259	Philippians	223n, 261
		1:10	257
1 Corinthians	204, 219, 223	1:27	257
2:6	257, 263	2	261
3:3	82n	2:1–11	258
7:26	204n	2:5	258, 262

INDEX OF ANCIENT SOURCES

2:5–11	261n		133, 134, 135, 136, 141, 142, 143, 144, 146, 147, 148, 149, 150, 151, 153, 154, 156, 159, 160, 168, 169, 170, 171, 174, 177, 179, 180, 181, 186, 187, 188, 189, 190, 192, 193, 195, 197, 198, 199, 200, 201, 202, 204, 205, 206, 207, 208, 209, 210, 213, 214, 215, 216, 217, 218, 219, 220, 221, 222, 223, 224, 225, 226, 227, 228, 229, 231, 232, 233, 234, 235, 236, 239, 240, 241, 242, 243, 244, 245, 246, 247, 248, 249, 250, 251, 254n, 255, 259, 260, 261, 262, 263, 264, 265, 266, 267, 268, 272, 273, 274, 275, 276, 277, 278, 279, 280
2:6	261		
2:6–11	261		
2:7–8	261		
2:8	258n, 261		
2:9	261		
2:11	256		
2:17	260n		
2:19–24	262		
2:20–21	262		
2:22	262		
2:25–30	262		
2:26	262		
2:29–30	262		
2:31	262		
3:4–17	262		
3:4b–7	262		
3:12–14	262		
3:15–17	262		
3:20	257		
4:18	53, 54, 57, 63, 260n		
Colossians	223n		
1 Thessalonians	223n		
2 Thessalonians	219n, 223n		
2:9	228n		
2 Timothy			
4:19	276n		
Philemon	223n		
Hebrews	vii, viii, 1, 2, 3, 4, 5, 6, 7, 8, 9, 13, 14, 15, 18, 19, 25, 27, 28, 33, 34, 37, 38, 50, 54, 55, 56, 57, 58, 59, 60, 61, 62, 63, 65, 66, 67, 68, 69, 70, 71, 88, 89, 90, 93, 94, 95, 96, 97, 98, 99, 100, 101, 102, 103, 104, 105, 107, 111, 113, 115, 116, 117, 118, 119, 120, 121, 122, 123, 124, 131, 132,		
		1	28, 141
		1–2	119
		1–4	91
		1–6	119, 122
		1–12	153
		1:1	94, 117
		1:1–2	245
		1:1–4	250n
		1:1–5	104
		1:1–13	104
		1:1–14	91
		1:1–2:18	91
		1:1–4:13	150
		1:2	99, 100, 117
		1:3	14, 67, 95, 120n, 172, 253n
		1:3–4	70
		1:4	261

INDEX OF ANCIENT SOURCES

1:5	94	3:7–4:11	87n, 94, 156, 157, 251, 253
1:5–14	123, 172		
1:6	71n, 96n, 117	3:7–4:13	91, 263n
1:7	96n, 117	3:8	99, 186
1:8	96n, 141, 172	3:10	117
1:10	261n	3:12	99, 120, 250
1:10–12	250	3:12–13	155n
1:13	141, 144, 250, 253n	3:12–4:11	91
		3:13	120n, 161
1:14	251	3:14	154n, 254
2	141	3:15	117, 186
2:1	117, 154n, 157	3:16–19	91
2:2	85, 117, 227	3:17	120n, 121, 186
2:2–3	119	4	186, 188
2:3	117, 134, 206, 227, 251	4:1	144, 156, 186, 188
2:3–4	156n, 228	4:1–3	28
2:4	262	4:1–11	120
2:5–8	91	4:1–13	121
2:5–3:6	252n	4:2	253, 263n
2:6	96, 97	4:3	117, 156
2:6–8	28	4:4	4, 96n, 97, 117, 120, 124
2:7	141, 172		
2:8	141, 250	4:6	188, 253, 263n
2:9	13, 70, 85, 87, 88, 172	4:7	96n, 117
		4:8	117
2:9–18	261	4:9–11	253
2:10	6, 144, 172, 205	4:11	156, 162, 186, 254
2:10–18	162		
2:10–3:6	70	4:12	94
2:11	172	4:12–13	120n
2:12	116	4:14	14, 154n, 187, 254
2:12–13	96		
2:14	57, 59, 85	4:14–15	155
2:14–15	253	4:14–16	133n, 149
2:14–18	229n	4:14–5:10	142, 252n
2:15	85, 144, 170	4:14–10:18	149n, 150, 251n
2:16	101, 263	4:15	120n, 155
2:17	94, 120n	4:16	62, 116, 156, 172, 188, 251n, 254n
2:18	155		
3	28, 186, 188		
3–4	100	4:19	62
3–6	119, 121	4:22	62
3:1	154n, 172, 187	5–7	92
3:1–6	91, 102	5–10	62
3:2	94	5:1	120n
3:2–6	261	5:1–6	91n
3:2c	91n	5:1–7:28	91
3:3	172	5:3	120n
3:3–6a	91n	5:4–5	172
3:6	94, 154n, 254	5:6	97, 117
3:7	97, 117	5:7	37, 38, 55, 56, 57, 61, 63, 229n
3:7–11	119		
3:7–19	121	5:7–9	155

INDEX OF ANCIENT SOURCES

5:7–10	91n, 142	7:22	60
5:8	261	7:24–8:6	252n
5:9	251	7:25	156, 251n
5:11	156n	7:26	6, 120n, 205, 261
5:11–6:2	116, 156n		
5:11–6:3	171	7:27	56, 57, 120n, 204
5:11–6:12	91n		
5:12	97, 116, 117, 134	7:28	92n, 117
		8	203
6:1	23	8–9	66, 196n
6:2	235	8–10	98, 99, 102
6:4	207, 208, 262	8:1	6, 14, 66, 155, 172, 202
6:4–6	154n		
6:4–8	6, 170, 207, 208	8:1–13	170
6:5	100	8:1–10:18	251n
6:6	13, 120n	8:1–10:25	158
6:7–8	123n	8:2	14, 66
6:9	170, 251	8:3	6, 14, 29, 66, 203, 204n
6:10	116, 161		
6:11	162	8:3–4	66
6:12	156n	8:3–9:10	66
6:13	263	8:4	67, 117
6:13–14	91n	8:5	19, 34, 66, 117
6:13–15	253	8:6	20, 52n, 60, 66, 99
6:13–18	79		
6:13–20	87, 88	8:7–13	263
6:14	79, 101, 117	8:8	117
6:15	186	8:8–12	98, 117
6:15–20	91n	8:9	117
6:18	6, 155, 207	8:10	66, 117
6:18–19	154n	8:12	21, 120n
6:19	155, 188	8:13	25n, 117, 225
6:19–20	229	9	21, 57, 59, 63, 69, 73, 83, 92, 143, 202
6:19–20a	251n		
6:20	19, 82n, 144, 156	9:1	66, 117
7	56, 92, 94, 202	9:1–5	67
7–10	73, 94, 122	9:1–10	21, 57, 67n
7:1	67	9:1–28	87
7:1–2	91n	9:2	57n
7:3	215	9:2–3	66
7:3–27	92n	9:2–5	143
7:4	154n	9:3	57n
7:5	117	9:4	117
7:11	87, 117	9:6	57n, 66
7:11–28	67, 170	9:6–14	158
7:12	117, 204	9:7	66, 67, 122
7:16	117	9:7–10	13
7:17	96	9:8	20, 22, 66
7:18	87, 117, 252n, 263	9:8–10	21
		9:9	21, 52n, 66, 173
7:19	117, 156	9:10	22, 117, 235
7:20–22	87n	9:11	60, 66
7:21	96n, 117	9:11–12	22, 70, 142

9:11–14	13, 33	10:1	22–23, 60, 117,
9:11–28	66, 67n		274n
9:11–10:18	252n	10:1–18	92, 142
9:12	14, 19, 57, 62,	10:2	20, 21, 23, 120n,
	66, 142		173
9:13	60, 66	10:3	21, 67, 87, 120n
9:13–14	60	10:4	6, 20, 60, 120n,
9:14	14, 23, 52n, 57,		207
	60, 66, 157, 173,	10:5	19, 61, 95
	250, 262	10:5–7	60, 96
9:15	4, 59, 66, 69,	10:5–10	61
	70, 81, 82, 83,	10:5–39	92
	85, 86, 87, 88,	10:6	95, 120n
	117, 251	10:7	61, 95, 96, 117,
9:15–18	3, 68, 69, 71,		142n
	72, 80, 85	10:8	117, 120n
9:15–22	3, 65, 73, 81	10:9	61, 144, 225
9:16	70, 71, 79, 80,	10:10	19, 61, 63
	82, 83, 85, 204	10:11	20, 60, 120n
9:16a	81	10:12	120n
9:16b	73, 82	10:12–13	70, 172
9:16–17	3, 59, 69, 71,	10:14	23, 85, 251
	72, 73, 74, 75,	10:15–17	85, 99
	79, 80, 81, 84,	10:16	117
	85	10:16–17	20, 117
9:17	70, 74, 80, 85,	10:17	21, 120n
	227n, 228	10:18	82n, 120n
9:17a	73, 83	10:19	62, 155, 156,
9:17b	74, 80, 84, 85,		157, 188, 251n
	88	10:19–20	19, 229
9:18	69, 70, 84	10:19–21	34
9:18–21	67, 85	10:19–22	19, 158
9:18–22	80, 82, 84	10:19–25	149, 254n
9:18–23	66	10:20	157
9:19	66, 67, 84, 94,	10:21	155
	102, 117	10:22	21, 34, 62, 156,
9:19–20	58, 229		173
9:20	97, 117	10:23	154n, 187
9:21	66	10:24	150, 155n, 161n
9:21–22	58	10:24–25	254
9:21–22a	58n	10:24–25a	161
9:22	85, 117	10:25	116, 150, 155n
9:22–23	66	10:26	120n
9:23	60, 66, 67, 204	10:26–31	120n, 170
9:24	19, 66, 191	10:28	85, 94, 102, 117
9:25	66	10:28–29	154n
9:26	22, 66, 120n,	10:29	117
	142	10:30	117
9:27	120n	10:30b	96n
9:28	22, 37, 38, 66,	10:31	250
	83, 85, 120n,	10:32	154n
	251	10:32–33	171
10	92	10:32–34	131n, 134, 144,
10–13	123		156n, 163, 253

INDEX OF ANCIENT SOURCES 299

10:33–34	152	12:1–4	254n
10:34	155, 226	12:2	13, 144, 162, 173, 261, 262
10:35	155		
10:37	123	12:2–3	154n, 172, 190, 252n
10:37–38	95		
10:38	95	12:3	120n, 262
10:39	170	12:4	120n, 134, 157, 226
11	6, 87, 100, 101, 180, 182, 183, 184, 185, 189, 190, 253, 262	12:5–6	92
		12:5–11	116
		12:12–14	157
11:1	173	12:14	99
11:1–40	155	12:15	155n
11:1–12:2	170	12:15–17	156
11:1–12:3	254	12:18–24	157
11:4–5	183	12:18	190
11:5	185	12:20	83n
11:6	6, 156, 207	12:21	97, 119n
11:7	183	12:22	116, 190, 250, 251n
11:8	157, 182		
11:8–10	157, 180	12:22–23	158
11:8–16	172	12:22–24	85, 251n, 254
11:8–19	92	12:23	71n, 116, 120n, 251
11:9	158, 181n, 182, 186		
		12:24	70
11:10	158, 184, 251	12:25	84, 154n, 250n, 253n
11:11	185		
11:11–12	186	12:25–29	120n
11:12	185	12:26	117
11:13	185, 186, 187	12:26–28	250
11:13–16	157, 180	12:28	144, 153, 157, 158, 168
11:14	158, 186, 188		
11:15	188, 189n	12:28–29	160
11:16	158, 172, 189, 190n	12:29	99
		13	6, 34, 150, 151, 153, 160, 161, 162, 190n, 192, 195, 196
11:17	87		
11:17–19	79, 87		
11:24–27	172		
11:25	95, 120n	13:1	162
11:25–26	189	13:1–2a	152
11:27	157	13:1–5a	160
11:29	157	13:1–6	161
11:32	218n, 265n, 276	13:1–7	197
11:36	152	13:1–9	197n
11:36–38	163	13:1–17	254
11:37–38	190	13:2	116, 163, 174, 189n
11:38	172		
11:39	190	13:2b	165
11:40	190, 251	13:3	116, 145, 163
12	92, 190	13:3b	165
12:1	120n, 155, 157, 190, 253, 262	13:4	120n, 150, 159, 164
	34, 155, 254, 262	13:4b	165
12:1–3		13:5	117, 155n

13:5a	164	13:18–25	221
13:5b–6	160, 165, 173	13:19	161
13:6	97	13:20–21	149, 265n
13:7	116, 117, 150, 154n, 156, 165, 166	13:20–25	104
		13:21	172
		13:22	6, 105, 116, 133n, 149, 161, 208
13:7–17	160, 165		
13:8	21, 166, 261n		
13:8–10	166	13:22–25	105
13:9	150, 161, 193, 196, 235	13:23	116, 134, 265n, 274
13:9–10	166	13:23–24	102
13:9–11	243	13:24	116, 135, 165, 166
13:9–16	191, 193, 195, 196, 197, 254n		
13:10	155, 196	1 Peter	179n, 180n, 181n, 191n, 216n, 220, 230n, 236
13:10–12	20		
13:11	120n, 191		
13:11–14	167		
13:12	63		
13:12–13	142	2 Peter	230n, 275n
13:13	20, 82n–83n, 157, 189, 191, 195, 197	2:11	80n
		3:11	99n
		3:15	219n
13:13–14	151, 157, 160, 172	1 John	
13:14	20, 158	1:5	50
13:15	34, 187n, 260n	1:7	50, 52, 54, 57, 58
13:15–16	20, 63, 168, 193, 196		
		1:10	51
13:15a	168		
13:15b–16a	168	Jude	150
13:16	116, 152, 153		
13:16a	152	Revelation	218
13:16b	168	3:5	51
13:17	116, 150, 165, 166	6:11	51
		7:9	51
13:18	21, 165, 166, 174	7:14	51, 52, 57, 58
		7:15	52
13:18–19	37n, 104	18:4	167

Jewish Literature

'Abot de Rabbi Nathan	270n	31b	112, 123n
		71	266n
Babylonian Talmud	110, 113		
Giṭṭin		Šabbat	
38b	115n	30b	266n, 268n
Megillah		Ta'anit	
7a	269n	12a	121
24a	111, 113	29a	121, 123
29b	110, 113		

INDEX OF ANCIENT SOURCES

Dead Sea Scrolls	vii, 215	Leviticus Rabbah	
CD		18:1	115n
I, 3	77n	28:1	266n
I, 17–18	77n		
III, 10–11	77n	1 Maccabees	
XV, 4–5	77n	10:24	208
1Q22 1 I, 10	77n		
4Q174	92	2 Maccabees	
4Q266 2 I, 21	77n	6–7	95
4Q269 2 I, 6	77n		
4Q390 1 I, 6	77n	3 Maccabees	
		1:16	55
Genesis Rabbah			
1:1	279n	4 Maccabees	
55:2–3	115	2:14	82n
		6:34	82n
Jerusalem Talmud		14:11	82n
Berakot		14:14	82n
2:4	123	14:19	82n
		15:2	95
Ta'anit		15:8	95
12a	121	17:22	241n
Josephus	108, 139	*Mekilta de Rabbi Yishma'el*	90
Antiquitates iudaicae			
1.154	181	Mishnah	112, 113,
1.157	181		115n, 123
16.43	109n	*'Abot*	
		1:12	99n
Bellum judaicum			
6.420	141n	*'Eduyyot*	
7.118	140	5:3	266n
7.121	138n		
7.123	139	*Megillah*	
7.123–162	139	3:4	111, 113
7.124–126	139	3:10	111n, 113
7.127–130	139	4:5–6	111, 112
7.137–138	140	4:6	123n
7.139–147	140		
7.148–150	143	*Roš Haššanah*	
7.148–151	140	1:1	121
7.152	139n	1:3	121
7.153	140		
7.153–155	140	*Ta'anit*	
7.156	140	4:6	121, 123
7.158–161	137		
		Yadayim	
Contra Apionem		3:5	266n, 268n
1.38–46	95		
2.77	225n	*Numbers Rabbah*	
2.175	108n	161b	266n
Lamentations Rabbah		*Pesiqta de Rab Kahana*	122
Proem 17	115n	101b	115n

Pesiqta Rabbati	122	*Seder ʿOlam Rabbah*	
10:6	119	6	121
10:9	119		
		Sipra	90
Philo	vii, 92, 93,		
	108, 181,	*Sipre Deuteronomy*	90
	192, 215	357	102
De Abrahamo		*Sipre Numbers*	90
62	181n		
		Sirach	
Quod deterius potiori insidari soleat		35:1–3	48
146	21	35:1–5	49
160	192n	35:4 (35:6–7^{ET})	49n
		35:5^{LXX} (35:8^{ET})	48
Quod Deus sit immutabilis			
74	97n	*Targum Qoheleth*	270
		1:1–2	270
De ebrietate		1:12–18	271
61	97n		
100	192n	*Testament of Simeon*	
		5:2	99n
De gigantibus			
54	192n	Tosefta	121, 123n
		Megillah	
Legum allegoriae		3:1–9	113
2.54–55	192n	3(4):10	111
		3:18	113
De opificio mundi			
71	19n	*Sukkah*	
		4:6	108n
De sacrificiis Abelis et Caini			
76–87	92n	*Taʿanit*	
		4:6	121
De somniis			
2.127	108n	*Yadayim*	
		2:14	270n
Qoheleth Rabbah	270, 279n		
1:3	266n, 268n	Wisdom of Solomon	
11:9	266n, 268n	7:25–26	95
		11:25	95

CHRISTIAN LITERATURE

Augustine	213	*Epistolae ad Romanos inchoata expositio*	
De civitate Dei		11.3–4 [PL 35.2095] 274	
10.5	213n, 274		
16.22	213n	*De haeresibus*	
		89	274
De doctrina christiana			
2.8.12–13	213n, 274	Barnabas	236

INDEX OF ANCIENT SOURCES

Clement of Alexandria		6.14.2	273n
Stromata		6.14.4	266n, 273n
5.10.62	273n	6.20.3	266n
6.7.62	273n	6.25.11–14	266n, 273
		6.25.14	275n
Clement of Rome	274n		
1 Clement	134, 183,	Ignatius of Antioch	219n, 220,
	184, 215n,		224n, 234
	219n, 220n,		
	224, 230, 236	Jerome	213, 271, 274
9–13	183, 184	*Epistulae*	
9.2	183	58	274
9.3	183	129.7	213n
9.4	183		
10	182	John Chrysostom	224
10.1	183		
10.1–2	182	Justin	236
10.4	182		
10.7	182, 183	Melito of Sardis	236
11.1	183, 184	*De Pascha*	222
12.1	183		
36.2–6	135n	Methodius of Olympus	
40	225n	*Symposium*	
55:1	80n	5.7	274n
Didache		Origen	224, 273
16:4–5	51	*Commentarii in evangelium Joannis*	
		1.20	273n
Diognetus			
3	225n	*De principiis*	
		1.5.1	273n
Ephraem of Syria	274		
		Polycarp of Smyrna	219n, 220
Epiphanius of Salamis	274		
		Theodore of Mopsuestia	
Eusebius	236		
Historia ecclesiastica		*In Epistolam Pauli ad Hebraeos*	
2.17.12	274n	*Commentarii Fragmenta*	
2.17.12–13	266n	PG 66.952	274n
3.3.1–7	266n		
3.3.5	274n	Tertullian	236
3.38.2	275n		
3.38.2–3	266n	*De pudicitia*	
5.26.1	266n	20	274n

OTHER WRITINGS

Anaximenes of		Aristotle	207
Lampsacus	202, 203	*Ethica nicomachea*	
Rhetorica ad Alexandrum	203n	4.2.2 (1122a)	205n
1.4 (1421b, 23–27)	203n		
1.12 (1422a, 20–21)	207n	*Poetica*	
		9.1 (1451a)	204

304 INDEX OF ANCIENT SOURCES

Rhetorica
1.3.5 (1358b) — 203
1.3.8 (1359a) — 208
1.4.2 (1359a) — 205
1.4.3 (1359a) — 207
2.18.5 (1392a) — 207

Cassiodorus
Variae
10.30.1 — 140n

Cassius Dio
Historia Romana
65.12 (epitome) — 138n

Cicero
De republica
6:23/25–6:24/26 — 173

Dio Chrysostom
Achilles (Or. 58)
3.7 — 145n
11.5–6 — 145n

De regno i (Or. 1)
9.4 — 209

Diodorus of Sicily
Bibliotheca historica
15.16.2 — 209

Hermogenes of Tarsus — 203
Progymnasmata
6 — 203n
11 — 206

Staseis
7 — 203n

Isocrates — 202

Lucian — 162, 163, 164, 169
De morte Peregrini
12–13 — 162, 171
16 — 163

Nikolaos of Myra
Progymnasmata — 204

Ovid
Metamorphoses
8.620–724 — 163

Paulus Orosius
Historiae
7.9 — 139n

Publius Rutilius Lupus — 205
Schemata Dianoeas et lexeos — 205n

Philostratus
Life of Apollonius
4.46 — 145n

Plato — 202
Crito
44c — 173
46c–47d — 173
Gorgias
526d–527e — 173

Pliny the Younger — 234

Plutarch
Moralia — 222n
De Superstitione — 222

Quintilian
Institutio oratoria
3.6.2 — 203
3.8.25 — 207
3.8.35 — 206
3.11.3 — 203
3.11.27 — 203
9.3.99 — 205
10.1.27 — 206
10.1.71 — 206

Suetonius
De vita Caesarum
8.6 — 138n

Tacitus — 234n
Annales
6.5.9 — 145n
15.44 — 134n

Xenophon
De vectigalibus
4.23 — 34n

www.ingramcontent.com/pod-product-compliance
Lightning Source LLC
Chambersburg PA
CBHW021819300426
44114CB00009BA/243